PRIMETIME BLUES

PRIME TIME BLUES

AFRICAN AMERICANS
ON NETWORK TELEVISION

BLUES

DONALD BOGLE

FARRAR, STRAUS AND GIROUX ■ NEW YORK

Farrar, Straus and Giroux
19 Union Square West, New York 10003

Distributed in Canada by Douglas & McIntyre Ltd.
Printed in the United States of America
First edition, 2001

Library of Congress Cataloging-in-Publication Data
Bogle, Donald.
  Primetime blues : African Americans on network television / Donald Bogle.— 1st ed.
    p.   cm.
  Includes bibliographical references and index.
  ISBN 0-374-23720-4
  1. Afro-Americans on television. I. Title.

PN1992.8.A34 B64 2001
791.45′089′96073—dc21

00-041700

Designed by Abby Kagan

To three terrific Bogles:

Roger, Jerry, and Jay

to Mark and Mechelle

to Bobby and Mariskia

to H. Alfred Farrell and Emery Wimbish

and

to my hero,

today, tomorrow, forever,

Roslyn Woods Bogle

CONTENTS

PRIMETIME BLUES

INTRODUCTION

rowing up in a quiet suburb of Philadelphia, where everything closed at nine in the evening and where life in the early 1960s moved at a fairly leisurely pace, I spent most of my spare time at the movies—and the rest of it plopped in front of the TV set. I saw just about everything that came on the tube, whether it was the variety shows, the nightly news shows, or the sports shows. But mainly I watched with sometimes rapt, sometimes casual attention the new primetime series, or even the old series, mostly sitcoms, that were already rerun in syndication, often five days a week.

From the first, I was struck whenever I saw an African American performer. It might be the exuberant and much maligned cast of *Amos 'n' Andy*, led by Tim Moore, Spencer Williams, and Ernestine Wade. Or it might be Eddie Anderson as the clever and confident Rochester on *The Jack Benny Show*. Or Ethel Waters, who had played the loyal maid on *Beulah*, in some of her guest appearances on programs like *Route 66* and *Daniel Boone*. Or later Bill Cosby on *I Spy*.

Even as a kid, I often found myself asking all sorts of questions about what I was seeing *and* enjoying. The friendly maid Beulah never appeared fazed by the fact that she was a servant in a household that clearly took her for granted. Didn't she ever grow tired of always smiling and pleasing the white Henderson family? As witty and resourceful and independent as Rochester was, wouldn't it have been delirious fun to see his life dramatized away from his boss, Jack Benny? Even the progressive Scotty on *I Spy* chummed it up with his white buddy Kelly without the subject of race—or the cultural distinctions that had to exist between the two men—entering into their friendship. Before I could consciously express it, I think I was aware, as was most of Black America, of a fundamental racism or a misinterpretation of African American life that underlay much of what appeared on the tube.

Yet I kept watching television. Because Black performers in series were still relatively rare, they always meant much to me, as they did to the rest of the African American audience. Usually, I liked the people I was seeing. Something about the warmed-over tones of Ethel Waters's voice or the cockiness of Anderson's Rochester or the shrewd intelligence of Scotty always intrigued and drew me to them. I already felt that way about many of the African American actors and actresses I had seen in old films, some of whom now appeared on television. Beneath the characters they played, there often appeared to be another person, one the actual text didn't seem to know much about.

Later, in the 1970s, like most of the nation, I was caught up in such television specials as *The Autobiography of Miss Jane Pittman* and *Roots*. Cicely Tyson, John Amos, Madge Sinclair, Ben Vereen, Leslie Uggams, and Olivia Cole gave masterly, thought-out performances that were often searing, poetic, and, rare for the tube, larger than life with movie-screen-size emotions and passions. But, frankly, during the era of shows like *Good Times* and *The Jeffersons*, I lost some of my interest in the tube. After all the social/political momentum of the late 1960s, the new primetime series seemed like dated throwbacks to the past. Too much clowning. Too many exaggerations.

Yet I was surprised by the people I knew who watched these shows and discussed the characters and story lines in such detail that it was obvious that they were connecting with the programs in a more personal way than they may have realized. Often, too, I noticed that even among those people who professed to hate television, except perhaps for some of the programming on PBS, there was a moment when they might mention some network primetime series with a surprising note of familiarity. Just about everyone seemed to have at least one show that they indulged in weekly, their guilty pleasure, a program they watched so intently that, during its broadcast, they did not want to be interrupted by phone calls or visitors. When I took another look at a show like *Sanford and Son* or *The Jeffersons*, I could understand why. I had to admit that while I grew weary of all the hootin' and hollerin', it was pretty hard to resist people like Redd Foxx, Sherman Hemsley, and Marla Gibbs.

In the 1980s, I found myself going back to television, relaxing in the rhythms of certain primetime series in a way I hadn't done since I was a kid. Programs as different as *Miami Vice* and *Dynasty* caught my attention, especially when their African American characters were on full view. But it was really *The Cosby Show* that reawakened something in me. At first I thought the series seemed too soft and agreeable for its own good without any social bite or political consciousness. Then, gradually, as I got to know its characters—their quirks, enthusiasms, follies, and passions—and its situations; even as I grew accustomed to the look of the series with its living-room sofa always facing the viewer, with the swinging door that led to the kitchen, with the refrigerator that Cliff loved rummaging through; as I came to anticipate the exchanges between Cliff and Clair and between them and their children, I found myself enjoying the series and actually missing it on those weeks when I had not been able to watch it.

What struck me most about *The Cosby Show* was that I had seen, during my suburban childhood, African American families similar to the Huxtables. But I had never seen such a family on television. Many critics might complain that the series was too idealized and too removed from the lives of most African American families. But there was a reason why it was popular with Black America as well as with white America; why, within the African American community itself, its appeal crossed lines of class and gender. *The Cosby Show* demonstrated the unique perspective that could be brought to the primetime series when an African American artist was in control of the material.

Afterward I thought more about the way the primetime series recorded or failed to record African American life. I began thinking again about my early childhood viewing experiences, what attracted me to tube characters, what disappointed me. I started making notes to myself on the way television's view of African Americans had changed over the decades, in large part because of the primetime network series, but also on the way in which some fixed images of African Americans had not progressed very far at all.

I became fully aware that, for better or worse, the weekly primetime series had a greater effect on viewer perceptions of African American experiences than almost any other form of television. That had probably been most apparent in the mid-1960s. In the early years of that politically restless era, there had been no new series starring African Americans. But throughout the era, as the nightly news recorded the boycotts, marches, and demonstrations of the civil rights movement, shocking the nation with images of fire hoses and billy clubs turned on African American protesters, mainstream America was jolted into a new awareness of a disenfranchised Black America determined to have full and equal rights. Yet much of mainstream America still thought of the new Negro as someone *out there* protesting, not as someone who might be a part of his or her community, someone he or she might actually know. With the absence of programs about African Americans, Black viewers felt that television was not fully and fairly representing them, not saying who they were and what their lives were like.

Those feelings—among Black and white viewers—changed during the mid and late 1960s when primetime television began to depict African Americans, more often than not, as Social Symbols in guest spots on general white series and in starring roles on such new series as *I Spy, Julia,* and *Room 222.* These new characters were signs of social progress, of a supposedly free and integrated America. Only as characters like Scotty, Julia, and Pete Dixon (on *Room 222*) arrived on the tube did African American viewers believe they were seeing some recognizable form of representation of themselves, no matter how idealized or evasive some of those representations ultimately might prove to be. Only then, too, did mainstream viewers feel they were coming to know the Negro as a person.

The primetime network series altered perceptions and attitudes by making African Americans a familiar weekly presence in American living rooms. With the primetime series, viewers could see the same Black characters in the same place with the same expected tangle of relationships at the same time week in, week out. Scotty, Julia, and Pete Dixon and his girlfriend, the high school counselor Liz McIntyre, as well as Linc on *The Mod Squad,* became neighbors of sorts. Of course, any threat or menace or dissent that actual African Americans might represent politically, especially in the 1960s, had to be simplified or nullified. Nonetheless, they helped lead the way for other tube neighbors, all tied into the social/political atmosphere of their times: the Jeffersons and the Evanses in the 1970s; the Huxtables, Deacon Frye and his daughter Thelma, and the women residing at 227 in the 1980s; the Banks family and their Fresh Prince in Bel Air, Martin in Detroit, as well as Moesha and those young women living single, all in the 1990s.

Throughout these eras, television's images of African Americans continued to be criticized. Criticism came not only from the intellectual community and organizations like the NAACP (which—from the early 1950s to the late 1990s—protested against television's treatment of Black Americans) but also from individual African American viewers. Even in the 1990s, with all the new channels, Black viewers still felt there wasn't a diversity of African American TV characters and situations.

Yet Black viewers kept watching. And more often than not, most still seemed to have a show they were devoted to. As in the past, what usually drew viewers in were the people on those programs. In many respects, television has always been a medium for writers rather than directors. What you hear can still be as important as what you see. Characters are created much as they once were in the theater: through dialogue and carefully crafted story lines rather than through strong visuals. But television, from the days of Uncle Miltie and Lucy and Desi or Gleason's Ralph Kramden, has also always been a medium of performers or personalities.

For African Americans, especially because writers rarely wrote with them in mind, the performers—their individual star personas or sometimes (as was the case with Ethel Waters) their personal stories—took on a greater significance. Black viewers might reject the nonsense of the scripts for some episodes of *Sanford and Son* or *The Jeffersons* or *Martin.* Or the evasions of an otherwise moving series like *I'll Fly Away.* But they never really rejected a Redd Foxx or a Sherman Hemsley or Martin Lawrence or Regina Taylor's Lily. What remained consistent throughout television history was that a group of dynamic or complicated or intriguing personalities managed to send personal messages to the viewers. From the days of Ethel Waters in the 1950s to the present, actors found themselves cast in parts that were shameless, dishonest travesties of African American life and culture. Yet often enough some of these actors also managed—ironically and paradoxically—to strike a nerve with viewers by turning the roles inside out. They offered personal visions and stories that proved affecting, occasionally powerful, and sometimes deliriously entertaining and enlightening. Sometimes, too, the viewers' knowledge of a performer's personal tensions or conflicts affected their responses to the character the performer played on television. Regardless, as Waters herself might have been the first to say, being colored, Negro, Black, or African American on the tube would never be a casual affair. Nor would it be without its complications, contradictions, and oddball achievements.

With all of that in mind, I added more notes. Then I began to look formally at the primetime weekly series: its images, its performers, its messages, its history. Thus came *Primetime Blues*. My focus here has been only on the networks, which include such new networks of the 1990s as UPN and WB, both of which built their power bases through African American programs.

Aside from the weekly primetime series, I decided it was important to comment on the rise—in the 1970s—of the primetime TV movie and the miniseries, both of which offered surprising counterpoints to the weekly series. There had been some indelible images in some of those TV films. Jane Pittman taking her walk to the fountain. Or Kunta Kinte fighting to preserve his sanity and sense of personal and cultural identity. Or Gale Sayers stoically remaining by his friend Brian Piccolo's side in *Brian's Song*. Or later Maya Angelou's sisters in *Sister, Sister* or Melvin Van Peebles's brothers in *Sophisticated Gents* or the women of Brewster Place. But again my focus has been on network programs with some occasional comments on cable movies and PBS.

In many respects, working on *Primetime Blues* has taken me back to my earliest days of television viewing. On the one hand, I think all of us still experience a sense of wonder at the rich talents inside that box. On the other hand, we still question much of what we see and remain disturbed by the way in which the more television changes, the more it also remains the same. Some fixed images never seemed to go away entirely. Television progresses only with the smallest steps. Yet even at that, we'll stick around the house on a Tuesday or Thursday night, watching in rapt attention, hoping the tube will take us to a place we know but which we've never before seen on that little screen in our living rooms.

1. THE 1950s: SCRAPS

At the tail end of the Depression, a former blues singer, then appearing in a Broadway drama, was asked by the NBC radio network to perform on an experimental broadcast for a new medium. She agreed—and made broadcast history. The year was 1939. The woman was Ethel Waters. The program was *The Ethel Waters Show.* The new medium then in development was called television.

On *The Ethel Waters Show,* Waters—along with the African American actresses Fredi Washington and Georgette Harvey—performed a dramatic sequence from her hit play *Mamba's Daughters.* Also appearing, in various skits, were actors Philip Loeb and Joey Faye. "Results offered sharp contrasts—all the way from deeply stirring drama to feeble slapstick comedy and not-too-effective scientific lecture," *Variety* wrote. "When it was good it was quite good but when it was bad it was capital B." Regardless, as the evening's headliner, the mighty Ethel Waters, midway in what would be a long, turbulent, and illustrious career, had become—at this very early time—the first African American to star in her own program on the tube. Television hasn't been the same since.

Ethel Waters would return to television—eleven years later—as the star of *Beulah.* As such, she would find herself saddled with a role, that of a warmhearted maid named Beulah, that misused her talents and, more often than not, distressed the actress herself. But her very presence led the way for everything of color to come over the next half century.

With that early *Ethel Waters Show*, a one-night-only event, the National Broadcasting Company hoped to see if such a television transmission could be effectively executed. The network also wanted to gauge how audiences would respond to this little box with the big window. By 1939, the idea of television had already been kicking around for years. The Radio Corporation of America, General Electric, and Westinghouse, which were NBC's parent companies, had funded important early research on television. In 1923, RCA's David Sarnoff felt confident enough about the new medium to write a memo in which he said, "I believe that television, which is the technical name for seeing as well as hearing by radio, will come to pass in the future." Four years later, A.T. & T. successfully transmitted pictures in a hookup between New York and Washington, D.C. By 1928, G.E.'s station W2XCW had begun broadcasting regularly from Schenectady. Three years later, the Columbia Broadcasting System opened its station W2XAB in New York. For almost twenty years, television broadcasting, sprouting up slowly here and there, would be experimental and noncommercial. All of that, however, changed after World War II.

By then, the new medium's technological kinks had been worked out, economically priced consoles had been manufactured, and television sets began turning up in American homes. The three networks that had controlled radio—NBC, CBS, and the American Broadcasting Company—dominated the new medium, along with a fourth network, DuMont.

From the start, television established itself by borrowing heavily from radio. Throughout the 1930s and 1940s, Americans had sought most of their nighttime entertainment at the movies, sometimes attending three or four times a week in record numbers. But on other evenings, they most likely sat huddled in their living rooms, listening to the radio. Some nights Americans would even forgo the picture show to tune in to an episode of their favorite radio program. Unlike the movies with their glamorous larger-than-life stars—those dazzling emblems of beauty, heat, and power that could be as threatening as they were charming—radio tended to tame situations and domesticate personalities. Coming into homes nightly, the voices—the ideas they represented, the situations they dramatized—conformed to set notions

Ethel Waters, star of nightclubs, records, movies, theater, radio—and television in 1939, when she appeared in an experimental broadcast of The Ethel Waters Show. *During the broadcast, she and actress Fredi Washington (right) performed a dramatic sequence from their Broadway play* Mamba's Daughters

that Americans had about themselves and their way of life. The ideal radio personalities were relatively plain everyday people without any great emotional disarray, political gripes, or social tensions. Just common folks like cornball Fibber McGee and Molly. Or a regular old cowpoke like Gene Autry. Or "ordinary" eccentrics like comic Jack Benny or George Burns and Gracie Allen.

Radio also prospered with its weekly, primetime programming staples: the dramatic show, the variety show, and a type of program it could be credited with having created: the sitcom. Sometimes loud and rowdy, sometimes providing a satiric comment on American manners and attitudes, the sitcom set up a problematic but funny situation within its first few minutes, then proceeded to develop and milk it for laughs through the use of familiar characters and settings. Finally, by the end of each episode, the situation was neatly resolved. Every joke, every line of dialogue, every incident, every action or even the mood of the characters went into building and then resolving the comic situation. A tightly wound cord, it could have no loose ends.

Radio's sitcoms were morality plays that dramatized issues about honesty, or loyalty, or maybe the importance of hard work or family ties. The sitcoms never presented the audience with any situation—any moral message—that might be unsettling or disturbing. The lessons were always familiar and predictable. Viewers just didn't know how the story would get around to making its point. During the Depression era and the postwar years, radio's sitcoms proved adept at reassuring a troubled nation that everything was fundamentally fine in the land of the free and the home of the brave; that order was maintained and justice was served.

Network programmers were keenly aware that radio had prepared audiences for television: the idea of solid entertainment in the home; of soothing, reassuring images; of well-packaged moral lessons in a fifteen-minute or half-hour timespan. And, of course, radio's basic staples—its dramatic shows, variety shows, and sitcoms—all moved comfortably to primetime television.

At first the commercial prospects looked dismal. Sponsors were skeptical about the medium's ability to sell their products. In early 1948, NBC lost $13,000 a day on television. On radio, $27,215 was considered a low advertising rate for a minute's worth of time. But in the early years of television, the rate for a sixty-second commercial was a piddling $1,510. No one was yet convinced that people would really sit at home and watch this little picture box.

After the glum postwar start, however, the tide soon turned as television programmers came up with hits in the late 1940s and early 1950s. The real turning point was *The Texaco Star Theater*, starring Milton Berle, known as Uncle Miltie and Mr. Television, which brought millions of new viewers to the tube. Other variety programs, such as Ed Sullivan's *Toast of the Town* and later Sid Caesar and Imogene Coca's *Your Show of Shows*, also clicked with viewers, as did sitcoms like *I Love Lucy* and *The Adventures of Ozzie & Harriet.* As the hits helped sell sets and hook an even larger audience on the box, they also brought in more sponsors, which eventually led to television's moneymaking powers—and its content. By the 1948–49 season, every network hour had a sponsor. Some critics of television came to believe that the networks cared less about the shows than about the sponsors. Some even argued that entertainment segments were there simply to make space in between the commercials. But TV was here to stay. In 1950, over six million sets were sold. By 1951, sales soared to sixteen million sets. Once coast-to-coast complex coaxial cable (which could carry broadcast video) was laid, television became a truly national medium.

POSTWAR BEGINNINGS

In the late 1940s, as this loose and free-flowing new medium struggled to work its way into the American home, not yet bowing to any particular social or political pressures, still hungry for material, and, most important, not yet driven by the concerns of big advertisers, postwar television sometimes took a chance on the offbeat and opened its doors to African American performers. Almost from the start, the variety shows featured Black guest stars. From Pearl Bailey to Marian Anderson to Ella Fitzgerald, Joyce Bryant, Sarah Vaughan, Pigmeat Markham, Eartha Kitt, Peg Leg Bates, and Cab Calloway, African American entertainers made their way into American homes through song and dance.

Occasionally, local programming could be important, especially in the powerful New York market. In 1948, the New York CBS affiliate hired Black entertainer Bob Howard to star in *The Bob Howard Show.* A fifteen-minute program that ran nightly (except for Saturday and Sunday), *The Bob Howard Show* was basically a one-man operation on which Howard sang and played the piano. Even then, his material was a familiar mix of the old and the (relatively) new. On his very first program, Howard performed the tune that Black actor Dooley Wilson made famous in the movie *Casablanca*, "As Time Goes By," as well as the old minstrel favorite "Dark Town Strutters." Aware of the demands of the new medium, Howard knew how to play to the camera. When he sang a number like "Them There Eyes," he widened his eyes exuberantly and smiled broadly. Between songs, he chatted and often promoted upcoming CBS shows.

For later generations, Howard's act would hardly look offbeat or unusual. Here was one more colored song-and-dance man, plying his wares. Yet strangely enough, *The Bob Howard Show* helped transform the American living room. For the first time, audiences could sit in their homes and *see* a Black man hosting the proceedings, calling the shots, and literally running the show. No one at CBS seemed particularly concerned about any adverse reactions, quite a contrast from what would happen only a few years later when another African American man, Nat "King" Cole, hosted his own show—with controversial and disastrous results. But television in 1948 seemed too much of a likable, bumbling kid just learning to walk and talk to be fearful of Howard; too busy to think that anything like color might stunt its growth. After thirteen months, *The Bob Howard Show* went off the air. Later, beginning in 1951, Howard hosted the show on another local New York station.

Other African Americans also turned up weekly. The same year that Howard's program debuted, the DuMont network broadcast a sitcom called *The Laytons*. Having first appeared as a local New York television program, it starred African American actress Amanda Randolph as a cheerful maid. Of course, the *uncheerful* Black maid was a personage that American films and now television rarely seemed to be aware of. *The Laytons*, however, had a quick demise, appearing first in August 1948 and then dropped from the network the following October. The program had so little effect on audiences that few people even remembered its having been on. But it introduced that tube staple: the Black domestic as TV personality.

In September 1949, CBS aired a national Black variety show, *Sugar Hill Times*, hosted by Apollo Theater emcee Willie Bryant. A live one-hour program that was broadcast three times a week at 8 p.m., each set of weekly episodes had a different title. It was *Uptown Jubilee* one week; then *Harlem Jubilee* another week; then *Sugar Hill Times*. The series went off the air by the end of October, 1950, but among its stars were comic Timmie Rogers, the Don Redmond Orchestra, and a handsome newcomer named Harry Belafonte.

THE HAZEL SCOTT SHOW:
AN UNEXPECTED FACE, AN UNLIKELY PRESENCE

In 1950, television took a more adventurous turn when the DuMont Network launched *The Hazel Scott Show*. Originally broadcast as a local New York program and then going network, running for fifteen minutes on Friday evenings—and later Mondays, Wednesdays, and Fridays—at 7:45, *The Hazel Scott Show* was yet another early program that used its Black host in an acceptable musical format. The show, however, broke ground. In an age when most TV hosts were men, its host was a woman, a Black woman at that, and a distinctive personality.

By 1950, Hazel Scott's background, which was already well known to viewers, made her something of a novelty on the entertainment scene. Born in Trinidad in 1920, Scott was the daughter of progressive parents: her father, a well-known Black scholar and college professor; her mother, a talented music student and later a professional musician. A child prodigy, Scott learned to read at age three, was discovered to have perfect pitch at three and a half, and soon afterward was playing the piano. By age five, she was improvising.

Later, when her family moved to New York City, a teenage Hazel, too young to attend the Juilliard School of Music, studied privately with a professor at the school. Still a teenager, she appeared at New York's chic supper club Café Society. There she became known for jazzing the classics, for turning the passionate chords of Rachmaninoff into a spicy boogie-woogie. Or giving a classical bent to a fast-moving pop tune. Film critic James Agee once criticized her for "niggery" antics during some of her boogie-woogie numbers. And African American writer Amiri Baraka once dismissed "the shabbiness, even embarrassment, of Hazel Scott playing 'concert boogie woogie' before thousands of white middle-class music lovers." But criticism aside, Scott—with her intelligence, her hauteur, her worldliness—was generally considered a progressive symbol for African American female entertainers.

From the clubs, Scott went to Hollywood in the early 1940s. There, she usually maintained her dignity and decorum, providing movie audiences with a counter-image to most of what Hollywood had said about African American women. No servile simpleton was she. No ditzy uneducated dunce. Her manager, Barney Josephson, had it written into her contracts that she could appear only as herself in such movies as *Something to Shout About, I Dood It, The Heat's On,* and *Broadway Rhythm.* Consequently, unlike most African American women in mainstream movies, Scott (like Lena Horne) was never cast as a maid. Instead she often appeared elegantly dressed in sophisticated settings, most impressively in *Rhapsody in Blue,* in which she coolly sang Gershwin's "The Man I Love" in French and English.

In her private life, Scott also maintained a composed and commanding image—with some political kick. As the second wife of fiery Black politico Adam Clayton Powell, she represented half of a new kind of Negro couple: educated, cultured, political, outspoken; a modern woman who didn't brook fools easily. Once when a restaurant refused to serve her, Hazel Scott sued and won. When appearing in the South, Scott refused to perform before segregated audiences. What always came across in her personal appearances was Scott's sense of her self-worth; her proud unwillingness to ever appear meek or submissive.

The Hazel Scott Show opened with the camera panning across an urban skyline, then revealing a set that was supposedly a room off the terrace of a posh penthouse. There sat the shimmering Scott at her piano, like an empress on her throne, presenting at every turn a vision of a woman of experience and sophistication. Energetically, she might perform Gershwin's " 'S Wonderful." Or "I'll Remember April." Or a swing version of Brahms's "Hungarian Dance Number 5." Or a torch song. Or a spiritual (on which she would accompany herself on the organ). Surprisingly, her urbane fare and style worked well for television. "Hazel Scott has a neat little show in this modest package," *Variety* wrote. "Most engaging element in the airer is the Scott personality, which is dignified, yet relaxed, and versatile."

The future looked promising for *The Hazel Scott Show*—and also for the image of African American women. But in the end, the very

Pianist Hazel Scott: bringing a cool elegance and sophistication to the tube as the star of The Hazel Scott Show

outspokenness that made Scott seem such a unique, contemporary woman also landed her in trouble. In June 1950, not long after her program's debut, Scott was listed in *Red Channels*, a compilation naming entertainers believed to be Communist or Communist sympathizers issued by the House Un-American Activities Committee. During the rise of McCarthyism in America—and the Communist witch-hunts that swept through the government and the entertainment industry—a number of careers were destroyed simply by the suggestion of "radical" ties. Almost immediately, Scott became "suspect" and felt the sting of the listing. By September, her show, which had scored well in the Hooper rating system of the day, was struggling to find a major sponsor. Without one, the program ran the risk of being canceled by Du-Mont.

Determined to fight the *Red Channels* listing, Scott publicly asked for a hearing before the House Un-American Activities Committee and went before the committee on September 22. Testifying that she was not a member of the Communist Party and "have never entertained the idea of being one, and I never will," she also lambasted *Red Channels* as "guilt by listing" and branded the publication "vile and un-American." Following her testimony, Hazel Scott called for the artists' and musicians' unions to boycott those networks or program sponsors which, without giving proof of disloyalty or providing a hearing, blacklisted entertainers in *Red Channels*. Her daring, courageous plea won her the admiration of other entertainers. But the die was already cast for *The Hazel Scott Show*. "Redlist Costs Hazel Scott Job," read the headline in *The Compass*. Her contract was not renewed, and her program, which had first aired nationally on July 3, 1950, went off the airwaves on September 29. The fate of Scott's show indicated even at this early stage that television would flee from any signs of controversy, especially political controversy.

But the demise of *The Hazel Scott Show* also indicated something else. Hazel Scott had carried her off-screen image—that of a political/ social firebrand—to the little screen. African American viewers watching her were aware of her past and what she might represent for the future, especially during the rise of the civil rights era. The modern Black woman—appearing regularly in American homes—had unexpectedly surfaced and then quickly disappeared. Had Scott survived, African American tube images might have veered in an altogether different direction; indeed they might have been in step with emerging postwar social attitudes.

Instead, playing it safe, keeping step with sponsor fears and conservatism, television reverted to the tried-and-true: those situations, characters, perspectives, and formulas that had already succeeded on radio's sitcoms (and in the movies too). And so came *Beulah*.

BEULAH: EVERYBODY'S FAVORITE NURTURER

Beulah told the story of Beulah, a Black maid; a warm and "winning," hefty, full-figured, and good-hearted "colored gal" with a deep hearty laugh. Employed by a middle-class white couple named the Hendersons, who had a cute little son named Donnie, Beulah was ever ready to solve the family's problems. She didn't seem able to exist without them.

Beulah had been around for years. The character had first appeared on the NBC Radio program *Homeward Unincorporated* in 1939. A few years later, Beulah drifted onto other programs: NBC's *That's Life* in 1943 and then *Fibber McGee and Molly*. Audiences liked the giggly, nurturing maid so much that finally in 1945 Beulah was spun off onto a show of her own on CBS Radio.

Neither programmers nor audiences seemed to think twice about the fact that this Black female lead character—one of the few on radio—wasn't played by an African American woman. Beulah was played by white actor Marlin Hurt, whose forced performance—with his use of a thick dialect—made the character all the more buffoonishly stereotyped. When Hurt suddenly died in 1940, another white actor, Bob Corley, took over the role. His antics matched his predecessor's. Finally, in 1947, someone had the bright idea of casting a real African American woman as Beulah. Actually, it might have been better had they decided to dump the character altogether. But Hattie McDaniel, the talented African American actress who had played comic servants in movies since the 1930s and won a Best Supporting Actress Oscar in 1939 for *Gone With the Wind*, stepped into the part and, for better or worse, made Beulah something of her own.

Beulah helped McDaniel hold on to her career. Following World War II, the befuddled or slovenly Black comic servant characters of the prewar years had been replaced in films by more adult and serious representations of African Americans. Such Negro Problem Pictures as *Pinky, Home of the Brave, Lost Boundaries,* and *Intruder in the Dust,* all released in 1949, explored the Negro Dilemma, the Color Question; focusing on issues of race and racism in America; establishing African American characters as brooding and troubled figures; bracing metaphors for a nation's social injustices and inequities. Yet while movie audiences were ready to accept new images of African Americans, radio audiences chuckled at the old corn and the familiar types of the prewar era. "Did somebody bawl for Beulah!" McDaniel belted out at the radio show's opening. Listeners howled. Beulah became a radio hit with McDaniel. And soon the character moved to TV land.

ABC launched the weekly half-hour sitcom in October 1950. Because the television show was filmed in New York rather than Hollywood (where the radio version of the show was still broadcast), ABC cast New York-based Ethel Waters in the lead role. Also in the cast were Butterfly McQueen as Beulah's high-pitched-voice friend Oriole; Percy "Bud" Harris as Beulah's boyfriend Bill (replaced in the second season by Dooley Wilson); and William Post Jr., Ginger Jones, and Clifford Sales as the Henderson family.

TV's Beulah wasn't much different from radio's. Usually, the show opened with some "pithy" comment made by Beulah. "She spends most of her time in the kitchen," Beulah said of herself at the opening of one episode. "But never seems to know what's cooking." Then she smiled broadly for the camera. "If marriages are made in heaven," Beulah lamented on another episode, "my guardian angel's sho' been loafing on the job." Then she burst into laughter. "Don't let nobody tell you I'm in the market for a husband," said Beulah about her love life. "Of course, I would be. But they don't sell husbands in a market."

Throughout *Beulah*'s three-season run, the expected adventures followed. On the very first episode, Beulah had to untangle a mess her employers had made with a business associate. In an attempt to impress the man, who hails from Mississippi, the Hendersons plan a fancy New Orleans-style dinner that turns disastrous. But just when all looks lost and the man is about to leave in a huff, the knowing, wise Beulah steps in to set things right. Good old Beulah knows what this Mississippi gent really craves in the cuisine department. She's prepared a dinner of corn bread and greens. He gets a whiff and immediately turns around to enjoy a *real* Southern-style dinner. Ah, that Beulah is really somethin'!

*Keeping the American family happy and well nurtured:
Louise Beavers (center) as the cheery domestic Beulah for
the Hendersons (Jane Frazee, David Bruce, Stuffy Singer)*

Beulah was *always* ready to save the day. One episode found Beulah and Bill trying to help little Donnie Henderson develop his social skills by teaching him to dance. "Donnie, when the beat's right, I just take off," she tells him. "When we get through with you, Donnie, you gonna be the struttiest cat in town." Beulah wouldn't be Beulah if she didn't know all about rhythm. On another episode, Beulah tried to inject some romance into the Hendersons' marriage because she feared it had grown complacent and stale. On another, Beulah—for the benefit of Mr. Henderson (whom she *affectionately* called Mr. Harry)—marched into the woods, where she struggled to catch a prize fish. She succeeds but not before providing laughs as she falls—a ton of fun—into the pond. Afterward she wants everyone to believe her boss landed the fish and therefore is as red-blooded and athletic as any other American male.

Even in the early 1950s, Beulah must have struck some television viewers as being from another decade. Here, during the era that marked the dawn of the civil rights movement, in the very year when poet Gwendolyn Brooks won a Pulitzer Prize, when President Truman ordered American troops into Korea, when Ralph Bunche won the Nobel Peace Prize for his work as a United Nations mediator in Palestine, Beulah seemed oblivious to current social/political realities. Content, proud of her work as a maid, and devoted to the Hendersons, she never complained. It never occurred to poor Beulah that she might be overworked or underpaid. Nor did she ever question the system that had designated her a servant.

Beulah, of course, was a type long present in American popular culture: the large, often dowdy, usually darker, all-knowing, all-seeing, all-hearing, all-understanding mammy figure, whose life is built around nurturing and nourishing those in the Big House. Lest she appear as a threat or rival to the white women she works for, the mammy, of course, has to be desexed; thus her large size and darker color. Her asexuality also makes her an ideal mother surrogate. Adolescent boys in her care don't have to struggle with any Oedipal feelings. Girls need not fret about an Electra complex. Long a cherished mainstream cultural icon, Mammy—thanks to the character Beulah—had found a place for herself on TV.

Both radio and television attempted to present Beulah within some semblance of an African American cultural context. Beulah's best friend, Oriole, who was a domestic for another family in the neighborhood, often hung around the Henderson kitchen, chatting away nonstop with Beulah. Nearby was Beulah's boyfriend, Bill Jackson, who ran his own fix-it shop. As might be expected, Beulah and Bill's relationship was a safe comic romance (not a vibrant adult coupling that might make us believe Beulah's got a sexuality after all) that was unfulfilling (and perhaps unconsummated) for Beulah.

Mostly, Bill pops up, like everybody else, for some nourishment from Beulah. But it's usually food that's on his mind. "Good morning, baby," he says one afternoon as he enters the Hendersons' kitchen, where she's cooking. He tells her he came to the house as soon as he heard she wanted to see him. But Beulah is wise to Bill. "Why, you's the fastest answering man at mealtime I ever did know!" she says.

When he's not trying to cop a meal, Bill seems to spend his time loafing. But then Bill isn't supposed to be too bright either. On one episode, when Mr. Harry tells Beulah he wants Bill to do various odd jobs for him, and then cites specific chores, Beulah slows him down. "Telling Bill one thing at a time is the best method. Too much stuff confuses him," she says. But what can you expect, the series implies, from a triflin' Black man anyway!

Beulah's ties with other African Americans may have partly accounted for her popularity with a segment of the Black audience. Her entire manner—her rhythm and perspective—is different when she's with the other Black cast members. She seems freer and astute. But never mind that. Beulah's purpose in life was maintaining order and decorum for those she willingly served. Snug as a bug with them good ol' white folks, Beulah was something of a simp joke.

"Except for a few spots, the comedy was weak with improbable situations and unconvincing characterizations," wrote *Variety* at the time of the TV series's debut, adding that Ethel Waters "lent the part warmth and humor." "With Miss Waters playing the title role, it had a number of amusing moments," wrote the television critic for *The New York Times*, "but on the whole the opening instalment suffered from a trite story and was regrettably stereotyped in concept."

ABC's decision to cast Ethel Waters proved a wise one. Improbable as it may seem, she truly lent the series some distinction and a lopsided credibility. Her presence also indicated—early on—that viewers might overlook weak story lines or poorly developed characters if they liked the people on-screen. Waters endowed the show with a subtext that made *Beulah* far more than it appeared on the surface.

By the early 1950s, Waters had long been a familiar and distinctive cultural force on the national landscape. She had been in show business since the teens, and her life and career—tough knocks and all—were well known to the public. Born out of wedlock and in poverty in 1896, ignored by her mother, feeling unloved and unwanted by almost everyone (save for her grandmother), she had married at thirteen. The marriage lasted two years. Afterward she worked as a chambermaid in a hotel. Then she slowly began to perform and build a career. As a slinky blues singer called Sweet Mama Stringbean, she worked her way up from honky-tonks and tiny theaters to sophisticated Harlem clubs in the 1920s. She became a major recording star with hits like "Dinah," "Am I Blue?" and "Stormy Weather." Later she won acclaim in such Broadway musicals as *Thousands Cheer* and *At Home Abroad*. Then she surprised the critics and public alike by shifting gears and showing the full range of her talents with a dramatic performance of fierce power in the play *Mamba's Daughters*.

But for all her success, Waters was dogged by professional and personal mishaps that sent her career into a rapid decline. By the mid-1940s, Waters, having fought for years with directors, producers, and club managers, had so many well-known outbursts on the set of the film *Cabin in the Sky* that she afterward was blacklisted in Hollywood for six years. No studio wanted to be bothered with her. She had also spent money wildly and recklessly—on men, on women, on friends. Near broke and struggling to find work in the postwar era, she somehow managed an extraordinary comeback, first in the film *Pinky*, for which she was nominated for an Academy Award as Best Supporting Actress of 1949. Then came her shattering performance in early 1950 as the one-eyed, emotionally frayed cook Berenice Sadie Brown in Carson McCullers's Broadway drama *The Member of the Wedding*. At first, she had balked at playing the role. "There is still no God in this play," she had told producer Bob Whitehead. "Berenice, the cook, is nasty. She's lost her faith. I won't play such a character. But don't get the wrong impression. I need the job and the money. Especially the money. I'm ten thousand dollars in debt right now, but I still can't be in a play without any God in it." Later McCullers "let me give the role my own interpretation," said Waters. Hailed by the critics, she portrayed a woman who, while working in the home of a white family and nurturing two troubled children there, nonetheless expressed the turmoil and tensions of her own life. Berenice was not simply a woman who carried a tray and smiled. A perceptive, bruised character, she broke the mold of the ditzy African American maid. Following this triumph, Waters had another the next year with the publication of her best-selling autobiography, *His Eye Is on the Sparrow*, which detailed her stormy life.

Occupying a unique place in the national consciousness, Ethel Waters was perceived as a woman of emotional depth and resilience; a woman whose spirit and drive had enabled her to endure in a sometimes tough and cruel world. ABC signed Waters for *Beulah* just at the time of her comeback (she was still appearing in *The Member of the Wedding*), when most Americans knew her name and something of her story. In the days long before Oprah, it was an extraordinary cultural position for an African American woman.

As played by Waters, Beulah is hard not to like. Gracing this nothing character with her own profound warmth and tenderness as well as a modicum of conviction, Waters transformed Beulah into a knowing earth mother, able to unravel life's tangled (albeit trivial) difficulties and to make everything right. Waters portrayed Beulah as a relaxed, older Southern Black woman, aware of the racial codes of the household in which she works—and fond of the family—yet not all-sacrificing for them. She seems very content to spend some time with her friends Bill and Oriole. Playing the character without a heavy dialect and a fake hearty laugh, Waters's Beulah (perhaps unintentionally) possessed sex appeal, even though larger and older women weren't supposed to. While the Hendersons strike us today as hopelessly plastic and phony, Waters's Beulah seemed a real person, trapped in an artificial world.

The viewers at home watching Waters understood—consciously or not—that she herself had taken on the real problems (of her own life) and overcome them. Those viewers, especially the African American ones, filled in the holes of *Beulah*'s story with their own sense of Ethel Waters. Waters, the woman, made the show work, and on a certain level made it appeal to its African American viewers. While that audience rejected much of the nonsense of the scripts, it couldn't reject Waters. Or, for that matter, the other African American performers in the cast. But it's not hard to understand, though, why Ethel Waters finally became fed up with the series. By the second season, she wanted out. Waters had decided she no longer wanted the "white folks kitchen comedy role."

But ABC wasn't about to give up on the series. Instead the network revamped the program. Now filming *Beulah* in Los Angeles, ABC hired Hattie McDaniel to play the title role. But looking tired, ill, and drained of her old energy, McDaniel played Beulah too broadly for her performance to work on the small screen with its demand for subdued intimacy. McDaniel was accustomed to keeping her audience at a distance, not letting it get too close to the real person inside. (Inside there might have been too much anger and frustration.) Hers is a vaudeville turn, fundamentally a pre-World War II reading of a prewar character. After she completed six episodes, McDaniel's illness forced her to drop out of the show. She died of cancer in 1952.

Character actress Louise Beavers was then cast in the role. Other new cast members included Ernest Whitman as Bill and Ruby Dandridge as the neighbor Oriole. The unexpected irony of actor Ernest Whitman (who portrayed Bill on radio) was that his character came across as anything but slow-witted. Whitman understood how to play with a line, and he was able to suggest a wily intelligence, leading the viewer to believe that Bill knew more than anybody thought. But Beavers—trying too hard to be a cheery Beulah—frequently came across as hopelessly childlike. On one episode, Beulah, with suitcase in hand, is prepared to leave the Hendersons' home, fearful she'll be fired because she's angered her employers and perhaps even caused a rift in their marriage. But, of course, Mrs. Henderson will hear no such talk.

Finally, Beavers, like Waters, grew uneasy with the show. Then ABC gave up. *Beulah* left the broadcast schedule on September 22, 1953. Beavers—who had appeared in movies throughout the 1930s and 1940s, and who was best known for her performance in the 1934 *Imitation of Life*—continued to work in television in such presentations as *Star Stage's Cleopatra Collins, Playhouse 90's The Hostess with the Mostes',* and *Walt Disney Presents Swamp Fox.* Still, it remains a sad irony that three of the most talented Black character actresses to work in American movies all ended up playing the same domestic, a role none appeared comfortable with.

Despite the actresses' talents, *Beulah,* as network television's introduction to the African American woman as popular nighttime series star, had presented the Black woman as a familiar nurturer, without a home or much of a life of her own; the African American man as neither husband nor father but triflin' roustabout; indicating early on the stereotypes and distortions about African American life that television would trade in for years to come.

That was true of the other series starring African Americans that appeared on television in the summer of 1951, the same time as the second season of *Beulah's* run. Almost twenty years would pass before two series starring African Americans would again run concurrently on television. And for the next twenty years—at least—no television series would be as controversial as this second program: *Amos 'n' Andy.*

AMOS 'N' ANDY:
PREWAR IMAGES IN A POSTWAR ERA

Amos 'n' Andy had also been a fixture on radio. The brainchild of two white creators, Freeman Gosden and Charles Correll, the series traced the experiences of two Southern Black men, Amos Jones and Andrew "Hogg" Brown, who had migrated from the South to the North, first to Chicago, later to Harlem. In and out of comic scrapes, the men were known for being bumbling, stumbling, dim-witted souls who had problems thinking straight and who constantly misused the English language. Gosden and Correll had first played the characters on a local Chicago radio show called *Sam 'n' Henry*. In 1928, the series was renamed and went network, running on NBC five times a week, from 7 to 7:15 each night. In the beginning, Gosden and Correll played all the roles, employing thick dialects and performing outlandish comic absurdities. Later African American performers such as Ernestine Wade, Nick Stewart, Wonderful Smith, Eddie Green, and Johnny Lee joined the cast.

No one could have predicted the extraordinary success of the show, which became a national cultural phenomenon in the first half of the twentieth century. During the fifteen minutes that *Amos 'n' Andy* was broadcast, America was said to just about close up shop. Department stores, restaurants, even movie theaters wheeled out radios, not wanting to lose customers who might otherwise rush home to listen to the program. It was said that on a summer night you could walk down almost any street in America and hear the sounds of the show blasting from radios. When the program aired, President Calvin Coolidge insisted that his staff not disturb him. Later Presidents Harry S. Truman and Dwight David Eisenhower were fans. So was First Lady Eleanor Roosevelt. George Bernard Shaw said, "There are three things which I shall never forget about America—the Rocky Mountains, Niagara Falls, and *Amos 'n' Andy*." Stock phrases from the show—"I'se regusted," "Now, ain't dat sumptin," "Splain dat to me," and "Check and double check"—entered the national lexicon. *Amos 'n' Andy*'s popularity peaked during the years of the Great Depression. Some twenty-five million listeners tuned in to hear it. Plagued by the same problems confronting most Americans at the time—unemployment, hunger, and the struggle to make ends meet—the two characters rushed into business deals or get-rich schemes that always failed. Or one might try to hoodwink the other in hopes of getting some cash. The characters' hopes for monetary success of course mirrored the lives and feelings of the down-and-out in America. But, no matter what the adversity, they laughed and cavorted. Somehow Americans reasoned that if these two colored fellows could make it through the worst of times, and do it with a joke and a big smile, why couldn't everybody else?

Television's most controversial series: Amos 'n' Andy *with (left to right) Spencer Williams as Andy, Tim Moore as Kingfish, and Alvin Childress as Amos*

In 1943, *Amos 'n' Andy,* then a half-hour show, moved to CBS, remaining popular as it kept pace with the nation's changing moods and dilemmas during World War II. In 1948, CBS paid Gosden and Correll the record sum of $2.5 million for all rights to the series. Soon a television version was planned. At first Correll and Gosden hoped to star on television—in blackface—but fortunately they dropped the idea. *Hearing* two white men playing colored clowns was one thing; *seeing* them playing colored clowns was another. So a search that drew national attention was on to find African American actors and actresses to play the now celebrated roles. Everybody in America seemed to have an opinion on the casting. Harry Truman suggested a comic at Texas State University for the role of Kingfish. Dwight Eisenhower, who was a golfing buddy of creator Gosden, recommended a Black soldier he had known during the war for the same part.

After two years and interviews or auditions with over five hundred African American actors, Gosden and Correll assembled their cast. Alvin Childress was hired as Amos, the most subdued character on the television series: a mild-mannered and sensible husband and father and the owner of the Fresh Air Cab Company. The role of Andy went to Spencer Williams. Born in 1889 in Vidalia, Louisiana, he had attended Wards Academy in Natchez, Mississippi, and later enrolled for two years at the University of Minnesota. After serving in the army, he went to Hollywood in the 1920s, where he worked on scripts for Octavus Roy Cohen stories and also scripted the comedies *Framing of the Shrew* and *Oft in the Silly Night.* Later he wrote and/or acted in such Black Westerns as *Bronze Buckaroo, Harlem Rides the Range,* and *Harlem on the Prairie.* He also directed the race movies *Go Down Death, The Blood of Jesus,* and *Juke Joint.* Having actually retired from show business to settle in Tulsa, Oklahoma, Williams returned to Los Angeles to play the role.

For the pivotal part of George "Kingfish" Stevens, veteran Tim Moore was hired. Born in Rock Island, Illinois, in 1888 (the fifth of thirteen children), Moore had left school at age eleven. A year later he began his show business career as part of an act called Cora Miskel and her Gold Dust twins. At thirteen, he was the star of a medicine show. At fifteen, he was a jockey. At seventeen, he was a boxer known as Young Klondike. For a time, he left show business to work in a factory in his hometown. Afterward he performed in vaudeville and in the hit Broadway show *Blackbirds of 1928,* which he later toured with in Europe. Returning to the States, he teamed with Vivian Harris in a comedy act that appeared with such big bands as Charlie Barnet, Jimmie Lunceford, and Erskine Hawkins. In the late 1940s, he performed in the race movie *Boy! What a Girl.* He also made it to Ed Sullivan's *Toast of the Town.* Like Spencer Williams, Moore came out of retirement to play what became his defining role.

The part of Kingfish's wife, Sapphire, went to Ernestine Wade, who had appeared on the radio program. Also in the cast were Johnny Lee as lawyer Algonquin J. Calhoun, Nick Stewart (billed as Nick O'Demus) as Lightnin', Amanda Randolph as Sapphire's Mama, and Amanda's sister Lillian Randolph as Andy's girlfriend, Madame Queen. All the cast had been entertainers for years. All were energetically revved up for the new medium which gave them a chance not only to revive their careers but also to reach a new and larger audience.

Ernestine Wade and Tim Moore —during a calmer moment—as the battlin' Sapphire and Kingfish

Spencer Williams (r.) with Charles Correll, the co-creator of Amos 'n' Andy

The show premiered on CBS on the evening of June 28, 1951, at 8:30. The episode *Kingfish Gets Drafted* was typical *Amos 'n' Andy* humor. When George "Kingfish" Stevens—who looks like he's well into his sixties—is notified that he's been drafted into the army, he becomes the hero of his neighborhood. Especially impressed are Sapphire and her Mama—who usually thinks her son-in-law is little more than a good-for-nothing shyster. When he learns that he mistakenly received a notice intended for a younger George Stevens, Kingfish, to save face in his community *and* his household, tries to enlist. But, of course, he's way too old. Finally, he fakes being inducted into the army. Later he fakes a furlough. When Sapphire and her Mama learn the truth, they bawl him out.

Most episodes focused on similar outlandish antics. In *Aunt Effie's Will,* Kingfish learns that Sapphire's recently departed aunt has left a will that specifies the sum of $2,000 is to be left to any heirs with a son. But Kingfish and Sapphire are childless. Determined to get the money, Kingfish adopts a son, none other than his forty-year-old friend Andy.

Kingfish's con-man exploits were also on display in an episode called *The Rare Coin.* Here Kingfish discovers that Andy has an old nickel worth $200. Immediately, he maneuvers to get the coin out of Andy's pocket and into his own. Thereafter he rushes to a pay telephone to call the rare coin dealer who will pay him the $200. But what coin does he inadvertently plop into the pay telephone? Why, the rare nickel of course! Then he tricks Andy into trying to pry the coin out of the phone box. The two are arrested and taken to court for damaging public property. There they are defended by their friend, the thoroughly inept lawyer Calhoun.

Another episode finds Kingfish and Sapphire invited to a hoity-toity society party at the Van Pelts'. Sapphire insists on a new dress. To purchase it, Kingfish, ever pressed for money, sells (without Sapphire's knowledge) her fur coat by claiming that it's mink. Who else but the dunce Andy buys it for his girlfriend, Rosemary. Then using the money to buy Sapphire the new dress, Kingfish ends up—unknowingly—in a department store's maternity ward, where he tells the clerk he wants a dress that his wife can do the rumba in! Matters become more complicated when Sapphire informs Kingfish that, along with her new dress, she wants to wear her fur coat to the party. She asks Kingfish to get it out of storage. To get the coat back, Kingfish has to stage a robbery in the park, where Andy and his girlfriend, who's wearing the coat, are out for an evening stroll. He enlists lawyer Calhoun to pretend to be a robber. But Calhoun is as inept as ever and botches the robbery. Afterward Andy informs Kingfish that Rosemary plans to attend the same society party and that she'll be wearing Sapphire's fur coat.

So it went on *Amos 'n' Andy* week after week. Forever trying to "get over" with one scheme or another and never appearing to have any kind of full-time employment, Kingfish spent most of his time at the lodge of his fraternal order, the Mystic Knights of the Sea. Usually, Sapphire was yelling and yapping at the top of her lungs about his shortcomings and shenanigans; so too was Sapphire's Mama. Also on hand was the slow-moving janitor Lightnin', a likable dimwit who is easily duped by Kingfish.

Viewers tuned in, laughed at the exploits, and turned the series into a ratings success. *Amos 'n' Andy*, which had entertained America through two national crises, the Depression and the war, looked as if it would answer the pop cultural needs of the new decade, the Fabulous Fifties. But protests sprang up immediately. Within hours of the airing of the first episode, New York branches of the National Association for the Advancement of Colored People criticized it for "the perpetuation of stereotyped characterizations." The local NAACP hinted at a boycott of the products of the show's sponsor—the Blatz Brewing Company—unless the series was terminated.

Reviewing the first episode, *Variety* was critical. "The fact remains that Gosden and Correll might have used their talents in projecting their Amos and Andy characters as warmer and more sympathetic people. The exaggerations were too pronounced." *Variety* added, "Considering that this is the first major use of Negroes in commercial broadcasting, the responsibility was twofold: (1) not to offend the sensibilities of a large segment of the U.S. population; (2) and to present them honestly without caricaturing weaknesses that are inherent in any human, regardless of race or color."

But most damning was the criticism at the NAACP's national convention in Atlanta on July 3, 1951, just days after the initial broadcast. Having protested against D. W. Griffith's *The Birth of a Nation* in 1915 and Hollywood's later stereotyped depictions of African Americans during the 1930s and early 1940s, the NAACP was fully aware of the power of the visual image, especially now that such images were coming into American homes nightly. The civil rights organization denounced the series. Later the NAACP listed its grievances in a paper titled "Why the *Amos 'n' Andy* TV Show Should Be Taken Off the Air":

> It tends to strengthen the conclusion among uninformed and prejudiced people that Negroes are inferior, lazy, dumb and dishonest.
>
> Every character in this one and only TV show with an all-Negro cast is either a clown or a crook.
>
> Negro doctors are shown as quacks and thieves.
>
> Negro lawyers are shown as slippery cowards, ignorant of their profession and without ethics.
>
> Negro women are shown as cackling, screaming shrews, in big-mouth close-ups, using street slang, just short of vulgarity.
>
> All Negroes are shown as dodging work of any kind.
>
> There is no other show on nation-wide television that shows Negroes in a favorable light. Very few first-class Negro performers get on TV and then only as a one-time guest.
>
> *Amos 'n' Andy* on television is worse than on radio because it is a *picture*, a living, talking, moving *picture* of Negroes, not merely a story in words over a radio loudspeaker.
>
> Millions of white Americans see this *Amos 'n' Andy* picture of Negroes and think the entire race is the same.
>
> Millions of white children learn about Negroes for the first time by seeing *Amos 'n' Andy* and carry this impression throughout their lives in one form or another.
>
> Since many whites never meet any Negroes personally, never attend any lectures or read any books on the race problem, or belong to any clubs or organizations where intergroup relations are discussed, they accept the *Amos 'n' Andy* picture as the true one.
>
> An entire race of 15,000,000 Americans is being slandered each week by this one-sided caricature on television, over the Columbia Broadcasting System, sponsored by the Blatz Brewing Company, to advertise and sell Blatz beer.

The NAACP called for letters of protest to be sent to the Blatz Brewing Company in Milwaukee and also to CBS in New York. The protests grew. One of the critical issues for TV's *Amos 'n' Andy* was that of choice. The NAACP believed African American viewers didn't have one on TV. Because television in the early 1950s carried only two shows starring African Americans—*Beulah* and *Amos 'n' Andy*—on an otherwise white programming schedule, the show took on a significance it otherwise wouldn't have had. When viewers suddenly saw Black faces rising from a sea of whiteness, those particular faces came to represent an entire race of people. (Had *I Love Lucy* been the *only* white sitcom on the air, it too would have been criticized.) As represented by *Amos 'n' Andy*, television's image of the Negro was the old stereotyped one. The blatant toms, coons, and mammies that had already disappeared from movies (or were being less obviously presented) had resurfaced shockingly in this new medium. The real failure was that, like *Beulah*, in a postwar era *Amos 'n' Andy* was trading in prewar images and ideas about ethnic humor.

For the NAACP and a new generation of African Americans about to launch the civil rights movement and demand that America become an open, fully integrated society—for a generation eager to prove itself just as "qualified," just as "educated," and just as "middle-class" as white America—*Amos 'n' Andy* looked like something out of prehistoric times. These characters were clearly *burdened* with their ethnicity and not ready to assimilate culturally. They were *colored* in an age of *Negroes.*

Loud, rowdy, and raucous, and too unknowing of the dominant culture, the characters of Sapphire, Kingfish, Andy, and lawyer Calhoun were not types to integrate a lunch counter at Woolworth's. The desire to be anywhere near white people was beyond their comprehension because white people—with few exceptions—still were not a part of their world. Interestingly and paradoxically, Beulah, as portrayed by Louise Beavers, was turned into an emblem of a budding Black middle class. More than either of the other actresses who played the role, Beavers often made Beulah a proper Black matron. Without any trace of a dialect, she was always well groomed, well coifed, and well mannered, looking like a woman ready to go off to church every Sunday. That may explain why, although *Beulah* was criticized, the show was never damned the way *Amos 'n' Andy* was. Beulah seemed capable of dealing with an integrated society, even though she could function only as a servant in that world. She knew how to behave around white people. The contradiction, though—again for the Black viewer—is that this otherwise possibly progressive Black woman has to perform such silly antics.

Yet despite the NAACP's criticism, a segment of the African American community had another view of *Amos 'n' Andy*. The *Pittsburgh Courier* columnist Billy Rowe called it "a cute and amusing show." "Negro audiences are going to find themselves in the healthy position of being able to look at people of their own color," he wrote, "performing for people of every color, without embarrassment." (Ironically, *The Pittsburgh Courier* had launched a petition drive in 1931 to have radio's *Amos 'n' Andy* banned from the airwaves.) Many African Americans from the 1950s remembered the TV series fondly. *Amos 'n' Andy*, while distorted and shameless, was also funny, clever, and brilliantly cast. The writers mastered the sitcom formula, creating half-hour comedies with every incident and line of dialogue fitting perfectly in presenting, developing, and resolving the comic situation. Yet the individual sequences were as funny as the episodes as a whole.

For a segment of the African American audience, *Amos 'n' Andy* also presented some authentic folk humor within a realm of total unreality. Both a braggart and a trickster, always stirring up problems for everyone, Kingfish was also something of a street hustler trying to live a

On the set with Tim Moore and Amanda Randolph, who played his nemesis, Sapphire's Mama

bourgeois existence. Kingfish and Andy were clearly old-style coon types—that familiar minstrel stereotype of the African American as lazy, ignorant, buffoonish. But because the characters operated in an almost exclusively Black world, some African American viewers were not disturbed or alienated by the very obvious stereotypes. Unlike Stepin Fetchit, who shamelessly clowned it up—dumbing himself down—for the benefit of whites in his Hollywood films of the 1930s, Kingfish, Andy, Calhoun, and Lightnin' clowned and kidded with one another. *Amos 'n' Andy* was dazzling communal coonery.

Though whites sometimes appeared on *Amos 'n' Andy*, usually the authority figures (the judges, policemen, and physicians) were Black. The series presented a world in which white people, for the most part, simply didn't exist. What emerged was a lopsided semblance of an African American community in which distinct social classes existed. When Sapphire wants that new dress for the society party at the Van Pelts', she's hoping to move into an upwardly mobile world. The recurring character Henry Van Porter (Jester Hairston) is an upper-class dandy, dressed to the nines with fancy suits, ties, and a monocle. (Hairston also played Sapphire's shiftless brother Leroy.) Sapphire's chief complaint to Kingfish is that his friend Andy is low-class, uncouth, and a no-account; not fit for the middle-class household she's striving to create. Part of the perverse appeal of Andy and Kingfish, of course, is that they haven't adopted—and don't care to adopt—middle-class values and virtues. Though Andy fell in love on various episodes, he never succumbed to the bourgeois institution of marriage. He saw what Kingfish endured!

For later generations, it may be surprising to see the way Kingfish and Sapphire live. In their Harlem apartment, totally unlike the ghetto residences on later shows like *Good Times* and *Sanford and Son*, everything was neatly ordered without any real suggestion of poverty or deprivation or of lives lived in any type of disarray or dysfunction. Nor were there cultural signs to indicate that African Americans rather than whites occupied the premises.

Though most of the men on *Amos 'n' Andy* speak in broad dialects with poor grammar, the women are sometimes drawn differently. On some episodes, Sapphire and her Mama are pure shrews—unable to breathe without raising their voices; unable to think without complaining about something. Henpecked Kingfish finds himself emasculated by them. But on other episodes (such as *The Society Party*) Sapphire and the other female characters are reasonable, intelligent, and really on the ball, able to see through the males' clownish charades. Here, of course, the series fell in line with traditional movie/radio images of Black women (in the past, usually those divested of their sexuality) as industrious and productive; and of Black men as lacking the skills and drive to function in the larger society. Yet the women sometimes mark something new, mainly because they articulated their feelings about a class system in the African American community.

The one mature and responsible male was Amos, who (as on the radio show) was depicted as a hard worker and dedicated family man with a wife named Ruby (Jane Ellis) and a daughter named Arbadella (Patty Marie Ellis). A memorable Christmas show spotlighted Amos's positive traits. His daughter Arbadella sees a doll she loves. But it is too expensive for the family to buy. Andy, who is Arbadella's godfather, takes a job as a department store Santa Claus to earn extra money to buy the doll, which he brings to Amos's home on Christmas Eve. Afterward Amos sits in Arbadella's bedroom as the girl goes to sleep. Reciting the Lord's Prayer, he tries to explain its meaning to her. It was a restrained, emotionally well-textured sequence. *Variety* called the episode "truly wonderful," "deeply moving," and "an almost classic bit," in which "the great value of showing a Negro family living normal lives in normal surroundings, sharing in the emotional and religious experiences of all people at Christmas time, became particularly evident."

The episode also remains the one most cited by *Amos 'n' Andy*'s defenders. If the series had done more of this type of show, it might have been a revolutionary program for television.

What remains odd and striking is that the subject of racism doesn't exist on *Amos 'n' Andy*, not only because of the absence of whites but also because of the characters' attitudes. Never does Kingfish decry the fact that he cannot buy Sapphire a new dress because he can't find work—because the Man runs the world. Never do we see some hostile white landlord demanding that George and Sapphire Stevens pay their rent. The series never expressed or even suggested anger or indignation about the system—racial, economic, or social. (Other television sitcoms didn't either.) It exists in a social/political vacuum. This very absence of comment on race—and racism—differentiates it from a later series like *Sanford and Son*, in which the characters were also sometimes lazy, triflin', and ignorant. But the later characters were so quick to voice their anger about the system's inequities and its racism that viewers seldom criticized them for trafficking in some of the same distorted tomfoolery as *Amos 'n' Andy*.

African American viewers no doubt had mixed emotions about the program. Aware that the show trivialized the experiences of the American Negro and fed into the worst racist stereotype of the Negro as illiterate, ignorant, and lazy, they also saw glimmers of African American humor and traditions, even if through a distorted lens. Actually, some of the humor and situations of *Amos 'n' Andy* had been lifted from a brand of African American comedy that had turned up in Black shows and clubs of the past. The African American comedy team of Flournoy Miller and Aubrey Lyles (who starred in and wrote the book for the groundbreaking 1921 Black musical *Shuffle Along*) specialized in playing off one another's wit—and in creating characters that frequently put some deal over on one another. They also created comic characters trying to make it through a world that seemed absurd and indifferent to their plight as African American men.

During *Amos 'n' Andy*'s radio days, Miller was stunned to hear material by his partner Lyles and himself—notably that of two Black men confused by simple arithmetic—lifted almost verbatim by Gosden and Correll. He threatened a lawsuit. Perhaps in an effort to placate him, Gosden and Correll later hired Miller as a writer for the radio and TV versions of the show. He also played a major role in helping cast the African American actors for the television series. But he always believed some of his act had been stolen and then popularized for a white audience without the distinct African American cultural demarcations that had originally appealed to Black audiences.

Perhaps the very aspect of *Amos 'n' Andy* that made it so enjoyable for some audiences in the early 1950s—namely, the performances—has made it somewhat alien to later generations. The work of the actors—the broad smiles, the double takes, the exaggerated dialects, the outlandish mugging, the timing, the energy level—was intentionally stagy and overblown, tied very much to vaudeville and ethnic theater, where Black performers often overplayed for their audiences. African American critic Margo Jefferson, who recalled enjoying the show as a child, once said that Lightnin' was her favorite character. He appealed to her because comedy itself "is such a mixture of empathy and superiority, identification and alienation." She found Lightnin' "provocatively unlike me (which let me laugh at him) and oddly like me (which let me laugh with him). For one thing, we were both cross-eyed. For another thing, which had precious little to do with race, I was a child, and his was the comedy of regression: broad, slow gestures; grimaces and double takes; sounds that broke language into vowels, syllables and tones."

Significantly, most of the performers on the series had built their careers in Black clubs and theaters. Accustomed to punching their lines for a Black audience (which didn't always laugh at the same jokes as a white one), they were also shrewdly aware that a gesture or a hand on a hip or a widening of the eyes immediately telegraphed an attitude or a mood or perspective that no piece of dialogue could ever hope to match. The cast worked together splendidly. Although each was a born scene stealer, none ever stepped on the others' lines; all in all, theirs was possibly the finest example of ensemble acting in the early years of television.

Curiously, though, as good as the actors were, they were not able to suggest another life for their characters. The extraordinary aspect of early African American film actors and actresses—McDaniel in *Gone With the Wind*, Bill "Bojangles" Robinson in his movies with Shirley Temple, Fredi Washington and Louise Beavers in *Imitation of Life*—was their ability to make us believe that their characters lived other lives away from the on-screen action; one often felt the text was not telling the entire story, not expressing the full range of these characters' emotions and motivations. The actors were able—also partly because of the narrative structure of the old films—to breathe life into their material. So strong and vivid was their work that the audience was compelled not only by what it saw but also by what it didn't see; what it believed the movie wasn't saying. That didn't happen on *Amos 'n' Andy*. What you saw was what you got.

Still, the actors' type of old-style ethnic humor and exaggerations might have succeeded in an African American forum. At New York's Apollo Theater, comics like Jackie "Moms" Mabley and Dewey "Pigmeat" Markham continued to perform this type of material. Black audiences accepted the exaggerations as precisely that and not as anything real. At the same time, at a theater like the Apollo, other African American performers would appear on display in a revue-style lineup of talents—musicians like Louis Armstrong and Miles Davis or bandleader

Earl "Fatha" Hines or singers like Sarah Vaughan, Betty Carter, and Nancy Wilson—thus presenting the audience with some diversity of images.

The protests against the television series continued for the next two years, until finally CBS, bowing to pressure, removed *Amos 'n' Andy* from its broadcast schedule in 1953. Here again television executives showed themselves to be terrified of controversy. *Amos 'n' Andy*, however, remained in syndication for years, becoming popular with younger viewers of the late 1950s and early 1960s. Then, in 1963, CBS revealed that the series had been sold to two African nations: Kenya and Nigeria. Afterward the Kenyan government announced that *Amos 'n' Andy* would be banned in the country. Protests sprang up the next year as a Chicago station was about to broadcast reruns. Finally, CBS withdrew *Amos 'n' Andy* from syndication in 1966.

Many of the *Amos 'n' Andy* actors saw their careers end with the series. Tim Moore, Spencer Williams, Alvin Childress, and Johnny Lee briefly toured, playing their *Amos 'n' Andy* characters. Afterward Spencer Williams went back into retirement. Alvin Childress performed later in episodes of *Sanford and Son, Good Times,* and *The Jeffersons* as well as the TV movie *Eleanor and Franklin.* Ernestine Wade rarely worked. Amanda and Lillian Randolph played roles in other series.

Tim Moore, however, who for African American viewers was an authentic television star, went into a sad decline. After years of struggle, the series had finally brought him a steady paycheck and national attention. But unable to find work afterward, he was plagued by financial and personal problems. In 1958, he made headlines after being arrested for assault with a deadly weapon. During a quarrel with his wife over a slab of roast beef that had disappeared, Moore fired a shotgun at her. He was jailed. Following a nonjury trial, Moore's charge was reduced to illegal use of a firearm. Fined $100, he was placed on one-year probation. Back in the news with coverage by both the mainstream and the African American press, Moore briefly got engagements. He made three appearances on *The Jack Paar Show* and then landed a booking at the Mocambo, the famed Los Angeles nightclub, where Frank Sinatra and other celebrities sat in the audience. There was talk of a series with Moore and George Jessel. But nothing came of that. Moore died penniless of tuberculosis in December 1958.

It would be years before the appearance of a new series starring African Americans. Yet both *Amos 'n' Andy* and *Beulah* left their mark on those Black shows that followed. Joyous Black nurturers like Beulah would turn up in other series of the 1950s as well as later shows like *Father of the Bride* and *Gimme a Break!* Bickering, hooting Black couples would appear in such shows as *Sanford and Son* and *The Jeffersons*. For years, a mature, sexual Black couple would be missing from primetime series. Responsible, adult Black males would also rarely turn up. Significantly, the acceptable format for a Black-cast series—for decades to come—would be the sitcom. There, the fundamentally happy-go-lucky Negro would never be perceived as a threat by the mainstream audience. In the world of the sitcom—with the fast-moving, unending stream of escapist jokes and gags—the idea of racial inequities and injustices or political resistance might, somehow, temporarily rear its head but then be brushed aside or laughed away.

OTHER ETHNICS

Surprisingly, despite the controversy, both *Beulah* and *Amos 'n' Andy* also indicated that the prewar movie and radio types might still win favor with television viewers during the Truman and Eisenhower eras. Prewar-style representations of other ethnic groups also aired. *The Goldbergs*—created by actress Gertrude Berg and a radio hit for almost twenty years—arrived on television in 1949. The story of a middle-class Jewish family in the Bronx, its central character, the mother Molly Goldberg—speaking in a Yiddish accent—was talkative, gossipy, meddlesome, and forever trying to solve the problems of her family and friends. Or just about anyone else around her. She, of course, was something of the traditional Jewish yenta. The syndicated series *Life with Luigi* dramatized the experiences of an Italian immigrant to Chicago, whose accent and problems with the language, naturally, were "hilarious." Actor J. Carrol Naish played Luigi. He also starred in the 1958 syndicated series *The New Adventures of Charlie Chan*—based on the hit movie series—which recounted the adventures of a wise and often *inscrutable* "Oriental" detective in San Francisco. The long-running *Lone Ranger* featured Jay Silverheels as the noble Native American Tonto, the perfect sidekick and loyal companion to the white man, whom he called Kemo Sabe (trusty scout), in this tale of a former Texas Ranger bringing order to the Wild West. Even *I Love Lucy*'s Ricky Ricardo was often a hot-tempered Latin, who, when excited, butchered the English language, speaking a polyglot of English, Spanish, and whatever.

Television didn't seem comfortable with ethnic groups unless these Others were turned comic or absurd. Any cultural experiences or attitudes—except those of the generic white American—remained a source of derision for years. Everything that seemed "foreign" or "alien" was fodder for laughs or condescension: from the way the characters spoke to the way they dressed to the ideas they espoused.

Still, once *Amos 'n' Andy* and *Beulah* were off the air, network television was almost lily white. Some syndicated shows (usually airing in the afternoons) like *Ramar of the Jungle* and *Jungle Jim* (each centering on a mighty white man on the dark continent of Africa, taming the restless or childlike natives) as well as *Sheena, Queen of the Jungle* (with a mighty white woman) were broadcast. Although *Ramar of the Jungle* was sometimes set in India, all these shows further contributed to a portrait of Africa as a savage, backward, cultureless continent.

COMIC SERVANTS: FAMILIAR ANTICS, FAMILIAR FACES

Television's audience continued to grow at a rapid pace. While only 3 percent of American households had television sets in 1949, 24 percent of homes had the tube by 1954. By 1956, the number had grown to 72 percent. During these years, weekly sitcoms or family dramas—such shows as *The Adventures of Ozzie & Harriet, Father Knows Best,* and *Leave It to Beaver*—often featured well-scrubbed, wholesome, non-ethnic, generically white households. Viewers, however, did see African American characters in supporting roles on such sitcoms as *The Trouble with Father, My Little Margie, The Danny Thomas Show,* and *The Jack Benny Show.* Updating old images and making them less offensive, the actors handled their modulated dialects well and managed to create characters that, though still distorted, were not blatant caricatures. But almost always their characters were comic servants. Like Hattie McDaniel and Louise Beavers, many of the actors playing these servant

Variety programs like The Ed Sullivan Show *brought a host of African American stars into American homes. Sullivan with Dorothy Dandridge. With Eartha Kitt. With a young Richard Pryor*

roles had already made careers out of such parts in Hollywood films in the 1930s and 1940s. Now they found themselves again stuck with scraps from the past. Yet many knew how to work their way around the roles.

That was certainly true of tall, lanky, half-asleep Willie Best—once billed as "Sleep 'n' Eat" and considered a Stepin Fetchit clone—who stammered, stuttered, and did wickedly timed double takes in scores of films during the Depression and war eras. His movie career ended right after the war with the release of his last films—*Suddenly, It's Spring* and *The Red Stallion* in 1947. But just when it looked as if he might have to pack up his bags and get out of the movie capital, Best, after a three-year hiatus, revived his career on television, appearing in two series in the early 1950s.

The forever startled or bewildered Willie Best as Charlie, the elevator "boy" on My Little Margie

He was best known for his role as the elevator "boy" Charlie on the sitcom *My Little Margie.* Best repeatedly bugged his eyes at the slightest provocation and looked stunned by the most ordinary of occurrences. On one occasion, upon delivering Margie Albright and her boyfriend Freddie to their floor, Best's Charlie becomes delirious over the sight of the two kissing good night. Widening his eyes, he goes into a romantic swoon. Apparently, he's never experienced love himself nor known much about sexual desire (or fulfilling it).

Best also performed on the sitcom *The Trouble with Father*, which aired under the title *The Stu Erwin Show* as well. Again cast as a likable childlike dunce, he's Willie, the family handyman, a nifty tagalong playmate for the family's adolescent daughter Jackie. Mostly called upon to react and to observe, he rarely initiates any action. Seen today, though, Willie sometimes strikes—for African American viewers—an ironic note. On one episode, when he finds himself near a city council building, Willie turns nervous. "The county jail is over there, isn't it?" he asks, looking as if he's about to tremble. "Well, this is as close as I want to get to it."

For white audiences of the time, Best probably seemed like the typical Black man, accustomed to getting in and out of trouble and fearful of heading back to a jailhouse that he's already familiar with. But for African American audiences, Best may have appeared to have some sense tucked inside his nonsense. Here's a Black man who just might understand it doesn't take much, perhaps not even a real crime, for him to end up in a jailhouse.

In this same episode, the writers may have unintentionally used Best as a counter-comment on the traditional white male view of things. The series' lead character, Stu Erwin, is a high school principal, forever involved in civic activities. He's also one of early TV's typical all-American doofus dads, which means that, like Dagwood Bumstead, he heads the household but is usually befuddled. Here his young daughter Jackie is angered to hear that the local playground keeper has lost his job because he's considered too old. No one, including her father as well as the president of the local city council, seems to care. But Jackie draws up a petition to have the man's job reinstated. The problem now is getting community adults to sign it. "Willie, you're an adult, aren't you?" she says to her Black buddy. Of course, the joke was that Willie was supposed to be as much a kid as young Jackie. He signs the petition but doesn't seem to know what he's doing. After all these years, the scene remains tough to watch. You feel the actor on-screen is being humiliated.

Nonetheless, Jackie enlists her mother's help in getting signatures— and also the help of Willie—who goes about his petition work with a surprising comic earnestness. In its own pop way, the episode suggests that those without power—women and here an unskilled Black man—are willing to fight against the status quo as well as a corrupt political figure and perhaps are the real agents for change in the future. As it turned out, the playground keeper's replacement was to have been the brother-in-law of the president of the city council. In the end, thanks to the petition drive, the older man gets his job back.

Of course, Willie Best always played his characters in a traditional asexual comic coon style. Though he was funny and knew how to get mileage out of the briefest moments on-screen by gracing his fool character with a kind of daffy enlightenment, he also looked tired, aware, certainly, that he had been playing the same fool role for almost twenty years. Best no doubt understood that if he petitioned anyone, he probably should have chosen the writers and producers of programs like *The Stu Erwin Show*.

Also working as regulars on sitcoms were the Randolph sisters—Lillian and Amanda. Having already appeared in such films as *At the Circus, It's a Wonderful Life,* and *The Bachelor and the Bobby-Soxer,* Lillian Randolph played the title role on the radio series *Beulah,* after Hattie McDaniel's death. But television viewers came to know her best as the audacious Madame Queen on *Amos 'n' Andy* and then as the good-natured housekeeper Birdie Lee Coggins on the 1955 syndicated sitcom *The Great Gildersleeve.*

This sitcom also centered on a "father" forever baffled by life's intricacies. A bachelor and the water commissioner in the mythical town of Summerfield, Throckmorton P. Gildersleeve (Willard Waterman) lives with his surrogate children—his niece and nephew. Birdie runs the household, at times even looking like a surrogate wife to Gildersleeve. But, of course, that thought was never supposed to cross a viewer's mind. (The same would be true years later with the Nell/Kanisky relationship on the sitcom *Gimme a Break!*)

Having played Birdie on the *Gildersleeve* radio show and in a low-budget movie series, Randolph sometimes performed as if she were retreading material. Birdie mainly has to smile, be agreeable, react to Gildersleeve, and, along the way, update the comic maid/mammy figure, making her less exaggerated and foolish. She's still not a person. And Randolph has none of the outrageous comic hauteur that made her Madame Queen so memorable.

Lillian Randolph (center with Mary Lee Robb and Willard Waterman), who appeared on radio, in the movies, and on television as the housekeeper Birdie in The Great Gildersleeve

Lillian Randolph, however, had staying power, working into the 1970s, almost up to the time of her death in 1980. Not only did she play small roles in the movies *Hush . . . Hush, Sweet Charlotte; The Great White Hope; Once Is Not Enough; The Onion Field;* and *Magic,* but in the late 1960s Bill Cosby cast her as his mother in *The Bill Cosby Show.* Randolph also turned up on such television programs as *Mannix, That's My Mama, The Autobiography of Miss Jane Pittman, Sanford and Son, The Jeffersons,* and *Roots.*

Her sister Amanda also fared well. Having begun her career in nightclubs and musicals in Cleveland, Amanda Randolph appeared on Broadway in the Black-cast musicals *Shuffle Along* and *Chocolate Dandies* and became a leading lady of the Alhambra Stock Company in Harlem. She eventually worked in such films as *No Way Out, She's Working Her Way Through College, A Man Called Peter,* and in Oscar Micheaux's Black-cast films *Lying Lips, Swing,* and as that comically hysterical landlady in *Underworld.* In 1953, after having played the maid on the sitcom *The Laytons* and then Sapphire's Mama on *Amos 'n' Andy* as well as having hosted her own local program, *The Amanda*

Show, she began an eleven-year run as the housekeeper Louise on *Make Room for Daddy,* later called *The Danny Thomas Show.*

In her earlier work, Amanda Randolph's characterizations sometimes were so broad that it was easy to think she didn't have any talent. Her Mama just seemed to shout and look tough and mean. But then the scripts for *Amos 'n' Andy* never gave her a chance to do much else. She could be hilarious when her Mama turned girlishly coy and demure, usually if she had an eye on some gentleman. You knew Mama was being phony. But you couldn't resist her mellow but futile game plans for romance. Always apparent were her expert timing and her great gift for ensemble acting. Ultimately, Randolph became a delirious scream on *Amos 'n' Andy.* But her performances on *The Danny Thomas Show* proved she could play other characters as well.

The series focused on Danny Thomas as Danny Williams, an entertainer coping with the demands of his profession and those of his family. Keeping the household in tip-top shape was Randolph's maid, Louise. Here again was an African American woman as the traditional homebound nurturing servant, who because we don't know much about her life away from the white family she cares for, seems inordinately caught up in them. Yet Amanda Randolph was able to inject some bite and a little sweetened vinegar into her character. Randolph's performances made Louise something of a shrewd realist who speaks with a casual authority.

On one episode, her employer Williams is laid up with a leg injury. Babying himself shamelessly, he lies around the house, deliberately taking his time to recover while lapping up as much attention and sympathy as possible. At one point he complains he can only do so much because "I have a broken leg." Louise, however, just looks at him and says, "You're not exactly on the operating table. That leg's been out of a cast for weeks."

When she's about to go home at the end of the day, Louise can't resist letting Williams know how well she's taken care of him while also getting in a little dig as well. "I guess you're all set for the evening," Louise says. "Cigars. Lighter. Kleenex. Snack for later on. Remote control for television. Candy. And fruit. You know, Joseph never prepared the Egyptians for the seven-year famine like you're prepared tonight."

Amanda Randolph (right) as the domestic Louise on **Make Room for Daddy,** *with Danny Thomas and Jean Hagen. The network received hate letters whenever any sign of affection was shown between Louise and her sitcom employers*

Of course, the writers threw a biblical reference into Louise's dialogue to better delineate her as a traditional churchgoing, no doubt God-fearing Black woman. Such biblical references were used for years with Black characters until finally even that would become an element in stereotyping African Americans.

Usually, when Louise had something to say to her employer Williams (and she was rarely at a loss for words), she looked him straight in the eye. Always pleasant but never sugarcoating her comments, Randolph's Louise emerged—in TV terms anyway—as a fairly assertive, intelligent character, and it was her realistic grasp of situations, compared with Williams's self-centered theatrics, that gave her appearances a nice twist and a sardonic flip. Viewers loved the fact that she could usually see through his every sham. Helping to shift the perspective on the series, Randolph's Louise was one of its realistic anchors. But, of course, the series was not built around Louise. Had she been the star, no doubt she would have had to endure the same simp maneuvers as poor Beulah.

Nevertheless, the writers of *The Danny Thomas Show* saw Randolph's skill. But even the slightest attempt to broaden her character met with resistance. "Whenever Danny or any member of his family showed physical affection for Amanda—a kiss on the cheek, an arm on the shoulder—I could count on a shower of hate mail," recalled the show's producer, Sheldon Leonard. One such letter read: "When I want to see a white man petting a gorilla, I'll go to the zoo." Another read: "I don't allow niggers in my living room and you have no right to put them there." "One of the peculiarities of this kind of mail, aside from its crudeness," said Leonard, "was that much of it was written in the same handwriting, and with the same postmark. The names were different. It was an obvious attempt by some sick people to make themselves seem like many more than they were." Yet such mail always made the networks nervous.

After *The Danny Thomas Show*, Amanda Randolph took whatever work she could find. But *Jet* reported in 1966 that "Miss Randolph, at 70, is not at all financially well fixed. In fact, the aging actress needs a couple of roles in shows to qualify for a pension she sorely needs." The next year Randolph died of a stroke.

Surprisingly less effective among the actors cast as servants was Clarence Muse. Having worked in movies since 1928—in such films as *Hearts in Dixie, So Red the Rose*, and the very entertaining race movie *Broken Strings*—and having scripted (with Langston Hughes) the Hollywood film *Way Down South*, Muse was one of Hollywood's most important African American actors in the 1930s. He also took himself very seriously, which didn't always help his performances.

In 1955, Muse appeared on the television series *Casablanca*, which alternated with the series *Cheyenne* and *King's Row* under the general title *Warner Brothers Presents*. In this small-screen version of the famous Bogart film, Muse portrayed Sam, who sits at the piano, where he plays and sings "As Time Goes By." Muse seemed like little more than a prop used to inject some energy and style into a lifeless project. The only problem was that Muse himself lacked the necessary style and effervescence to pull the thing off.

Worse was that the TV version failed to re-create what made Sam so interesting in the film: his relationship with leading man Rick (now played by Charles McGraw), who owns the Club American, where Sam works. The movie had toyed with the idea of interracial male bonding. Aware of Rick's history and his vulnerabilities, Sam was able to tap the hero's emotional core with his song "As Time Goes By." But television's Rick and Sam seemed simply to go through the motions of friendship and camaraderie without insights into one another's character.

Most interesting on the television version was what transpired when a love interest turned up for Rick. On one episode, a young woman (played by Anita Ekberg), who is mad for Rick, confides her feelings and fears about her life to Sam. Or so we are told. Suggested was the idea of an emotional rapport (a white woman opening her heart to an African American man) but no such rapport was actually dramatized for the viewer, which might have raised the idea of Black male/white female intimacy (whether it be sexual or emotional). Instead we hear her speak of their encounter. "I saw Sam," she tells Rick. "We talked." Throughout, Muse was a bit of a blank. Though he wants to hold the screen and make a scene all his own, he doesn't have the drive or imagination to do it in the way that even a Willie Best did.

EDDIE ANDERSON'S ROCHESTER: OUTWITTING MR. BENNY

Of all the actors to play early TV servants, the one clearly ten steps ahead of the others, as he had been in films, was Eddie "Rochester" Anderson. Born in Oakland, California, in 1905, Eddie Anderson had grown up in a family of entertainers. His father, Big Ed, was a minstrel performer; his mother, Ella, a circus tightrope walker. As a teenager, Anderson formed an act with his older brother Cornelius. Later he traveled with Cornelius and another young man as part of a trio called Three Black Aces. During these early years, Anderson sang and danced, not yet realizing his comedic talents. In the Depression era, he appeared in bits in films and then caught the attention of moviegoers when he played Noah in Hollywood's 1936 Black-cast film *The Green Pastures*. But his great success came in the late 1930s when he teamed with white comedian Jack Benny, one of the nation's most popular radio stars.

Searching for an actor to play a porter on a train skit for his radio program, Benny went with this unknown who auditioned on an open call and whose most distinguishing characteristic was his gravelly, sandpaper-like voice. As a twelve-year-old hawking newspapers, Anderson had strained his vocal cords, which left him with the distinctive throaty sound that he would become famous for.

Eddie "Rochester" Anderson and Jack Benny, perhaps America's first interracial comedy team

With his first appearance—on Easter Sunday 1937—Anderson was such a hit that he was immediately signed as a regular on Benny's show. Somehow it was decided to call the character, now Benny's manservant, Rochester. No one remembers why. In the beginning, Anderson wasn't billed on the Benny program. Some radio listeners actually thought Rochester was Benny's servant who somehow showed up in the radio studio each week and caused a laugh riot. Anderson as the character—on radio and then films with Jack Benny—clicked so strongly that he thereafter became identified by the name, till finally he was billed in his films with and without Jack Benny as Eddie "Rochester" Anderson.

On the television series—from 1950 to 1965—Anderson's Rochester was again an audience favorite. Perhaps because roles appeared to be tailor-made for Anderson, he rarely had to go through any demeaning or fake cheery antics and dialogue. Consequently, the African

American audience didn't feel that sense of unease it experienced when certain other Black actors appeared in comedy sketches.

Lena Horne once said Anderson was the first modern Black comedian. There was nothing servile or submissive about him. He neither spoke in dialect nor was stooped over. Nor did he ever suck up to Benny or back off from telling him the truth. He always gave a furiously funny spin to the words "boss" and "Mr. Benny." Cocky and confident, always resourceful and witty, Rochester seemed his own man and usually behaved as if he were the boss in the Jack Benny household; an idea that the scriptwriters played with time and again in the series.

On the premiere episode of Benny's television program (which included individual sitcom-like sequences within a variety show format), Rochester's confidence and his carefree attitude about his work in the Benny household were on prominent display. Practically given the opening half of the show all to himself, he was first seen propped up on a window ledge, cleaning the window. But no ordinary window cleaner is he. He's dressed in neat shirt and tie. And he's singing "My Blue Heaven"!

From there, Anderson's given a chance to show his gift for visual/physical comedy as he gingerly uses a feather duster to dust around the room. As he does so, he dances in his inimitable style. What made his dance steps such a surprise was that at first glance he seemed too sturdy and heavy-footed a guy to have any grace or agility. But in a very athletic, masculine manner, he's unexpectedly light on his feet, able to slide, glide, turn, and tap with the greatest of ease. "Work. Work. Work," he says as he moves about. "That's all I do around here. Seven days a week."

Throughout the episodes, there were built-in nods to the audience's awareness of Rochester: his character traits, habits, idiosyncrasies. As series always do, the episodes allowed the audience to delight in its own anticipation of how Rochester—with or without Benny—would behave. He could always be counted on to make cracks about Benny's well-known vanity. Or Benny's stinginess. On the premiere episode, when Jack Benny's phone rings, Rochester answers, "Mr. Benny's residence." Then he adds, poking fun at his boss, "Star of stage, screen, and radio and television." Of course, as it turns out, the call is not for Benny but for Rochester.

On another episode, Rochester comments on his boss, the cheapskate. Benny wants to know what Rochester would like for Christmas and what he gave him the previous year. Without missing a beat, Rochester answers, "A brand-new dollar bill! And a lecture on the evils of wine, women, and song."

Unlike other African American male comics (like Willie Best and Tim Moore's Kingfish), who seemed sexually neutralized or asexual, Rochester, on TV as in the movies, was permitted to have lady friends. Part of the joke was he was usually trying to maneuver his way out of the boss's pad in order to make a little time for a girlfriend. On the premiere episode, Rochester has a telephone conversation with his girlfriend Susie, who asks if he can get Mr. Benny's car for the evening. "*We* have a rule in this house," he replies. "If we take the car anyplace and it brings us back the same day, we don't press our luck any farther."

When he wants Susie to wear a certain dress that evening, she says, "But, Rochester, that dress is so tight."

He just growls and says, "Yes!"

On another episode when Benny and Rochester are packing for a trip to New York, Benny tells his manservant, "As soon as we get there, you'll go to Harlem, and that'll be the last time I see you. You'll be spending all your time with your girlfriend Dorothy."

"Oh, boss, you know that isn't true," says Rochester.

"It isn't, hey. The last time we went to New York, you didn't even wait for the train to get into Grand Central Station. You pulled the emergency cord at a Hundred Twenty-fifth Street."

"I know."

"All right. So what was the big emergency?"

"I had to get to Dorothy's house fast," says Rochester. "Her boyfriend was a porter on the train."

Rochester neither over- nor underplayed his sexuality. Never did he permit himself to become something of a comic buck (as did the character Martin in the 1990s, who seemed to have nothing but sex on his mind). Rochester was never coarse or vulgar. Nor did he objectify women.

His work with Benny broke precedents and cultural taboos. The two were television's first interracial comedy team (just as they'd been in the movies). Like the best comedy duos, they complemented each other splendidly. Exchanging barbs, they understood one another's persona, one another's rhythm, one another's timing. Benny could be uptight and tightfisted. Rochester was loose and at ease with himself and the world. Benny could have doubts and always questioned himself and the situations he got himself into. Rochester was too assured to ever question anything. Benny seemed anal-retentive. Rochester wouldn't even harbor such an idea about himself. In a way, they were the Oscar and Felix of their day, the original odd couple. And while the crux of their relationship was that they were master and servant, Rochester never seemed to serve anybody other than himself. At times, he appeared to feel downright sorry for Benny.

The series, of course, spotlighted the idea of interracial male bonding. Race and culture were subjects that occasionally made their way into the episodes. There were references to Rochester and Harlem. Rochester also didn't hesitate to let it be known that where he came from, they did things in a different way. But the two men respected each other. Significantly, too, whereas later bonding dramas often emphasized the theme of the African American man sacrificing himself for his white friend, Rochester never appeared to sacrifice or deny any integral part of himself for the boss or anyone else. He liked Benny. But he liked himself better.

Eddie "Rochester" Anderson wasn't the greatest Black star of the era. That distinction would belong to Ethel Waters. But he was one of the best-known Black players, one of the best-paid, and one of the few series performers to do guest spots on other programs. Later in the decade he would be the big name in the special telecast of *The Green Pastures*.

Looking back on these early servant characters, one might want to dismiss all of them. Yet the Black actors and actresses of these early series enlivened television with a different type of style and presence. Their dialects, double takes, attitudinizing, their body language were all cultural signs that energized the early series, sometimes giving them an edge, sometimes spicing up otherwise routine and bland material. Had television given them something different to express, there's no telling what they might have accomplished.

Givin' 'em dat ole-time religion—and dem ole-time images, too: The Green
Pastures *with William Warfield as De Lawd with two heavenly attendants*

Wouldn't it have been deliriously jolting to have seen Louise
Beavers's Beulah turn *evil* on the Hendersons? Or what if Beulah and
Bill or even Beulah and Willie Best's Charlie from *My Little Margie*, in
their private quarters, had the opportunity to mock the Hendersons or
the Albrights, poking fun at their pretentions or follies—just as real
Black servants did when away from their employers? Had we seen their
lives in their own homes with their own families and their own honesty
about the work they did, the people they served, and the nation in
which they lived, these actors would have had the chance to boldly
(rather than covertly) open the eyes of television viewers.

So rare was the appearance of African Americans on a medium that
remained almost exclusively white that Black viewers always registered
excitement at the sight of a Black performer on that box in their living
rooms. In the early days, there was usually someone in a Black neighborhood with a television set, and often enough various neighbors
piled into that house for a gander. For Black Americans, early television
could be both a family and a communal affair.

More significantly, Black viewers often intuitively responded to the
personal messages the performers brought to their roles. White and
Black viewers would read the performers on these shows in entirely dif-

ferent ways. Singer Etta James remembered that in the Los Angeles of her childhood "all the black actors were heroes. They might play fools on the screen, but the folks in the neighborhood knew it took more than a fool to break into lily-white Hollywood."

Still, in the mid-1950s, television remained locked in a time warp; not yet ready to present—on a regular weekly basis—dramatic or more complicated African American characters. The African American publication *Jet* reported that when Black actress Maidie Norman appeared on the cop show *Dragnet* in 1956, she was the first African American performer cast (in a guest spot) in the series. Hy Gardner, the editor of the *New York Herald Tribune*'s radio-TV magazine, wrote of the "wall of frustration that faced such black stars as Lena Horne, Dorothy Dandridge, Billy Ekstine, Duke Ellington, Ethel Waters, Marian Anderson, Pearl Bailey and Harry Belafonte. Television will throw them a bone from time to time but the meat, a program of their own, remains hidden away in the deep freeze of intolerance. Whether the fault lies with the networks or the sponsors, whether they fear possible public reaction in certain quarters, is immaterial. The viewing public is being cheated of many hours of enjoyment." Serious African American characters on the primetime series were almost nonexistent. So too was any serious thought that the mass audience might give to African American life—or the place of the Negro in American society.

By the mid-1950s, television's African American characters looked all the more hopelessly, disturbingly anachronistic, especially in light of political and social developments in American society. In 1954, the Supreme Court decision in the case of *Brown* v. *Board of Education* had ruled that segregation in public schools was unconstitutional. A year later, seamstress Rosa Parks refused to sit in the back of the bus, and consequently sparked the Montgomery bus boycott that in turn helped lead to the rise of the civil rights movement. Soon America would see a series of other boycotts, protests, demonstrations, and sit-ins while a lineup of new African American leaders would come to national prominence: Martin Luther King Jr., Thurgood Marshall, Medgar Evers.

The movies were reflecting the changes of American life—and also of Black America's evolving view of itself. Following the Negro Problem

Pictures of 1949, Hollywood had continued to present more progressive African American images. Joseph L. Mankiewicz's *No Way Out* dramatized the plight of a young Black doctor, falsely accused by a racist of killing a white patient. The film climaxed with a city so torn apart by the case that a full-fledged race riot erupted. In films like *Bright Road* and *Carmen Jones*, Dorothy Dandridge had drawn portraits of modern African American women: sensitive, intelligent, dramatic, determined to make their own decisions. But if one were to come to any conclusions about the place of African Americans in American society judging by television images, it would be that Black citizens—for the most part—were contented souls. If they existed at all.

Even when the African American character was not presented as a clown or a caricature, he or she was still a marginalized figure in a white world. Such was the case with the adaptation of John O'Hara's novel *Appointment in Samara* that appeared on the series *Robert Montgomery Presents*. Robert Montgomery starred as a troubled businessman about to lose everything. In a sequence at an exclusive men's club, when an argument breaks out between Montgomery and another man, a waiter intervenes and stops the two men from fighting. The waiter, played by African American actor P. Jay Sidney (also billed as Jay P. Sidney), uttered such lines as "Can I bring you something, Mr. English?" No one would think twice about the role—it's so slight—were it not for the fact that it was one of the few that featured a serious Black actor during the era; and the drama itself was one of the few to incorporate the Negro in some manner into American life.

On occasion, dramatic episodes presented the Negro as social symbol or even as a representation of a moral code. That occurred on the 1955 episode *Breakdown* on *Alfred Hitchcock Presents*. Here Joseph Cotten stars as a ruthless businessman who is in a car accident in an isolated area. As the man lies with eyes open, unable to move or speak, we hear him in voice-over commenting on the world around him. He appears to be badly injured. But we also have the eerie feeling he might be dead. Nearby are three convicts on the run—two white, one Black. They see him lying helpless in the car, assume he is dead, and then proceed to ransack the vehicle.

Once they leave, two other convicts—one white, one Black—approach and also search the car for any valuables. "Ain't nothing left," says the Black convict, played by James Edwards. "They took everything." Studying the face of the seemingly dead man, Edwards says he thinks the man might still be alive. But his comment is brushed aside by the other convict, who reminds him that they've come to take the man's clothes. Once they've removed the man's sports jacket and shirt, Edwards says simply, almost tenderly, "I've done a lot of things. But I've never robbed a dead man."

For this brief moment, the African American character becomes the conscience of the drama. Written by Frances Cockrell and Louis Pollock and directed by Hitchcock himself, the episode uses Edwards's character to articulate what the audience is supposed to feel. Intense and intelligent, Edwards's performance suggests another life for the character; an inner life the script has no time or desire to dramatize. A brief dramatic interlude like this one always struck African American viewers as a dose of reality. Yet the Black character was, nonetheless, presented as an outcast from the dominant culture; another African American male who has been such a threat to mainstream society that he has had to be removed from it.

JAMES EDWARDS AND THE NEW-STYLE DRAMATIC ACTORS

Finally, television began to acknowledge the presence of the Negro and African American culture—with occasional special presentations that featured African American actors either in important dramatic roles or in Black-cast productions. Usually, such presentations were aired as part of the adventure series or the dramatic anthology series that flourished in the 1950s: such programs as *Studio One, Fireside Theatre, Philco Television Playhouse,* or *General Electric Theater.* As predecessors to TV movies, the anthology series presented a new drama each week and were generally considered "quality" productions. Such series moved African American characters from the sidelines to front and center, starting in 1955, which proved to be a banner year. They also provided a lifetime for such new dramatic actors of the postwar era as Ossie Davis, Sidney Poitier, and especially James Edwards.

For a spell, Edwards was the Black actor that everyone kept their eyes on. Born in Muncie, Indiana, he had studied at Indiana and Northwestern Universities as well as at Knoxville College. Having spent a year as a professional boxer, Edwards first startled movie audiences in

1949 with his performances as a prizefighter in *The Set Up* and as the troubled soldier struggling with racism in the military in *Home of the Brave*. An altogether new kind of presence on the pop-culture landscape, he was a serious dramatic film actor with a bruised, hurt-boy quality unlike that of any other African American actor in Hollywood before him. His intelligent characters also often appeared to be the embodiment of the postwar Negro ready for a new day in America. Edwards—tall, lean, muscular, and athletic—also had the looks of a leading man. The Black press eagerly publicized him while African American moviegoers enthusiastically supported him. But his film career stalled, due in large measure to a lack of roles, but also to his own demons. He became one of those doomed young men of movie history.

For a time in the 1950s and early 1960s, however, Edwards was able to keep his acting career alive, thanks partly to television. In the 1955 *General Electric Theater* presentation *D.P.*, he played an embittered American soldier stationed in Germany. His life is transformed when he befriends an orphaned boy who is the son of a Black man and a young German woman. Another important role for Edwards was as the young Ralph Bunche on *Toward Tomorrow* on the *DuPont Cavalcade Theatre* in 1955. He also appeared in the *Volcano Seat* episode of *Climax*, *The 20th Century Fox Hour* presentation of *The Last Patriarch*, the *Desilu Playhouse* drama *Silent Thunder*, and the *Mission* episode of *Zane Grey Theater*. Most of these productions may now seem slight and dated without any of the punch they initally delivered. But just the fact that the sometimes explosive Edwards appeared in them lent the dramas a contemporary edge. "I was totally bowled over by James Edwards," Diahann Carroll once said. "He was, at the time, the only really famous black actor. He was strong, sexy, and mysterious." Often Edwards's very persona—that of a restless, searching young man, seemingly alienated and isolated and always perhaps a tad too sensitive— suggested, for Black viewers at least, that he might be a victim of American racism. Though the 1950s dramas in which he appeared often didn't focus on race, his very presence always gave them a racial subtext.

Edwards continued working into the next decade in episodes of such series as *Peter Gunn*, *The Eleventh Hour*, *The Outsider*, *The Outcasts*, and *The Virginian*. His performance as the troubled prizefighter in the *Decision in the Ring* episode of *The Fugitive* was both moving and disturbing—a portrait of someone about to crack up because of his experiences as a Black man in America. But the Edwards career never soared the way it should have. Most of the plum Black movie roles of the era went to Sidney Poitier. Many of the important TV roles in the 1960s also went to younger Black actors like Greg Morris and Lloyd Haynes. Diahann Carroll recalled that Edwards was "half crazy with frustration and rage from not being able to work." She realized that "there was really no place for him in the industry, and his career gradually ground to a standstill." But for Black TV viewers, Edwards must have briefly appeared to be the great Black hope. He died in 1970.

Another production that sought to bring theater, along with a compelling Black protagonist, to the tube was the 1955 *Kraft Television Theatre* version of Eugene O'Neill's *The Emperor Jones*, directed by Fielder Cook. Known to theatergoers for decades—primarily because of Paul Robeson's stirring performance in the title role (repeated in an independent 1933 film version)—O'Neill's drama traced the fortunes and tragic fate of a Black convict named Brutus Jones. After escaping from a prison chain gang, Jones swims to safety on a tiny Caribbean island. There he is greeted as a god by the naive natives. He becomes their Emperor Jones. But power corrupts. By the drama's end, Brutus Jones has undergone another transformation: he is reduced to a powerless state, a man destroyed by his own "primitive" fears and superstitions.

Newcomer Ossie Davis was cast as Brutus with a supporting cast that included Rex Ingram and Everett Sloane. Parts of television's *The Emperor Jones* were strong for the period, especially when Davis tells the white character Smithers, "Talk polite, white man. I'm emperor here now. Don't you forget it!" *Kraft Television Theatre* clearly intended to do something provocative for TV while also—because by then the play had become part of the American dramatic canon—playing it safe. The critical response was mixed. "A good try, and in spots quite powerful, but it didn't come off with continuity and impact," wrote *Variety*. "Ossie Davis, though at times powerful and moving as Jones, couldn't overcome what at times amounted to incoherence in the scripting and staging." But the review concluded, "A show like 'Jones,' even if it didn't come off quite expertly, rates a bow from the waist for exploring the offbeat and the new in television. More of it is welcome, and better luck next time."

Today most of *The Emperor Jones* looks hopelessly stagy. And provocative as the character may once have been to theatergoers, Brutus Jones strikes many as one more dated portrait of a Black man as a naive and half-crazed brute. Still, the drama was another move in a new direction.

A MAN IS TEN FEET TALL:
BONDED BUDDIES FOR AN INTEGRATIONIST AGE

Few television productions of the era, however, were more important in altering African American images than the *Philco Television Playhouse* live presentation of *A Man Is Ten Feet Tall*. Written by Robert Alan Aurthur and directed by Robert Mulligan, it told the story of the friendship of two young men. One is a troubled fellow named Axel North, who has deserted from the army and arrived in New York, where he lands a job as a longshoreman. The other—Tommy Tyler—is a longshoreman who befriends him. Tommy shows Axel the ropes on the job, takes him home to meet his wife, and peers into his soul. Sensing Axel's doubts and insecurities, Tommy repeatedly seeks to boost his confidence. In the climactic sequence, when Axel becomes embroiled in a heated quarrel with another worker, Tommy comes to his friend's defense and is fatally wounded—with a longshoreman's hook thrust in his back. He dies in Axel's arms.

What made *A Man Is Ten Feet Tall* provocative in 1955 was that the young men were of different races. Axel (played by Don Murray) is white; Tommy, Black. Aurthur's teleplay sought to explore the type of warm and meaningful relationship that can develop between decent people, regardless of race. Its subtext was a liberal plea for tolerance and understanding of African Americans. Tommy Tyler represented a new-style common African American Everyman—honest, sensitive, and, of course, *worthy* of acceptance by white America. There were even glimmers of a mature African American male sexuality. Fortunately for the production, the role of Tommy was played by an African American actor then still struggling to make a name for himself, the young Sidney Poitier.

A Man Is Ten Feet Tall was praised as an early television milestone. "As nearly as can be recalled," wrote the reviewer for *Variety*, "this was the first and certainly major instance wherein a Negro was unqualifiedly integrated into a teleplay." The reviewer added that such "integration which nearly everyone among the high brass in tv and elsewhere talks about but seldom practices, set 'Ten Feet Tall' apart." *Variety* called Poitier's performance an "articulate and even superlative characterization."

Sidney Poitier with Martin Balsam and Don Murray in the groundbreaking 1955 drama A Man Is Ten Feet Tall

Today, *A Man Is Ten Feet Tall* shows its age. It is hard to fully believe in the two men's friendship because race and cultural differences are never really addressed by them; in fact, as if to alleviate mainstream viewers' fears in 1955, such differences and distinctions are usually avoided. One of the few comments on cultural distinctions is almost funny. In the dinner sequence at Tyler's home, what does Tommy do to introduce some new culture into the poor white guy's life? He teaches Axel how to play the bongos! When Tommy and his wife dance that evening, the effort to show their love of music and movement just about backfires. It almost appears as if we're being reminded that Negroes *really* do have rhythm.

A Man Is Ten Feet Tall now looks like a prototype for Hollywood's fake idealized method for handling such Black/white friendships. Tommy Tyler strikes us as a mighty noble soul, almost saintly, a symbol of the perfect Good Negro, who doesn't make waves and has no real gripes with the system. Hoping to encourage his new friend, Tommy is quick to express his own contentment with life in America. "Listen, I wanted to be a musician. I wanted to go to Juilliard," he says of his early, perhaps unrealistic aspirations. Though that hasn't worked out, he's neither bitter nor resentful. Instead he's accepted what life has given him. "That's why I don't care if I never become a doctor or lawyer. And, man, I don't care if the furniture is broken-down." He adds, "I've got a woman who loves me. And I got kids who love me. And I don't have to walk the streets of no city."

Tommy as social symbol represents the ordinary Black man, who wants a home and family like everyone else but who doesn't have any great burning—and perhaps threatening—ambitions. He deserves a place in the system, the drama says, yet he in no way challenges that system's inequities because he doesn't appear to see them clearly.

But he is able to reach out and touch the troubled white man. On Axel's first day on the job, Tommy, seeing Axel's hesitation when he has to move a stack of boxes, asks warmly, "Don't you know how to lift?" He then shows the man how to maneuver the boxes with a longshoreman's hook. "Man, you look beat. How'd you like some soup?" he later says to Axel, ready to share his lunch with the new worker.

Before long, he's taken Axel completely under his wing, showing him the ropes on the job and, as a wise Negro, preparing the young man for the future with some philosophical advice. When he has to cope with a badgering co-worker, Tommy tells Axel, "You take that Charlie. You're either going to laugh at him or beat his brains out. That's the lowest form of animal life." He adds, "Sometimes a man's gotta make a choice." "You go with the men and you're ten feet tall. You go with the lower forms and you're down in the slime."

Eventually, Axel feels so relaxed with Tommy that he confides that he wants to tell him something but is afraid Tommy won't like him. But Axel need have no such worries. Says Tommy, "You couldn't say anything that'll make me not like you. So don't bother to try."

A comforted Axel eventually reveals his past and his present: the fact that he's deserted from the army; the fact that he has problems with his girlfriend in another city; the fact that now he is mostly lonely, spending much of his free time walking the streets or sitting in movie houses on 42nd Street.

Part soul mate, part familiar nurturer, Tommy looks a bit as if he were the well-brought-up offspring of that life-enhancer Beulah. Yet because Tommy always seems unique and upbeat and Axel is such an unrelentingly dreary sad sack, you can't help but wonder why Tommy is so keen on developing a friendship with him. Axel doesn't seem to offer much. At times, what with the camera's intimate two shots of the men, audiences may have intuitively wondered if there was some sexual attraction between the two men. As if anticipating and then promptly dismissing such thoughts among viewers, writer Aurthur makes sure to give us a married Tommy with two children and an Axel very much interested in a young woman. But for contemporary viewers, *A Man Is Ten Feet Tall*'s latent gay subtext gives it some punch.

The most puzzling—and frustrating—aspect of *A Man Is Ten Feet Tall* is its failure to create a sense of Tyler's feelings, and possible psychological tensions, as an African American man functioning in a sometimes hostile white working-class environment. Tommy is never shown with other Black dockworkers. In fact, he appears isolated from them.

"Stay away from him," the worker Charlie (played by Martin Balsam) warns Axel about Tommy on the first day at work. Racial tensions seem to be suggested, especially when we hear Tommy's comments during an argument with Charlie. "You're a little, frightened, gasping man," says Tommy. "You close your eyes and you hate, hate, hate. And like everybody in the world who hates, you're afraid somebody's going to take something away from you. Well, I got news for you, daddy, you can relax, 'cause you ain't got nothing I want."

Later, in the climactic scene, Tommy says to Charlie, "Why don't you lay off that kid."

"Outta my way, *boy*," Charlie says to Tommy.

Tommy doesn't challenge him at first. Afterward, when he breaks up a fight between Charlie and Axel, he's told by Axel, "It's my fight, Tommy."

"No, it isn't. It's me he wants."

Throughout, racism is woven into the fabric of the drama as subtext. But *A Man Is Ten Feet Tall* never explores or examines the underlying topic that gives the drama its real drive, energy, and *possibilities.*

At the conclusion, when Tommy has been killed by Charlie, Axel attains a new maturity. Challenging the dockers' code of silence about the killing, which is adhered to even by the few Black longshoremen, Axel turns Charlie in for the crime. Afterward, he's quick to say, "You can't hurt a guy who's ten feet tall." Axel has learned from Tommy. Because of his African American friend, he's able to live by his conscience and assume his manhood. What more could any white person ask of Black America?

A Man Is Ten Feet Tall marked an important shift in television history. Finally, television drama was at least acknowledging the presence of a different, though idealized, kind of Negro in American society: an articulate, hardworking, nonbuffoonish family man; as much the embodiment of traditional middle-class values as anyone else in America. Finally, primetime seemed to be catching up with the changes coming about in society as African Americans became more outspoken about their rights and the system's racial inequities. But not all viewers were ready for the change.

A Man Is Ten Feet Tall met with controversy and opposition in the South. Hilda Simms, a light-skinned African American actress, was cast as Poitier's young wife. Some viewers mistakenly assumed that Simms was white and that *A Man Is Ten Feet Tall* depicted an interracial marriage. *Jet* reported that the *Jackson* (Miss.) *Daily News* was outraged because "programs such as this are part of the brain-washing scheme to prepare southern minds to accept the monster of integration and intermarriage."

"Philco was threatened with cancellation of many of its franchises," recalled Sidney Poitier. "The Philco Playhouse people hastened to explain that she wasn't white, but it made no difference to the hard-core dissenters whose pressure threw an economic scare into the Philco Manufacturing Corporation. This pressure was brought to bear not only because a black actress was thought to be white, but also because the Philco Playhouse producers had the courage and sense of fairness to examine universal human questions in a black show when large segments of the viewing audience were unaccustomed to black shows."

Such reactions merely reinforced the networks' fears of experimenting with any new or distinctive material about African Americans. And advertisers, noting audience reactions, also hesitated to sponsor racial material.

Nonetheless, *A Man Is Ten Feet Tall* became important to Sidney Poitier's career. Previously, Poitier had performed in the television productions *The Parole Officer* and *Fascinating Stranger*. But more important, having appeared in films—as a young doctor in *No Way Out*, as a sensitive South African priest in *Cry the Beloved Country*, and perhaps most startlingly as a troubled, rebellious student in *Blackboard Jungle*—the Miami-born Poitier had begun ushering in a distinctive postwar image of the African American male able to operate in an integrated society and also forced to react to American racism. James Edwards was the first African American to play such roles in films. But Poitier was on his way to playing such roles consistently in films.

Yet in the mid-1950s, Poitier found new film work scarce. And so while actors generally were not prone to accept television roles after an early movie success, Poitier found he had little choice and was happy to have the chance to play Tommy Tyler on television. "For me," said Poitier, "it was a personal triumph." So impressed was producer David Susskind with the production (and the critical response) that he expanded the drama into a feature-length film. The new version was titled *Edge of the City*. John Cassavetes replaced Don Murray as Axel. But Poitier repeated his role as Tommy. The critical reception to the movie led to Poitier's appearance in *The Defiant Ones*, which firmly established him as a major American film actor. The movies' gain was television's loss. Poitier appeared in the television special *The Strolling Twenties* but he didn't return to a dramatic television role until almost forty years later when he appeared as Thurgood Marshall in *Separate But Equal*.

Excited by such productions as *A Man Is Ten Feet Tall* and a broadcast of *Tosca* starring Leontyne Price and white tenor David Poleri, *Jet* ran a cover story on the Poitier drama with a 1955 article titled "TV's New Policy for Negroes." The magazine noted that "television in its infancy was shunned by top white actors, who feared loss of prestige or movie contracts in the new medium. Thus, the vedeo [sic] floodgates were expected to be thrown open to experienced Negro actors. It never happened. But today, a startling new change is swiftly taking place on the TV screen."

ETHEL WATERS: TUBE DRAMATICS, TUBE CONFESSIONS

That same year, Ethel Waters appeared in several other dramatic pre-sentations. *Speaking to Hannah* seemed a trifle. But the *General Electric Theater*'s presentation of *Winner by Decision* on CBS cast her as the strong-willed mother of a conflicted young Golden Gloves boxing champion, played by Harry Belafonte. The mother, who believes a world of opportunities await a new generation of African Americans, wants him to turn in his boxing gloves to become a doctor. Though *Winner by Decision* was often enough a routine melodrama, its Black leads lifted it out of television's ordinary nightly grind.

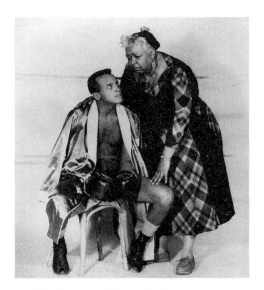

*Ethel Waters with Harry Belafonte as her son
in the drama* Winner by Decision

More important was Ethel Waters's appearance in NBC's broadcast of excerpts from William Faulkner's *The Sound and the Fury* on the anthology series *Playwrights '56*. Considered adult material, the television version primarily dramatized the fourth section of Faulkner's novel, which centered on the Black matriarch Dilsey. This was probably television's first attempt at drawing a complex African American woman.

By now Waters was an even more extraordinary physical and visual presence, heavier, weighing well over two hundred pounds, with almost completely white hair. Her face was fuller and weathered but retained its luminous glow and unusual beauty. Everything about Waters suggested that she had survived pain and heartache—and that her knowledge of life's vicissitudes and cruelties had been hard-won. She had also continued to invest her profound religious faith into just about every character she played. Director Fred Zinnemann recalled, when directing her in the 1952 movie version of *The Member of the Wedding*, that she was "a very headstrong lady. If she took three steps to the right, and I'd ask her to move to the left instead, she'd stand perfectly still, point at me, and say, '*God* is my director!' "

But despite Waters's gifts—and her eagerness to play a complicated heroine—television's *The Sound and the Fury* was sanitized and compromised. If anything, the production revealed some of the medium's greatest fears about race and the power of African American women. In the novel, the fiercely strong Dilsey—perceptive and outspoken—was a force to be reckoned with. Clearly, the novel's moral center (and again a portrait of the Negro as the conscience of a decadent Southern culture), she engendered an open terror in the white Southerner Jason Compson. But the TV production avoided any suggestion of Dilsey's power. Waters was given little more to do than to stand around and *look* strong—and occasionally to react. Sadly, what could have been a great role for Waters turned into little more than a lightweight dramatic version of Beulah.

The critics bemoaned television's missed opportunity.

"Ethel Waters regrettably had only a relatively small role," wrote Jack Gould in *The New York Times*. "Courage should be made of sterner stuff," *Variety* wrote. "But if this, the less purply Dilsey section of the novel, were important to do, then why not at least be a good reporter and make the corrupt, scheming, thieving Jason live in mortal fear of the matriarchal Negress. In the tv edition, Jason, played by Franchot Tone, showed neither by word nor deed that he feared Dilsey." *Variety* complained that "Miss Waters' role was too thin to supply the element of 'taking command.' In short, Dilsey came out almost diametrically opposed to her weight in the novel, so that even this small sensitive area of white man vs. Negro was emasculated."

Even so, the production's potential didn't go unnoticed. Four years later, Hollywood produced a similarly disappointing movie version of the Faulkner novel starring Yul Brynner, Joanne Woodward, and Ethel Waters.

Ethel Waters as Faulkner's Dilsey, a role she played on television and in the movies in the 1950s

Still, Ethel Waters continued to occupy a unique position in American television in the mid and late 1950s. Following *Beulah*, her appearances on such variety shows as *This Is Show Business* and *The Jackie Gleason Show* showed that her voice could still entrance. With her performances in such TV productions as *The Dance, Sing for Me*, and later *Good Night Sweet Blues*, she emerged as perhaps television's most distinctive and important African American star of the Eisenhower decade; not only the one African American actress immediately known by face and name to the ever-growing television audience but also the one Black actress who played a series of dramatic roles. Most significantly, Ethel Waters helped bridge the prewar and postwar eras, leading to more modern depictions of African American women. Almost always she represented, as an actress and as a personality, the strong, long-suffering Black woman, whose purpose fundamentally was to serve, nurture, and ultimately impart wisdom. What lifted her out of the old-style mammy category was that her dramatic matriarchs could be troubled, restless, searching, clearly aware of moral choices to be made. Her important appearances—even in a half-baked production like *The Sound and the Fury* or a routine melodrama like *Winner by Decision*—altered the idea of the African American woman as a simple soul without any real reasons to sing the blues.

During the Eisenhower era, she remained the one Black performer whom viewers connected to in the most personal way. Unlike Eddie Anderson, who was a star known mainly because of his character Rochester, Waters was still known because of her personal tensions and her ever-unfolding personal drama, which television capitalized on. Yet though she won more major dramatic roles than other African American television performers during the period, Ethel Waters was still struggling to find work. During two startling television appearances, she starred in her own personal psychodrama, revealing her eagerness for employment—and also her near desperation.

The first was her appearance—in early 1954—on Edward R. Murrow's *Person to Person*. On this popular program, journalist Murrow did live interviews with celebrities: Murrow in the studio with cigarette in hand; the stars in their homes. To his credit, Murrow interviewed not only the expected stars like Marilyn Monroe, Elizabeth Taylor and husband Mike Todd, Fidel Castro, and Senator John F. Kennedy, but also such African American celebrities and artists as Duke Ellington, Cab Calloway, W. C. Handy, Roy Campanella, and Sammy Davis Jr. Television had already brought the Negro into white households. Now it was taking mainstream viewers into African American homes. Waters's appearance on *Person to Person* was considered a prized, high-status event, much like the Barbara Walters celebrity interviews of the late 1970s.

Murrow opened his interview with a quote: "A drama critic once wrote, 'There are a goodly number of proficient actors on our stage but precious few who are interesting people.' He was writing about Ethel Waters, who can look back on forty years on the stage. She has almost become a legend as the one who in 1917 was the first woman to sing 'St. Louis Blues'—to record it."

Once introduced, Waters responded, "I'm here. All 253 pounds of me." At the time, she was living on the second floor of a red-brick house in Brooklyn's Crown Heights. Hardly the expected residence of a star. The interview soon delved into personal areas. When asked what she did for relaxation, Waters gave an unexpected response. "There's a compulsory relaxation. And then there's a voluntary relaxation," she said. "Right now I'm on the compulsory one. So while I'm waiting for the phone to ring for me to get some employment while I'm in between dates—that's the celebrity way of expressing it—I just waste away my time reminiscing."

Waters discussed her childhood with Murrow, explaining that she was a Dead End Kid, who didn't fit in, who was in and out of school. She was saved by the nuns who took an interest in her at a Catholic school. A moving moment occurred when Waters played her 1929 recording of "I Got Rhythm." She sang along with the music, still able to give her throaty blues growls. But her sadness and her longing for a happier time showed whenever she spoke.

The evening's most powerful moment came when Murrow asked what had given Waters her greatest professional satisfaction. Without hesitation, she answered the play *Mamba's Daughters*, in which she had played her first great dramatic character, Hagar. Recounting the scene in which Hagar learns her daughter Lissa has been raped, Waters explained that in Hagar's "slow, inarticulate way, she's trying to rebuild the girl's courage and her morale." At that moment, Ethel Waters assumed the character of Hagar and quoted: "Lissa, listen, we Black folks have one ting over white folks and that is, there ain't no trouble so big we can't sing 'bout 'em. Best ting for trouble, honey, is singin' and workin'. And your work is singin'. Then you is holding a chile against trouble."

Today the *Mamba's Daughters* dialect seems dated; so, too, the sentiments expressed. But Waters delivered the lines with such heartfelt sincerity—and a dramatic intensity totally unlike the typical underacting that television already required of actors—that she must have shaken the average television viewer out of his or her general stupor.

"Do you want to do another play, Ethel?" Murrow asked.

She answered yes, adding that she'd had offers for work abroad but that she preferred performing in the States. Yet she didn't want to do a serious drama because she feared the emotions it might pull out of her.

"I constantly can't live in my tragic past. And it has been tragic," she said. "I have to get away from it at times because it undermines me."

This was the stuff of real drama, worlds removed from everyday 1950s bland television fare. Here was a woman down on her luck, openly revealing her fears and her great vulnerabilities. Few primetime programs could ever hope to emotionally match this one, which might well have been the first of television's confessional interviews; long before interviewers like Barbara Walters or Oprah Winfrey mastered the art of drawing personal stories out of their subjects; long before TV had its daily stream of talk shows in which private stories often appeared exploited or trivialized. Waters used the medium to speak directly and seriously to viewers. TV had known fake intimacy. But here was the real thing, unadulterated, and worlds removed from the standard *Person to Person* fare. Most such Murrow interviews were light-hearted celebrity chatter. The only other interview to touch the viewer as Waters did was Murrow's conversation with a haunting, melancholic Marilyn Monroe.

But Ethel Waters's personal television psychodrama didn't end with the appearance on *Person to Person*. By 1957, Waters was heavily in debt and hounded for payment of back taxes. When the Internal Revenue Service seized the royalties on her autobiography, *His Eye Is on the Sparrow*, she announced publicly that she had worked only nine weeks during all of 1955, mainly in summer stock productions of *The Member of the Wedding*. Waters told the press she was broke. "I am unemployed," she said. "No job. I don't have a quarter to my name." Then, desperate for some income, Waters appeared on the NBC quiz show *Break the $250,000 Bank*. There she answered questions about music. "The woman who, during forty-seven years as a performing artist, has had stellar roles on stage, screen and vaudeville," reported *The New York Times*, "entered the contest to try to raise funds for taxes the Federal government said she owed."

For Ethel Waters, the appearance on *Break the $250,000 Bank* must have been humiliating. But it became part of a national spectacle as viewers tuned in to see if the fallen star would be able to get back on her feet. Somehow she managed to maintain her dignity and come through the quiz show experience with her self-respect intact. Waters won $10,000 on the program.

Two years later Mike Wallace interviewed Waters. At the time, she was starring on Broadway in *An Evening with Ethel Waters*. Aware that the most effective conversation with Waters would be one that focused on her tensions and problems—and that steered clear of celebrity fluff—Wallace read a passage from *His Eye Is on the Sparrow*, in which she wrote of feeling like an outsider. "You're regarded as the foremost actress of your race," he said. "Do you still feel an outsider?" Though Waters said she no longer felt the outsider, it was hard to believe her. Afterward Wallace questioned her about changes in show business since her early years as a blues singer. He also spoke of the long barren periods in her career as well as the fact that she had turned down a major role in the play *A Raisin in the Sun*. Then he grilled her on her financial problems. "You want to talk about money?" he asked. "Yeah. I ain't got none," Waters answered. "So why not talk about it."

She gave a compelling but evasive interview. When Wallace referred to a *New York Times* book review of her autobiography, which commented that Waters appeared to believe she could not count on anything in the white man's world, she dodged his question, stating that her best friends were not of her nationality. Often she spoke of her religious beliefs. She had declined a role in the television version of *The Green Pastures* because, she said with anger, "they were belittling my Lord. Do you realize what the Supreme Being is, Mike?" She also believed that the "only thing that's lasting, Michael, is beyond. It's eternity. So when I say I'm passing through, I'm trying to get my house in order to meet the great stage manager." Poignant but never pathetic, Ethel Waters remained a striking and unusual larger-than-life presence for television; a woman who refused to indulge in small talk and who instead used the medium to express her highly idiosyncratic view of the world.

THE NAT "KING" COLE SHOW:
CHALLENGING MADISON AVENUE AND THE SOUTHERN MARKET

In 1956, the forecast looked promising with the debut of the fifteen-minute primetime program *The Nat "King" Cole Show*. The Black press excitedly reported that it was the one network series at the time to star an African American. Already African American entertainers appeared regularly as guest stars on the nation's most popular variety programs. Performers like Bob Howard and Hazel Scott had hosted their own programs. So, too, had singer Billy Daniels—star of the 1953 *The Billy Daniels Show*—for a thirteen-week run. But singer Nat "King" Cole was the first to appear when the medium's future was assured, and when fewer risks were taken with weekly programs.

Cole himself was a model star. Unlike the era's African American rock-and-rollers like Little Richard and Chuck Berry who were now popular with American teenagers and who with their sexy moves and fast-paced music represented a frightening sign of unruly, funky rebellion for many parents, Cole's style—soothing, smooth, and refined—was compared with that of Sinatra and Bing Crosby. With his mellow hits "Nature Boy," "Mona Lisa," and "Young at Heart," Cole could be enjoyed by audiences both young and old. NBC appeared to have selected an ideal Black star for its new series.

Nat "King" Cole on his short-lived TV show with guest Harry Belafonte

Weekly, Cole performed standard pop tunes. Also featured were such guest stars as Peggy Lee, Pearl Bailey, and Cab Calloway. Airing on Mondays from 7:30 to 7:45 p.m., *The Nat "King" Cole Show* was greeted enthusiastically by the critics as sophisticated, elegant fare. "He was completely at ease on the opening stanza and dished out lotsa charm in song and speech," wrote *Variety*. "It's all Cole's show, and he keeps the quarter-hour rolling in a tasteful, melodic manner." But from the beginning, the show's ratings were low. NBC didn't help matters by airing it opposite CBS's very popular *The Adventures of Robin Hood. The Nat "King" Cole Show* averaged only 19 percent of the viewing audience while 50 percent of television viewers had tuned in to *The Adventures of Robin Hood.* It looked as if the network expected to lose in that time slot regardless of what aired; so why not sacrifice Cole's show rather than one the network considered more important. NBC had always been concerned that its Southern affiliates might object to a weekly program starring an African American—especially a program that was not a comedy. The concerns proved justified. Many Southern stations refused to carry the show. In Birmingham, Alabama, one television station manager, who dropped the show, informed *Jet*, "I like Nat Cole, but they told me if he came back on they would bomb my house and my station."

Sponsors also stayed away from *The Nat "King" Cole Show*, assuming there was no audience for it and also fearing that Southern viewers would boycott their products. "I think Nat could do a fine sales job on a product," one advertising executive told *Jet*. "Somebody ought to buy him. My outfit won't because things are considered too fluid down South. They might resent the show." Although the program was worth $85,000 a week in advertisement revenues, it was offered to sponsors at advertising rates of $45,000 an episode.

Still, NBC stuck with *The Nat "King" Cole Show*. In July 1957, the network even expanded it to a half-hour program and aired it in a special summer time slot on Tuesday evenings, from 10 to 10:30. The following September, NBC broadcast the program on Tuesdays from 7:30 to 8 p.m. in seventy-seven stations, half of them in the South.

Because Cole was well liked within the entertainment industry itself, many stars rallied around him and offered to perform for scale wages. Harry Belafonte, who generally received $50,000 for a television guest appearance, accepted a scale payment of $155. So too such big names as Ella Fitzgerald, Tony Bennett, Peggy Lee, and Mel Tormé. Sammy Davis Jr. accepted a Leica camera as payment. Gospel star Mahalia Jackson requested a color television set. Few shows in television history had as loyal a following among entertainers.

Changing the time slot helped a bit, especially in some urban areas. The American Research Bureau reported *The Nat "King" Cole Show* eventually rose to the Number One position in New York in its Tuesday night slot. In Los Angeles, the program became the eighth most popular show. According to Cole, the Trendex rating system reported that the program was viewed in between three and four million homes. But still *The Nat "King" Cole Show* suffered from poor national ratings.

In a last-ditch effort to save the show, NBC decided to change its time slot to Saturdays at 7 p.m. Eastern Standard Time. But Cole objected. "If I could have continued at 7:30, I would have suffered the thing through," he said. "But the Saturday slot was a TV horse of another color. At that hour (6 p.m. in the Midwest and 5 p.m. in some areas) most people are eating or shopping." *The Nat "King" Cole Show* went off the air in December 1957 after sixty-four weeks. The national audience itself didn't appear ready to accept a sophisticated African American male hosting his own program.

Cole publicly blasted Madison Avenue for his program's embattled history. The advertising agencies had failed to find him a sponsor. "Madison Avenue, the center of the advertising industry, and their big clients didn't want their products associated with Negroes," Cole told *Ebony*. "They scramble all over each other to sign Negro guest stars to help boost the ratings of white stars, but they won't put money on a Negro with his own program. I'm not a chip-on-the-shoulder guy, but I want to be frank about this. Ad Alley thinks it's still a white man's world. *The Nat "King" Cole Show* put the spotlight on them. It proved who dictates what is seen on TV: New Yorkers and particularly Madison Avenue. They control TV. They govern the tastes of the people."

LOOKING BACK: THE NOT SO GREEN PASTURES

The year that Cole's program was canceled, NBC appeared to retreat comfortably into the past with *Hallmark Hall of Fame*'s Black-cast production of *The Green Pastures*, which garnered great attention. Based on the Southern sketches of Roark Bradford, this comedy/drama by white writer Marc Connelly had been a Broadway hit in the Depression era as well as a successful Hollywood movie. Excerpts from the play were also broadcast on television in 1951. Considered something of a classic, *The Green Pastures* was a fantasy about an all-colored heaven, in which charming, giddy Black angels flounced around in wings and chattered about fish fries and custard pudding. *The Green Pastures* also dramatized Black versions—as seen through the eyes of a colored

Southern Sunday school class—of such biblical stories as Adam and Eve, Noah's Ark, Moses and old Pharaoh, and Hezdrel. Reigning over all creatures great and small was a heavenly host called De Lawd. The cast included William Warfield as De Lawd, Earle Hyman as both Adam and Hezdrel, Frederick O'Neal as Moses, Terry Carter as Gabriel, Richard Ward as Pharaoh, and, repeating the role he had played in the film, Eddie "Rochester" Anderson as Noah.

The critics loved it. Hailing the production as "unquestionably one of the most magnificent evenings that video ever has experienced," the *New York Times* critic Jack Gould wrote that the staging was brilliant and "contained some of the season's finest acting." "If *Green Pastures* does not receive recognition in the Peabody and Emmy Awards next spring—with a special citation to Mr. [H. C.] Hallmark Hall [president of Hallmark] for his vision in supplying the funds which made possible a major contribution to the art of television—the video industry has run completely amok."

Though likable and graced with moments of warmth and insight, *The Green Pastures* was perfectly safe and by now perfectly predictable and dated fare. Frequently, the characters spoke in dialect. De Lawd himself was something of a Southern backwoods preacher. Always the joke—for the mainstream audience—was the mix of high and low; the high being the great biblical stories; the low being that they were brought to life not in the traditional stately, grand manner but rather in this "common Black folk" style. Though African American viewers could find pleasure in seeing African American performers working together in a big production, they (as well as mainstream viewers) had no doubt begun to tire of this type of ersatz Black drama. *The Green Pastures* suffered in the ratings. Most viewers watched the show's competition: another network's broadcast of producer Mike Todd's lavish party—with his wife Elizabeth Taylor in attendance—to celebrate his hit film *Around the World in Eighty Days*. Afterward the *Hallmark Hall of Fame* series did something unprecedented. Almost two years later it broadcast a second live version of *The Green Pastures* with virtually the same cast. Again the critics were beside themselves with praise.

"The initial performance of Marc Connelly's adaptation of his own play occurred on Oct. 17, 1957, a night when a majority of viewers elected to tune in an indescribably cheap item of motion-picture exploitation at Madison Square Garden," wrote Jack Gould in *The New*

York Times. "Last night's performance was touched by the same irides-cent glow that made the TV premiere eighteen months ago so unfor-gettable."

Rather than reflect the ever-widening racial divisions in national life and the growing Black dissent of the rising civil rights movement, tele-vision still preferred to promote images of cutesy Black angels.

LOOKING FORWARD: DRAMATIC POSSIBILITIES

Some dramatic African American actors and actresses, however, were able to find employment. Madame Sul-Te-Wan and Roy Glenn made the best out of bits on an episode of a series like *Medic* in 1955. Suzette Harbin drew some attention from the Black press for her role on *The Charles Maury Story* episode of *Wagon Train* in 1958. Other times, though, performers were able to do more substantial work. Singer Eartha Kitt played Salome on an episode of *Omnibus* and a native queen on *Playhouse 90*'s adaptation of *The Heart of Darkness.* Earle Hy-man, who decades later became known as the father of Cliff Huxtable on *The Cosby Show*, not only appeared in *The Green Pastures* but also played the title role in *Camera Three*'s production of *Othello* (which was not aired, however, during the important primetime hours). Fred-erick O'Neal appeared in the drama *Danger* as a detective who helps solve the mystery murder of a woman who had been involved with a jazz musician. O'Neal also chalked up credits in such *Playwrights '56* productions as *The Battler* and *The Undiscovered Man* as well as the *Play of the Week* production of Langston Hughes's *Simply Heavenly.* Rex Ingram appeared on such dramatic presentations as *The Intolerable Portrait* and *Black Saddle.* That robust actor William Marshall—re-membered for his movie roles in *Demetrius and the Gladiators* and *Ly-dia Bailey*—was an impressive presence in *Omnibus*'s *Othello* as well as the New York local series *Harlem Detective.* Light-skinned actor Frank Silvera was fortunate in being able to play not only African American characters but also other ethnics (Native Americans and Hispanics) in such specials as *The Skin of Our Teeth* and *Studio One*'s *Guitar* as well as in episodes of the series *Captain Video, The Big Story, Wanted Dead or Alive, Perry Mason,* and *Ellery Queen.* And actor P. Jay Sidney had the distinction of appearing in some seventy productions during television's early years, although he usually played supporting or minor parts. He also made appearances on the series *You'll Never Get Rich.*

One of the more unusual performances by an African American actor in the late 1950s was that of Juano Hernandez in *Studio One*'s production of *Escape Route.* Though it was a drama about international intrigue (Caribbean death squads in the United States), *Escape Route*'s plot was really irrelevant. Writer William Mourne and director Fielder Cook were more interested in exploring such favorite liberal themes of the 1950s as those of personal involvement and individual responsibility; of nonconformity in a conformist age; and of everyday all-American prejudice. Set in New York City, *Escape Route* focused on the investigation of the death of a college professor named Vargas who has been shot under mysterious circumstances. While dying, he utters a few words in a foreign language to a fellow white professor named Tucker (James Daly).

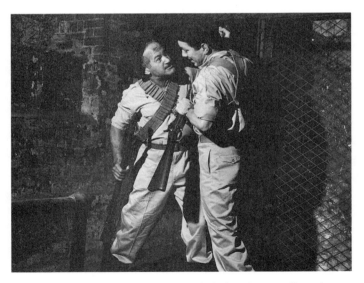

Frank Silvera (left), who often played Black characters as well as other ethnics, in The Quiet Spaniard

A detective named Calador, played by Hernandez, investigates the Vargas shooting. He relentlessly questions Tucker, who refuses to become involved in the investigation. From his first appearance, coolly dressed in suit and tie, Calador looks completely different from just about every other African American male TV character of the era. It's his manner that sets him apart, and the great self-assurance that the actor himself brings to the role. Methodical and focused, Hernandez's Calador seems oblivious to the fact that he's a Black man challenging a white one. "I'm trying to tell you courteously, Mr. Tucker, that you will be available if we want you," says Calador firmly. "Physically. Geographically. Not preferentially." He also tells the professor, "You and I do not click. My feelings tell me not to trust you, Mr. Tucker, even though my head tells me that here's a man, not exactly your type of man, but an honest man, a teacher. Perhaps I do not enter your head at all."

Once he has seen the tenement where Tucker lives, Calador challenges Tucker to examine his feelings about the Caribbean immigrants around him. Calador explains that he too comes from a Caribbean culture where, he says, "my smallest brother died of typhus. Who dies of typhus here? There, my father ate sugarcane pulp for lunch. Who has to do that here? He died also. Across the back of his neck, a machete in a small uprising. To whom does that happen here? I repeat, Mr. Tucker. It is not we who lived on an island. But you. And even when you go there, you go with the eye of a tourist. You see only that which is pretty and picturesque as if typhus and sugarcane pulp and a military government never happened."

Viewers in 1957 may have wondered what this dialogue was doing in this particular drama. But writer Mourne and director Cook were using what might have been a standard television mystery to make a statement on a system of exploitation and cruelty. Interestingly, the exploitation here is in an island culture, not America, the land of the free and the home of the brave.

Hernandez's Calador was something of a liberal archetype for the 1950s: a rugged individualist, both perceptive and philosophical, determined to uncover the truth of a situation while stating his view of the world. Repeatedly, he pushes Tucker, this timid "ordinary" white male, to take a stand. In the end that's precisely what Tucker does, thanks to the guidance of Calador, who in some respects once again represents the Negro as moral conscience. But Hernandez plays him as a man, not a social symbol.

Escape Route was neither great nor compelling drama. But it afforded Juano Hernandez, one of America's unacknowledged great dramatic actors, a rare opportunity to play a shrewd, ironic character

Juano Hernandez, the star of Escape Route

on television. A towering, muscular, broad-shouldered, "mahogany-skinned" man (as the press liked to describe him), the Puerto Rican-born (1896) Hernandez had been a jack-of-all-trades for years. With very little formal education but with a thirst for knowledge that stayed with him throughout his life, Hernandez began his career in an acrobatic act in Rio de Janeiro. Later he became a professional boxer called Kid Curly. Then he sang in a minstrel show, entertained in a circus, and performed dramatic sketches in vaudeville. With performances in such Broadway productions as *Show Boat, Strange Fruit*, and *Let My People Go* and such Oscar Micheaux films as *The Girl from Chicago* and *The Notorious Elinor Lee*, he seemed to have found his calling. In the 1940s, Hernandez turned to radio, where he acted and wrote scripts. But, finally, the full range and power of Hernandez, the dramatic actor, was revealed with his performance in the film adaptation of William Faulkner's *Intruder in the Dust*. Film critic Pauline Kael wrote that Hernandez's stubborn and insufferable character Lucas Beauchamp "is very much like another modern example of pride, isolation, and intransigence—De Sica's great Umberto D." Afterward there were supporting dramatic roles in the films *Stars in My Crown, The Breaking Point, Young Man with a Horn, Ransom*, and *Trial*. Later, when Hernandez appeared in *The Pawnbroker*, Kael wrote: "The great Juano

Hernandez, as the man who wants to talk, gives the single most moving performance I saw in 1965."

Hernandez's television appearances continued in such dramas as *Studio 57*'s *Goodwill Ambassadors* and an episode of *Alfred Hitchcock Presents* titled *Josh*. He also portrayed the Native American Standing Bear in the drama *The Dispossessed*. Hernandez appeared to relish his scenes as the Ponca chief who stubbornly defies the law to lead his people off their disease-ridden reservation. In television roles that were never complex, Hernandez often managed nonetheless to suggest a proud, disciplined man, slightly battered by life, greatly disillusioned, yet making his way through with confidence and a quiet power.

Though Hernandez later worked in such other television dramas as *Black Monday* (a *Play of the Week* production) and in episodes of such dramatic series as *Route 66, The Dick Powell Show, The Defenders, Adventures in Paradise,* and *Naked City,* his career on the tube was littered with waste. Not his. But the medium's.

SAMMY DAVIS JR.: LIFE ON THE TUBE

For a time, the African American press thought Sammy Davis Jr. might become the most important Black actor (rather than Harry Belafonte or Sidney Poitier) to work in television. By the mid-1950s, Davis was already a star but not yet the superstar icon he would later become. Born in a Harlem tenement in 1925, he had been in show business almost from the time he could walk. While little Sammy was left in the care of his grandmother, his parents—the entertainers Elvira Sanchez and Sammy Davis Sr.—had traveled in a vaudeville act. But when his mother left his father, Sammy, then three years old, was recruited to perform as a singer and dancer with his father and Will Mastin, an entertainer whom Sammy always called his uncle though in fact they were not related. The act was called the Will Mastin Trio.

For years, the three traveled around the country on the chitlin circuit—those Black clubs, theaters, and other venues that mainstream America knew nothing about but where African American audiences gathered for first-rate, highly energetic, highly innovative entertainment. Singing and dancing with a ferocious energy, Davis was clearly a child prodigy whom audiences immediately took to. In 1933, he sat on

Sammy Davis Jr., singer, dancer, impressionist, drummer, and guest star on an array of variety programs. With Elizabeth Taylor and Richard Burton on The Sammy Davis, Jr. Show *in 1966. With Rosey Grier and Rat Pack pal Peter Lawford*

Ethel Waters's lap while she crooned him to sleep in the short film *Rufus Jones for President*. It was a fit pairing because, eventually, like Waters (and another former child star, Dorothy Dandridge), Davis served as another important bridge between prewar and postwar African American entertainment images. Both he and Waters were among the last of a certain breed of all-around entertainer; performers who appeared able to do just about anything, easily (and sometimes brilliantly) making a transition from song and dance to dramatics.

By the late 1940s and early 1950s, the Will Mastin Trio had begun to cross over, playing important white clubs in Las Vegas and Los Angeles. Helping to make them even better known and bigger stars were their appearances on early television variety programs. By then, Sammy also played the drums and did wickedly clever impressions of some of Hollywood's biggest white stars: James Cagney, Humphrey Bogart, James Stewart, and Edward G. Robinson. For the first time in pop culture history, white audiences saw a Black man openly (but gently) mock a white one. By then, everyone knew that without Sammy, Davis Sr. and Mastin would not have much of an act. Though urged to go out on his own, Sammy stayed with the trio. With hopes of becoming a dramatic actor, he turned to television, setting his sights, wrote *Ebony*, "on becoming the first bigtime Negro television personality."

In 1954, the Black press reported that Davis had signed a contract with ABC to do a series pilot. Called *Three's Company*, it was to be a sitcom about a family of entertainers (Davis Jr., Davis Sr., and Mastin) called the Lightfoots. Also signed as co-stars were dramatic actor Frederick O'Neal and actress Ruth Attaway, along with former Katherine Dunham dancer Frances Taylor, who was cast as Sammy's love interest. *Three's Company* would have musical entertainment but also some heartfelt drama. A chorus of Black and white dancers and singers would appear, making it technically an interracial production. Over an eight-month period, $20,000 was spent to make the pilot, which afterward sat on the shelf while ABC tried to find a sponsor. But none would touch it, and finally plans for the series were dropped. Two years before *The Nat "King" Cole Show*, it was a clear sign that by now, with major advertisers as much as network programmers dictating what viewers would see, a primetime show starring African Americans was considered commercially infeasible.

With the trio, Sammy chalked up more guest appearances on such variety programs as *The Walter Winchell Show, The Jerry Lewis Show, The Frank Sinatra Show, The Big Record,* and *The Milton Berle Show.* But the ambitious and aggressive Davis didn't give up his search for dramatic parts. He managed to find roles that, for the time, were considered important. The first was on *The General Electric Theater* presentation of *Auf Wiedersehen* in 1958, in which he played a young GI assigned to postwar duty in Germany. There, he tries to adopt a Black child (played by Steven Perry) in an orphanage.

Sammy Davis Jr., the dramatic actor, with Steven Perry, on General Electric Theater's Auf Wiedersehen

Then, as the era drew to a close, Davis appeared in a predominantly Black episode of the Western series *Dick Powell's Zane Grey Theater.* The half-hour episode was called *Mission.* Though Westerns were frequently broadcast on TV and though it has been estimated that 20 to 30 percent of the actual cowboys in the Old West were Mexicans, Native Americans, or African Americans, *Mission,* which aired in 1959, was a rare production that acknowledged a Black presence on the American frontier. *Mission* dramatized the heroic exploits of the real-life Buffalo Soldiers, the all-Negro 10th unit of the United States Cavalry in the 1880s. Davis Jr. starred along with James Edwards, Ernie Anderson, and Hari Rhodes. On a mission to transport a Comanche chieftain to a U.S. fort for the signing of a peace treaty, the Buffalo Soldiers are attacked by Apaches who oppose the treaty. Thereafter *Mission* focused not on tensions between Native Americans and the U.S. government but rather touched on the psychological dilemma of Black soldiers engaged in a war with another minority, their "red" brothers.

Early on, when the chief has been captured by the Buffalo Soldiers, the character played by Davis expresses his anger about their prisoner; his feelings echo those expressed in past films and past mainstream interpretations of American history. "Ain't but one way to bring in a Comanche," says Davis. "And that ain't on a horse. It's across one." Later an Apache meets with the Black soldiers. "You are brave soldiers," he tells them. "You are fools to die for a land that does not want you. You are our brothers. We do not wish to kill you." He urges them to turn the chief over. That was the kind of dramatically telling moment that African American viewers in 1959 must have been waiting for, and briefly they may have assumed *Mission* was going to make a perceptive comment on Native American/African American relations. But the Buffalo Soldiers are depicted as *loyal* (and unquestioning) Americans who will not abide such foolish talk.

By the episode's end, when the Indians ask for a trade—they'll return a wounded Black soldier if the Comanche is turned over to them—Davis agrees to their demands. He appears to have put aside his supposedly justified anger about Native American brutality—for the sake of peace. We then see the Buffalo Soldiers send a Native American—presumably the Comanche chief—on a horse toward the braves, who in turn send back their Black captive.

But soon the camera cuts to a close-up of Davis—on horseback—dressed as the chief. The real leader is being taken to the fort by the other Buffalo Soldiers for the signing of the treaty. Once Davis's true identity is discovered, he will no doubt die at the hands of these "red savages."

African American viewers must have had mixed feelings about *Mission*. It exploited its Black characters, repeatedly using their loyalty to their country as a way to deny the obvious parallels between the plight of the American Indian and the American Negro. Still, *Mission*, written by Aaron Spelling and directed by William Dario Faralla, has to be credited for incorporating African Americans into American history. The Black man has nobly sacrificed himself for the good of his country. "Naughty little television comes clean," wrote *Variety*. "By breaking the racial barrier that has, up to now, existed in video's somewhat rigged version of the early American west." *Variety* wrote of the actors, "All these men deserve bigger and even better parts."

Mission gave Davis a showcase for his budding dramatic skills. "Davis, who probably hasn't even scratched the surface of his talents yet," wrote *Variety*, "gives a convincing performance throughout." Though never an actor in the league of a Poitier, Davis was a strong, commanding personality. Sometimes he looked as if he was trying too hard, as if he wanted the viewers to appreciate and *like* him. Yet he held the screen.

In the next decades, Davis appeared in *The General Electric Theater*'s *Memory in White* as well as *The Dick Powell Show*'s *The Legend*. He turned up in episodes of the Western series *The Lawman* and *The Rifleman* as well as in such popular dramatic series as *Ben Casey, The Mod Squad, The Name of the Game, Charlie's Angels*, and *Hunter*. Davis also guest-starred in episodes of such sitcoms as *The Patty Duke Show, Batman, I Dream of Jeannie, The Beverly Hillbillies, The Wild, Wild West, Here's Lucy, Chico and the Man, The Jeffersons*, and a very famous episode of *All in the Family* in 1972 in which he kissed Archie Bunker. He even made appearances on the daytime soap opera *One Life to Live* in 1978. He also hosted his own talk show (at a time when such programs were rarities for African American performers), *The Sammy Davis, Jr. Show* in 1966. Though that show was short-lived, Davis came back later as the star of the talk program *Sammy and Company*.

In the long run, the medium enabled Davis to maintain a vital career; to keep his name and face out there. He proved to be one of TV's early and enduring African American stars, although never a *genuine* television star like a Tim Moore or later like Bill Cosby, Redd Foxx, Flip Wilson, or Sherman Hemsley; the kind of performer viewers welcomed in their home week after week. Never able to fully scale down his dramatic performances the way an Ethel Waters did, Davis may have been too *big* or too *hot* a personality for that.

Still, he remained a television fixture for the next four decades and, surprisingly, even in the midst of his well-publicized personal troubles and controversies. Ultimately, his television appearances became a revealing document on his life. After Davis lost an eye in a car accident in 1954, he made a triumphant comeback—wearing a black eye patch—at the club Ciro's in Los Angeles. Then he appeared on a succession of variety shows. For viewers, the sight of Davis in the eye patch simply made him all the more a larger-than-life figure; a man who had survived an ugly tragedy. Later television recorded his appearances with the Rat Pack: Sinatra, Dean Martin, Joey Bishop, and Davis, those devil-may-care buddies who carried on with a nutty abandon as if they couldn't wait for tomorrow so they could do it all over again. When Davis married the blond Swedish actress Mai Britt in 1960, no one was sure how the public would accept this union. While campaigning for presidential candidate John F. Kennedy, Davis had been asked not to attend the Democratic convention because it was feared—especially with all that television coverage—that Southern delegates would be offended by his presence. Davis was then asked not to attend Kennedy's inauguration. Yet the marriage didn't seem to seriously affect his appeal to TV viewers.

His career probably suffered more during the 1970s. As the war raged on in Vietnam and Watergate scandals erupted almost daily, Davis remained a staunch supporter of Richard Nixon. When newspapers throughout the country published photographs of Davis hugging Nixon, Davis was labeled as the worst type of tom within the African American community. Yet Sammy's television appearances continued.

In time, Davis's dramatic work was forgotten. Instead television, which had been crucial to the survival of his career, also led to the perception of Davis, the entertainer, as a grinning, eager-to-please accommodationist, who joked with white hosts and sometimes playfully used a thick Kingfish-style dialect ("Holy mackerel!") to get laughs. He often looked needy of love and approval. Though Davis had always been a strong supporter of the civil rights movement, he became—for a new generation of Black Americans—a shameless, bejeweled sellout. Television never captured the complexities of this rather tormented figure, who kept most of his real fears hidden. Even in more serious TV interviews, he could not get past the established image. He could not startle TV viewers by letting them know there was a person inside the entertainer. The closest he came to that was with a 1969 interview on a local New York show, Gil Noble's *Like It Is*. Davis's last major appearance was on a two-and-a-half-hour special, *Sammy Davis Jr.'s 60th Anniversary*

Celebration. Looking frail and ill and obviously suffering the ravages of throat cancer, he received tributes from a long list of celebrities that included Frank Sinatra, Michael Jackson, and Eddie Murphy. A few months later he was dead at the age of sixty-five.

In the Eisenhower era, though, Sammy Davis Jr., along with Waters, Poitier, Juano Hernandez, and James Edwards, was among the few performers whose dramatic roles on primetime television challenged the accepted view of African Americans as members of that contented servant class. But, significantly, none of these actors appeared weekly in a dramatic series. The tube's dramatic African American remained something of a special event and therefore—in the minds of the mainstream audience—not truly representative of the Negro in everyday American life. Images of comic Black performers, even from expired shows, dominated.

By the close of the 1950s, the new series and the special dramatic presentations made it clear that television was a writer's medium *and* also an actor's medium. The early television writers on weekly series realized their work had to showcase a TV star's persona because viewers still tuned in to see *people*, be it Lucy or Robert Young as Jim Anderson on *Father Knows Best.*

But in the early years, little was written that dealt honestly and perceptively with African American characters. Black characters—and personalities—on the weekly series still rarely had lives of their own and were there to provide some laughs or to give a little nurturing to a white character in distress. The Black performers, however, had understood (at least intuitively) that rather than play a character (as written), they had to play *against* the role. And so they used or created personas that were always bigger than the parts themselves. During the Truman and Eisenhower 1950s, it was the *presence* of actors like Ethel Waters, Juano Hernandez, and Eddie Anderson—rather than their roles—that had begun to exert a power over viewers, especially African Americans. If Anderson hadn't infused the role with his own personality, the character Rochester wouldn't have worked. And eventually even the writers knew they had to create routines around Anderson's assertive personality.

As the era closed, television remained a mixed blessing for African

American viewers. Nightly, the news shows were beginning to report on the civil rights movement. It was a historic event when TV cameras recorded troops sent by President Eisenhower to prevent violence during the desegregation of Central High School in Little Rock, Arkansas. (Television also noted Eisenhower's reluctance to do so.) African American leaders such as Martin Luther King Jr. and Roy Wilkins were also seen on television. In a 1958 five-part series that CBS's Mike Wallace did on "Negro racism" in America, viewers had even seen coverage of the growing Nation of Islam—the new Black Muslim movement—with its leaders Elijah Muhammad and Malcolm X. (A few years later, Malcolm X would comment on the biases and distortions of the CBS special, which he believed fed a national hostility against the movement.) But no indication of this changing social/political/racial climate had turned up on the primetime series, which steadfastly avoided any serious comment on African American life or on the nation's race problems. Though it would often be argued that television gave people what they wanted and that the programs that won the ratings represented the medium's democratization, that concept never applied to African American viewers, who (as the NAACP had well understood) had no choices on the little box. Only in the next decade would television begin to reflect the new racial attitudes in America.

2. THE 1960s: SOCIAL SYMBOLS

On the streets of America, the 1960s opened with a bang. Four Black students from North Carolina A&T sat at a lunch counter at a five-and-ten-cent store in Greensboro and refused to budge until they were served. The sit-in had been born. Less than two weeks later, sit-ins had spread to fifteen Southern cities in five states. Soon afterward the Student Nonviolent Coordinating Committee was founded, Freedom Riders set out on buses in the South, and in 1962 Supreme Court Justice Hugo Black ruled that the University of Mississippi must admit James H. Meredith, an African American air force veteran. "There is no case in history where the Caucasian race has survived social integration," fumed Mississippi governor Ross Barnett, who personally denied Meredith admission to the university. Later federal marshals escorted Meredith to campus for registration.

The tide was turning. President John F. Kennedy issued an executive order that prohibited racial and religious discrimination in federally financed housing and—in a 1963 historic television and radio address—declared to the nation that segregation was morally wrong and that it was "time to act in the Congress, in your state and local legislative body, and, above all, in all of our daily lives." That same year, the Reverend Martin Luther King Jr. gave his stirring "I Have a Dream" speech in front of the Lincoln Memorial as more than 250,000 Blacks and whites descended on the nation's capital to demand equal rights. It was the largest civil rights demonstration in the country's history.

And so the nation—in the early years of the restless, turbulent 1960s—had witnessed the start of some of the most sweeping social and political changes in its history. Before the era ended, disorders and riots would explode in ghettos throughout the country—and Americans would be stunned by the political assassinations of John F. Kennedy, his brother Robert Kennedy, NAACP activist Medgar Evers, Malcolm X, and the Reverend Martin Luther King Jr.

Throughout the decade, the images in the tiny box were affected by new attitudes toward the Negro and the American system—and by Black America's growing (and vocal) political disaffiliation and dissent. The evening news would document the extraordinary events of the rising civil rights movement in startling detail: the desegregation of schools, the use of billy clubs and fire hoses on protesters, the vicious taunts and cries of white Southern crowds opposed to integration. In 1962, the very nature of the news itself would be altered when the first African American network correspondent, Mal Goode, was hired by ABC. In time, primetime series would feature African American guest stars in an effort to reflect the mood of a nation forced to take a new look at itself, to question its traditional values and outlooks, and to re-examine its history. Though those primetime series would also set out to reassure their viewers that despite the appearance of social changes and new political attitudes, all was really well in America—in essence, to deny the racial conflicts and divisions that were very much on the minds of most Americans—a lineup of dramatic African American actors and actresses would eventually find interesting work on television. Ossie Davis, Ruby Dee, Cicely Tyson, Robert Hooks, Lou Gossett, Ivan Dixon, Diana Sands, Brock Peters, Billy Dee Williams, Al Freeman Jr., Ellen Holly, Denise Nicholas, Lloyd Haynes, Diahann Carroll, and a new comic making a name for himself, Bill Cosby, all became known to television viewers in the 1960s. The medium's altered reflection of American life wasn't immediate, and it wasn't always clear and sharp. But there were significant comments—whether subliminal or direct—on America and the way in which the country wanted to see itself. A new day in television slowly emerged.

At the start of the 1960s, the primetime schedule looked the same as ever. Still a lineup of sitcoms—like *My Three Sons, Dennis the Menace,* and *The Beverly Hillbillies*—with untroubled families living in plastic lily-white worlds that were politically evasive and socially reassuring. Variety and sports shows still spotlighted the Negro entertainer or Negro athlete. Series that featured a regular Black cast member still chose the familiar roles of contented servant or loyal friend. A series like *Father of the Bride* cast Ruby Dandridge as the giggly, chunky maid Delilah to a white family, the Bankses. Like everyone else in the household, Delilah was worried about the daughter of the house, pretty Kay, who was a newlywed. Poor Delilah—not much different from Beulah—still didn't seem to have anything better to do. Rochester remained Jack Benny's clever, manipulative manservant on *The Jack Benny Show*. Amanda Randolph still played the pragmatic Louise on *The Danny Thomas Show*.

On a new series like *Car 54, Where Are You?*—the story of police officers in New York's 53rd Precinct—two African American actors, Nipsey Russell and Frederick O'Neal, appeared regularly. Rather than focusing on crime (as you might expect from the setting), *Car 54, Where Are You?* spent much of its time on the slapstick antics of the cops. The Bronx itself looked like a mighty tame place. And the Black cops didn't have any gripes with the system or their colleagues.

A CHANGING OF THE GUARD: GUEST STARS IN THE SOCIALLY CONSCIOUS DRAMATIC SERIES

Signs of change, however, turned up in some of the guest appearances on the new dramatic series. By now, the live dramatic anthology shows like *Playhouse 90* and *Studio One* were either dead or on their last legs. Production of most dramatic programs had moved from New York to Los Angeles. Film replaced the live tape drama. On the surface, TV dramatic programs looked more like movies with varied and dramatic camera angles, tighter editing, better lighting and sound, and more realistic sets. In some cases, episodes were shot on location. Though most dramatic series sought to be entertaining, others, following in the tradition of the anthology series, strove to comment on societal problems and conflicts. A program like *The Defenders* addressed social issues in an evolving, more adult manner. A series like *The F.B.I.*—a rather standard cop show that patriotically saluted J. Edgar Hoover's corps of crime fighters—sometimes in spite of itself, attempted to uncover the forces that could lead a character into a life of crime. Another, *Route 66*, questioned—in a brooding manner—the way of life in America.

Though rebellion was not yet fashionable and dissent was still considered to be something voiced only by misfits or bohemians, both subjects were beginning to be expressed—albeit tentatively—in weekly series. When that happened, the Negro guest star—often as social symbol—played an important part.

Perhaps no early 1960s series better captured the growing sense of isolation and loneliness among the American young—and a reexamination of traditional American values—than *Route 66*. Its heroes were two young men of vastly different backgrounds: Tod Stiles (Martin Milner), the son of a wealthy family who, following his father's death, discovered himself left with almost nothing; and Buz Murdock (George Maharis), a former kid of the streets who had grown up in New York's rough Hell's Kitchen. Having become friends, they traversed the country in Tod's Corvette in search of adventure, romance, danger—and meaning. Just two white guys seeking to expand their horizons and to somehow find themselves.

One of *Route 66*'s most memorable episodes, the 1961 *Good Night Sweet Blues*, centered on the efforts of Buz and Tod to reunite a jazz band. The two young men, while traveling in Pittsburgh, come across an elderly Black woman who has fallen ill in her car. "Are you in pain?" they ask. "It's gone away," she responds, after taking her medication. Then she perceptively asks, "How about you? Yours gone yet?"

Once they help get her safely home, the woman, Jennie, sits in bed with the two men by her side. When Tod and Buz let her know they are jazz buffs, aficionados, she asks sweetly what that means. Once they've explained, she tells them, "Could be the good Lord had in mind for us to meet today." Buz and Tod feel so at ease with her that they tell her they have no family. "We're sort of looking for a place where we fit," one of the young men says. She knows what that means, Jennie tells them.

She speaks of her past as a blues singer with a band called the Memphis Naturals. "We was like one big family," she says. "And, oh, wouldn't I love to see them all together again one more time." She asks Tod and Buz to track down the former band members, whom she has not seen in thirty years. She wants a final jam session before she dies.

Thereafter Tod and Buz embark on a search, which carries them to Philadelphia, Chicago, Kansas City, New York, and San Francisco. One former band member is in jail. Another is found working as a shoeshine man in a public park in San Francisco. Another has left music to become a successful attorney. Buz and Tod succeed in gathering all the band members—except two. One has died. His embittered son, however, plays in his place. The other—called King—comes to see Jennie, but says he cannot perform.

Directed by Jack Smight and written by Will Lovin, *Good Night Sweet Blues* was not earth-shattering drama. Some of the dialogue is endearingly corny. But it was still above par for television drama. Simply by building a story around jazz musicians and the drift of their lives, the episode suggests the importance of jazz in American cultural history. It also acknowledges the individual pain and disappointment that the musicians have experienced. Missing, however, was the type of racial fireworks you might expect from a drama of the 1960s. *Good Night Sweet Blues* never makes a concrete comment on the discrimination that African American jazz artists endured as they struggled to find work and recognition and often as they watched less talented white musicians achieve great fame and praise. The episode's strength lies mainly in its racial subtext, in what it *suggests*, not in what it is willing to come out and say directly. Like much of television fare to follow, *Good Night Sweet Blues* set out to soothe and comfort its mainstream audience by ultimately creating a world of order and harmony where Black (the musicians) and white (the sensitive Tod and Buz) are united in a society that is apparently free of deeply ingrained racial conflicts.

Still, thanks to the performances and a sensitive director, *Good Night Sweet Blues* had a wonderful feel to it, warmer and emotionally more textured than most primetime dramas. The actors themselves appeared almost relieved at having the chance to play roles they didn't feel embarrassed by. Portraying the band members were Frederick O'Neal (as the musician turned lawyer) and the actual jazz musicians Jo Jones, Coleman Hawkins, and Roy Eldridge. (The presence alone of these jazz greats made *Good Night Sweet Blues* worth seeing.) Also cast were P. Jay Sidney, actress Billie Allen, and a very young Bill Gunn, who later wrote the screenplay for the film *The Landlord* and wrote and directed the Black cult movie *Ganja and Hess*.

But the dramatic standouts were two of Hollywood's veteran African American performers: Juano Hernandez as King—one of his last important television roles—and in the pivotal central role of Jennie, Ethel Waters. Both were able to work wonders with their material, infusing fundamentally flat characters with a sense of urgency and vitality. Especially memorable was the sequence when Hernandez's character, King, was finally found, shining shoes in the park. Having given up all thoughts of his career long ago, he has hocked his horn. "You're asking me to do the one thing that will destroy me," he says in response to Buz's request that he play for Jennie. Drinking, bad luck, and bad health didn't destroy him, he explains. Nor did the time when his wife left him. But playing with the group will. Though he has whipped his alcohol problem, he doesn't have a lip anymore. "I'm just afraid to touch that horn," he says. Everything about Hernandez suggests a broken-spirited man. At times, his eyes turn blank, almost cold, and we can sense he's withdrawn to protect the little part of himself that remains alive. Yet there is always that element of basic humanity to a Hernandez performance, so that we feel he will eventually do what he knows is morally right, even if it tears him apart to do so.

Throughout *Good Night Sweet Blues*, the script stamps the character Jennie with Waters's then well-known religious attitudes. At every turn, there are references to Jennie's faith and the God she believes in so fiercely. On her deathbed, as she is about to hear the final jam session, Jennie says, "Thanks, Lord. . . . God bless you, Buz. And you too, Tod. And thank you, dear Lord." Had any other actress uttered these lines, the dialogue would have sounded patently phony, perhaps even campy.

Ethel Waters was once again something of an all-knowing, all-hearing, all-seeing Black earth mother, who is able to intuitively understand private hurts and fears but who refuses to judge those who stand before her. It's a very seductive, double-edged fantasy, both pleasurable and dangerous.

Following *Good Night Sweet Blues*, Waters had but one other important television performance in the 1960s, as a lonely old woman in an episode of the Western series *Daniel Boone*. Afterward, she found herself becoming something of a social/political anachronism. Her long-suffering heroines struck younger African American viewers as passive conciliatory bystanders, who comforted rather than challenged an older racist generation, who didn't understand what fighting for one's rights meant. Waters eventually retired from show business. But she continued to appear periodically on the tube in the crusades of evangelist Billy Graham, where she praised the Lord without commenting on the wrongs of the system. For older viewers she remained a legend, whose appearances were a part of her ongoing personal/public story.

Another drama with a jazz artist protagonist and a racial subtext was the 1962 *Blues for a Junk Man* episode of the series *Cain's Hundred*. The series starred Peter Mark Richman as Nick Cain, a former mob lawyer who is now a federal agent tracking down members of organized crime. On this episode, Nick comes to the aid of a friend, jazz singer Norma Sherman, played by guest star Dorothy Dandridge. Recently released from prison on a drug charge, an emotionally fragile Norma tries to pick up the pieces of her career. But because of her past drug conviction, she cannot get a cabaret license. As she fights to stay free of drugs, she also struggles to save her marriage to a jazz musician (Ivan Dixon).

Often Norma Sherman's story seems to spring from all those tabloid headlines about Billie Holiday in the 1940s and 1950s. Holiday had died not long before in 1959. *Blues for a Junk Man* was a great opportunity for an edgy comment on an artist's life and the toll that bigotry and discrimination took on her. Instead viewers saw a straightforward, well-controlled, smoothly directed and acted drama that refused to delve into the race-specific aspects of its Holiday-like heroine's troubles. Nowhere in this hour-long drama did viewers see the kind of incidents that helped drive the real Billie Holiday to the end of her rope: the occasions when she had to use back entrances at nightclubs where she worked, when she was told by club managers not to mix with the whites who came to see her perform, when—during a performance—she was once called a nigger by a white patron. (Dandridge had endured some of these same indignities in her nightclub career.)

Even so, *Blues for a Junk Man* was often engrossing, simply because of the casting and what viewers consequently read into the story. (A longer version was filmed as a feature called *The Murder Men* to be released in Europe.) Had Norma Sherman been a white heroine, *Blues for a Junk Man* still would have been an effective melodrama. But the fact that its heroine was played by African American actress Dandridge made it compelling. Surely, as African American viewers and perceptive white ones watched the story unfold, they understood that as an African American woman working in white clubs, Norma Sherman had to have experienced both race and gender discrimination. They also understood there had to be a reason why the woman had

Dorothy Dandridge, in her last dramatic role,
as troubled singer Norma Sherman, with Peter
Mark Richman, in the Blues for a Junk Man
episode of Cain's Hundred

succumbed to drugs in the first place. Black viewers tended to sub-consciously rewrite the script with the kind of historical details offered by the real-life Holiday's story. Dandridge herself looked weary and lost, sad and disillusioned; viewers were aware that she was an-other African American artist whose film career had been cut short by a Hollywood that didn't make a place for an authentic Black movie goddess.

At the same time, the drama indicated the problems confronting a professional Black woman struggling to have a stable personal relation-ship. The scenes between Dandridge and Dixon were especially strong and convincing. His character can't forgive her for her past failures. We may also wonder if he can forgive her for her past professional success. Though *Blues for a Junk Man* doesn't show much of the new woman in Dixon's life, you still feel she's less demanding and assertive than Norma. When Dixon is packing his clothes, about to walk out on her, Dandridge's Norma can only respond with her exhaustion. She doesn't have the energy to put up another fight even to save something she loves.

"You think it's been easy for me?" Dixon asks. "Look, you know I'd give you my right arm. You want my right arm?"

"I don't want anything from you," she says. Director John Peyser pulls in for a close-up. "Then get out. Get lost. And forget you ever knew me," Dandridge tells Dixon. Soon afterward another close-up captures her conflicted emotions. *Blues for a Junk Man* dramatized a fairly tense adult relationship between an African American man and woman, a rarity for television at the time.

Interestingly, whenever Peyser and his director of photography, William Spencer, moved in for close-ups of Dandridge, they also revealed their infatuation with her—and their awareness that hers was a type of beauty television rarely paid tribute to. Dandridge herself played the role in true movie star fashion, knowing when to turn on the charm, when to highlight the dreamy despair without ever losing her innate glamour. Ironically, for a woman born for the movies, Dandridge's last important dramatic role would be in this television drama. Three years later she was dead at age forty-two from an overdose of an antidepressant.

Other series used African American characters to make social comments. A program like the legal drama *The Defenders*—which centered on a father-and-son defense team, Preston and Preston, who were champions of liberal causes—examined such controversial issues as abortion, euthanasia, the rights of the poor, the legal system itself, and even the entertainment industry's blacklisting era. In some episodes that featured Black characters, *The Defenders*, however, chose not to focus on racial tensions. Rather it acknowledged the presence of the American Negro in national life.

The episode *The Star-Spangled Ghetto* featured an unusual Black character, an unyielding, strictly-by-the-book Black prosecutor played by Ossie Davis. A white couple is on trial for a liquor store robbery. She's nineteen. He's twenty. As it turns out, the two, hoping for a fresh start, had stolen in order to marry and to escape from their poverty-laden lives. Preston and Preston decide to base their defense on the social conditions that led the couple to the crime.

But the African American prosecutor will accept none of that. "Do you mean they deserve a better shake just because they're poor?" he asks.

"If a man wakes up by the rules and lives his day by the rules, he's dead," the elder Preston tells the prosecutor. "There are no juices of life left in him. You suffer from that."

The white lawyers are the progressives, reexamining and challenging traditional values. Both sound like the rebellious young of the 1960s. The elder Preston says things must change within the system. When the judge on the case asks, "What's so bad about what we've got?" Preston replies, "What's so great about it? If it were perfect, we wouldn't need courts at all." He goes on to explain: "We live in a materialistic society where ownership is what rules and lives. And if we can't own what we are told we must own, we can become miserable, unhappy . . . then some of us retaliate against the society that imprisoned us in its own peculiar ghetto—the ghetto reserved for people who are unable to own the proper possessions."

Watching the episode, you may cheer the sentiments expressed but you may also prefer that those sentiments be articulated by the Black character. Rather than depicting the prosecutor as a man who might have experienced hardships himself (and perhaps also the stinging effects of racism), the episode chooses to present a reactionary who reinforces traditional values that are in need of an overhaul. While *The Star-Spangled Ghetto* was forward-looking in dramatizing the Negro as an able-bodied professional, the episode might have meant more to an African American audience had the Black prosecutor been able to show some signs of empathy and tolerance. Instead he seems to have been created (or cast with a Black actor) to alleviate any fears the mainstream audience might have of an educated African American professional who might use his smarts to subvert the system.

The Defenders, however, proved adept when it did focus on the race theme in an episode titled *Non-Violent*. A young white man from a prominent family has been arrested during a protest. So, too, has a Black minister (James Earl Jones), who is calling for more jobs for Blacks in the construction business. He explains that in their community 32 percent of the residents are Black and 59 percent of them are unemployed. During the past two years, he has petitioned the city council twelve times about this matter. Yet the mayor has done nothing.

Nor have his allegations about job discrimination been covered by the press, at least not until this recent protest; without it, he would not have been able to bring the discrimination to the attention of the citizens of the community. But while *Non-Violent* was quick to point out the grim statistics and struggles of African Americans, it went further in exploring America's complicated attitudes on race. The father of the young white man prides himself on being a liberal. He's donated to the NAACP and been on the fund-raising committee for the United Negro College Fund. Yet he doesn't understand why his son is determined to sit in a cell to uphold his convictions rather than agreeing to a release.

In an intriguing scene, the Black minister argues with his mother, who also cannot understand why her son, a man of God, has broken the law. But her son informs her of a new day for Black people. "It's no longer good enough for one Negro from the town to go to the college," he tells her. "Or for one colored man to succeed in business. Or one singer. Or one ballplayer. That's all past now, Mama. We've all got to work together now. The college graduates. And the doctors. And the women working in the white folks' kitchen. And folks chopping cotton." Here the episode was touching on the rarely explored issue of class within the African American community. Despite a hokey ending, the *Non-Violent* episode of *The Defenders* was 1960s-style liberal television at its most effective, both entertaining and thoughtful.

On other series like the medical drama *The Nurses*, the Negro was again acknowledged as a part of American life and the working world, which would remain an important point to be made throughout the 1960s and into the 1970s and 1980s. Often enough the problems confronting such a character would be social rather than racial. Appearing on one episode of *The Nurses*, Diana Sands, as a young nurse in training, was simply an educated, hardworking young woman like any other student nurse. On another episode of the series, she played a young nurse who has to deal with the rude, abusive behavior of a young (white) resident who embarrasses her before a class of students she is teaching. When she testifies before the hospital board about the young man, her gripes are social ones, not racial. It never enters her mind to play the race card. Here African Americans were drawn as everyday figures in a society that was becoming increasingly more integrated.

The same was true of the appearances of Hilda Simms, who had a recurring role on *The Nurses*. She endures the same fatigue and hassles as the rest of the overworked staff at the big-city hospital where the series was set. She was just a typical professional young Black woman on the job. General audiences may not have even known that the light-skinned Simms was African American. But the Black audience knew, and that put her appearance in *The Nurses* in a whole other context.

The Nurses did directly address racial issues in the episode *Express Stop from Lenox Avenue*. The series leads, Shirl Conway and Zina Bethune, remained in the background while African American guest stars Ruby Dee, Claudia McNeil, and Carl Lee assumed center stage. The episode explored the conflicting emotions of a young Black nurse, portrayed by Dee, who fights to be treated with respect and dignity by the hospital staff. *Variety* wrote that the episode, which moved many viewers, was "persuasive and mature in its treatment as any probing of the Negro problem attempted on Broadway in recent years." Dee, McNeil, and Lee were all nominated for Emmys for their performances.

Gradually, race relations became an "acceptable" topic on the primetime series. An episode of the series *The Eleventh Hour* examined race in the corporate world. A young Black female executive—at a white company—must deal with the pressures of her job and also the attitudes of her moody young husband. An episode of *Mr. Novak*—the story of an English teacher at Jefferson High School in Los Angeles—focused on racial divisions among the American young. When a teenaged Black girl is pelted with garbage by a group of unruly whites, other white students are forced to confront their own feelings about race. Ultimately, they give themselves high marks as the student body of the school denounces the incident. The episode might have been more realistic had it not been so quick to congratulate itself on its own liberalism. Its optimistic ending seemed to minimize the very conflicts it initially set out to explore.

Rarely would television indict American society, which in effect would be an indictment of its mainstream audience. Frequently, the race theme drama avoided at all costs a full exploration of the subject. That was evident in the 1964 episode *To Set It Right* in the series *The Lieutenant.* When two young marines—a Black named Ernest Cameron (Don Mitchell) and a white named Peter Devlin (Dennis Hopper)—report to a new military base, they immediately clash and break into a fight. The lieutenant of the platoon—the series star, Lieutenant Rice (Gary Lockwood)—asks what the problem is.

"We went to high school back home," the Black marine tells Rice. "There were just a few of us—Black monkeys. But there was a lot of white apes. And Devlin was the king of the apes." Cameron then reveals some of the indignities and cruelties he suffered at the hand of Devlin and others. One night six white guys with bicycle chains jumped him in an alley. "I was just another nigger who didn't know his place," he says.

Rice inquires about Cameron's treatment in the military. "Has anyone said that since you joined the Marine Corps?" he asks.

"No, sir," Cameron is quick to answer. "I liked the Corps fine until a few minutes ago." He adds that while in boot camp he did not see an ounce of prejudice.

The exchange puts its viewers at ease. There is no reason to feel guilt or embarrassment about Devlin's behavior, which is a case of individual bigotry. The Marine Corps itself (and perhaps, by extension, the culture at large) is free of such racism.

Thereafter, *To Set It Right*, written by Lee Erwin and directed by Vincent McEveety, focuses on Rice's determination to teach the two men something about Black/white brotherhood. Little attention was given to the white Devlin: his motives, background, irrationality. Instead the focus was on Cameron, who seems to represent the new Negro of the civil rights era. At first, Cameron strikes us as a very hip, assertive young man. But the more you see of him, the more troubled he appears. Here is a young Black man who is unable to have even a simple conversation—or relationship—that doesn't touch on race in one manner or another. A romantic afternoon with his girlfriend, Norma (Nichelle Nichols), becomes an occasion for a harangue—about what else but race. Norma is smart, attractive, levelheaded, and even-tempered. When she casually informs Cameron of her new job, he asks if it's in her field of accounting. She answers that she hasn't yet found such a job. "Sure," he tells her. "Meanwhile scrub floors." Norma counters that she's working as a waitress. "Have they got any white college graduates working there?" he asks. Norma points out that Cameron has a grudge about almost everything. "Everybody's got a right to settle scores but us," he tells her. "I'm nobody's Uncle Tom, Norma. I'm a man." Exasperated, she then attempts to make Cameron see that he's as prejudiced as those whites that he despises.

Explaining to Norma that they are living in a new age, Cameron tells her that their folks—the previous generation of Black Americans—wouldn't fight back. They just took it. "We were born losers," he says. "And we'll stay that way till we change it ourselves."

Finally, Norma realizes she is unable to reason with Cameron. But no one else can either. A Black sergeant on the base (played by Woody Strode) believes Cameron is creating problems for himself. Things were fine in the platoon, he says, before Cameron came along with this chip on his shoulder. Though *To Set It Right* had some fairly strong language and appeared eager to face racism head-on, it also lost its nerve and ultimately undermined the feelings—the very strong, modern Black perspective—of its character Cameron. The fact that Norma and the Black sergeant don't agree with him makes Cameron appear to be a Black man at odds with the Black community itself. Ultimately, he comes across as one more Angry Young Negro with unjustified racial hostility, perhaps even irrational or paranoid racial fears.

Ironically, where *To Set It Right* proved really effective was in a sequence with Rice and Norma. Rice says there might be fewer problems if people stopped acting as if they were different.

"We are different," Norma says.

"You mean the color of our skin is different," he tells her.

"And that's all?" she asks.

"Well, there are, of course, sociological factors. Economics plays a part in it too. Certain groups have their traditions and mores. I guess I sound a little like a textbook."

"Yes, you do," says Norma. Then by way of explaining Cameron's perspective, she tells Rice that Cameron has "been a Negro a lot longer than you've been thinking about his problems."

Finally, when Rice complains about Cameron's anger, Norma asks if he would prefer that Cameron be childlike, laughing and happy always, with a grin pasted on his face. "I know he's a proud boy," says Rice.

"He's a proud man," says Norma.

In this quiet exchange, Norma—the Black woman—is able to articulate Cameron's dilemma in a more thoughtful and mature way than Cameron himself has done.

The episode ended with Rice forcing Devlin and Cameron to work together during a military exercise in which their very survival depends on their cooperation. Of course, his strategy works. By episode's end, Cameron and Devlin come to some understanding and are even able to joke with one another.

Though *To Set It Right* earnestly set out to say something to its au-dience about race in America, it refused to unsettle its mainstream viewers. White bigots like Devlin, *To Set It Right* seems to say, can be ex-pected in a free, democratic nation, as exceptions to the rules that most fair, just Americans live by. But the real problem of this new age seems to be hostile young Blacks, who have to be willing to put aside their anger and their own set of biases. In essence, the Black community must now deal with its own bigotry.

Black bigots showed their faces on other dramas during this time. In the *Allie* episode of the doctor series *Ben Casey*, Sammy Davis Jr. portrayed a baseball player who had lost an eye. He was treated by an antiwhite physician, played by Greg Morris. On an episode of the series *Channing*, which was set at the fictional Channing University, James Earl Jones appeared as a professor who's a bigot of another sort. Alien-ated from most faculty members because of his own hang-ups (not theirs), he is also unusually demanding of a bright young Black stu-dent, who he blindly does not believe can meet the university's high academic standards. It takes a feisty, nonconformist professor (played in high style by Agnes Moorehead) to bring him to his senses; to show him the way his own racial paranoia has entangled him in emotional knots and led him to treat another Black American unfairly.

Though primetime still shied away from stories exploring the ef-fects of racism or even dramas that uncovered any of the nation's other festering social problems, throughout the era episodes of such series as *The Defenders, Cain's Hundred, Route 66, The Lieutenant, The Nurses, Channing, Naked City,* and *Mr. Novak* proved important. Americans were seeing articulate, active, and troubled new-style African American characters, who weren't waltzing about as if they hadn't a care in the world. That was even occasionally true of a series like *The Fugitive*. On the *Decision in the Ring* episode of *The Fugitive*, James Edwards ap-peared as a disillusioned young prizefighter who had forsaken his dream of being a doctor because of the medical profession's racism. Now suffering memory loss, he believes his bouts in the ring have left him brain-damaged. A year later, on another episode of *The Fugitive*, Ivan Dixon appeared as a doctor (without any racial problems in his profession) who treats the series' hero, Richard Kimble. Yet another episode of *The Fugitive* featured Dixon and Diana Sands as an African ambassador and his wife. In most cases, African Americans on such programs were again social symbols; indications that Negroes were worthy of integration (just as Poitier's character had been in *A Man Is Ten Feet Tall*) and that society had to make a place for them.

Even when depicted as criminals, Black characters were handled sympathetically, often presented as pawns in an inequitable social system in which they had little or no control. An episode of *The F.B.I.* featured Robert Hooks as a gas station attendant caught in the grip of pressing financial problems. He is behind on his rent, his wife (Cicely Tyson) is pregnant, and he hopes to get a college education as a way out of his social/economic rut. When he serves on a jury in a case involving a Mafia criminal, he succumbs to a $10,000 bribe to cast a ballot for the man's acquittal. His wife suspects he has done something wrong. Finally, tormented by his decision, he cooperates with the FBI in their investigation of jury tampering. Another episode of *The F.B.I.* featured Billy Dee Williams as an escaped convict with a conscience. At one point while on the run, he phones his wife, yearning simply to hear the sound of her voice and to know how she and his son are doing. During a climactic robbery sequence, he pleads with another convict not to shoot two guards. Throughout, Williams shows us a sensitive, loyal man, who somehow went wrong in life.

But there were not enough of such new roles. Nor in the early years of the new decade was there a serious African American character appearing as a regular on a weekly series. Though television had brought the social/political messages of such figures as Martin Luther King Jr., Malcolm X, Rosa Parks, and Fannie Lou Hamer into the nation's homes, those activists who turned up on the nightly news were essentially, like the serious Black characters of the dramatic series, still *guest shots*, not primetime regulars. Only the series character could be the kind of familiar presence that might in time alter viewer perceptions. But in the early 1960s, it still looked as if the networks feared mainstream viewers would reject anything *but* a comic African American character coming weekly into their homes. Finally, though, there appeared a little series, *East Side, West Side*, that briefly looked as if it would break some of television's long-standing rules, if not its racial taboos.

EAST SIDE, WEST SIDE: URBAN REALITIES AND GLIMMERS OF A NEW KIND OF AFRICAN AMERICAN LEADING LADY

Premiering on September 23, 1963, at 10 p.m. on CBS, *East Side, West Side* starred George C. Scott as Neil Brock, a New York City social worker. His office was faced with the problems of urban renewal, prostitution, blockbusting, rape, and appropriate treatment for the mentally disabled. Working with Brock were the head of the welfare branch played by Elizabeth Wilson and a young Black social worker named Jane Foster, played by Cicely Tyson.

East Side, West Side received wide coverage upon its debut. In *New York Newsday*, critic Barbara Delatiner wrote that it "made an auspicious bow. If the same quality can be maintained and a few writing difficulties ironed out, the new series could be the best of the season." Some reviewers, however, complained that the series failed to deliver on its promise of adult, realistic drama. "A sensational phoney," was the way the critic for the *New York Herald Tribune* described it. But almost every critic noticed two episodes totally unlike anything else then appearing on the network primetime schedule. The episodes—*Who Do You Kill?* and *No Hiding Place*—dealt in explicit terms with America's growing racial problems.

Directed by Tom Gries and written by the series's executive producer, Arnold Perl, *Who Do You Kill?* told the story of a couple living in a Harlem tenement while struggling to make ends meet. The husband, Joe (James Earl Jones), having recently come North from the South, is unemployed and in school. During the evenings the wife, Ruth, works in a bar/restaurant to keep the family afloat while Joe cares for their young child. Theirs is a grim existence of decaying buildings and battered dreams. Garbage fills a nearby lot. Inside their tenement, plaster falls from the ceilings. Paint peels on the walls. There are always the sounds of rats too. "Listen at them," Joe tells Ruth. "It's their house. Not ours." In their tiny, cramped apartment, a curtain is used to partition a room for their child in her crib.

Almost overwhelmed by financial pressures, Ruth and Joe argue about their future. He informs her that he has quit a course at school, believing he won't be able to find a decent job regardless of whatever training he has. She worries about him being swallowed up by the temptations and despair of the streets. "I want you away from those street boys, the ones with the needles, the pipe jobs," she tells him. "As strong as you are, they'll suck you under." Their lives, however, are irrevocably changed following a chilling moment when—hearing a cry from their baby—Joe discovers his daughter has been gnawed, in her crib, by a rat. He uses a broom to beat the animal. Then, in a frenzy of desperation and panic, he picks the child up and runs out onto the street. But no taxicab will stop and take him to the hospital. Finally, he walks to the hospital, carrying the bleeding baby in his arms. But the child dies. Afterward Joe and Ruth must pick up the pieces of their life together.

At times, *Who Do You Kill?* faltered in the manner in which well-intentioned dramas often do. "I don't think any white man knows what it's like—the life of a Negro," social worker Neil Brock tells the distraught father, Joe. "We can sympathize, project, understand. But know?" Such dialogue sounded as if it "came right out of a textbook, empty and practically meaningless," wrote critic Barbara Delatiner of *New York Newsday*. The episode's efforts to dramatize a protest movement led by a local Black minister also at times seemed patronizing. "Patience. Nonviolent determination," the minister tells a group of African Americans. "These are our weapons." That was all well and good, and the sentiments were certainly those of a segment of Black protesters at the time. But then the minister adds, "We must unite and survive through dignity. . . . And the greatest gift of all. Laughter. Laughter to keep from crying." At that point, viewers may have wanted to cry out themselves. Enough already. *Who Do You Kill?* also failed to incorporate Cicely Tyson's character Jane into enough of the action. Though she had more to do in this episode than in others and though she is shrewdly shown to be a part of the African American community, about the most she can do is to console the heartbroken father, telling him, in essence, to have hope. If ever a program cried out for a telling comment from a Black character, this was it.

Still, shot in New York in a gritty, highly realistic style by cameraman Jack Priestly (who had previously filmed the stark-looking *Naked City*), *Who Do You Kill?* dazzled the critics.

"Drama of protest, a theme rarely found on television, made an impressive and moving appearance last night on *East Side, West Side*," wrote *The New York Times*'s Jack Gould, who hailed the production for its "lean and perceptive understanding" of the "erosion of the human spirit that accompanies exploitation of a minority."

"For the first time 'the winds of change,' marking the Negro protest movement in this country, won a dramatic outing on a network," wrote *Variety*. *The Village Voice* called the drama "as forceful a piece of social propaganda as has been on TV for a long time." As Jack Gould had noted, this was the first predominantly Negro-cast TV drama since *The Green Pastures*.

Who Do You Kill? was powerful adult television; the performances—strong, intense, direct, deeply felt—were far better than those usually seen on television. Both James Earl Jones and Diana Sands were relative newcomers then working in New York theater. Fresher and more convincing here than in some of his later inflated performances, Jones had performed in such theater productions as *Moon on a Rainbow Shawl*, *A Midsummer Night's Dream*, *The Merchant of Venice*, and *The Tempest*. Diana Sands was a highly touted stage actress who looked as if she could do almost any role, whether it be the lead in James Baldwin's play *Blues for Mister Charlie* or Cleopatra in Shakespeare's *Antony and Cleopatra* and Shaw's *Caesar and Cleopatra*. In the 1960s, she brought her usual vitality and gritty style to such television programs as *The Nurses*, *The Outer Limits*, and later *Dr. Kildare*, *The Fugitive*, *I Spy*, and *Medical Center*. Watching Jones and Sands in *Who Do You Kill?*, viewers saw two young skilled performers testing one another and pushing an intelligent script to its limits. Somehow their theatrical flourishes—they *sound* more like theater people than film/television performers—worked. Both were nominated for Emmys for their performances. Director Tom Gries won an Emmy for his work on the episode.

Who Do You Kill? ran into problems with network affiliates. In Atlanta, CBS's WAGA-TV refused to air it for fear that it might spark racial tensions. "We feel this city has made excellent progress in race relations," said the station's general manager, "and it is our conclusion that this program might well impair that progress." The program also was not shown in Shreveport, Louisiana.

East Side, West Side's other important episode, *No Place to Hide*, written by Millard Lampell, focused on the social upheaval—the meanness and the petty vindictiveness—that occurs when a Black couple, played by Ruby Dee and Earle Hyman, moves into a white suburban neighborhood on Long Island. The white residents are terrified by the mere thought of this type of social integration. Unscrupulous real estate agents attempt to frighten families into leaving the area, buying up their homes at low prices, and then selling those same homes at inflated prices to Black families. The Black couple, though, is revealed as decent, educated, and really far more of a credit to the community than many of the white residents.

For its time *No Hiding Place* addressed very real social attitudes. CBS took precautions, however, to ensure the episode would not be *too* controversial. Originally, George C. Scott's character danced with Ruby Dee at a social gathering. The sequence was cut—for dramatic purposes, said CBS, rather than any network taboo against mixing the races. But star Scott as well as others publicly criticized the network for caving in to its fears of possible audience reactions, again especially in the South.

But the most important aspect of *East Side, West Side* was its casting of Cicely Tyson. *The Village Voice* complained that Tyson, "a good actress," was handed "a part so shallow as to confirm everything derogatory one has ever heard Negroes say about Negro social workers." But most viewers were struck by her presence. Pauline Kael found Tyson's control and "her tight reserve slightly antipathetic; she seemed to be holding back from us—not yielding her personality, not relaxing within the minuscule demands of the role. Now I think I can see why. It was a role in which a beautiful pinheaded actress might have been perfectly content, and her contentment might have made her seem delectable. Those secretary roles, black and white, are generally played for comedy or for sex; the black girls are plumped down in an office—to fill the quotas—but they're playing classy maids. What Tyson's strained manner in that series was saying to us was 'I can't give myself to this role—I have more than this in me.' And, despite her magnetic glamour, she wouldn't give us more than the cold efficiency of the secretary she played—which could only make a viewer slightly uncomfortable."

African American viewers also had another response to Tyson. Just the fact that she was there week after week in a professional setting was a breakthrough. "I really didn't do much on the series," Tyson said years later. "But people always remember me in it." In this small, seemingly throwaway role, Tyson ushered in a whole new bearing and aesthetic for African American women on television. Slender and taut, neither grinning nor performing domestic duties, here was a dark African American woman who was the complete antithesis of the long-cherished mammy figure. Tyson wore her hair in a *natural* (becoming the first Black woman to do so in a weekly series), before the Afro had widespread acceptance, even within the African American community. With her flawless skin, chiseled features, and luminous eyes, Tyson was a beautiful woman but not in the traditional Western sense. She may well have made viewers rethink their definition of beauty.

Though often an observer on the series, she nonetheless appeared to understand every move and gesture of those around her. And despite the fact that the story lines didn't acknowledge her sexuality, she herself came across as a sexual young woman. She had a glowing intensity that made viewers, even when they didn't know her name, realize that here possibly was a remarkable actress who was bigger and better than the part she played.

Tyson's strong sense of herself may have contributed to some of the series's problems. *East Side, West Side*'s producer, David Susskind, charged that CBS dumped the series because twenty-six Southern affiliates refused to air an integrated program. "A Negro actress was an integrated member of the *East Side, West Side* company," said Susskind, "and in her role as a social worker's aide, had frequent disputes with her white co-star. They don't like that down South." He said that the Southern affiliates had dropped the show because of its "Negro characters. We've had Negro actors playing doctors, architects, lawyers." Denying Susskind's charges, CBS insisted that twenty stations had been added to the *East Side, West Side* lineup, about half of which were in the South. But the network admitted that several Southern affiliates had also refused to carry the series all year. In the end, said CBS, *East Side, West Side* died—after only one season—because of its poor ratings. Many observers believed the network had not given the series time to develop a following, and several critics mourned its removal from the primetime lineup.

"Two years ago, if any television executive had suggested a dramatic show with Negro actors and a Negro theme, he would have been quietly transferred to the mailroom," wrote Barry Farrell in *Life*. "In the season just past, half a dozen such shows were attempted by the major networks, and that is progress. But now that the season is ending, it is clear that the nice tries meant far less than the demise of the one show that not only tried but actually said something worthwhile. Throughout the season, *East Side, West Side* served as the conscience of television." He added that with the series's cancellation, "television appears to have given up on the racial problem as a source of serious drama." Ironically, on the day that the series was canceled, it received the National Television Critics' Best Film Series award.

Still, *East Side, West Side* had taken the primetime series in a new direction. Some twenty million viewers had seen the episodes *Who Do You Kill?* and *No Hiding Place.* And Cicely Tyson's presence had led the way to a new type of Black cast member on the weekly primetime series schedule.

NEW FACES

Other African American supporting characters appeared in new series. On the sitcom *Hogan's Heroes,* which revolved around the "funny" exploits of American prisoners of war in a Nazi POW camp during World War II, Ivan Dixon played Sergeant James Kinchloe. Though the American soldiers, led by Colonel Robert Hogan, frequently came across as clever adolescents as they outwitted their German captors, Colonel Klink and Sergeant Schultz, Dixon managed to keep his cool. But on most episodes, he was kept on the sidelines. "Ivan felt very unused," said *Hogan's Heroes* co-star Robert Clary. "He really had very little to do every week." Twice Dixon was paired with attractive African American actresses: Barbara McNair (as a Black American working with the French Resistance during the war) and Isabelle Cooley. Having just given a highly acclaimed performance in the independent movie drama *Nothing But a Man,* Dixon always looked as if he were too smart for this type of adolescent farce. Perhaps it wasn't surprising that he left the series after its fifth season, replaced by Kenneth Washington.

Shrewdly, Dixon used *Hogan's Heroes* to do more serious work. Having grown up in Harlem, the son of a grocer who had been awarded the Croix de Guerre during World War I, Dixon had graduated from North Carolina Central University (with a degree in political science), then earned a Rockefeller Foundation scholarship that enabled him to enroll in graduate studies at Western Reserve University. Afterward he trained as a director at Karamu House in Cleveland and New York's American Theater Wing. But unable to land directing jobs—"When I started," he once said, "you couldn't get in those pro-

Actor Ivan Dixon (left with Bob Crane) in Hogan's Heroes, before he emerged as an important TV director

duction areas"—he found work as an actor on the stage (in *The Cave Dwellers*) and films (*Something of Value, Porgy and Bess*, and repeating the role he had created on stage of the African student Asagai in *A Raisin in the Sun*). But his career was kept alive and thriving by his appearances in such TV shows as *The Big Story*, the *DuPont Show of the Month*'s production of *Arrowsmith, The Twilight Zone, The Eleventh Hour, The Outer Limits*, and *The F.B.I.* Dixon also gave a widely praised performance in the *CBS Playhouse* Vietnam drama *The Final War of Olly Winter*.

In television and films, he projected a quiet sensitivity (without the bruised quality of a James Edwards) combined with a relaxed virility rarely exhibited by African American males. Dixon's contemporary and friend Sidney Poitier commented, "Ivan was a truly talented actor whose potential was never realized. . . . The industry wasn't ready to cultivate two of us at the same time."

But Poitier also recalled "the triumphant arrival of the motion picture director Ivan Dixon." In the 1970s, Dixon directed the films *Trou-*

ble Man and *The Spook Who Sat by the Door*. But he fared far better as a television director, beginning with episodes of *The Bill Cosby Show* and continuing for the next three decades with episodes of such shows as *Get Christie Love!*, *Snoops*, and *Brewster Place*. He also became one of the first African American television directors of such non-Black programs as *The Waltons* (fifteen episodes), *Magnum, P.I.* (twelve episodes), *The Rockford Files* (eighteen episodes), *The Mod Squad*, *Starsky and Hutch*, *In the Heat of the Night*, and *Quantum Leap*.

A different type of African American character appeared in 1965 during the last season of the Western series *Rawhide*. Joining the production that starred Eric Fleming and newcomer Clint Eastwood was Black actor Raymond St. Jacques as Simon Blake, one of the men traveling cross-country with a massive cattle drive. Like Cicely Tyson on *East Side, West Side*, St. Jacques's Blake didn't have much to do, but his very presence said volumes. In this high-testosterone series, with its endless salutes to traditional masculine heroics and the never-ending myth of the old frontier, St. Jacques, with his upright proud bearing, injected color into what was usually an all-white male world.

BILL COSBY AND *I SPY:* A COOL HERO IN A HOT AGE, FIGHTING FOR TRUTH, JUSTICE, AND HIS BEST BUDDY

The weekly series underwent its most dramatic color change with the 1965 debut of an adventure series about two international intelligence agents of an unspecified U.S. government agency, traveling undercover in foreign lands and fighting for the American Way. The series might have been mildly diverting and quickly forgotten were it not for the casting. One agent was white; the other, Black. The series was *I Spy*, which introduced the mainstream audience to a rising twenty-seven-year-old comic, Bill Cosby. In temperament, image, and outlook, he proved to be the right actor in the right place at the right time.

Before his appearance on *I Spy*, Cosby had already crafted an unusual comic persona that appealed to audiences Black and white. Born in 1937 in Philadelphia, Cosby was the son of a navy mess steward; his mother was a housemaid. Quitting high school after the tenth grade,

Cosby joined the navy for two years. Through a correspondence course, he acquired his high school equivalency diploma. Later he attended Philadelphia's Temple University. While in his mid-twenties, he began performing stand-up comedy in small clubs, quickly moving up the ranks to earn between $3,000 and $10,000 a week. With two hit comedy albums and appearances on such programs as *The Tonight Show* and *The Jonathan Winters Show*, Cosby was among a new generation of Black comedians that included Dick Gregory, Godfrey Cambridge, and a very young Richard Pryor. Each had a distinct comic persona.

Dick Gregory dealt specifically with racial matters in a satiric, sometimes biting manner. One of Gregory's most famous comic lines had

Bonded buddies, fighting for truth, justice, and one another: Bill Cosby and Robert Culp as the undercover agents in I Spy

him seated at a lunch counter in the South during the era of sit-ins. When the white waitress told him, "I'm sorry but we don't serve Negroes," he answered, "That's all right. I don't eat 'em." Influenced by

Jack Benny and Fred Allen, satirist Godfrey Cambridge often performed nonracial stand-up comedy. Yet he also injected racial comments into some of his routines, although he once said, "If I would do
just racial material, I would go out of my cotton picking mind." The
young Pryor, still not having found his comic identity (for years he said
he wanted to be just like Cosby), was known for an almost manic drive
and intensity. Appearing boyish and even a tad preppy in his suits and
ties, he also looked as if he might flip out on you at any moment.
Though these new comedy stars appeared on television, none was able
to successfully star in a series. Once he found his comic identity, the ex-
plosively satirical Pryor proved too hot a persona for television. His
1977 variety program, *The Richard Pryor Show*, would last for only five
episodes. During that short time, he repeatedly had problems with
NBC's censors. On the opening of one episode, Pryor, appearing to be
nude but actually wearing a body suit, indicated there was only one
way to please television censors: the camera panned down to reveal a
seemingly emasculated Pryor.

Bill Cosby, however, was the coolest of cool, the most laid-back of
comedians. His monologues were explicitly *nonracial*. He told cute tales
about Fat Albert, Dumb Donald, Weird Harold, and the perils of growing up. In anyone else's hands, the material might have been mundane
or downright corny. But Cosby perfected the persona of a man puzzled
and frazzled by life's little absurdities and domestic headaches but always in control of his emotions. He couldn't comprehend why common sense didn't prevail (it made life so much easier). Yet he was never
angry. To his great credit, Cosby himself—the master of nonethnic
anecdotes—never came across as a Black man trying to be white. He
managed to hold on to his ethnic grit—through his rhythm and his *attitude*. In the 1960s and in the years to come, audiences Black and white
identified with his material—and responded to his timing, delivery,
and personality. Still, it might strike some as odd that Cosby—with his
seemingly politically neutral persona—became a star in the politically
restless 1960s.

While developing *I Spy*, Sheldon Leonard (the series co-creator and
executive producer) had been impressed by Cosby's rapid career rise
and his remarkable rapport with mixed audiences. Then one night
Leonard happened to see Cosby on television. "He was doing a stand-
up comedy routine on a Jack Paar special," Leonard recalled. "He was

just what we needed for *I Spy*, except for one thing. He was black." For later generations, the idea of co-starring an African American actor opposite a white one in a dramatic role might almost seem a cliché. But when Leonard discussed casting Cosby (who had not acted before), the concept was considered so daring that *I Spy* almost didn't happen. Network executives grew uneasy. Sponsors were not sure such a series would work.

Producer Leonard, however, felt confident. He had been watching viewer responses to the question of race. He hadn't forgotten the letters that had criticized Amanda Randolph on his earlier series *The Danny Thomas Show*. But he was also aware of the reactions to an episode of *The Dick Van Dyke Show*, which he had produced.

In the episode, Rob and Laura Petrie were parents of a newborn son. But Rob suspected there had been a mix-up in the hospital. His son looked nothing like him and he believed that he and his wife had been given the son of a couple named Peters. Already at the hospital the Petries had received gifts and flowers intended for the Peters couple. In turn, the Peters family had received gifts intended for the Petries. Never having met the couple, Rob called them. "Hello, Mr. Peters?" he said on the phone. "I think we have something of yours, and you have something of ours. . . . Mr. Peters, may I ask you a personal question? Who does your baby look like? . . . Well, that's what I thought, because our baby doesn't look like either of us either. . . . You're taking this pretty lightly. . . . Okay. We live right around the block. . . . Okay. I'll expect you." Shortly afterward, the doorbell rang at the Petrie home. To Rob's surprise (and the audience's), Mr. and Mrs. Peters (played by Greg Morris and Mimi Dillard) were a good-looking, young African American couple.

The representative for the sponsor, Procter & Gamble, protested, "We're afraid of that script. You're making fun of the fact that the couple is black." Leonard said that wasn't the case at all. "We're making fun of the fact that Rob Petrie is a dope." Later the network objected, fearful of responses from their Southern affiliates. But Leonard won out. "When the handsome couple made their entrance, there was a moment of shocked silence, then the audience went crazy," said Leonard of the show's taping. "It was the longest laugh in the whole five-year history of *The Dick Van Dyke Show*—so long that it had to be trimmed to fit the episode into its allotted air time."

"I had a computer readout," said Leonard, "analyzing the mail we had gotten after the *Van Dyke* episode in which Greg Morris had made a schmuck of Dick. It indicated that out of nineteen hundred and sixty pieces of mail, seventeen hundred and eighty-two had applauded our presentation of the black man, two hundred and one were hostile, and the balance were indeterminate. I was prepared to claim that this showed the attitude of the viewing public was much more enlightened than it had been in the Amanda Randolph days."

But questions arose at NBC as to what could and could not be shown on *I Spy*. When Cosby and white star Robert Culp were traveling together, would the two men ride together in the front seat of the car? If so, would Southern audiences object to seeing a Black man sitting right next to a white one? When the two men checked into a hotel together, would they share a room? Would there ever be an incident when a hotel denied a room to Cosby because of his race? Said Leonard, "I had reason to expect such questions as 'You mean to say that these two fellas, the white man and a negra, are gonna go out on dates together? Sleep in the same room? Sit on the same toilet seat?' "

Eventually, the producers worked around such problems. Most episodes of *I Spy* took place in foreign countries. (Its first nine episodes were shot on location in Japan, Hong Kong, and Mexico, which gave it an exciting realistic look for television.) Consequently, it was felt audiences would never question such matters as hotel accommodations in these foreign lands.

Still, after the pilot episode had been filmed, edited, and scored, the NBC brass, recalled Leonard, "loved it with one reservation. They didn't like Cosby. They wanted to replace him. It wasn't just that he was black, which was risky enough to start with, but his acting was amateurish. Unfortunately, that was true. His inexperience showed." But Leonard told NBC not to worry. "He'll get better. He's a natural. This was his first shot at acting in front of a camera. Naturally, he was uptight, and I didn't have much time to help him. As soon as he relaxes he'll light up the screen." But the executives were insistent. "We still think you should replace him. There must be some guy out there who can do better. He doesn't have to be black." Leonard replied, "If you replace him, you better figure on replacing me, too." Cosby stayed.

On *I Spy* Robert Culp portrayed agent Kelly Robinson, a former Princeton law student and professional tennis star who had played on

Davis Cup teams. He went undercover as a tennis champ. Cosby played agent Alexander Scott, who feigned the role of Kelly's trainer and companion. It proved a perfect cover, although even here some African American viewers may have grumbled that this new-style Black character still had traces of the old servant syndrome. Otherwise Cosby's Scott was a wholly new kind of Black man on television. A man of many talents, Scott was a graduate of Temple University and a Rhodes Scholar who spoke seven languages and was also a karate master and a sharpshooter. A very cerebral, resolutely middle-class African American action hero. The exploits of both Kelly and Scotty grew out of the James Bond movie series, then very popular, and also the highly rated television series *The Man from U.N.C.L.E.*

The hour-long series premiered on September 15, 1965, at 10 p.m. on NBC. Its first episode—*So Long, Patrick Henry*—took Kelly and Scotty to Hong Kong, where they meet up with a disillusioned Black American Olympic star, played by Ivan Dixon, who has decided to defect to Red China. Trying to persuade him to do otherwise is his young fiancée played by Cicely Tyson. Eventually, the two undercover agents help the athlete have a change of heart.

Written by Robert Culp, *So Long, Patrick Henry* had a politically astute premise: an African American man who sees no future for himself in his own country might turn to Communism with its promise of equality for all people. But the episode was more interested in chase sequences and karate chops and kicks than in exploring and explaining its rebel character's perspective. It also failed to probe the athlete's ultimate decision *not* to defect. Still, Black audiences had seen a trio of serious dramatic Black characters—played by Cosby, Dixon, and Tyson—and had also been presented at least with the *idea* of possible Black political dissent.

Most critics liked the Black performers. "Ivan Dixon, in a guest role, gave a strong performance as an American defector. And it was good to see comedian Bill Cosby working regularly, even though he didn't get a laugh," commented the *New York Herald Tribune.* "Cicely Tyson was cool and attractive in the role of Dixon's fiancée," wrote *Variety.*

But otherwise for a series that would eventually be remembered fondly by millions of viewers, *I Spy* got some fairly lousy reviews. "Whatever the cause of the trouble, this series, in its opening segment, has failed to communicate," wrote *The Christian Science Monitor. The*

New York Times called *I Spy* "a show in search of an attitude and also the style to go with it."

But perhaps most telling was *Variety*'s comment: "The network and producer Sheldon Leonard have, with more guts than ordinary observers could imagine, cast Negro comedian Bill Cosby in a feature role, then turned about in the premiere stanza and racked another ethnic group, the Chinese, with casting that was a throwback to Fu Manchu and dialog [sic] that would be more likely on the washroom walls of a southern bus station—'give Charlie Chan a fortune cookie and he goes away happy.' " While heralding a new day for images of one minority group, *I Spy* had obviously fallen into the trap of rigidly stereotyping another.

But the series improved. The ratings kept it in the top twenty shows (not the top ten), and *I Spy* was popular with the young—white and Black—and also proved successful abroad. During the first season, NBC was quick to announce that 180 of its affiliates carried the program. But the network admitted that it failed to secure clearance for *I Spy* in Albany and Savannah, Georgia; Daytona Beach, Florida; and Alexandria, Louisiana. The series did find advertisers (a factor the television industry was watching closely). "Everybody told us we were going to have trouble with the sponsors," producer Sheldon Leonard told *Ebony*, but "we have more sponsors than we need."

What propelled *I Spy*'s success, what gave it definition and distinction amid the wave of bland television entries of the season, was indeed its Black/white combo. During a time when the Negro Problem was stamped more and more on the national consciousness, the mainstream television audience clearly still had a "curiosity" about the Negro: who he/she was, what he/she thought, what he/she was really fighting for. *I Spy* answered those questions in terms that were acceptable and nonthreatening. In essence, the Negro was a friend, a buddy, a defender of the American way of life.

I Spy brought the theme of interracial male bonding into clear focus. Throughout Kelly and Scotty are perfectly attuned to one another's moods, attitudes, likes, and dislikes. Sometimes the men didn't even seem to need to talk; instead each appeared to always know what was on the other's mind. (Off the set, the two actors became friends.) They were forever coming to one another's defense. On an episode like *Bet Me a Dollar*, mainstream audiences must have felt very relieved to see

Scotty vigilantly fighting to save Kelly's life after the latter unknowingly suffers from a potentially deadly infection. On an episode like *It's All Done with Mirrors*, Scotty has to rescue Kelly, who has been brainwashed by a sinister doctor. Though Kelly is believed to be a traitorous double agent, Scotty is determined to prove otherwise. In the climactic sequence, Kelly has been programmed to kill Scotty. But he can't put a bullet into his buddy. "You missed six times, Kelly. You're a disgrace," says Scotty. "You couldn't hurt a hair on my head." Even a brilliant master of brainwashing hasn't been able to destroy the affection these two guys have for each other.

Ironically, at the time of *I Spy*, mainstream America was witnessing a dramatic change in the direction of the civil rights movement. Martin Luther King Jr.'s nonviolent, passive resistance philosophy was being rejected by a younger segment of Black America, which had turned its ears to the words of a more militant leader like Malcolm X. The system itself, which Black America had fought to desegregate, was now being questioned. Why integrate with blue-eyed devils? The doctrines of cultural separatism and Black Nationalism were taking root. Much of white America grew fearful of the new radicalism—and the young African American males like Stokely Carmichael and H. Rap Brown who espoused its causes. The very year that *I Spy* debuted also marked the assassination of Malcolm X.

None of this new social/political momentum showed up on primetime. Instead the loyal, warmhearted, good-natured Scotty removed any fear of Black male rage and anger at the system. Both Scotty and Kelly were cultural anomalies; men who had transcended their country's attitudes on race. That might have been an enlightening premise—had the audience ever seen the racial system and the racial history that these seemingly remarkable men had transcended. But the topic of race was usually nowhere to be found on *I Spy*, at least not as a part of the conscious text of the episodes.

Cosby himself vetoed any dialogue based on racial issues, so *Ebony* reported, because he had already created a career based on nonracial material. Cosby acknowledged that his success was partly a by-product of the Negro "revolution." Doors had been opened to him because of Black protest. He might never have had a forum to display his talent without those who had joined the bus boycotts and the sit-ins. "Negroes like Martin Luther King and Dick Gregory; Negro groups like the

Deacons and the Muslims—all are dedicated to the cause of civil rights," Cosby told *Ebony*. "But they do their jobs in their own way. My way is to show white people that Negroes are human beings with the same aspirations and abilities that whites have."

Cosby had his point, which was why—even at this time with the new protest movements within Black America—*I Spy* still meant a great deal to African American viewers. Cosby projected an image of a supremely *qualified* Black man, again like the other TV social symbols of the era, an educated, intelligent, articulate young man, able to function in and contribute to American society. Playing the character with a casual assurance, Cosby never let any type of submissive gesture creep into his acting. Scotty could never even imagine calling any white man the Boss. Week after week, he unraveled intrigues, asserted himself, and, along with Kelly, saved the day for his country. Unlike later Black heroes, such as Avery Brooks's Hawk on *Spenser: For Hire*, his main function never appeared to be to simply save the white hero at a crucial moment, then go his way. The heroes of *I Spy* worked out problems together.

Cosby took his role—and his image as a new kind of Black male on television—very seriously. He also spoke up and demanded certain changes in the story lines and the motivations of his character. At first, his Scotty didn't have love interests. In part, this seemed important because no one wanted to see Scotty depicted as an oversexed or forever horny Black man, more interested in seducing a pretty woman than in solving the crime. Ironically, on certain occasions, Cosby had an almost grim seriousness, as if he couldn't fully relax, so determined was he to do a solid job. Kelly, however, seemed looser and had all sorts of pretty women vying for his attentions, and he took them up on their offers.

After a time, it looked as if Cosby's Scotty might become another type: the decent Black man who, while not sexually neutered, appeared sexually neutralized. It was reminiscent of some of Sidney Poitier's and Harry Belafonte's movie characters: here were Black men considered to be sexually attractive but rarely permitted to be sexually aggressive. Surely, an African American male's sexuality could be presented as one component in a fully developed personality. A Black man could be intelligent, sensitive, emotional, *and* sexual (as had been the case with Ivan Dixon's character in the film *Nothing But a Man*). Cosby sought to bring that realistic middle ground to the series.

Jet reported a "toe-to-toe slugfest" between Cosby and producer Sheldon Leonard. Cosby wanted Scotty to have a leading lady on some episodes. He felt the character was being depicted as a "jovial, good-natured celibate." Even when a snazzy lady showed up, romance seemed out of the question. On an episode called *The Loser*, Scotty attempted to break up a ring of heroin dealers who captured him and tied him up in the dressing room of a singer at a nightclub, played by guest star Eartha Kitt. The singer helped Scotty escape. The two could easily have developed a romantic relationship. But she was a heroin addict. Usually, a little loving can redeem shady ladies in TV and the movies. But no such thing happened here. Cosby told a newspaper columnist, "We travel to countries in Latin America, the Orient and Europe. I could get a girl any place. I don't care what she is."

Finally, Cosby won out. Jazz singer Nancy Wilson was brought in as Cosby's love interest for an episode called *Lori*. So important an event did this seem that *Jet* ran a cover story on it. Wilson played a Las Vegas singer who is suspected of aiding her brother (Greg Morris) in subversive activities. Cosby's Scotty clearly seems interested in her, and the two have a parting kiss at the conclusion of the episode. But for most of the time, they were adversaries. Cosby worked with other leading ladies like Cicely Tyson and Barbara McNair. Yet despite his victory on *I Spy*, women never pursued him the way they did his co-star, Culp. Romantic Black heroes mostly remained a taboo for years to come. (*Room 222* was a notable exception.)

For his work on *I Spy*, Cosby was awarded an Emmy as Outstanding Actor in a Drama Series for the 1965–66 season. This type of recognition was also a breakthrough. Emmy wins were still a rarity for African American performers. Harry Belafonte had walked off with the award for Outstanding Performance in a Variety or Music Program or Series in the 1959–60 season. Though dramatic stars like Ruby Dee, Diana Sands, and James Earl Jones had earned nominations, none had won the big prize. Cosby's award indicated the industry was taking the work of dramatic Black stars seriously. Eventually, African American performers would receive far greater recognition from Emmy voters than from those who cast ballots for the Oscars. Later Cosby picked up two more Emmys for his role on the series.

At the series' end in 1968, Cosby had become one of the medium's best-known performers. Years later, speaking of some of the pressures he experienced filming *I Spy*, he admitted that he was often on edge. "Because I was first, the network and the advertisers were nervous about how I should act, on camera *and* off," he said. "I was not supposed to be anything other than what they wanted a Black man to be at that time. And that changed by the week." He understood that despite the rise of the civil rights movement and the "pressure groups" that were on NBC's back, the network's only fear was that "the old silent majority would reject me and the show." He believed there were a "dozen thin lines" that he was supposed to walk.

"I had to dress and talk like 'them' or I was considered uneducated," he said. "But if I dressed or spoke too well, as in *better than*, then I was threatening and that was no good. With all of this, I still had to live with me in that role, making the character acceptable not just to white America but to me and to Blacks everywhere. It was a box I was in. It could also have been a bag. But it wasn't 'cause I chose to deal with the facts of network life, of Madison Avenue. Had I not dealt with it, I'd have been fired and others who were waiting in line behind me might still be waiting. So, I tried to handle it as quietly and as diplomatically as possible." He also recalled, "I had an idol . . . Jackie Robinson. He made it happen for Blacks in baseball by using his talents, never his rage, to express his Blackness. I felt that if in my ballpark I did my job as well as Robinson did his, I would also therefore be moving us down the road a piece." This would be Cosby's philosophy for the duration of his career.

THE NEW NEGROES ARRIVE:
DAKTARI'S MIKE, *MISSION*'S BARNEY, AND *STAR TREK*'S UHURA

Cosby's role on *I Spy* broke the mold for Black television characters. The educated, middle-class African American had now found a place on the weekly primetime series schedule. The season after *I Spy*'s debut, other series featured dramatic Black characters as regulars. So "many" new Black characters appeared (three, to be exact) that some critics called the 1966–67 television season the Year of the Negro. Though without the far-reaching effect of Cosby's Scotty, the series proved important nonetheless. In an increasingly separatist age, the new characters remained integration-style figures who worked harmoniously with their white compatriots.

Among the new series was *Daktari*, the story of an American veterinarian who runs a center for animals in Africa. Assisting him are his daughter, a fellow American named Jack Dane, and a local native intern named Mike. Today *Daktari*—the Swahili word for doctor—seems like a shrewd update of the 1950s series *Jungle Jim* and *Ramar of the Jungle*: yet another portrait of a mighty white man bringing insight and knowledge to the dark continent.

Nonetheless, actor Hari Rhodes, who played Mike, like Cosby projected an image of a new-style Black man: intelligent, perceptive, and relatively assertive. Rhodes himself had been on the Hollywood scene for over ten years. Having grown up in Cincinnati, he had quit school, joined the Marines at age fifteen, and served in Korea, where he had participated in the historic Inchon landing. He completed his high

Part of the team: Hari Rhodes as the intern in Daktari
with Cheryl Miller, Marshall Thompson, Yale Summers,
and Hedley Mattingly

school education in the military. Afterward he returned to Cincinnati, studied drama, and supported himself by working as a radio sportscaster. Then, in 1956, he moved to Los Angeles with only twelve dollars in his pocket. He won a stage role at the *Ebony Showcase* theater, which was run by former *Amos 'n' Andy* actor Nick Stewart. Rhodes's pay was one dollar a day. To earn that, he also had to sweep up the theater. He lived in the rear of a Model A Ford—along with a friend. His first brush with the Hollywood system occurred shortly after he had read of a training program for young actors offered by a major studio. "I got on the phone and called the man in charge," he said, "and asked if he would interview me, and he told me to come around to the studio. I said, 'By the way, I think I should tell you that I'm a Negro.' He said, 'Don't waste your time. We don't take Negroes in this program.' I hung up the phone. Almost tore the cradle off the thing."

Eventually, he found work in such movies as *Blindfold*, *Drums of Africa*, and *Return to Peyton Place* and on such TV programs as *Dick Powell's Zane Grey Theater*, *Peyton Place*, *I Spy*, *My Three Sons*, *Ben Casey*, and others. He also wrote a novel, *The Chosen Few*.

But *Daktari* proved his most important credit. Watching him, one sees a handsome young man (if ever anyone looked like a leading man, he certainly did) who clearly was playing a part that demanded little of his resources. Mike would have been a stronger and more interesting character (and perhaps more challenging for the actor himself) had the writers developed a greater sense of his cultural binds and, dare we say it, of his political consciousness. There, in the wilds of Africa, where natives can still be restless or appear as a benign form of the dark Other, Rhodes's Mike was very much a part of the team effort at the animal center. Rhodes later appeared as a regular on *The Protectors* episodes of the series *The Bold Ones*.

Also debuting in the fall of 1966 was one of television's most popular (and enduring) series, *Mission: Impossible*, a drama about highly specialized government undercover agents who looked like prototypical Cold War heroes as they foiled the sinister plots of small Communist foreign nations. *Mission: Impossible* opened in the same way each week. The leader of the Impossible Missions Force, first Dan Briggs, later Jim Phelps, listened to a tape-recorded message of his assignment. "Your mission, Briggs, should you decide to accept it, is . . ." The message concluded: "This tape will self-destruct in five seconds." Then Briggs/Phelps would flip through photographs of possible operators to help on the assignment. Among them were cast regulars: agent Rollin Hand (Martin Landau), who was a master of disguises; muscleman Willie Armitage (Peter Lupus), who could be counted on to use his brawn to get the group out of trouble; Cinnamon Carter (Barbara Bain), a coolly beautiful young woman who sometimes used her seductive powers to ensnare corrupt political leaders; and an engineer and ace electronics expert named Barney Collier, played by African American actor Greg Morris.

Morris's Barney Collier was one of the few characters to appear for the entire seven-year run of *Mission: Impossible.* The backstory on Collier was that he was the son of middle-class parents, both of whom had been teachers. Having become the president of Collier Electronics, he was independently wealthy. Otherwise little definition was given to Collier (or to any of the other characters, for that matter). The scripts presented him as something of an acultural, nonracial Black man.

The creators of *Mission: Impossible* had decided from the beginning that race was not to be a factor for the character. Creator Bruce Geller said he chose Morris because of his acting ability and—standing six

Mission: Impossible's agents of international intrigue: Greg Morris (center) with Peter Lupus, Barbara Bain, Peter Graves, and Martin Landau

feet two—his athletic ability. "If Greg Morris turned down the role of Barney," said Geller, "my next choice was a blue-eyed, blond Scandinavian."

Still, race was a factor for viewers. "Some people wrote resenting my relationship to Barbara Bain," said Morris. "It was funny because our relationship was like brother and sister." Black viewers found themselves watching Barney even more closely to see how he related to such African American guest stars as Cicely Tyson, Billy Dee Williams, Brock Peters, Georg Stanford Brown, and Barbara McNair.

Collier was smart, shrewd, resourceful, and not easily flustered. Never questioning the team effort that he was so much a part of, he was something of a pop precursor to Colin Powell. Like Cosby's Scotty, he was cooler than cool in the midst of some very hairy situations. His expertise included "demolition, construction, counterfeiting, metallurgy, special effects, puzzle solving, safecracking, lock picking, computers, robot technology, criminology, and codes." Often performing his technical heroics to the beat of Lalo Schifrin's famous *Mission: Impossible* score, he worked unseen "in tunnels, elevator shafts, walls, rafters, and basements, often secreted in false filing cabinets, packing cases, limousines, trucks—just about anything that could conceal a human being." During the seven-year run, he was also "shot (three times), beaten, blinded, poisoned, brainwashed, left stranded in a live minefield, and caught in a firetrap." Throughout, said Morris, "the one thing Barney never did was show fear."

The first episode created around Barney—titled *Death Squad*—didn't come until the 1969–70 season. Here, while on vacation with Jim Phelps in the Caribbean, Barney saves his girlfriend (Cicely Tyson) from a young man about to attack her. When the young man is accidentally killed, Barney is arrested and ends up in a prison cell, about to be hanged. Well written and well directed, the episode provided Barney with a love interest but didn't supply any new startling insights into the character.

On another episode, *Cat's Paw* (during the 1970–71 season), viewers learned that Barney's older journalist brother, Larry Collier (originally, Barney was supposed to have been an only child), had been murdered just when he learned of a link between a tainted police officer and a local ghetto mob boss (Hari Rhodes). Out to avenge his brother's death, Barney, pretending to be a crooked accountant, is hired by the mobster. He seduces the mobster's secretary (Abbey Lincoln) in the hope of getting information out of her. *Cat's Paw*, written by Howard Browne, gave Morris a chance to flex his acting muscles as well as to be teamed with an attractive African American actress.

For Black viewers, no matter what the scripts did or didn't say about Collier, he would always be *Black*. The smooth nonchalant style that Morris exhibited—as well as his good looks and polite middle-class demeanor—made him a bona fide TV star for the African American audience.

For Greg Morris, the role of Barney, limited as it was, was the break he had been looking for. A native of Cleveland, he had spent part of his childhood in New York City, where his mother was a secretary to the African American labor organizer A. Philip Randolph. Upon graduating from high school, Morris joined the army. Later he enrolled briefly at Ohio State University. There, he was a basketball star. He also took a course in speech that apparently struck a chord. When he transferred to the University of Iowa, he majored in drama.

Afterward he lived in Seattle, where he worked in a lumber camp and appeared in theater productions. Once he moved to Los Angeles, he found television parts. His first important role was as a fireman on an episode of *Ben Casey*. When he returned to the series for another guest appearance, he appeared to move up in the world: he played an ophthalmologist. The change, of course, reflected the altered views of the television industry—and the nation—as to roles in which African Americans could realistically be cast. Other television appearances included *Dr. Kildare, The Dick Van Dyke Show* (the Mr. Peters episode), and *The Twilight Zone.*

Once *Mission: Impossible* went off the air, viewers didn't see much of Morris until he played a supporting role in the Robert Urich series *Vega$* in 1979. *Mission: Impossible* was rerun in syndication for years, then revived as a new series in 1988. Greg Morris's son, Phil Morris, was cast as Barney's son, Grant Collier, also an electronics wizard.

Created by Gene Roddenberry, *Star Trek* was the third important series to appear in 1966. Though initially a ratings disappointment, *Star Trek*'s reruns enjoyed immense popularity in syndication for decades to come. So, too, did the crew of this science fiction drama about the starship USS *Enterprise*—traveling in the twenty-third century to unexplored worlds. The cast included: the dashing Captain Kirk (William Shatner); the wise half-breed Vulcan, Mr. Spock (Leonard Nimoy); the sardonic surgeon Dr. Leonard "Bones" McCoy (DeForest Kelley); the engineer Scotty (James Doohan); the chief navigator Sulu (George Takai); the assistant navigator Chekov (Walter Koenig); McCoy's assistant Nurse Christine Chapel (Majel Barrett); and Uhura, the communications officer, played by African American actress Nichelle Nichols. As their spaceship transported supplies to Earth colonies in space, the crew was always on a voyage to new territory where they were exposed to alien cultures.

Star Trek was conceived as a series of morality tales that addressed—in a universe safely ensconced in the future—then-current issues. Though the series didn't directly deal with America's racial problems, many episodes explored themes about tolerance, difference, and compassion in a universe that could be insensitive and cruel. Difference was not to be feared. Often it was valued. The character Spock was himself a type of "different" miscegenated being; part Vulcan, part Earthling with pointed ears and a green complexion. Yet beneath the alien exterior was a man of vision and understanding.

Like Barney Collier, Uhura was written as another team player without greatly distinguishing racial characteristics. In this futuristic drama, she too might be viewed as a generic character. That, however, was never the way actress Nichelle Nichols conceived Uhura.

Soaring into the future: William Shatner as Captain Kirk, Leonard Nimoy as Mr. Spock, and Nichelle Nichols as Uhura on Star Trek. *Part of the fun was often watching to see if Kirk stole any furtive glances at the voluptuous Uhura. The two had television's first interracial kiss in the episode* Plato's Stepchildren

Originally, Nichols had almost not been cast in the series. A native of Chicago, she had toured as a singer/dancer with the bands of Duke Ellington and Lionel Hampton. But except for work as a dancer in the 1959 film *Porgy and Bess* and some theater roles, her career in Hollywood didn't seem to be going anywhere. Her first television part was in the *To Set It Right* episode of the series *The Lieutenant*, which had been created by Gene Roddenberry. The two became friends and later lovers. For a while, she left the States to perform as a chanteuse in Europe. When she received a call from her agent telling her to return immediately for an audition for a new series, she balked at the idea. Finally, she showed up at MGM studios, where, oddly enough, she was asked to read the part of the male Spock. The role had already been cast, but the producers wanted to see how she'd come across. Impressed, they hired her to play a character which had not yet been created. All that Gene Roddenberry knew was that he wanted a certain kind of woman on the basically male spacecraft.

He and Nichols discussed her role and came up with a surprisingly well-detailed backstory for the character. "Gene and I agreed that she would be a citizen of the United States of Africa," said Nichols. Her name would be Uhura, which was derived from *uhuru*, the Swahili word for freedom. "According to the 'biography' Gene and I developed for my character, Uhura was far more than an intergalactic telephone operator," recalled Nichols. "As head of Communications, she commanded a corps of largely unseen communications technicians, linguists, and other specialists who worked in the bowels of the *Enterprise*, in the 'comm-center.' A linguistics scholar and a top graduate of Starfleet Academy, she was a protégée of Mr. Spock, whom she admired for his logic." Roddenberry even outlined "where Uhura had grown up, who her parents were, and why she had been chosen over other candidates for the *Enterprise*'s five-year mission."

Afterward Nichols went into the series optimistic about playing an unusual kind of African American woman; one better defined (on paper) than any in television history. But Roddenberry's plans for the character met with resistance by the network brass, who at first assumed that Uhura would simply provide a little "color" on the bridge, a type of set decoration. "The network men had a fit when they saw that not only was there now an important woman in the command crew and on the bridge, but a Black one!" said Nichols. "When they realized that Uhura's involvement would be substantial and her lines went well beyond 'Yes, Captain!' they furiously issued Gene an ultimatum. Get rid of her! Gene flatly refused."

On the premiere episode, Uhura briefly spoke Swahili with another Black character. But otherwise the original conception of Uhura was nowhere in sight. Usually, Nichols found herself reacting to events and, indeed, being a form of very elegant, sexy set decoration. Part of the fun for viewers, though, was looking for those moments when handsome, straitlaced Captain Kirk cast a furtive glance at the voluptuous Uhura. Here the casting provided an intriguing subtext. Two attractive people out there in space, away from the restrictions and taboos of contemporary American society. Why shouldn't they have a little fun!

One of *Star Trek*'s most important episodes played on the possible attraction between the two. Titled *Plato's Stepchildren*, the episode centered on the starship's visit to an unknown planet. Residing there is a eugenically near-perfect race that calls itself Platonians. This race of people had settled on Earth during the time of Plato but left after the decline of ancient Greece. Exploring the planet, Captain Kirk, Mr. Spock, and Bones learn that the Platonians discovered plants that have endowed them with hyperkinetic powers. But this seemingly superior race has one flaw. They have no immune system.

The Platonians also have become corrupt and starved for diversions. When the Platonian King Parmen demands that Bones remain on the planet to tend to its people's medical needs, Bones refuses. Thereafter, the king devises a series of cruel and humiliating ways to torture Kirk and Spock. Parmen pairs Spock with Nurse Chapel and Kirk with Uhura in a Greek arena. There Kirk cracks a whip near Uhura while the Platonians, apparently devotees of S/M entertainment, eagerly watch. But most important, Kirk is made to kiss Uhura.

"Given the fact that we were in the twenty-third century," said Nichols, "and that it was quite clear from the story that Kirk and Uhura are kissing against their will, I didn't see a problem." No one else in the cast seemed to mind either. Originally, Spock was to have planted the kiss. But actor William Shatner insisted, "If anybody's going to get to kiss Uhura, it's going to be me—I mean Captain Kirk."

During the filming, the director, however, became apprehensive and rushed to the front office to discuss it. Said Nichols, "The network suits, who probably would not have noticed it otherwise, began to get cold feet, since the director was concerned. Yes, they thought, what would the viewers say? What about the Southern affiliates?"

Finally, a compromise was worked out. Two versions of the scene would be shot: one with a kiss, one without. Then Roddenberry arranged to have the scene shot near the end of the day. William Shatner goofed around so much that numerous retakes were required of the kiss sequence. Several takes actually were fine. Finally, just when the studio day was about to end, Shatner and Nichols did the kissless shot. As it turned out, that shot was terrible. The executives then went with the kiss. And so television audiences got to see the first interracial kiss in a primetime series.

"*Plato's Stepchildren* first aired in November 1968 and provoked a huge response," recalled Nichols. "We received one of the largest batches of fan mail ever, all of it very positive, with many addressed to me from girls wondering how it felt to kiss Captain Kirk, and many to him from guys wondering the same thing about me. Interestingly, almost no one found the kiss offensive."

Roddenberry did show Nichols one letter that read: "I'm a white Southern gentleman, and I like *Star Trek*. I am totally opposed to the mixing of the races. However, any time a red-blooded American boy like Captain Kirk gets a beautiful dame in his arms that looks like Uhura, he ain't gonna fight it." Still, while a white male star might kiss a Black woman in a fantasy sequence, the mere idea of an African American male even touching a white woman could send a deadly panic into the hearts of network executives. In 1968 the brass at NBC went into conniptions at the sight of blond British pop star Petula Clark—on her special *Petula*—actually holding the arm of Harry Belafonte while performing a duet with him. This instance of interracial contact was considered controversial for mainstream viewers.

Ultimately, *Star Trek* was the victim of poor Nielsen ratings. Demographics revealed that most viewers were teenagers and young children, who were mesmerized by this futuristic drama that stressed universal brotherhood. It was the perfect tale for a restless and questioning generation; a drama that appealed to those in the growing Youth Movement, the Antiwar Movement, and the Black Movement as well. Thus in spite of her near invisibility, Uhura had made more of an impression than those network executives had figured on. When a despairing

Nichols was planning to leave the series, Martin Luther King Jr.—a fan of the show—told her, "You cannot, and you must not. Don't you realize how important your presence, your character is?" He liked the series message of "men and women of all races going forth in peaceful exploration, living as equals."

Though Uhura rarely had much to do, the important factor once again was that the audience was seeing here, as with *Mission: Impossible*, an intelligent Black character incorporated into the action, a part of the very fiber of the series itself. Young African American viewers (some older ones too) were intrigued by the idea of who Uhura might *really* be. So eager, too, was that audience for the presence of an African American woman on the weekly primetime schedule that Uhura's role was considered a breakthrough. Nichols as Uhura ended up on the cover of *Ebony* with an article titled "A New Star in the TV Heavens."

At that time, however, advertisers were not interested in such young viewers—or African American ones. *Star Trek* went off the air in 1969 following its third season. But in syndicated reruns, it became television's first cult series, eventually spawning successful *Star Trek* feature films and also the spin-off series *Star Trek: The Next Generation* and *Star Trek: Deep Space Nine*.

Other African American performers appeared regularly on dramatic primetime series in supporting roles. In the short-lived 1966 police drama *Hawk*, Burt Reynolds starred as an Iroquois Indian named John Hawk, who works out of New York's district attorney's office. His partner was a likable, sensitive African American detective played by Wayne Grice. A year later, the drama *Ironside* starred Raymond Burr as a police detective paralyzed after being shot by a would-be assassin. Featured was newcomer Don Mitchell as Mark Sanger, a former delinquent, who became an aide and bodyguard for Detective Ironside. Viewers probably remember the character best as the man behind Ironside's wheelchair. Though Mitchell's Sanger later went to law school and got married, for many, this new-style bright Black character seemed like another updated servant figure minus the dialect and the comic antics. Still, the African American audience enjoyed seeing Mitchell on the show. This type of loyal, sometimes ego-boosting sidekick for the white hero would appear for years to come and would be popular with older Black viewers in such series as *Matlock* and *Walker*.

In 1967, a grittier and more complicated new-style character appeared on the police series *N.Y.P.D.* Negro Ensemble Company co-founder Robert Hooks was cast as a New York City police detective, along with white actors Jack Warden and Frank Converse. Shot in New York City with the cooperation of its police department and endorsed by the city's mayor, John Lindsay, some episodes were based on actual cases. Hooks had more to do than most African American actors on the other new series. But if anything, his character in *N.Y.P.D.*, like Wayne Grice's in *Hawk*, indicated a shift in "appropriate" roles for Black actors: now the cop—the man not out to tear the system down but to enforce its laws and to maintain its order—had become a wholly acceptable role for the Black actor.

Then there was the 1967 series *The High Chaparral*. Something of a clone of the hit Western *Bonanza*, it featured two powerful families— the Cannons and the Montoyas—both landowners in the 1870s. Most television viewers were probably unaware that the actor playing Don Sebastian Montoya was African American performer Frank Silvera. But the light-skinned Silvera had long known he might not have much of a career if he waited for Black roles. No doubt he was well aware of the way Hollywood's color caste system had stunted the promising career of a light-skinned African American beauty like Fredi Washington. In the early 1950s when he had read for the part of a Black elevator man in the play *Blind Spot*, the producer had said, "He's great but he's too light." Said Silvera: "Ask him if I'm light enough for the lead." He ended up playing the elevator man. But he also played other ethnics in such films as *Viva Zapata!* (as Mexican general Huerta), *Hombre*, and *Che!*

The Jamaican-born Silvera, a Boston University graduate who attended Northwestern's law school, also appeared as the father of Ben Gazzara in Broadway's *A Hatful of Rain*. As he had done in the 1950s, Silvera played diverse non-Black characters in such television dramas as *Bonanza*, *The Defenders*, *Rawhide*, and *Gunsmoke*. Yet he had a strong commitment to improving the lot of African American performers. Among his many credits was that of director of the Los Angeles and New York productions of James Baldwin's play *The Amen*

Corner. As co-founder of the Theatre of Being, he announced that he hoped to train performers toward the establishment of "a new criteria concerning the Negro image" and "to advance the cause of African American talent." As Montoya on *The High Chaparral*, Silvera was a supremely confident presence, savoring every gesture and flourish of his wealthy aristocratic character. Of course, many African American viewers knew precisely what he was up to. His appearances on *The High Chaparral* were cut short by his tragic death in 1970 when he was accidentally electrocuted at his home in Los Angeles.

During its 1968–69 season, the nighttime soap *Peyton Place* also added a Black family to its roster of troubled small-town residents. Percy Rodriguez played the physician Harry Miles. Ruby Dee was cast as his wife, Alma. And Glynn Turman played their teenage son Lew. Unfortunately, the Miles family was marginalized without enough story lines developed around them. It turned out that they appeared during the final season of the series. Eartha Kitt also appeared as Catwoman—cunning and forcefully campy—in episodes of the pop extravaganza *Batman*.

Of the post-1966 series's supporting characters, few drew more attention than Peggy Fair, who joined the cop show *Mannix* during its second season in 1968. Series lead character Joe Mannix (Mike Connors) was a Los Angeles private detective. His secretary, pert Peggy, was played by African American actress Gail Fisher. Her husband, who had been a cop with Mannix, had been killed. At first glance, poor Peggy, who didn't have much of a life of her own, may have looked as if she had little more to do than answer the telephone, reassure Mannix of his powers, and help keep his life in order; something of another updated servant with a series of set expressions and attitudes. There was the Concerned Peggy. The Slightly Agitated Peggy. The Sweetly Comforting Peggy. The Always Efficient Peggy. Surprisingly, these worked well for this action series. Upon closer view, Peggy was also important to various plot lines. Some may have wondered why the good-looking Mannix never took a romantic interest in the good-looking widow Peggy. Part of the kick was waiting—in vain—for Mannix to make a move on Peggy. (It wasn't too different from the response to the Captain Kirk/Uhura pairing.) On one episode, after Mannix has recovered from a bout of amnesia, he sits in his hospital bed talking to the understanding Peggy. But warmhearted Peggy and manly Mannix always mind their manners. Any thoughts that the two might have a warmer, more intimate conversation were quickly dispelled when Mannix is visited by another woman. Peggy discreetly leaves. It's Joe Mannix's loss.

Such romantic undercurrents were also at the heart of the episode *The World Between*, which focused exclusively on Peggy. When she defends Mannix and herself against a gunman in their office, Peggy is shot and then hospitalized. A glimpse into her "other" life occurs when she's visited by her son Toby and a neighbor. Peggy, however, becomes concerned about a mysterious Black man in the room across from hers. Fearing that he might be planning to kill her, she phones Joe Mannix at the office. She's surprised when a sexy young woman (viewers see that she's a voluptuous redhead) answers the phone and informs her that she's Mannix's secretary. Peggy promptly tells her that *she* is his secretary, then hangs up. For a few seconds, viewers saw two women (one Black, the other white) fighting over the same man. When Mannix visits Peggy at the hospital, they exchange words about the young woman as well as about the man across the hall. Mannix dismisses her fears of the man. An annoyed, huffy Peggy tells him, "You'd be perfectly relieved if he would come in here and snuff me out. You've obviously got a new secretary that you're perfectly delighted with!" Though Joe assures Peggy that once she's well the young woman will be discharged, Peggy doesn't want to hear it. "Good night, Mr. Mannix!" she tells him. Here viewers were clearly seeing a Jealous Peggy.

When she meets the man across the hall (played by Hari Rhodes), Peggy's intrigued by him, especially once she detects his accent.

"But you're African," she says.

"Like you, sister," he replies.

"Right on, brother."

It's a dopey, hokey moment that today seems funny because the language and expressions are so much those of the late 1960s/early 1970s. But the exchange contextualizes Peggy in a purely pop manner with the new sense of pride and unity then sweeping through Black America. Thereafter it's revealed that the man is the premier of a newly independent African nation. He has come to the United States for medical treatment. Yet political opponents plan to assassinate him. He and Peggy fall in love. "You are very charming and very lovely," he tells her, and Peggy is ready to chuck everything to go to Africa with him. She even has him meet her two aunts (Maidie Norman and television veteran Lillian Randolph). But Mannix is as jealous of the African premier as Peggy was of his temporary secretary. "You cannot afford to fall in love with him," an agitated Joe tells Peggy. Of course, the series could not afford to let Peggy run off with the premier. Assassination attempts fail. But the premier's illness has advanced to the point where there is no hope. "The operation was a complete success," Peggy says. "But the patient will die. That's it, isn't it?" "My body fails me," he tells her. "But my heart—my heart is with you. Please understand. I must put what's left of my life into my country." The episode ends with a saddened Peggy back at her desk in Mannix's office.

The World Between episode was the type that could invigorate a series by touching on taboo subjects that viewers had, at least unconsciously, always thought about. There really was a deeper attraction between Peggy and Mannix. Peggy herself was a sensual woman, not as tightly bound to her job as most episodes led us to believe. She had a private life, and she was not isolated from then current political/social ideas and sentiments. This aspect of Peggy, though, was rarely seen.

Fisher herself usually seemed a tad smug, almost too much of a proper middle-class lady, who knows she looks good. Yet slight as the character might seem to later generations, Fisher's Peggy appealed to viewers of her age, especially African Americans. Gail Fisher ended up winning an Emmy for her performance as Outstanding Supporting Actress in Drama for the 1969–70 season.

As the 1960s were nearing an end, other African American actors and actresses were able to find dramatic work on the primetime schedule; a direct result of the still changing political atmosphere in America. By the late 1960s, the nation had gone from a civil rights era of passive resistance to a more assertive form of protest with the rise of the Black Power Movement. Black America had become even more vocal about its demands for equal rights. During the years of the Johnson administration, with its talk of the Great Society and its War on Poverty, riots erupted in ghettos around the country: in Newark, Detroit, Harlem, and Watts.

In 1968, the National Advisory Commission on Civil Disorders, headed by Otto Kerner (the former governor of Illinois), whose conclusions were generally referred to as the Kerner Report, examined the causes of violence in America. It studied twenty-three cities in which disorders had sprung up. "What white Americans have never fully understood is that white society is deeply implicated in the ghetto," reported the commission. It added that there existed two Americas: one Black, the other white. One of its conclusions was that the media contributed to the tensions and disruptions within Black America, and had a responsibility to make the Negro more visible and a part of American life. There was a need for more programming not only about Black Americans but also by and for Black Americans. Afterward government officials met with network executives to discuss the role of the media in covering racial problems. An outgrowth of these discussions was the rise of public affairs shows. In New York, programs like *Inside Bedford-Stuyvesant* and later *Black News* with Marian Etoile Watson and Bill McCreary appeared. Nationally, a show like *Soul*, hosted and executive-produced by Ellis Haizlip, focused on the Black arts. A program like National Educational Television's *Black Journal*, under the guidance of its second executive producer, William Greaves, covered a range of social, political, and artistic issues pertaining to America's Black community. It won an Emmy for excellence in public affairs television. *Black Journal* also provided a training ground for such young African American directors/producers as St. Clair Bourne, Tony Brown, Madeline Anderson, and notably Stan Lathan, who later directed a host of network programs, including episodes of *Sanford and Son, Hill Street Blues, Barney Miller, Cagney and Lacey*, and *Remington Steele* as well as the series *The Steve Harvey Show*.

JULIA: AN ODE TO INTEGRATION IN A SEPARATIST AGE

Television already had begun to respond to the new political/social climate by offering its 1966 Year of the Negro. But that clearly was not enough. Though the primetime network series had carried the new Negro into American homes, no weekly series was yet centered on Black American life—with an African American performer as the series star rather than co-star or supporting player. In some respects, it looked as if the primetime series went out of its way *not* to focus on an African

American household. *I Spy* mostly kept the new Negro in foreign lands. So did *Mission: Impossible*. *Daktari* took the new Negro back to the dark continent. And *Star Trek* projected the new Negro into outer space. Finally, NBC announced plans to air a new series centered on a Black nurse living with her young son in Los Angeles. The series was *Julia*, starring Diahann Carroll. "We're going to show it like it is," producer/creator Hal Kanter proudly told the press once the series went into production.

Julia would tell the story of Julia Baker, whose husband—an air force captain—had been killed in Vietnam. Beginning a new life for herself and her six-year-old son Corey (Marc Copage) in Los Angeles, Julia lands a job at Astrospace Industries and settles into a comfortable existence in an integrated apartment building. Her son becomes best friends with a little white boy named Earl J. Waggedorn (Michael Link), who lives in their building. Julia herself becomes friendly with Earl's mother, Marie (Betty Beaird). Though life for Julia would have its ups and downs, basically it would be good and not greatly troubling.

Diahann Carroll, the star of Julia, *with Lloyd Nolan as Dr. Chegley*

Once word leaked out about the sitcom's story line, even before the show aired, criticism arose about its basic premise and its characters. Those who had anticipated an edgy series that would tap the still-growing unrest in America's urban centers realized that *Julia* would not be *that*. In *The Saturday Review*'s April 20, 1968, issue, columnist Robert Lewis Shayon wrote that the sitcom's middle-class situation "is a far, far cry from the bitter realities of Negro life in the urban ghetto, the pit of America's explosion potential." He denounced *Julia* for its sugarcoated portrait of Black lives completely untouched by contemporary politics or current history.

"I would think that [Mr. Shayon] might give us the courtesy of seeing our show before he criticized it," responded Diahann Carroll. "We're dealing with an entertainment medium. *Julia* is a drama-comedy; it isn't politically oriented. Because I am black that doesn't mean I have to deal with problems of all black people. That's not my sole responsibility . . . all TV is divorced from reality. *The Beverly Hillbillies* don't go back and show you the life they came from in the Ozarks; their business is to make people laugh. . . . It isn't our business to 'tell it as it is.' Look at *East Side, West Side* . . . it only lasted a short time. . . . Maybe people just don't want to see things like that after they've had a pretty grim day themselves."

The discussion didn't end there. In a later issue of *The Saturday Review*, Shayon responded to Carroll's comments. "*Julia* is politically oriented, contrary to Miss Carroll's conviction—but in the wrong way," wrote Shayon. "It distorts reality and deals in double-truth. The business of TV comedy is not primarily to make people laugh: it is to manage consumption; and if in so doing it dulls critical sensibilities in people who have 'had a pretty grim day,' it contributes its share to the rigidity of a way of life in which black Americans suffer more severely than others."

Others were also critical. Actor Harry Belafonte "launched a full-scale assault on *Julia*, then asked me not to do it," recalled Carroll. Thus before *Julia* even aired, it had entered the arena of a national debate.

Julia premiered on September 17, 1968, at 8:30 p.m. on NBC. The first episode established the characters and situation. Julia and Corey have just arrived in Los Angeles. Their new apartment looks well furnished, well decorated, and spacious, hardly the kind of ghetto flat some might have expected. But once Julia hits the pavement in search of a job, she experiences a covert form of racism during an interview at Astrospace Industries. The personnel interviewer named Colton is obviously shocked to see a young Black woman standing across from his desk, applying for a position as a nurse.

"May I sit down?" Julia asks. "I take it this interview means my application met with your approval?"

"Yes," he replies.

"My background. Education. References. They're all acceptable," says Julia.

"Training. Experience. Naturally, yes. Before we conduct personal interviews, they have to be," Colton tells her. But he adds, "Frankly, you're not exactly what I expected."

"No?"

"No. Not from what I read here."

"Did you expect me to be older or younger?"

When Colton leaves his office for a few minutes, Julia is briefly alone with an older Black man, who is a janitor at the company. He asks what she does. "I'm a registered nurse," she says.

"You're not going to register with Mr. Colton," he tells her frankly.

The interview gets Julia nowhere. But later, when she speaks over the telephone to a Dr. Chegley at Astrospace, she has better results. He tells her to come to his office. "Be here at nine," he says. "And make yourself as handsome as you can manage. I'm tired of looking at ugly nurses. I married one."

"I'll do my best, sir," says Julia, overlooking a remark that a later generation might well consider a form of sexual harassment. "But has Mr. Colton told you?"

"Told me what?"

"I'm colored," Julia says.

"What color are you?" Dr. Chegley asks.

"I'm a Negro."

"Have you always been a Negro?" he wants to know. "Or are you just trying to be fashionable?"

That premiere episode was the prototype for the way the series usually handled the race theme. It acknowledged that *prejudice* existed. But ultimately Colton's race prejudice was of no significant consequence in Julia's life once the crusty but fair-minded Dr. Chegley appears. Because Chegley was a cast regular whom mainstream viewers had to identify with in some way (or at least not be alienated by), any apprehension that viewers had that Chegley might be a bigoted man—and that Julia might really be encountering a biased world at Astrospace Industries—was brushed aside with their initial telephone conversation.

In another sequence on the premiere episode, Corey plays with white neighbor Earl J. Waggedorn. As the two boys talk, Waggedorn looks at Julia and then asks Corey if that's his mother. Corey says yes.

"You know what?" Waggedorn says innocently. "Your mother's colored."

"Of course. I'm colored too," says Corey.

"You are?" Waggedorn asks in amazement.

"Yeah."

"Oh, boy!" says Waggedorn.

The two laugh and resume their play.

Today even the way the series premise had been established—with its use of the word *colored*—seems soft and dated. Diahann Carroll herself believed that in 1968 *colored* "seemed a bit stretchy and out of step, but I understood that the joke was trying to make a very mild racial statement."

Nonetheless, thanks to Chegley, Julia gets the job. Thereafter episodes dealt with Julia and Corey. Julia and employer Chegley. Julia and co-worker Nurse Hannah Yarby (Lurene Tuttle). Julia and her neighbors. Corey and Earl Waggedorn. Some episodes also dealt with race. But race/racism was never a major problem for the Baker family.

Julia met with mixed reviews. "The star, Diahann Carroll, is charming and beautiful," *Cue*'s reviewer wrote. "The little boy, Marc Copage, who plays her son, is adorable. The fact remains that, if they were white, *Julia* would never have gotten to the pilot stage." "Watts it ain't, Orange County maybe?" wrote *Variety*. "In matters as sensitive as race relations, even sitcom characters will have to have a little substance."

Some reviewers, however, felt that demands were being made of *Julia* that were not required of typical primetime fare. "For years we've been looking at escapism television," wrote the reviewer for the New York *Daily News*, "so why, when a Negro actress is starred in the same kind of a series does she suddenly have to carry the weight of the whole racial question on her delicate shoulders? *Julia* pretends to be nothing more than a pleasant, charming half-hour situation comedy, and it should be judged as such. We've read so many ridiculous articles on it, the next thing we know Diahann will be asked not only to solve the racial question but also the Vietnam war. It's enough that an attractive talented actress has been cast in the part and is doing a good job."

"Meant to be both amusing and touching, the story projects a somewhat fictionalized everyday living pattern of middle class Negroes in an integrated, middle class environment," commented *Ebony*, which, like most of the Black press, supported *Julia*. "To the ghetto Negro who, despite his poverty, has vast television reception, this may not be telling it like it is. But for television it is showing it like it has never been shown before."

Airing opposite *The Red Skelton Show* and *It Takes a Thief, Julia* won its time slot and did well in the ratings. For a time, it found favor with older Black audiences too, as eager as ever for a program that acknowledged in some manner or another that African Americans had friends of their own, homes of their own, lives of their own. Of early episodes, Diahann Carroll remembered thinking, "Well, I suppose this is a kind of progress. First television pretended there wasn't any prejudice. Then it pretended there weren't any racial differences. Now it has reached the point where it can not only acknowledge there *are* differences, but a white man can write jokes for a Black woman to say about them."

But the criticism continued. There were complaints about Julia's lifestyle and the fact that the show had no strong Black male in the household. "By now there was an entire chorus of critics complaining about *Julia's* harmful inadequacies," said Carroll. "I thought the criticism was wildly overstated, but it troubled me deeply, especially the accusation that the series failed to offer a proper role model to Black children."

When Carroll met with producer Hal Kanter to discuss this latter charge, he stressed that the lack of a father had nothing to do with race. Instead it was part of a trend in television. Sitcoms revolving around single-parent households had proven popular. That very season Hope Lange, Doris Day, and Lucille Ball starred in new shows about widowed mothers. Kanter failed to see, however, that there were alternative TV images of white households where white fathers did exist. No such alternative Black household existed on television.

"There was no question in my mind that *Julia* had the responsibility to set a positive example in the way it presented the Black family," said Carroll. "And it didn't take long to realize that it was largely up to me to try to make that happen. For all Hal's good intentions, it became increasingly difficult for him to write meaningfully about Black people. How could he? He had never really been exposed to Blacks. It was inevitable that as the season progressed the writing would become more and more problematic."

Such African American writers as Robert Goodwin, Harry Dolan, Gene Boland, and Ferdinand Leon were brought on the series. And Carroll pored over the scripts of other writers, searching "for blatant examples of racism or just plain ignorance." Though Kanter listened to her comments, "sometimes we ran into serious problems."

On one episode Carroll took issue with a seemingly innocuous line of dialogue. The script called for Corey, while playing with a friend, to say, "I'm John Wayne and you're an Indian, and bang-bang, I just shot you dead."

Carroll objected. "Hal, Corey cannot say that!" she told the producer.

"Why not?" asked Kanter.

"Because John Wayne is not the idol of Black children. Because Black parents don't think of him as a role model."

"Diahann, John Wayne is the most famous cowboy in the history of motion pictures."

"That may be true. That may be absolutely true. But I have to take the responsibility for those words."

"Well, look, we can't use Roy Rogers's name," said Kanter. "Roy Rogers retired years ago."

Of course, Carroll hoped to give *Julia* something it was in desperate need of: an African American cultural context for the Black characters—with references, language, attitudes, and values distinct unto Black Americans. Within much of the African American community at the time, John Wayne was considered a right-wing hawk who represented the values of the conservative political establishment that young Blacks (and whites) were protesting against.

On the occasions when it attempted to address the theme of bigotry, the results were sometimes dismal. On one episode, Corey returns home from school upset because a classmate has called him a *nigger*. This prompts Julia to have a discussion about race with her neighbor, who asks, "When did bigotry come into your life, Julia?" Julia explains that when she attended her high school prom, her mother had made her a beautiful yellow organdy dress to wear. But once at the school gym, Julia stood alone because no one asked her for a dance. That was her first exposure to racism. Diahann Carroll said she fought with producer Kanter about the episode, saying it was completely unrealistic that Julia hadn't experienced bigotry before then.

Other episodes handled the race theme or the theme of discrimination more effectively. One of the better episodes finds Julia dealing with discrimination on her job. When denied a security clearance at Astrospace Industries, Julia finally confronts a supervisor. "I've discovered, Mrs. Baker," he tells her, "you belong to an organization so suspect we haven't even been able to uncover its activities." "I belong to several organizations. Which one are you specifically suspicious of? The YWCA?" she asks him. When he explains that he knows she belongs to a group called ANTI, an angered Julia tells him, "The American Negro Training Institute. A nonprofit group of volunteers who teach our professions to underprivileged children, of all races. It's anti-ignorance! And it's no more subversive than the PTA." Thereafter Julia quits. By the episode's end, Dr. Chegley straightens things out, and we know Julia will return to work. Perhaps most interesting is Diahann Carroll, the actress, during her confrontation scene. Watching her (with the awareness of her problems on the set), you feel that Diahann Carroll enjoys these moments when she can let loose. Without losing her ladylike cool, she still can get effectively hot under the collar. In fact, she's at her best when she can let off some steam.

On another episode, Julia is confronted with the "prejudice" of a neighbor in her apartment building. The Bennetts are an older couple whose young granddaughter Pamela is visiting them. Mr. Bennett suggests that Corey and Earl play with Pamela. But Mrs. Bennett doesn't seem eager for the children to spend time together. The little girl, however, wants to play house. "Okay," says Corey, "she can be the mother, and I'll be the daddy." But a nervous Mrs. Bennett objects, "No, Earl will be the daddy."

Later Mrs. Bennett sees that a child has used crayons to draw all over a wall in the building's hallway. "It's absolutely shameful. This place is turning into a ghetto," she tells her husband. "It had to happen sooner or later. And this is just the beginning." "Beginning of what?" he asks. "Turning this house into a tenement. It always happens when those people move in." "What people?" asks Mr. Bennett. Both he and his wife are unaware that Julia is in the hallway and has overheard their conversation. "I believe, Mr. Bennett, the reference is to me and my son," says Julia. Without directly stating it, Mrs. Bennett is convinced that Corey has defaced the wall. An angry Julia, however, also knows there is nothing she can do to change the woman's mind.

Later in her apartment, Julia expresses her anger to Corey. "Poor Mrs. Bennett is a sad lady. She thinks that you and I are different," she says. "What I mean is, we are dark-skinned. And people like Mrs. Bennett think that Afro-Americans like you and me and Uncle Lou and Aunt Emma—that we are different." Corey tells his mother that he overheard Mrs. Bennett telling her granddaughter that people like the Bakers "move into nice, clean places and make them dirty." "Our house isn't dirty," he says. "Of course not," says Julia. "But Mrs. Bennett doesn't know that. She's never been to our house. And it's up to you and me and all of us to help teach her and other prejudiced people how wrong they are."

"What's prejudice?" Corey wants to know.

"Let's say prejudice is when some people think they are better than other people."

Corey doesn't understand. But when he says he doesn't like Pamela, he stops himself. "I guess I'm prejudiced too." "You shouldn't be. Prejudice is what causes all the problems of the world."

Later Mrs. Bennett tells the building's landlord, Mr. Cooper, that she's concerned that he may let other colored people move into the building. He responds that she thinks she's superior because she's white. But he doesn't have such feelings because he knows "if I'm superior, what's Edward Brooke doing in the United States Senate instead of me. If I'm superior, why didn't I get the Nobel Prize instead of Martin Luther King. And if I'm superior, how come the Giants got Willie Mays playing center field instead of Carl Cooper."

The episode ends on a note of reconciliation. Mr. Bennett rushes to Julia's apartment, asking for her help. He knows she's a nurse, he says. His granddaughter is choking. Julia goes to the Bennetts' apartment, where she discovers that a crayon was caught in the girl's throat. It's then revealed that Pamela had drawn on the hallway wall. "Mrs. Baker," says Mrs. Bennett, "I've been a very stupid woman. You've opened my eyes. I hope you can open your heart enough to forgive me." We know Julia will.

Of course, you would prefer that Julia, rather than the landlord, had the big confrontation scene with Mrs. Bennett. (Actress Carroll may have preferred that confrontation too.) The idea that Julia, by example, must also *teach* prejudiced people must have seemed dated even in the late 1960s. The episode also lessens some of its sting with the idea that Corey (and other Negroes) are prejudiced too. When Corey says he doesn't like Pamela, he's referring to the little girl's behavior. He's not basing his judgment on her race or gender. He is, after all, best friends with the white Earl. But the script doesn't permit Julia to make such distinctions.

Providing Julia with some soul: guest stars boxer Sugar Ray Robinson and Diana Sands with Diahann Carroll

At times, *Julia* was successful at creating a semblance of an African American community for its heroine. Diana Sands appeared as Julia's cousin in thirteen episodes. During one season, Black actress Carol Deering was a cast regular, playing Allison Mills. Actress Virginia Capers also appeared as Julia's mother in some episodes. Small African sculptures could occasionally be glimpsed in her apartment. Julia also had boyfriends, played by actors Paul Winfield, Fred Williamson, and Don Marshall. Some of Diahann Carroll's scenes with former football star Williamson still sparkle and resonate. Here are two gilded narcissists, each confident of her/his appeal, each recognizing the other's sexy powers, but neither willing to concede defeat in the gender games that men and women play. (Carroll was far more relaxed with Williamson than she would be years later when cast opposite that other assured narcissist Billy Dee Williams in *Dynasty*.) It's sheer fun to watch this sophisticated, mature African American couple. Had the series cast them as man and wife, they might have provided the elegant domestic battle of wits that movie audiences had seen decades before with Nick and Nora Charles in the *Thin Man* series. But television wasn't ready for that kind of weekly Black couple.

Still, despite the race-theme episodes, the problem was that *Julia* worked very hard to show that its central character had transcended racism and cultural differences. America, too, the series said, had transcended such matters. Julia spoke the right way, dressed the right way, behaved the right way, thought the right way, and even looked the right way. By casting Diahann Carroll, a light-brown-skinned Black woman with keen features, the show's producers had come up with an acceptable heroine. Mainstream audiences might not perceive her so much as the Dark Other. Thus having met the standards—beauty and otherwise—of the dominant culture, Julia was depicted as living in a free and open society.

Had the series appeared at the start of the integrationist movement in the late 1950s, it would have been forward-looking and daring. But, ironically, *Julia*'s integrationist-style heroine arrived during an era when a segment of Black America—young Black America in particular—was loudly calling for cultural/racial separatism; during a time when African American students were taking over administration buildings on campuses throughout the nation, when they were wearing dashikis and cultivating Afros, when the slogan "Say it loud/I'm Black/I'm proud" was heard daily. But untouched by all of this, Julia Baker lived in a fantasy version of Los Angeles where the uprisings and disorders in ghettos around the country, including Watts, didn't appear to exist at all. One critic wrote that Julia "would not recognize a ghetto if she stumbled into it."

However, *Julia*—a sitcom—would never have found an audience if *every* episode had focused on America's race problem. Perhaps the very nature of the sitcom (plenty of laughs, a resolution at the end of the half hour) isn't conducive to weekly doses of a *specific* social ill. The audience would have wearied of the same old Black problem week after week. Then, too, an episode about race every week would have trivialized the race problem. Yet young viewers of the day could never forgive the show for not being hard-hitting about race. Ultimately, *Julia* became a victim of its historical era.

Carroll, however, still believed *Julia* had value and significance. "What captured my attention was Julia herself," said Carroll. "Behind the stylized cuteness of the dialogue, Julia's conversations with her son reflected many of the same middle-class attitudes toward everything I experienced in my own childhood. I could relate to that very easily, just as I could relate to Julia's desire to make a place for herself in the world. She wanted a good job. She wanted a nice apartment. She wanted to give her child a decent education."

Of course, Carroll had a point. It was important that television comment in some way on African American middle-class life. At the same time, *Julia*'s controversy pointed up another fact: that a Black audience, still starved for some representation of itself on television, might expect one series to answer all its needs. But no series could be all things to all African American viewers. Neither *Julia* nor later *The Cosby Show* could ever satisfy everyone. Both had a burden placed on them that general white series didn't. *The Cosby Show*, however, could carry the burden. *Julia* could not.

By the third season, Diahann Carroll felt she was sleepwalking her way through the show. The daily grind exhausted her. The unending criticism and the battles with Hal Kanter "had also worn me to a frazzle," she said. "It seemed to me that the show's format had become very dated." When the time came to renew her contract for the fourth season, Carroll asked for a release. *Julia*'s last broadcast was on May 25, 1971.

AN ASSIMILATED GODDESS IN A SEPARATIST AGE

Julia established Diahann Carroll as a television star. The medium, however, had already proved important to her career. Born Carol Diann Johnson in the Bronx in 1935, the daughter of a New York City subway conductor and a nurse, she had grown up in Harlem. At the age of six, she began singing. At ten, she won a Metropolitan Opera scholarship. At fifteen, she won a beauty contest at her father's Masonic Temple in Harlem. Two years later, she changed her name to Diahann Carroll when she performed on *Arthur Godfrey's Talent Scouts* and won first prize. By the time she appeared on the television talent show *Chance of a Lifetime* and won $3,000 and a booking at New York's Latin Quarter, show business was in her blood, and she knew what she wanted to do with her life. She struggled, however, to please her middle-class parents, who wanted to see her live a more traditional middle-class life. Upon graduation from New York's High School of Music and Art, Diahann Carroll entered New York University with plans to study sociology. But she dropped out of college to put all her energy into her career.

Fiercely ambitious, she modeled, sang, and acted. She won supporting roles in the films *Carmen Jones* and *Porgy and Bess*. She also appeared in the Broadway show *House of Flowers*. Then came a steady career climb that led to appearances at top nightclubs like the Persian Room in New York, the Sands in Las Vegas, and the Caribe Hilton in San Juan, Puerto Rico. But the breakthrough was the starring role—as a fashion model involved in an interracial love affair—in the Broadway musical *No Strings*, which won her a Tony Award. Throughout, she worked on TV, not only on variety programs (*The Danny Kaye Show, The Judy Garland Show*, and, as a regular, on *The Jack Paar Show*) but also in dramatic roles on *Peter Gunn, The Eleventh Hour*, and in the *Horse Has a Big Head* episode of *Naked City*, which won her an Emmy nomination.

She also appeared in the Black-cast TV specials *The Strolling Twenties* and *A Time for Laughter: A Look at Negro Humor in America*. The latter showcased the rich comedic styles of different generations of Black comics—from the old-style ethnic stars like Jackie "Moms" Mabley, Dewey "Pigmeat" Markham, and Redd Foxx to such newcomers as Godfrey Cambridge, Dick Gregory, and Richard Pryor. By the time Carroll starred in *Julia*, she had also logged up to sixty appearances on primetime variety shows.

Of those years, as she crossed over, appearing more and more for integrated, then mostly white audiences, Diahann Carroll admitted, "I was always torn, and the confusions have always remained. The conflict first took the form of music. The music we all listened and danced to, rhythm and blues . . . I never *sang* that kind of music. I never had a jazz feeling, a blues feeling, and I still don't. I had a very strong resistance to that kind of music because it was *racial.* I saw the other kind, my kind, as a move to *assimilation.*" During the 1950s and early 1960s, an era in which integration was very much a desired social goal for Black America, Carroll's *assimilated* image was viewed positively, as were those of Lena Horne, Eartha Kitt, and Dorothy Dandridge (although Dandridge, especially in the film *Carmen Jones,* had such a glorious ethnic beat and rhythm that she never seemed to have lost her roots).

Carroll also had conflicted feelings about her sexy image. "How could I portray all those different roles before audiences, in revealing gowns and a lot of makeup, and still maintain an image that was pleasing to my parents?" she said. That uneasiness may account—despite her sensuality—for her rather prim and proper demeanor in nightclubs and on variety shows. There was always a part of herself that Diahann Carroll, especially as a singer, seemed to be holding back. She had none of the queenly, rather icy haughtiness of a Lena Horne. Nor did she have the sophisticated sensual vitality of a Dorothy Dandridge.

In her dramatic television performances as well as in *Julia,* Carroll seemed eager to please yet reserved, never quite giving herself fully to her characters. Looking as if she refused to do anything that might seem unladylike or undignified, she sometimes seemed fake to the core. Yet you always felt there was more to her than what you were seeing. (The same could be said of Gail Fisher.)

Julia proved a mixed blessing. Millions of viewers around the country now knew who Carroll was. But the series also contributed to her *image* problem. During the separatist late 1960s and early 1970s when African American viewers were looking for more ethnic stars with a sense of their cultural identity, Diahann Carroll—on-screen in *Julia* and off-screen—struck some as being too much a conciliatory figure, *too* assimilated. Her well-publicized romance with British interviewer David Frost contributed to that impression.

But the public perception of Diahann Carroll wasn't helped by some of her other statements to the press, especially in a 1970 interview with *TV Guide.* "I ask what she thinks—as a black—of her position in the entertainment world," the *TV Guide* reporter wrote. "Since the success of *Julia*, she has been called a 'sellout' to the white Establishment by some of the more militant blacks. Does she consider herself so?"

"Of course! *Of course, I'm a sellout.* What else would I be? I've sold my talents for a job I'm not particularly crazy about," she responded, catching the reporter and no doubt *TV Guide* readers off guard. "*Isn't that what you do? Isn't that what most people do?* I've been operating in the white world for 15 years." She added, "I'm a black woman with a white image. I'm as close as they can get to having the best of both worlds. The audience can accept me in the same way, and for the same reason. I don't scare them." Diahann Carroll may have later regretted that statement. Or perhaps the way it was perceived. Those words "I'm a black woman with a white image" hovered over her career for some time to come.

"Times have been trying for Diahann Carroll in recent years not because of a faltering career," wrote *Jet* in 1975, "but because of the constant criticism she has received throughout the Black community as a result of her associations with white men and, perhaps in a real sense, her image as a 'white folks' nigger' which apparently stems from her great degree of acceptability by white audiences." "Her critics argue that the actress left her Blackness in Harlem," the magazine added.

Diahann Carroll countered her critics. "I am not about to go out and defend my Blackness to anyone," Carroll told *Jet*. "Each one of us tried to do what we thought was the best thing to do as we came along. And that's all you can ask of anyone. To put somebody down for that is not only unfair, it's ridiculous. . . . *I* know I've been Black all the time. And I'm comfortable with that."

After *Julia*, Diahann Carroll continued working in television, hosting her summer variety program *The Diahann Carroll Show* in 1976. Ironically, in the 1970s, Carroll's best film performance—in *Claudine*—was as a working-class welfare mother, doing her best to hold on to her dignity and self-respect. Later her best TV performance was in Maya Angelou's 1982 *Sister, Sister*, in which she played an achingly inhibited middle-class woman who is jolted (by her sister) into dropping her protective social mask and defense mechanisms to reveal her deepest emotions and fears. Carroll seemed thrilled to finally shed her pretenses with a performance (in the big scenes) that came from her gut. She also appeared in leading roles in the miniseries *Roots: The Next Generations* and such TV movies as *I Know Why the Caged*

Her rise to stardom: Carroll, the ingenue. Carroll, the singer promoting an early album. Carroll, the glitzy glamour goddess

Bird Sings, From the Dead of Night, Murder in Black and White, Having Our Say: The Delany Sisters' First 100 Years, and *Sally Hemings.* Ultimately, she held on to her career—having made shrewd but subtle image changes—and outlasted even some of her toughest critics.

POP GOES THE POLITICAL HERO:
THE MOD SQUAD AND *THE OUTCASTS*

The same year that *Julia* debuted, another new series, *The Mod Squad,* reached younger viewers by touching on the new social/political landscape. Its lead characters were three young dropouts—"one Black, one white, one blonde." The blonde was Julie Barnes (Peggy Lipton). The runaway daughter of a San Francisco prostitute, she was arrested in Los Angeles for vagrancy. The white, Pete Cochran (Michael Cole), was the son of a wealthy Beverly Hills couple, who left home and stole a car—and also was arrested. The Black, Lincoln or Linc Hayes (Clarence Williams III), was one of thirteen children living in Watts. He was

One Black, one white, one blonde: those intrepid counterculture cops—Clarence Williams III, Michael Cole, and Peggy Lipton—on The Mod Squad

taken into custody during the Watts riots. An enterprising police captain, Adam Greer (Tige Andrews), recruited the three to become undercover cops for the Los Angeles Police Department. Their assignment: to weed out criminals preying on the young of America.

The Mod Squad provided a mix of action adventure and liberal politics. Some episodes were the standard cops-and-robbers type of yarns: dramas about drugs, Mafia kingpins, motorcycle gangs, cop killers, and blackmail. Others were "socially relevant" dramas. But always the creators of The Mod Squad hoped to establish Julie, Pete, and Linc as counterculture heroes, expressing the disaffiliation and disillusionment of the era's youth movement. Somehow the formula worked. The Mod Squad soared to success. At its peak, the series won a 45 percent share of the television viewing audience, usually staying in the Top Ten shows of the week, or at least the Top Twenty.

So much about the show—perhaps best exemplified by the huge Afro of star Clarence Williams III—looked new and hip. Young audiences liked the idea of seeing young rebellious edgy heroes, arguing with one another, questioning each other's motives, and usually fighting for the underdogs. The producers also shrewdly decided early on not to bite the hand that fed them: the series could not offend the delicate sensibilities of its young audience. "We were stuck with that stigma of the kids being undercover dragnets, kids finking on kids," said producer Aaron Spelling. "We got letters before we went on the air saying, 'You dirty cop finks!'" Consequently, the mod squad never betrayed its young friends.

Yet older audiences could take comfort in the fact that these revolting young-uns were not tearing the system down but—like Scotty on *I Spy* and Barney on *Mission: Impossible*—ensuring that things didn't fall apart. Despite its counterculture appearance, The Mod Squad was still a cop show.

Some critics argued that The Mod Squad exploited the counterculture of the period. "Here was the TV industry, based upon a middle-class, consumption culture, transforming one of the fiercest attacks upon its values into pleasing entertainment," wrote Robert Lewis Shayon in *The Saturday Review*. "On Mod Squad, non-manipulative modern youth—caring so much about highly personalistic trusting relationships, so committed to nonviolence—have been embraced, vulgarized, and assimilated by the professional sheriffs of society and turned into Establishment 'finks.' " Or, as another critic said, "*The Mod Squad* was probably the ultimate example of the establishment co-opting the youth movement of the late 1960s." True. In its cover story on the series, *Jet* reported that "Black militants" were critical of *The Mod Squad* because it gave "aid and comfort to a fat majority that believes, because it really wants to believe, that everything is in apple pie order and, hence, do nothing to help alleviate the oppressed and hateful position Blacks are left in." Also true. But *Jet*—which titled its story "Why Mod Squad Turns on Young TV Viewers"—also reported that *The Mod Squad* had a large Black viewership.

The Mod Squad effectively tapped some of the political fervor of its era. In an early episode, the three young cops went undercover at a high school in search of the murderer of a popular history teacher. Linc pretended to be a substitute teacher; Julie, a student; and Pete, a gym teacher. While solving the crime, the three were exposed to current social attitudes. The kids revealed their suspicion of the police. Tension broke out between the students and the Black substitute teacher because of his discussion of the Civil War. Another episode commented critically on the My Lai massacre in Vietnam. Others focused on campus upheavals, slum landlords, the problems of ghetto youths, and the Supreme Court's Miranda Rights decision. Eventually, *The Mod Squad* emerged as a quintessential 1960s-style show. Later generations wouldn't be able to watch an episode without being aware of some of the passions, yearnings, and idealism of the period.

The Mod Squad also showed the young of that era crossing lines of gender and race to solve the nation's problems. The language—with the use of then-current slang and African American expressions and colloquialisms like *solid, soul,* and "*ain't it the mother truth*"—may strike later viewers as hokey. But the writers were attempting to dramatize the way the young were transforming the culture itself. Even Robert Lewis Shayon conceded that ultimately "*The Mod Squad* was constructively anti-establishment."

For the African American audience, *The Mod Squad* also offered episodes that dealt with race in a manner that shows such as *I Spy* and *Julia* seemed worlds removed from. One episode, *When Smitty Comes Marching Home,* told the story of a Vietnam vet (played by Lou Gossett) who left America a second-class citizen and returned home a third-class one.

Producer Aaron Spelling once proudly announced that about 25 percent of the actors—guest stars, supporting players, extras—on the series were Black. "I try to keep away from Negro secretaries with one line to speak," said Spelling. "A lot of producers in this town are using Negroes because it's the 'in thing.' I think we must present them as intelligent people with the terrible needs they have."

But the character that most impressed African American (and younger white) viewers was Linc. With his puffed-up Afro, his wire-rimmed glasses, his inquisitive eyes, and his unrelenting scowl, Clarence Williams III created a vivid portrait of an intense young African American man, searching and restless; aware of America's attitudes on race; and unwilling to compromise himself. His quiet fire captured some of the militant spirit sweeping through the Black community. Though he worked with his two white friends, Linc projected a strong cultural identity and sense of his roots. Williams appeared to delight in dialogue like "I don't fink on soul brothers." Though he played a cop, he also managed to make viewers believe in Linc's integrity. That was no small feat. Linc was for many the small tube's first African American political symbol.

Williams, the actor, was also an unusual presence on a medium that preferred small emotions. He mastered the *slow burn*, meticulously building on his character's frustrations or tensions to the point where one felt he might explode right into your living room. Yet he never lost his cool, which in a sense made him all the more threatening. A native New Yorker, Williams had appeared in the films *The Last Angry Man* and *The Cool World*. But his training ground had been the theater, both on and off Broadway, in such productions as *Dark of the Moon, King John*, and, most impressively, *Slow Dance on the Killing Ground*. The *Mod Squad* scripts never afforded Williams the opportunity to fully express the tensions within him; sometimes he seems like an inactive volcano, but you can always see the steam rising from the pit. Later in a film like *52 Pick-Up* and his Emmy Award-winning performance in the TV movie *Wallace*, Williams's talents were brilliantly utilized.

Another political symbol in this era of social symbols was the character Jemal David, played by actor Otis Young, on the series *The Outcasts*, which debuted in 1968. A Western set in the post-Civil War years, it centered on a former plantation owner, Earl Corey (Don Murray), and a freed slave, Jemal David, who form an unlikely partnership: together they roam the West working as bounty hunters in search of criminals. Young's Jemal David was possibly television's angriest African American protagonist; a defiant man who refused to forget the indignities and humiliations of slavery. He also never let his partner's racism go unchallenged. David and Corey were constantly at one another's throats, arguing and fighting. "You do have a natural advantage in the dark, boy," Corey tells Jemal at one point, "unless you happen to smile." "That's mighty white of you," Jemal responds. Jemal refuses to kowtow to his white partner. Nor will he permit any other Black to do so. In one episode, Corey runs into an old man named Gideon, who once had been a faithful slave on his family's plantation. Poor old Gideon doesn't seem to realize that the South lost the Civil War. Jemal lashes out at the Black man's willingness to still accommodate and please his former master.

Actor Otis Young believed *The Outcasts* was important "because for the first time in American television they didn't deny that when a Black man went into Western towns he was going to run into trouble, and they didn't deny that the white men he ran into might be bigots." But Young also clashed with the series's producers over various scenes and dialogue. On one episode, Young held up filming because he refused to say the line "Ain't nothin' like darkies for prayin'."

"I, Otis Young, Black man in America, 36 years old, who suffered and scuffled for 14 years in the theater, said that the line is an insult to Negroes," Young told the press. "I said that if I had to say the line I would not do the series. This, of course, would ruin my career, but I'd rather ruin my career than continue to perpetuate this phony attitude about the Negroes. . . . If this line went through, the next they'd have up there is Stepin Fetchit. If I compromised myself on this script, it would be a little easier next time, and in three or four years I'd wake up one morning and be a wealthy Negro who forgot who he was."

A graduate of New York University (who also studied theater with Frank Silvera), Young had begun his career in such stage productions as *Tambourines to Glory* and *Blues for Mister Charlie*. On television, he appeared in the *Hallmark Hall of Fame* production of *The Green Pastures* as well as episodes of *East Side, West Side* and, later, *Get Christie Love!, Columbo, Cannon,* and *Ellery Queen.* Off-screen, he was one of television's most outspoken critics. Of Cosby on *I Spy*, he said, "Bill did not play the nuances that a Negro would feel. His lines were interchangeable with Robert Culp's." Needless to say, Young's comments—as well as his interpretation of his character—didn't win him many friends in Hollywood. Said one producer on *The Outcasts*, "We didn't want the show quite so angry." *The Outcasts*, suffering poor ratings, died after one season.

During the last year of the decade, three other series appeared starring African Americans: *Land of the Giants*, *Room 222*, and *The Bill Cosby Show*. *Land of the Giants* was a science fiction tale about a group of seven Earthlings on a flight from the United States to London in the mid-1980s. En route, their craft is downed. Afterward caught in a "space warp," they discover themselves in a land where the inhabitants are twelve times their size. Black actor Don Marshall was featured as a member of the flight. The series lasted two seasons.

ROOM 222's PETE DIXON AND LIZ MCINTYRE: A HIGH SCHOOL KID'S DREAM TEAM

Room 222 had a longer run and is remembered with affection. Created by James Brooks, the series centered on the experiences of a young Black teacher named Pete Dixon (Lloyd Haynes) at an integrated Los Angeles high school called Walt Whitman High. His colleagues included the school's guidance counselor, Liz McIntyre (Denise Nicholas), who was also Pete's love interest; a feisty principal (Michael Constantine); and a young student teacher, who later became an English teacher, Alice Johnson (Karen Valentine). There were also several student regulars on the series. Pete's homeroom number was 222.

Room 222 was in many respects an old-style high school drama, a gentle amalgam of *Blackboard Jungle* and *To Sir, With Love*, updated with problems and issues that preoccupied viewers in the late 1960s. On the premiere episode, Pete discovers that a Black student named Richie is ineligible to attend Walt Whitman High because he lives in another district. But the student explains he can't cope with the problems at his old school: the half days; the split sessions; the fights; the cops in the halls. Rather than go by the book, Dixon works to keep Richie at Whitman. Naturally, he succeeds. Pete—with the help of the

Love and politics at the American high school: Lloyd Haynes, Denise Nicholas, Karen Valentine, and Michael Constantine on Room 222

principal—finds a loophole whereby transfer students are accepted to take classes not offered at their own schools. So what's the course Richie takes at Walt Whitman that he can't get back home? It's Hebrew.

Race was also acknowledged on that first episode, albeit gently. "I know I have a lot of the middle-class hang-ups," the ingratiating student teacher Alice tells Dixon. "I went to a segregated school."

"It's okay—so did I."

"I think it's so significant that you're colored," she says, then adds, "I meant it as a compliment. Oh, did I use the wrong term? Well, I'd better ask you straight out—do you prefer 'colored' or 'Negro' or 'Black'?"

"I've always preferred Pete," he tells her.

During an era when *colored* and *Negro* Americans were still fighting to be called Black and when the use of the word indicated a political consciousness and a cultural definition, Pete's response seemed compromised. A *real brother* would very definitely have let her know that he was both Pete *and* Black. As was true of the series itself, an issue had been raised and then softened in a comforting manner meant to entertain mainstream viewers. Realistic in its aspirations, the series often had unrealistically neat solutions.

African American novelist John Oliver Killens observed that *Room 222* was "a nice, liberal-oriented, interracial, innocuous show" with "Black folk" that were "full of understanding and wisdom, sympathetic all the way." But Killens also believed that the series suffered because it depicted no basic problems between the races. "All men are brothers," he said. "Right? An undramatic, middle-classish situation that hardly has anything to do with the Black experience." For Killens and others within the Black community at this time, the series lacked a certain cultural authenticity because its primary Black characters were middle-class rather than gritty urban protagonists who clearly could be seen as victims of a racist system. During this period when the ghetto experience was glamorized, when the language, style, and attitudes of urban African Americans seemed the voice of the true Black America, there was the feeling that those of the middle class were in some way sellouts and accommodationists. But the real point of Killens's perspective was that the Black characters of *Room 222* were never fully enough contextualized so that viewers might have understood that while characters like Pete and Liz indeed were middle-class and seemingly removed from a harsher urban experience, they still were connected to other African Americans (through history and cultural demarcations). This, of course, had been the problem with *Julia*, and it would plague other middle-class Black series to come in this decade and the very early 1970s.

Still, *Room 222* brought something new to the primetime series. Because the series was actually shot at the 3,000-student Los Angeles High School, *Room 222* had a realistic look and feel, making it appear as one more example of the 1960s gritty "relevant" style. *Room 222* also brought African American actors and actresses into an integrated setting, stressing the idea of people working together—just, of course, as *Julia* had done. But like *The Mod Squad*, *Room 222* presented both a tougher and a more culturally diverse world with students Black, white, and Asian American. Various episodes examined issues of drugs, dropouts, parental abuse, school integration, and racial conflicts. The relationship between Dixon and girlfriend Liz was also fairly adult: two people who, although they might disagree about professional or personal matters, liked and respected one another—and whose strong attraction overrode their differences.

But where the series may have succeeded best was, thanks to Lloyd

Haynes's performance, in its realistic depiction of a rather "average" African American male. Lloyd Haynes played Pete in a low-keyed, laid-back manner. Not a terribly exciting character (or performance), Pete ran the risk at times of becoming a tad dull. But that was part of his appeal. Unlike Ethel Waters, Eddie "Rochester" Anderson, Louise Beavers, and Tim Moore as Kingfish, the new stars were hardly *hot*, larger-than-life personalities with outsized emotions. Nothing about them was outlandish or scary. What distinguished Haynes—in a medium that now clearly preferred *cool* images—were indeed his cool style and his looks. In *Cue*, Joan Walker called him "an extraordinarily attractive young actor who should set race relations forward by decades." Yet even his good looks seemed safe and without any irregularities. (The same had been true of Hari Rhodes and Greg Morris.) Haynes, like other new stars, always seemed like a guy anyone might know, who simply wanted to do the best job possible. That paradoxically *special* "ordinary" quality contributed to the success of the series.

Denise Nicholas, however, had sparks and suggestions of deep fires waiting to erupt. A light brown African American woman with striking eyes and a sexy smile, she was more sensual than most television heroines and not plastic (as Carroll sometimes was on *Julia*). Nicholas might have become important in movies had the Hollywood system been different. She had come to television after a career on the stage with the Negro Ensemble Company in New York and then the Free Southern Theatre. With that kind of background, she knew how to strike a pose for an African American audience, and she understood very well the importance of *attitude* in getting a message across.

Following *Room 222*, which aired for five seasons on ABC, Haynes almost looked as if he had abandoned his career. For a time, he worked with youth groups, trying to reach troubled, underachieving teenagers. He also joined the United States Naval Reserves. Later he appeared on such television shows as *T. J. Hooker, Look What's Happened to Rosemary's Baby, Marcus Welby, M.D., Harold Robbins' 79 Park Avenue, The Kids Who Knew Too Much, Born to Be Sold,* and (in the role of Major Ken Morgan) *General Hospital.* Haynes died of lung cancer in 1986 at the age of fifty-two. Nicholas appeared with Sidney Poitier and Bill Cosby in the films *Let's Do It Again* and *A Piece of the Action.* Later she returned to series television in *Baby, I'm Back* and *In the Heat of the Night.* Both Haynes and Nicholas, like other stars of successful series, may have discovered that audiences identified them as the characters they had once played and needed time to accept them as different characters. Then, too, as African American performers, neither had the options of their white counterparts.

THE BILL COSBY SHOW:
COSBY ON HIS OWN, TESTING THE WATERS

That didn't happen with the other African American actor starring in a new series at the close of the decade. Bill Cosby's personality was strong enough to dominate and define every character that he played. Just as Lucille Ball always did Lucy, Cosby always played himself, Cos: a very likable everyday sort of guy who, perhaps surprisingly, didn't take any guff from anybody but who was always calm, collected, and somehow *racially correct*. When he appeared in *The Bill Cosby Show* in 1969, the audience may have rejected the series but not the star.

Cosby returned to series television a year after *I Spy* went off the air. By then, he had hosted several primetime specials. He may already have become television's most familiar Black face. When he signed to do *The Bill Cosby Show*, he was shrewd and sophisticated enough to know the key to survival on TV was controlling his image. Not only did he star but he also was the executive producer, which was something no African American star before him had done. In time, Cosby hired other African Americans (like Ivan Dixon, then beginning his directorial career) to work behind the scenes. He also brought in veteran actors like Lillian Randolph.

The series revolved around Chester "Chet" Kincaid, a physical education teacher and coach at a Los Angeles high school. Chet deals with the expected unmotivated students as well as the school's levelheaded guidance counselor (Joyce Bulifant) and its principal, Mr. Langford (Sid McCoy). Away from work, Chet, a bachelor, courts various girlfriends and contends with his family, including his mother, Rose Kincaid (played the first season by Lillian Randolph and the next by Beah Richards), his brother Brian (Lee Weaver)—a sanitation worker—and Brian's wife, Verna (Olga James).

The Bill Cosby Show's first episode neatly summed up some of the series's forthcoming assets and shortcomings. It opened with Chet ca-

On his own: Bill Cosby as Chet Kincaid on The Bill Cosby Show

sually out for a jog. When he hears a public phone ringing, he picks it up. A woman (whom Chet knows) is on the other end, asking him to look for her husband, Calvin, who works at a nearby garage. But Calvin, says Chet, is not at the garage. He's at Birdie's—a poolroom.

Chet seeks out Calvin at Birdie's. Calvin, however, is upset that his wife now knows his whereabouts. He asks Chet to phone his wife and say he's not in the poolroom. But Chet doesn't want to become involved in their domestic squabble. He returns to his jog. Then two cops stop him, saying he fits the description of a man who just robbed a store. Taken to the police station, Chet calls Calvin to verify his whereabouts at the time of the robbery. But now Calvin doesn't want to get involved. When he does show up at the police station, Calvin's suspected of being an accomplice in the robbery! Everything works out when the police apprehend the real robber. To Chet's surprise, the man is Chet's double.

The episode moved along like an unfolding anecdote being told by a laid-back raconteur—on an off day. It's amusing but long-winded and not greatly compelling. Yet Cosby—as Kincaid—holds things together beautifully and makes the whole episode work on a certain level. Cosby is the master of the little situation; of dramatizing the concerns and comic foibles of "ordinary" people. Pulling off neat characterizations of Calvin and his missus (who are white and easy for the white viewer to identify with), the episode reaches for something else with Chet's arrest by the police. Cosby appears eager to comment on a race-specific situation: the idea that African American males are targets for a bigoted police force. It's wonderful to see that topic presented—in a rather relaxed tone—in the sitcom format.

But ultimately the episode undercuts any political points it wants to make and is insistent upon *not* rattling its mainstream viewers. First, the cops are an integrated pair, one Black, the other white. Finally, they are revealed as justified in having arrested Chet because he really does look like the actual robber. Again, television played it very safe. Again, the model African American television hero proved himself safe too. The subliminal message may even have been that those African Americans who think the cops are out to get Black men are being paranoid!

Yet other aspects of Cosby's show made it a marked departure from general television fare and also possibly a culturally more significant show than *I Spy*. While Scotty often appeared in a cultural vacuum,

Cosby set out not only to culturally contextualize Chet but also to present a very normal African American life. Chet is in so many respects just like any guy. But Cosby refuses to let us forget he is Black. Sporting an Afro, he relates in both a warm and a loose way to other African American characters, including those who are more ethnically defined. He doesn't live in some culturally isolated cell as poor Julia had to. Yet that world is also an integrated one; not just Black and white but also Latino and Asian. Cosby told the press that, being the series's executive producer, he now had the "opportunity to give minority groups—all of them—a chance to work in this industry. I'm tired of seeing a Chinese hired to run a laundry or a Mexican hired to act silly. In the classroom of my show we're going to mix up all the races. You'll see every type: Japanese, Mexican, Indian, Negro, down to white."

Cosby even played with the idea of distinct generational and perhaps even cultural/class differences among African Americans. On one episode, the veteran Black performers Jackie "Moms" Mabley and Mantan Moreland make guest appearances as Chet's cranky Aunt Edna and Uncle Dewey. One evening, they arrive unexpectedly at Chet's home when he is alone with a girlfriend. Chet is annoyed not by their surprise visit but by their bickering. Their insults are fast and furious. Edna says of Dewey, "There's a man that gets out of breath putting on his pajamas at night. That's a man who has to take naps so he'll be rested when he goes to sleep." Dewey counters, "I wouldn't keep my eyes closed so much if my eyes had something to look at." "Your shadow's better-looking than you," Edna tells him. "I used to stay home from work just to keep from kissing you goodbye," Dewey says. As they leave Chet's home, they invite Chet and his girlfriend to come to dinner. The aunt promises a soulful meal of black-eyed peas, sweet potatoes, and greens.

Before the dinner, Chet visits his aunt and uncle. Reprimanding the pair as if they were children, he tells them he wants no more of their fights and insults. Embarrassed, they agree to behave differently with one another. On the evening of the dinner, Chet and girlfriend arrive to find a very restrained pair, excessively courteous to one another, almost obsequious in their attempts to please—and to present themselves as something of a de-ethnicized, modern, middle-class Black couple. They've been stripped of the very qualities that gave their relationship its spark and energy.

Later Chet comes to the conclusion that some people need a certain kind of tough combative push—to make a relationship work. He goes to the couple's apartment and releases them from their fake bonds of domesticity. The two are once again yelling and yapping and having the time of their lives.

By bringing on guest stars Mabley and Moreland, Cosby was acknowledging a certain cultural tradition of the past. Here were two skilled comics who had worked the chitlin circuit. Mabley had performed stand-up comedy at Black clubs and theaters (like the Apollo) for decades. Moreland had worked in supporting roles in Hollywood movies and had also starred in Black-cast race movies. Both spoke with warm dialects, sprinkled with African American colloquialisms. Both were accustomed to punching their lines (much like the cast of TV's *Amos 'n' Andy*) for Black audiences.

In this era of Black middle-class social symbols, their loud, lowdown ethnic humor belonged to the past. But Cosby brings it back to indicate that with a diversity of African American images in a show like his, perhaps this kind of humor can work. And it does. The couple uses old-style Black cultural references, from the food they eat to their attitude toward one another. Their very comments are a form of *the dozens* or *signifying* whereby African American participants play a verbal game of topping one another with insults. A grunt or a groan or a *hmmmm* or a perfectly timed double take said volumes more than a page of dialogue. The aunt and uncle—spontaneous, outspoken, true to themselves—are contrasted with Chet and his girlfriend. The younger couple speaks without a dialect and without any grammatical mishaps. During their initial appearance, they are discussing a foreign film they've seen. They strike us as very controlled emotionally and as assimilated products of an integrated system.

In most episodes, though, Cosby was interested in expressing—without simplifying—the important values, outlooks, and norms of an emerging new Black middle class. Cosby wanted to depict Black Americans who in many respects were no different than white Americans. Family life was important. Education was important. A good job with a good income was important too. They experienced many of the same "little" daily problems that everyone else did in America. Yet at key moments, he wanted to show the very real and important differences that existed in the Black community, even if it merely be an aunt and uncle shooting the dozens. He also gave Chet a love life. Various actresses appeared as his girlfriends, including a young Cicely Tyson.

The Bill Cosby Show wasn't interested in the race theme. That was clear from Chet's encounter with the police in the first episode. And from another early episode when the subject of discrimination comes up after a Black student is rejected for a spot on the basketball team. As it turns out, the boy, who is five feet one, accuses Chet of being *prejudiced* against short people.

Cosby hadn't yet worked it all out. In *The Bill Cosby Show*, he wasn't able to deliver a fully developed and entertaining series based on his views of African American life and culture. But his attempt at expressing a generic American experience and a specific African American one in the very same show would finally flower in the 1980s when he would completely alter the very concept of the Black sitcom with *The Cosby Show.*

The Bill Cosby Show aired only two seasons. Viewers didn't then seem particularly interested in Black middle-class life. At a time of continued social unrest, a younger generation of African Americans called into question the values of the Black bourgeoisie; accusing it of having forgotten its cultural roots; of adopting white manners and mores. For the new generation in this increasingly separatist age, that's what integration seemed to be all about.

By the end of the 1960s, African American images had clearly changed. In their guest appearances on series, African American actors and actresses had ushered in protagonists whose tensions and troubles were directly related to their status in American society. In starring roles in series developed around them, other African American actors had created characters who were capable of functioning in—and contributing to—mainstream life in America. Throughout the era, the performances of actors like Cicely Tyson, Ivan Dixon, Bill Cosby, Diahann Carroll, Lloyd Haynes, Denise Nicholas, and Clarence Williams III had made the African American character seem less of the Other. These were flesh-and-blood people—not carrying a tray with a smile pasted on their faces but living with daily goals and aspirations—that viewers felt they knew and understood and, for better or worse, could identify with. Yet primetime television still failed to present African American cultural references and perspectives. A search was on for ethnic heroes and heroines on the primetime series. That search would lead to some surprising new hit shows starring African Americans in the next decade.

3. THE 1970s: JOKESTERS

At first, the 1970s looked as if it would be a replay of the 1960s. The war raged on in Vietnam. So did the demonstrations against it. The feminist movement gained momentum as women questioned their place in American society. Campus protests continued as students, Black and white, rebelled against the policies, procedures, and fundamental curricula of their universities. Daily newspaper headlines chronicled this new era's turbulence. During a racial disturbance at Jackson State University in Mississippi, two Black students were killed. In San Rafael, Marin County, California, four people, including a judge, were also killed during a courthouse shoot-out. Afterward there was a nationwide search for Angela Davis, a college professor and activist accused of providing the weapons used by the convicts in the shoot-out. During a clash between the police and the Black Panthers in Philadelphia, a police officer was killed and six others were wounded. Later the break-in of the Democratic headquarters in Washington, D.C., led to the Watergate scandal, which culminated in the resignation of President Richard Milhous Nixon. In the early 1970s, Americans still appeared to be restlessly debating their nation's values, traditions, attitudes—and history.

But within a few years, much of that early political drive and energy evaporated. In what came to be known as the "Me Decade," many Americans appeared to withdraw from social and political issues to concentrate instead on more personal needs. The rise of the discos—those Friday and Saturday night emporiums of frenetic music and dreamy escape—was probably the most apt symbol of that political withdrawal. Here Americans looked determined to push pressing problems aside—and literally to dance their lives away. Other trends and fads were also signs of the decade's new interest in self. The fitness craze took off as Americans rushed to health food stores, took up jogging, worked out in the gym, or studied transcendental meditation, all in efforts at self-improvement. Or they focused more on the effects of the environment on their daily lives.

Again television images reflected the new atmosphere.

Just as the movies had started to change in the early 1970s with the rise of African American directors like Melvin Van Peebles, Gordon Parks Sr., and Gordon Parks Jr., and with the assertive and aggressive heroes and heroines (Shaft, Superfly, Foxy Brown) of the Blaxploitation era, television also made a place for an assortment of new Black faces. More African Americans appeared in primetime series than at any other time in television history: not only in supporting roles on general white-oriented programs but also in a lineup of Black-cast series that became highly popular. Viewers also saw the emergence of African American television stars: Flip Wilson, Redd Foxx, Cicely Tyson, Gary Coleman, Esther Rolle, Sherman Hemsley, John Amos, and Marla Gibbs. These immensely talented performers with striking personalities were followed closely by the press and became household names throughout the country—even when they had to maneuver their way around dubious or disparaging roles. For a spell, that 1960s saying—Black Is Beautiful—seemed to be the attitude of network programmers *and* viewers. But it took a period of adjustment before the networks were able to come up with winning combinations of stars and programs.

Most striking at the very start of the decade was the weekly appearance of "serious" and "committed" African American characters. On *The Young Rebels,* Louis Gossett Jr. (then billed simply as Lou Gossett) appeared as Isak Poole, a former slave fighting for his nation's rights during, of all periods, the Revolutionary War. Judy Pace played a hip, young, socially conscious attorney on *The Young Lawyers. The Silent Force* cast Percy Rodriguez (formerly of TV's *Peyton Place*) as one of a trio of government agents battling organized crime. Newcomer John

Amos was a fresh and disarming presence as Gordon (Gordy) Howard, the television weatherman, on *The Mary Tyler Moore Show*. Black characters were also featured on such series as *The Interns* (Hal Frederick), *The Storefront Lawyers* (Pauline Myers), and *Matt Lincoln* (Felton Perry and Chelsea Brown). Black supporting characters seemed to be in fashion; as if a series without one was a tad dated and even déclassé. Yet, with the exception of Amos's Gordy on *The Mary Tyler Moore Show*, none of these series featuring these characters lasted longer than one season.

That was also true of the new Black series *Barefoot in the Park*, which ABC launched in 1970. Based on Neil Simon's hit Broadway play that had also been adapted as a movie starring Jane Fonda and Robert Redford, *Barefoot in the Park* told the story of a newlywed New York couple, ensnared in a web of comic entanglements as they coped with one another—and various friends, relatives, and associates—while struggling to live on a tight budget.

The idea of a TV version had been kicking around for a while. Earlier a pilot for the series had been filmed with white performers. But it was turned down by CBS for being "too risqué." Then TV executive Douglas Cramer, who had been associated with *Julia*, had the idea that viewers would tune in to a program with a Black couple if it was "honest and true to their situation." A Black-cast pilot was filmed for ABC with Tracy Reed as the ditzy wife, Corie Bratter; Scoey Mitchell as her lawyer husband, Paul Bratter; Thelma Carpenter as Corie's control freak mother; and Nipsey Russell as the mother's ardent suitor, Honey Robinson. When it was shown to its affiliate executives, they gave it a standing ovation. At the screening, a Southern gentleman approached actress Tracy Reed. "I want to tell you that I love you in spite of myself," he said. "Do you realize what that means for me to come out here from my part of the country to tell you that I love you? Do you realize how *fantastic* that is and what a *great* vehicle this is going to be." Why shouldn't he have liked her? Reed asked. But for ABC, the more important issue was that the Southern market seemed to have changed its attitude about certain Black programs. *Barefoot in the Park* looked promising.

Most viewers at home, however, took one look at *Barefoot in the Park* and never came back. Again here was a series that failed to give its characters a distinct African American cultural identity; to create situations, antics, and dialogue that grew out of an African American experience. The original writers (both white) prided themselves on a research visit to a Watts drama workshop. "We wanted to find out as much as possible about the relationship Black people have when they're alone without white people around," one said. Good idea. But they should have hung out at the workshop with the brothers and sisters a little longer. Their few attempts at contextualizing the characters proved all wrong.

In the original Simon comedy, the young couple's neighbor Robinson had been a sophisticated bon vivant. But apparently the writers didn't find that "realistic" for a Black character; so the character became the owner of a pool hall. Previously, Corie's mother had been a suburban matron. On the series, she worked as a maid for a white family. On the one hand, *Barefoot in the Park* tried breaking away from old images with its bourgeois leads. On the other hand, the creators of the series had no idea what the real Black bourgeoisie was like and relied (with its older characters) on trite, hand-me-down depictions from the past.

Ultimately, *Barefoot in the Park* seemed a standard, generic white middle-class comedy that was hopelessly out of sync with contemporary outlooks and interests. Its lead characters were as culturally adrift as poor Julia—without any of the fire, grit, and ethnic thrust of the era. (Once the series was in production, *Barefoot in the Park* at first had only one Black writer.) Actor Scoey Mitchell openly complained that he was being forced to do "the Uncle Tom bit." Eventually, he was fired. Neil Simon's other hit play *The Odd Couple* also came to the small screen in 1970 but with far different results. With characters fully contextualized, it proved to be an enduring hit into the 1980s. If someone had perceptively fiddled around with the concept, the Black version of *Barefoot in the Park* might have survived. But then, considering what did succeed in this era, maybe not. In retrospect, viewers just didn't seem interested in a series built around middle-class Black characters.

FLIP WILSON: THE VARIETY SHOW GOES ETHNIC

It's doubtful if anyone could have predicted the type of Black-oriented program that would find favor with viewers. The primetime network television series soon did a surprising turnaround. Suddenly, in place of the social symbols that had dominated in the 1960s and the politically oriented dramatic African American characters that appeared on shows like *The Mod Squad* and *The Outcasts*, the old-style broad ethnic humor resurfaced and became popular. *The Flip Wilson Show* marked its return.

Its star, Flip Wilson, was an energetic, inventive comic, known best for funny, colorful tales rather than jokes or punch lines. Born Clerow Wilson in 1933 in Jersey City, he was one of twenty-four children (eighteen of whom survived) of a troubled couple. His father, a janitor, was an alcoholic. His mother, so the stories went, abandoned the family. Growing up, Wilson once said he had been "so poor even the poor looked down on me." Shifted from one foster home to another (thirteen in all), young Clerow frequently ran away, spent time in a reform school, and at sixteen joined the air force, where he was known for "flipping out" people with his jokes and funny stories.

Flip Wilson's bodacious Geraldine with guest star Bing Crosby on the surprise hit
The Flip Wilson Show

Afterward he bummed around and lived in San Francisco, earning forty dollars a week as a bellhop at a hotel. When a dance team performed in the hotel's floor show, Wilson persuaded them to let him do comedy while they changed costumes. Later Wilson performed with the dancers in Stockton, California. He earned one dollar a night. From 1954 to 1963, he played small Black clubs (part of the chitlin circuit) and "sweat-stained" saloons but without much success. Living like a nomad, he sometimes slept in bus stations. He had two short-lived marriages; the first to a dancer named Peaches whom he met in the Bahamas; the second to a woman named Blondell who bore him four children. Both ended on a sour note. Throughout his career, Wilson shied away from any discussion of his personal life.

Serious about the art of comedy, Wilson studied Max Eastman's *Enjoyment of Laughter*. "Generally, it only takes one thing that's different to be great," he later said. "I don't think there's anything that can compare with Charlie Chaplin's walk and remarkable use of the body. With Bob Hope, it's timing; with W. C. Fields it's complete effortlessness." Early on, Wilson realized "what my thing was and I eliminated everything else. I used to work with a partner, but he'd get drunk and forget his lines. No partner. I eliminated the orchestra because I didn't sing or dance. I used to wear a ratty old coat and a funny hat. I threw those away. No props. Just me. Flip Wilson."

The direction of his career changed when Monte Kay, the husband of Diahann Carroll, became his manager in 1963. Booked by Kay into New York's Bitter End and the Village Gate and into San Francisco's hungry i, he became known in show business circles. During an appearance on *The Tonight Show*, comedian Redd Foxx was asked by host Johnny Carson to name the funniest comic around. He answered, "Flip Wilson." Afterward Wilson was booked for an appearance on Carson's show. He performed a routine about a Black woman buying a wig. "You sure it don't make me look too Polish?" she asked the store clerk. He broke the house up. On that single appearance on *The Tonight Show*, he performed before more people than he had during his entire eleven years of club work. Other appearances on *The Tonight Show* followed. Then he subbed for Carson as a guest host. He also performed on *The Carol Burnett Show*, *The Dean Martin Show*, *Laugh-In*, *The Ed Sullivan Show*, *The Merv Griffin Show*, and *The Mike Douglas Show*. He recorded best-selling comedy albums too, including *Flip Wilson, You Devil You*, which won a Grammy Award for Best Comedy Recording in 1968. Always Wilson specialized in whimsical, lighthearted narratives. One of his most famous monologues was the story of Christopher Columbus's discovery of America, which was history told from an African American perspective. Queen Isabella—Queen Isabel Johnson—decides to finance his trip upon learning that in the New World he will find Ray Charles. "He in America?" she exclaims. "Damn right," Chris replies. "Chris goin' to America in that boat. Chris goin' to find Ray Charles." Once he reaches his destination, Columbus encounters a West Indian maiden who has her own ideas about the European discovery of America. "What the hell you want comin' round in them ships?" she asks. "We don't wanna be discovered. You better discover your ass away from here."

By now, NBC executives had taken notice of him and signed him to a development deal. He taped a special for the network in 1968. But the show was so poorly done that NBC shelved it. Then Wilson hosted another special, *The Flip Wilson Show*, in September 1969. This time he came up with a winner that captured a 42 percent share of the audience. Afterward NBC developed a sitcom around him, with Wilson playing a deejay. But that proved disappointing and was dropped.

Then came his variety show series.

Variety programs were losing their popular appeal. Past variety programs starring any African American—like *The Nat "King" Cole Show*, *The Sammy Davis, Jr. Show*, and *The Leslie Uggams Show*—were all considered failures. But producer Bob Henry, a television veteran who had worked on *The Nat "King" Cole Show*, decided to make *The Flip Wilson Show* a different type of program. Shrewdly, Henry insisted that the show be shot in the round before a live studio audience, which created the perfect type of intimacy for Wilson's particular style. The comedian was also filmed in full shots. "The head-to-toe selling was important," said Henry. "What Chaplin's legs were to him, Flip's body is to his program." Banished were the familiar chorus lines, production numbers, and windy introductions that were so much a part of variety shows at the time. Simplicity became crucial to Wilson's effects.

On *The Flip Wilson Show*, Wilson brought on an interracial mix of guest stars that included Lena Horne, Lucille Ball, Diahann Carroll, Bing Crosby, Jack Benny, Stevie Wonder, and James Brown. More important, Wilson created a rich gallery of characters: the bopping

Wilson with guest star Lena Horne

Reverend LeRoy of the Church of What's Happening Now; Freddie the Playboy; Sonny the White House janitor; and Herbie the Good Time Ice Cream Man. But the centerpiece of his comic creations—and *The Flip Wilson Show* itself—was the character Geraldine Jones, a sometimes loud, raunchy, gregarious, fun-loving, sassy lass equipped with a knowledge of the streets *and* of men. Usually strutting about in wigs and short dresses, Geraldine had a boyfriend named Killer, who sounded as if he were a pretty tough, hot customer. Geraldine's lines were punctuated by a snap of her fingers or a shake of her hips.

After its premiere on September 17, 1970, at 7:30 p.m., *The Flip Wilson Show* surprised industry experts as it drew (at its peak) an audience of forty million people weekly and became the number one variety show on the air—as well as the number two show of any kind. One minute of commercial time cost advertisers $86,000. No African American performer had ever had this type of TV success. Exerting a great deal of creative control over the series, Wilson won an Emmy (along with his other writers) for Outstanding Writing in Variety or Music Programs in 1971. He ended up on the cover of *Time* with a banner that read: "Television's First Black Superstar."

In most respects, *The Flip Wilson Show* was a safe program. At a time when comics like Lenny Bruce, Dick Gregory, and Godfrey Cambridge performed biting or edgy, satirical monologues—humor infused with political awareness—Wilson's characters were hardly rebels with gripes to unload. "It should be noted that, to a vet of the VARIETY Apollo Theatre beat," the critic for *Variety* wrote, "there is something more often than not missing in tv's burgeoning Negro humor. The mocking of Negro family life and mores has been preserved while the ever-present barbs at Whitey's ways seemed to have almost vanished. Wilson and others may find themselves becoming strangely popular in Crackerville." Wilson's characters were "ordinary," "little" people who spoke with traces of the familiar dialect and whose lives were seemingly uneventful and untouched by any larger social issues. Their "safeness" grew out of their docility; the fact that they lacked anger and threat; the fact that these characters, who seemed predictably triflin' and lazy, rarely rattled any preconceived notions about Negro behavior.

For Black America's intellectual community, Wilson's characters were a collection of repackaged stereotypes that belonged to another era. "There is a certain grim white humor in the fact that the Black marches and demonstrations of the '60s reached artistic fulfillment in the '70s with Flip Wilson's Geraldine and Melvin Van Peebles' Sweetback, two provocative and ultimately insidious reincarnations of all the Sapphires and Studs of yesteryear," Lerone Bennett wrote in *Ebony*. "Who would have believed that the Afros and dashikis would lead to Geraldine? . . . Such a preposterous reversal of images could only happen in a community without a sure sense of the meaning of its experience and the overwhelming power of electronic and film media to distort and debase even the best artistic intentions." Others believed that the Geraldine/Reverend LeRoy antics were funny when performed within the Black community. Taken out of an African American context and put on white television, this kind of humor could be misinterpreted. Some Black viewers would never feel comfortable seeing this kind of material, no matter how entertaining, on television. The response to many of Flip Wilson's characters was not that different from the response to *Amos 'n' Andy*—and not different from the response to later shows like *Sanford and Son*, *In Living Color*, and *Martin*.

In response, Wilson told the press, "I have feelings about these things, but I'm selling professional entertainment. Politics is for politicians. Each man has his own style. Mine is that 'the funny' has no color. I do these characters because they're what I know. But people are just people to me. The way I see it, I don't have to think Black—or not think Black. I just have to entertain. I'm just a comic."

Yet despite the critics, African American audiences appeared to relish the rich ethnic humor and the Black communal atmosphere that surfaced as Wilson joked and laughed with such guests as Richard Pryor, or Bill Cosby, or Lena Horne. Through Wilson's impeccable timing and brilliant delivery, his memorable idiosyncratic characters like Reverend LeRoy and Geraldine—with their language, gestures, and even body movements—encapsulated an aspect of the African American experience that a program like *Barefoot in the Park* couldn't begin to fathom.

Geraldine embodied a certain type of Black assertion and assurance. Supremely confident of her powers and her appeal, Geraldine never felt she had to prove anything to anybody. "When you're hot, you're hot!" she often said. "When you're not, you're not!" She was always eager to *announce* herself (and her satisfaction with herself) to anyone, whether he/she cared to listen or not. "What you see is what you get!" she exclaimed. And if anyone dared get out of bounds on *her* turf, Geraldine informed *him*, "Whooo-eeeee! Watch out, honey! Don't touch me. Don't ever touch me!" The audience knew she meant it. Geraldine kept audiences cued in to the fact that she was a Black woman able to take care of herself; who perhaps *had* to take care of herself.

Both a caricature and a pointed parody, Geraldine was indeed part Sapphire from *Amos 'n' Andy*; loud and raucous but with a built-in awareness of her effect on the audience. She also was part of the best of what Hattie McDaniel represented: a powerhouse who couldn't abide pretense nor would she be trifled with; a woman determined to do things her way and on her terms; a woman with a particularly American brand of aggressiveness and audacity. Yet Geraldine also had a sexuality missing from earlier comic Black females. When she rolled her eyes and swung her hips, she delighted in her sexual power and in the joy her boyfriend Killer brought her. She was clearly a precursor to Martin Lawrence's coarser, outrageously bodacious Sheneneh in the 1990s.

Wilson's skits also permitted Geraldine to be far more outspoken with white characters. The hostile edges of McDaniel's heroine were never explained by the scripts. It was the actress's own invention; her way of rebelling against and overturning (as best she could) America's stereotyping. But rebellious independence was *scripted* into the Geraldine skits. Who could ever forget the exchange between Geraldine and any of the white guest stars—when she told them not to touch her! She might as well have been addressing all of white America. In the end, Geraldine was a reconfigured caricature yet graced with character details that the African American audience could respond to.

After four seasons, an exhausted Wilson left the series. He appeared occasionally on specials for NBC. In 1981, he made newspaper headlines when he was arrested and charged for possession of cocaine. He was then dropped from a Seven-Up advertising campaign. In 1984, he hosted a revival of the Art Linkletter program *People Are Funny*. A year later, he returned to series television as the star of the short-lived *Charlie & Co.* But never again was he able to directly address and engage an audience as he did with his variety show, which ultimately proved the highpoint of his career. In 1998, Wilson died of liver cancer at the age of sixty-four.

The Flip Wilson Show brought the old-style ethnic humor—the outrageous antics, the dialects, the mugging—out of the closet and back into vogue. For better or worse, the show said it was all right to laugh at the simpleton shenanigans of a Black character as well as to laugh about race and ethnicity. Helping to usher back in the racial joke, the show also indicated that now viewers would accept Black stars as jokesters. No longer did Black performers—on the weekly series—need be high-minded, earnest social symbols who could fit into the system. Instead, at a time when the system itself was still being called into question, viewers often preferred stars who seemed outside the system.

ALL IN THE FAMILY: THE BIGOT AS POP HERO

Six months after the debut of *The Flip Wilson Show*, ethnic humor of another sort was repopularized on *All in the Family*. Some might say it simply represented old-style comic racism. Created by Norman Lear and based on the British series *Till Death Us Do Part, All in the Family* focused on the Bunker household in Queens. Archie Bunker (Carroll O'Connor), the blue-collar working stiff who headed the home, was an unapologetic bigot unable to accept the social changes coming about in American society. His wife, Edith (Jean Stapleton), whom he called the Dingbat, was a kindly, gentle soul baffled by the changes but willing to adapt to them. The Bunkers' daughter, Gloria (Sally Struthers), and her husband, Mike (Rob Reiner), "the meathead," who lived with the Bunkers while Mike worked on his college degree, were 1960s-style liberals.

Throughout the series, the Bunkers were a marked departure from those previous perfect TV nuclear families living in bland, politically neutral suburbs, divorced from the gritty realities of everyday American life. They shouted at one another. They flushed toilets. They didn't live in a home that was immaculately clean and ordered. *All in the Family*, which (with various cast changes) ran until 1983, de-idealized television's traditional white American family and opened a window to the world that had been firmly shut and shuttered in the past. Weekly, Archie, who yearned for the good old days, clashed and argued with

Mike and other family members about everything: Vietnam, Watergate, Death, Poverty, Menopause, Impotency, Women's Rights, and Religion. Ultimately, *All in the Family* took the sitcom in a new direction with topics that would have been wholly unacceptable in earlier decades. The series also broached a subject no one had ever thought fit for laughter on a sitcom: racism in America.

On the premiere episode, Archie called son-in-law Mike "the laziest white boy I ever met." Mike protested that the comment was a covert way for Archie "to put down a whole race," implying that all Blacks were inherently lazy. Archie countered: "I didn't say that. You're the one who said that. I never said your Blacks were lazy. I never said that at all . . . of course, their systems is geared a little slower than ours, that's all."

Unneighborly neighbors: Archie Bunker (Carroll O'Connor) and George Jefferson (Sherman Hemsley)

On other episodes, Archie proclaimed that "Jesus was white and so was Santa Claus," and naturally that "spooks" could run faster on the football field because "they've got it in their bloods . . . inherited from the time their forefathers were in the jungles running barefoot through all them thorns and thickets." Believing Blacks had no business in neighborhoods with whites, Archie was rankled that a Black family, the Jeffersons, lived next door. Mike became friends with the son of the Jeffersons, Lionel (Mike Evans), who often slyly poked fun at Archie and got the best of him. Edith was also friendly with Louise Jefferson (Isabel Sanford). During the first seasons, Archie crossed swords with Henry Jefferson (Mel Stewart). In the fourth season, his nemesis was Henry's brother and Louise's husband, George Jefferson (Sherman Hemsley), who was just as antiwhite as Archie was antiblack. Throughout, Archie seemed eager to vent against any kind of ethnic differences. For Archie, Blacks were spades, Asians were Chinks, Jews were hebes, Italians were dagos, and Puerto Ricans were spics. He was also homophobic and sexist, refusing to hear any talk of the woman's movement.

Nervous about the program, CBS's switchboards were ready for complaints the night the series premiered in January 1971. But the program was barely noticed and did nothing in the ratings. *All in the Family* looked as if it might bomb. Then came the Emmys. Jean Stapleton walked off with the award for Outstanding Actress in a Comedy Series. *All in the Family* itself won Outstanding Comedy Series. During summer reruns, *All in the Family* picked up a large audience. Afterward it reigned at the top of the Nielsen ratings for five consecutive seasons with an audience of some sixty million viewers. *The Wall Street Journal* reported that at its peak *All in the Family* was seen by nearly one-third of all Americans. Of its viewers, 35 percent saw nothing wrong with Archie's attitudes. Archie became so popular that during the 1972 presidential campaign, bumper stickers and buttons popped up that read: "Archie Bunker for President." A record album was released with thirteen cuts of Archie's best lines. The paperback book *The Wit and Wisdom of Archie Bunker* also appeared. A bigot had become a pop icon.

With *All in the Family*'s great popularity came a closer examination of its premise and its hero. Critics complained that by depicting Archie as a lovable bigot, rather than a hateful, limited man, the series condoned his behavior. Bill Cosby commented that watching it was like seeing "a junkie shoot up." Lucille Ball compared the show to the days of ancient Rome when "the Romans let human beings be eaten by lions, while they laughed and drank—that was entertainment. But I'm tired of the ugly."

Debating the series's influence on the young, Black and white, *Ebony* questioned why a television program chose to use such a deplorable racist character as a source of humor. "He's a wholly ignorant, lower-middle-class, white Anglo-Saxon Protestant, beer-bellied bigot," the magazine commented. "This hero, this St. Archie, must be dealt with seriously for he has become much more than a mere television character; he has become a social force engaging the minds and hearts of vast millions of Americans—many of them the people who will significantly control Black lives . . . from behind desks in employment offices and welfare aid bureaus in City Halls and police stations, in state legislatures and the Congress, in the White House."

As much as other characters might argue with him, Archie remained the series hero: the man the audience usually rooted for; the man who appeared to speak a truth that others denied. It didn't help matters that Carroll O'Connor played the role so brilliantly (and was supported by an excellent cast), drawing us to Archie even when we were repulsed, etching in a vulnerability that we may have felt the character had no right to. Had Archie not been made so likable, the series might have struck some serious blows at racism. But then had he not been likable, viewers would not have watched him weekly. In *The New York Times*, writer Laura Z. Hobson, the author of the novel *Gentleman's Agreement*, which had attacked American anti-Semitism in the 1940s, pointed out the series's fundamental "dishonesty." *All in the Family* was considered groundbreaking partly because of its frank language; the idea that here was a show daring to, well, "call a spade a spade." But Hobson commented that by using such words as "hebe" and "coon" rather than harsher, more realistic terms such as "kike" and "nigger," the series softened Archie and made him a more acceptable hero. Ultimately, Archie's weekly presence legitimized a certain brand of racism.

Initially, even CBS's chairman, William S. Paley, thought the show was vulgar and offensive. But he changed his mind once *All in the Family* became such a hit. Aware that some social critics felt the show was healthy because it helped audiences deal honestly with their suppressed feelings, Paley commissioned a study of the series's effect. He assumed it would prove that the program opened people's minds—and thus silence its critics. But the study claimed just the opposite—that rather than eliminating misconceptions and prejudices, *All in the Family* simply reinforced long-standing attitudes. Sally Bedell Smith reported that a CBS executive said to Paley, "What shall we do with it? If we release it, we'll have to cancel the show." Paley responded, "Destroy it. Throw it out."

Toward the end of the series—once Mike and Gloria moved out of the Bunker household, once Edith had died, once Archie was left to raise little Stephanie Mills on his own—other African American characters such as Polly and Ed Swanson (Janet MacLachlan and Mel Bryant) and Ellen Canby (Barbara Meek) appeared. Some of the sting was taken out of Archie's bite too. He looked a bit pathetic. But his bigotry remained as acceptable as ever.

In retrospect, the series remains an innovative piece of work that brought racism front and center in the daily lives of sitcom characters. *All in the Family* indicated that perhaps the American family could never be completely understood without examining its attitudes about race. Through the neighbors the Jeffersons, *All in the Family* also presented assertive Black characters, well aware of their supposed place in American society and not ready to accept the same old crap. George, Henry, and Lionel Jefferson all let Archie know their feelings. That may explain why the series appealed to some African American viewers. Racial confrontation (as well as all sorts of other confrontations) had become a part of the most engaging and escapist of television formats, the sitcom. In a sense, it had succeeded in a way that some had hoped *Julia* might: social issues were now raised weekly on a sitcom. In the end, *All in the Family* led the way to significant spin-offs, including *Maude*, based on the experiences of Edith's very liberal cousin Maude; *Good Times*, centered on the family life of Maude's outspoken black maid, Florida; and *The Jeffersons*, built around the lives of the Bunkers' next-door neighbors. But even before those series, the success of *All in the Family* led the way for another Norman Lear sitcom spotlighting some of the old ethnic humor and jokes, *Sanford and Son*.

REDD FOXX: THE WORLD ACCORDING TO FRED SANFORD

Like *All in the Family*, *Sanford and Son* sprang from another British sitcom, *Steptoe and Son*. There had been hopes for an American version for years. White actors Lee Tracy and Aldo Ray had made a pilot for the series that didn't sell. Then Norman Lear and Bud Yorkin planned to do it with Barnard Hughes and Paul Sorvino. But that didn't work either. Finally, Lear and Yorkin decided to re-create it as a Black show, which in the early 1970s was considered daring. Both men had noticed the altered perspectives already then taking root in popular culture. Not only had *The Flip Wilson Show* proved that a Black TV star could appeal to a mainstream audience but so too had such crossover music stars of the 1960s and early 1970s as Motown's Supremes and Temptations as well as Atlantic's queen of soul, Aretha Franklin. Younger audiences were conferring superstar status on African American entertainers who in the past would have been denied such a broad audience. The success of Black movies like *Shaft* and *Cotton Comes to Harlem* was also a sign of a new African American audience.

Premiering on NBC in January 1972, *Sanford and Son* revolved around the exploits of a Los Angeles junk dealer, Fred Sanford (Redd Foxx), and his adult son, Lamont (Demond Wilson). At age thirty-four, Lamont, often at odds with his father, yearned to be out of his father's home and on his own. But every attempt by Lamont to leave was thwarted by the scheming, cantankerous, elder Sanford. Fred's favorite ploy, whenever confronted with Lamont's rebellion, was to lean back, clutch his chest, feign a heart attack, and cry out to his deceased wife, "Elizabeth, it's the big one! I'm coming to join you, honey!"

Redd Foxx and Demond Wilson in the sitcom
that soared in the ratings

Also on hand was a rowdy network of Sanford and son cronies: Bubba (Don Bexley), Melvin (Slappy White), Julio (Gregory Sierra), the white police officer Swanhauser (Noam Pitlik), and Fred's attractive lady friend, the nurse Donna Harris (Lynn Hamilton). Later the show brought on Whitman Mayo as the slow-moving Grady and that deliriously crafty scene-stealer LaWanda Page as the infamous Aunt Esther, Fred's sister-in-law, who couldn't abide him. Whenever she was upset by Sanford's antics, Aunt Esther would give him a mean look, raise her handbag, and warn, "Watch out, sucka!"

Sanford and Son soared in the ratings and became the most successful Black-oriented series in television history. *Ebony* called it "one of the brightest half hours to grace the TV tube." But as with *All in the Family, Sanford and Son* had its critics, who complained that here were two childlike Black men with almost no ambition or drive. Fred Sanford—lazy and conniving—seemed like little more than the familiar coon figure, forever scheming to get out of work, forever trying to *get over* on someone.

Sensitive to the criticism, Foxx wanted it known that he paid attention to racial comments in the scripts. When a line referred to a sapphire ring, he objected because that had been the name of Kingfish's wife. "I called it a red ruby. I just don't want the word *sapphire* on my show," he said. "I don't want the show to be *Amos 'n' Andy*." But that seemed to be missing the real point. Fred Sanford's arguments with Aunt Esther were the loudest and most cantankerous verbal slugfests since the days of Kingfish and Sapphire; in fact, they seemed like little more than a replay. As played by the brown-skinned Page, Aunt Esther was one more in a lineup of old-style hootin' and hollerin' desexed mammy-like figures, battling a triflin' Black male. And Grady, who talked as slowly as he moved and often was almost unintelligible, at times seemed like a shocking update of Stepin Fetchit.

In a stinging article in *The New York Times*, African American writer Eugenia Collier accused the show of being "white to the core," of "encasing whiteness in a black skin." Missing altogether, she complained, was an African American consciousness. "There is nothing here that has traditionally motivated black humor—no redemptive suffering, no strength, no tragedy behind the humor," Collier wrote. "Fred Sanford and his little boy Lamont, conceived by white minds and based upon a white value system, are not strong black men capable of achieving—or even understanding—liberation. They are merely two more American child-men. We—all of us—need to be surrounded by positive—and *true*—images of blackness based upon black realities, not upon white aberrations."

Other aspects of the series would trouble later generations. Fred Sanford—who we know has himself encountered discrimination—was sometimes a very intolerant, bigoted man. One might not object to Fred's lack of tolerance for his oppressor, the generic white man. But his comments about other minorities were not as funny as the writers may have thought. Fred's primary opposition to Lamont's friendship with the character Julio seemed to be that the latter was Puerto Rican. Today one cringes at some of the dialogue. When Lamont told his father that Julio had borrowed his truck, a testy Fred said, "Now you gone and got Puerto Rican all over our truck."

Sanford also made cutting remarks about Asians. "I can't eat that Chink food," said Sanford. "Those people do their cooking and laundry in the same pot." Other times, his homophobia came to the fore. When Lamont planned to leave Watts to become a seaman, Sanford promptly warned him that all seamen were gay. Lamont couldn't be asking for a worse fate, Fred seemed to be saying. Sometimes chuckling at Fred Sanford was like laughing at Archie: you did so at your own peril; and you might be shocked to discover what you had been programmed to think of as funny.

What can account for the fact that this series was so "beloved" by viewers, Black and white? Some might argue that the white audiences felt comfortable because none of its perceptions (or rather misconceptions) about African Americans was challenged by the series; the images alleviated white fears of Black anger. Watching *Sanford and Son*, all that political dissent and turmoil of the 1960s seemed like no more than a bad dream. These old-style genial Negroes had *some* gripes but posed no threat. Once again, here were entertaining people not about to disrupt the system; they were living in their own universe, which in essence was a fun place. Of course, all of that was partly true.

But for the African American audience, something else transpired on the show. No white critic may ever understand the pleasure the African American audience still experienced (at this time in history) at again seeing African American performers relating to one another, establishing a semblance of a Black community and an approximation of Black life and culture. On this level, *Sanford and Son*'s appeal was similar to that of *Amos 'n' Andy* and *Beulah*. Sanford, that lazy good-for-nothing schemer, seemed to live on his own terms; and was willing to fight to the end to preserve those terms. Nor was he ever as docile as one might have thought. There was the pleasure of seeing Sanford speak his mind, especially about race. When Fred's sister married a white man, Fred couldn't come up with enough nouns to describe the man: "Mr. Intermarry," "Paleface," "Snow Whitey," "Honky," and "White Tornado" were just a few. On another episode when a white nurse was about to give Fred a chest X-ray, he cried out, "I ain't going in there with that ugly old white woman." Sometimes the racial comments were more subtle, more biting, and more significant. When a white police officer, investigating a burglary, asked if the felons were "colored," Sanford answered, "Yeah . . . *white.*" Redd Foxx delivered the line as if he'd been waiting all his life to say it.

This was the crucial difference between *Sanford and Son* and *Amos 'n' Andy*. *Sanford and Son* frequently acknowledged racism, even when it didn't challenge it. Unlike the heroine of *Julia*, the characters had no desire to integrate. The lives of Sanford, Aunt Esther, Melvin, and Lamont were complete without the presence of whites, who were automatically viewed suspiciously. *Sanford and Son* never paused long enough to deliver stinging covert comments on racism and its effects. But the very nature of Fred and Lamont's lives—the junkyard that they lived in—indicated they had to make do with the few bones thrown their way. Had they expressed real anger about that, the series would have gone in a different and provocative direction. Still, racism always seemed to hover above their lives. The series's perspective was also strengthened by the work of African American director Stan Lathan on some episodes and also the Black writer Ilunga Adell.

Aunt Esther, Bubba, Grady, and the others (who were hardly upwardly mobile or middle-class) seemed—through their language, gestures, mannerisms—rooted in a shared cultural identity. The problem, however, with the ethnicity of the characters on *Sanford and Son*, as well as with characters on other series to follow, was that it was often forced and exaggerated—and it was treated exclusively in comic terms. By not showing a great enough diversity within the African American community (ethnicity could be conveyed in many different ways),

Sanford and Son never accurately expressed what the African American audience then thought. But the series touched on the needs of a new segment of the African American audience of its time.

On another level, *Sanford and Son* was a sad series; its Fred and Lamont were just sitting, waiting for something to happen in their lives. Fred was amusing but he couldn't see any new possibilities for himself. Lamont became pathetic because, though still a young man, he was too weak to break away and establish a new life. Only late in the series did Lamont become engaged to a divorcée named Janet (Marlene Clark), who had a young son. But then the series went off the air. For the most part, Fred and Lamont were like Beckett's two tramps, Vladimir and Estragon, confined to a just as hopeless, if cluttered and claustrophobic, rather than minimalist, landscape. They too seemed to wait for a Mr. Godot to alter *something* in their paltry existence.

Sanford and Son left the airways after five seasons—and many disputes. Foxx fought with the NBC brass about his salary, his dressing room, his treatment. During the 1974–75 season, he didn't appear in the first two (and some later) episodes because of contractual disagreements. Later he signed to star in a variety show for another network. Then Demond Wilson demanded more money. Finally, NBC shut down the show.

But that was not the end of the *Sanford* story. A few seasons earlier, NBC had launched a *Sanford and Son* spin-off, *Grady*, which recounted the adventures of Sanford's buddy Grady Wilson. It folded after less than four months. But NBC still didn't want to give up entirely on the *Sanford and Son* franchise. In the fall of 1977, the network aired *Sanford Arms*, which starred Theodore Wilson as Phil Wheeler, a widower with two children who puts down a mortgage on the Sanford property and opens a hotel. LaWanda Page appeared as Aunt Esther, still feisty as she collected the monthly payments from Wheeler. Other supporting characters from the old show appeared: Grady, Bubba, Woody (Esther's husband). But without Fred Sanford, viewers had no interest in *Sanford Arms*. NBC dumped it after less than a month.

Sanford and Son's stars struggled to keep their careers alive. Georgia-born Demond Wilson had begun his career as a child performer in a Broadway revival of *The Green Pastures* and later in a television production of *The Children's Hour*. After studying acting at the American Community Theater and Hunter College, he served in Viet-

NBC tries holding on to the Sanford *franchise:*
LaWanda Page as Aunt Esther in
Sanford Arms

nam, then resumed his career on stage in *The Boys in the Band* and *Ceremonies in Dark Old Men* and on television in daytime soap operas and episodes of *Mission: Impossible* and *All in the Family.*

After leaving *Sanford and Son*, Wilson starred opposite Denise Nicholas in the series *Baby, I'm Back*, premiering in January 1978. It was the tale of a Black father who deserts his wife and children only to resurface years later—just when she has had him declared legally dead. What was dead was the series concept: one more image of an absentee African American father. The show went off the air in August 1978. Four years later, Wilson appeared with Ron Glass in *The New Odd Couple*. Though he made guest appearances on other programs, he never attained the kind of television stardom he'd had in the past.

Sanford and Son brought Redd Foxx the mainstream stardom that had been a long time coming. Foxx had already been in show business—in a career fraught with many ups and downs—for over thirty years. Born in St. Louis in 1922, he was the son of an electrician. His real name was John Elroy Sanford, which the producers later used for the series. (His older brother was named Fred.) He came up with his stage name after friends told him he was sly as a fox. He also admired the baseball player Jimmie Foxx.

As a teenager, he ran away to Chicago to be with his mother, who worked there as a domestic. After a year in high school, Foxx quit to play with two friends in a washtub band. They entertained on street corners. In the summer of 1939, the trio went to New York to break into show business. There, they also performed on street corners, sometimes earning as much as fifty dollars a night each. When World War II broke out, the group disbanded. Many lean days followed. Foxx sometimes slept on rooftops and in doorways. Arrested for having slept in a hallway and stealing a bottle of milk, he spent a short time incarcerated on Rikers Island. Afterward, to make ends meet, he worked as a short-order cook, a busboy, and a cart pusher in the garment district. In Harlem, he washed dishes and was called Chicago Red because of his hair. He became friendly with another redheaded young man from Michigan, Malcolm Little, who was called Detroit Red. Foxx was "the funniest dishwasher on this earth," said Detroit Red, who later became known as Malcolm X.

After the war, Foxx teamed with Slappy White in a comedy act. For a spell, they were successful, earning about $450 a night in 1947. But a big engagement at Broadway's Palace Theater flopped. Afterward they performed with singer Dinah Washington in her show in California. In 1951, their act broke up. Foxx kept performing but to stay financially afloat he also worked as a sign painter in Los Angeles. He didn't know it but another twenty years would pass before he made it to the big time.

Nonetheless, on he plowed, appearing at clubs and theaters on the chitlin circuit, slowly building a following at theaters like the Regal in Chicago, the Howard in Washington, and the Uptown in Philadelphia. By 1956, he cut the first of his comedy party albums, *Laff of the Party*, for Dooto Records. On his recordings, Foxx told scatological jokes that shocked listeners but kept them in hysterics. Before Lenny Bruce, he had broken one of the comedy establishment's golden rules, having mastered not only the dirty joke but also the risqué story—and with language that would never be acceptable in polite circles. Following a contractual dispute, he quit the Dooto label but was prohibited from recording for any other company. Frank Sinatra intervened and worked out an arrangement for Foxx to record on Sinatra's Reprise Records. Foxx made forty-nine albums that sold over 10 million copies.

Working his way up from the chitlin circuit: Redd Foxx, whose "blue"
comedy albums were best-sellers within the African American
community for years, but who was almost
unknown by the cultural mainstream

Foxx became well known within Black America and also within the hip circles of the entertainment industry. "Redd was the comedic father of us all," said Bill Cosby. "He was the first of the *urban* Black comics, and Dick Gregory and Flip Wilson and all the others who came later took from *him*," said Quincy Jones.

A break across the color barrier came when he was booked into New York's Basin St. East in 1959. Trying to keep the act clean, he almost bombed. But Steve Lawrence and singer Eydie Gormé, who were in the audience, shouted, "Do your *real* act, Redd." "I was scared," said Foxx, "but I did it, and the people loved it." Later NBC host Hugh Downs brought Foxx on *The Today Show*. Foxx again cleaned up his material but was funny and clicked.

After other television appearances, including *A Time for Laughter* in 1968 and *Soul* in 1969, Foxx was offered more lucrative club bookings.

He became a regular at Las Vegas's Hilton International Hotel, signing a $960,000-a-year contract. When Bud Yorkin saw him as a junkman in the 1970 film *Cotton Comes to Harlem*, he knew he'd found the character for the series he was about to produce. Afterward even Foxx was surprised by the tremendous success of *Sanford and Son*, which "made it in twelve weeks," he said. "Yet Redd Foxx has been around for thirty-three years. What took so long?" He brought his friends Slappy White and LaWanda Page (who had gone to school with him in St. Louis) onto the show. Viewers saw that these were performers attuned to one another's moods, rhythms, and timing, which helped make *Sanford and Son*, like *Amos 'n' Andy*, one of television's best ensemble casts.

Foxx's endurance and his long years as an icon in the African American community made *Sanford and Son* all the more significant to the Black television audience. Even without the blue humor, he was still funny, but older and irascible, demanding and eccentric, and operating like the king of his own universe. For the Black audience, watching Foxx was like seeing itself finally triumphing after so many turns and disappointments. Maybe hard work and resilience did pay off.

Once Foxx left *Sanford and Son*, he starred in the ABC variety program *The Redd Foxx Show*, which lasted a little over four months. Making amends with NBC, he had another stab at his Sanford character in the series *Sanford*, debuting in March 1980. Now Fred Sanford was back in his Watts junkyard. But Lamont, on his own at last, was working on the Alaska pipeline. Sanford's partners were Rollo (Nathaniel Taylor), from the original series, and Cal (Dennis Burkley), an overweight white Southerner. Fred courted a wealthy Beverly Hills widow, Evelyn "Eve" Lewis (Marguerite Ray). Also around were Aunt Esther's son Cliff (Clinton Derricks-Carroll); Eve's daughter Cissy (Suzanne Stone); Eve's brother Winston (Percy Rodriguez); and Eve's feisty maid Clara (Cathy Cooper). It wasn't a very good mix. NBC tried to fix the show, but it soon left the network lineup.

Afterward, Foxx was beset by personal and financial problems. A big spender, he went through much of his fortune. Of his three marriages, two ended in divorce, with alimony payments that also dwindled his finances. Millions in recording royalties, he complained, had never been paid. Known as a soft touch, he had also lent money to friends. "I've been cheated more than most people because I'm gullible and I'm a target," he once said. The Internal Revenue Service demanded nearly $3 million for back taxes, penalties, and interest. Eventually, the IRS entered Foxx's Las Vegas home, taking his possessions. Afterward Eddie Murphy cast Foxx in his film *Harlem Nights* and in the 1991 CBS series *The Royal Family*. Performing opposite Della Reese, Foxx was as feisty and engaging as ever. But during a 1991 rehearsal of the new show, Foxx suddenly collapsed and was rushed to the hospital, where he died of a massive heart attack. He was sixty-eight years old. Foxx was never able to duplicate his astounding Sanford success, but he didn't have to. Having created one of television's most memorable characters, he had become one of its greatest stars.

MAKE WAY FOR FLORIDA, J.J., AND THE NEW SITCOMS

The extraordinary success of *Sanford and Son* led the way for other Black sitcoms that followed throughout the decade. During any given week, viewers could tune in to such series as *Roll Out!*, *Good Times*, *That's My Mama*, *What's Happening!!*, *Grady*, *Sanford Arms*, *Baby, I'm Back*, and the immensely successful *The Jeffersons*. Suddenly, the African American series—or at least the sitcom—had commercial validity.

Among the first to appear was another Norman Lear production, *Good Times*, which premiered in the fall of 1974. Its central character, Florida Evans, played by Esther Rolle, was already known to viewers, having first appeared for two seasons as the maid on the sitcom *Maude*. The ninth of eighteen children, Rolle was the daughter of poor Bahamians who had moved to Pompano, Florida, where she was born. Once her parents saved enough money, they bought a small truck farm. But Rolle grew up under harsh conditions. She watched her mother give birth to triplets, all of whom died within twenty-four hours because there were no hospitals for Blacks in the area. After moving to New York, Rolle enrolled in a drama course at the New School for Social Research. An original member of the Negro Ensemble Company, she also appeared on Broadway in such productions as *The Amen Corner*, *Blues for Mr. Charlie*, *The Crucible*, and *Purlie Victorious* and worked on television (the daytime soap *One Life to Live*). Then came her critically praised performance in Melvin Van Peebles's Broadway drama *Don't Play Us Cheap*. Afterward producers Norman Lear and Bud Yorkin approached Rolle about the part on *Maude*. But she turned them down. "I kept telling them, 'I won't leave New York to go out there and be a Hollywood maid,'" Rolle recalled. "Then Norman said, 'We don't want a Hollywood maid, Esther, we want a human being.' I said, 'You gonna let me have a say?' When he said yes, I accepted, because people follow images."

On *Maude*, Rolle's Florida was outspoken, clever, realistic, the embodiment of 1960s-style political correctness, yet at times a surprising symbol for preserving the status quo. During her first appearance when interviewed for a job in the household of Maude Findlay, Florida was told by Maude that she wouldn't have to do any of the things maids usually did. Maude insisted that Florida could use the front door rather than the back one. Not only could she take her meals with the family, she could also have cocktails with them every day.

But Florida would have none of that! She informed Maude that she'd prefer using the back door because she could carry the groceries in more easily there. She wanted to eat by herself. And as for cocktails—well, she didn't drink in the middle of the day.

Florida preferred to be a traditional maid *except* when it came to expressing her views. Weekly, she did so, and it was funny to see an African American woman so readily and knowingly matching wits with her employer. The difference between Rolle's maid and Hattie McDaniel's was that the *Maude* scripts stated emphatically that she was intelligent and assertive. Otherwise, though, Florida was not doing anything any "newer" than what McDaniel and Eddie "Rochester" Anderson had done years before. The scripts just congratulated themselves on their own liberalism. Quiet as it was kept, the scripts were also sometimes condescending in trumpeting the character's assertiveness. What a surprise, the writers seemed to be saying, to find a middle-aged African American woman who could actually think for herself! Still, in the tradition of talented African American performers clutching tenaciously at dialogue or scenes that gave them a chance to develop self-empowered characters, Rolle played the role to the hilt. No entrance or exit ever went unnoticed. She seemed to be waiting to deliver a zinger—and viewers gleefully waited right along with her. She never disappointed. Her performance on *Maude* was often better timed and more intensely felt than some of the performances on *Good Times*.

On her last appearance on *Maude*, Florida made plans to leave the

Findlay home in Tuckahoe, New York, to be with her husband, then called Henry (and played by John Amos) in Harlem. He didn't want her to work anymore. Florida and Maude promised to visit each other. But Florida suddenly looked at Maude and said, "Mrs. Findlay, you know we'll never visit each other." "I know," Maude replied. It was a genuinely realistic moment.

On *Good Times*, Florida resided in Chicago rather than Harlem. There, she lived in a tenement on the South Side with her husband, now named James, and her three children: seventeen-year-old James Jr., called J.J. (Jimmie Walker); sixteen-year-old Thelma (BernNadette Stanis); and ten-year-old Michael (Ralph Carter). Weekly, the children argued with one another. Weekly, they were disciplined by their parents. Weekly, their lively neighbor Willona Woods (Ja'net DuBois) popped in to tell them all about her problems with men or life.

Good Times was considered a breakthrough because it acknowledged poverty and other urban ills confronting a segment of the African American community. Unlike *Sanford and Son*'s soft treatment of life in Watts, *Good Times* was edgy, pushy, and in-your-face about its issues. The opening theme song told of "temporary layoffs and easy-credit rip-offs" and "keeping your head above water." Various episodes dealt with teen alcoholism, gang warfare, unemployment, and busing.

Created by African American writers Eric Monte and Mike Evans (who had played Lionel Jefferson on *All in the Family*) and then developed into a series by Norman Lear, *Good Times* was also a TV rarity that presented a two-parent African American family household. John Amos played James with warmth and intelligence. What made his character all the more affecting was that he was no blind victim of the system. James understood its workings, which made him feel at times all the more trapped and frustrated. Yet he was the head of his household. The children treated him with respect. And Florida seemed determined that his home be his castle; that while the outside world might try to emasculate him, within the walls of their apartment, he would always have the last word.

The dialogue could be biting and was often laced with topical political references. While James, always in and out of work, struggled to hold his family together, he was quick to articulate his plight as an untrained Black man in America. Returning home after unsuccessfully searching for a job, he told his wife, "I lost out on the last one by only four years of college, four years of high school, and two years of grade school." On another occasion, unable to find a better job, James recalled that "the President said he was going to bring us all together, but no one told us it would be on a breadline." Florida also got to comment on the President and foreign policy. "Mama, if the President made two hundred thousand dollars, how come he only paid seven hundred dollars in taxes?" the daughter Thelma asked. "Maybe he took Israel to lunch," Florida replied. Racism hovered over the family's lives. So did the aftermath of Watergate and Vietnam. Traditional American values were openly questioned. And the series touched on some of the disillusionment that Americans, Black and white, felt about their nation during the post-Nixon years of Gerald Ford's presidency in the mid-1970s.

Generally, *Good Times* was praised by the critics. "On the one side, Black viewers are being afforded material that provides immediate personal and psychic identification," wrote John J. O'Connor in *The New York Times*. "They no longer have to be content with *Father Knows Best*, which was unreal even for many white Americans. On the other side, whites are being given glimpses of Black life that, however simplified, can't help but weaken artificial racial barriers." *Ebony* said it offered "the tube's best effort to date at showing a real slice of ghetto Black life."

Yet provocative as *Good Times* sometimes appeared, it was never as good as most of us wanted to believe, even in its first two seasons. Too often it relied on typical television-style humor. Someone might ask Willona, "Don't you ever come in without making a joke?" Her response: "No, but last night I went out with one." Thelma might tell J.J., "If you was born in Detroit, you'd have been recalled for being dangerously ugly."

Seen today, poor Florida appears to go overboard to stand by her man. On one episode, Florida returned to school to get a high school diploma. She then was so busy correcting James's grammar and discussing child psychology that he became opposed to her continuing education. Were the writers suggesting that an educated woman runs the risk of disrupting a happy marriage? Finally, Florida and James have a fight. Afterward she comes to the conclusion that "what's right is my husband and family, what's wrong is anything that comes between us." Then the writers, having made their real point, tried to weasel out by making another. James comes up with a better idea. Why don't they both go back to school? To boost the African American male's manhood, must the African American woman subjugate herself? Must she always let him make the important decisions? Too often that's precisely what *Good Times* seemed to say.

The series also delighted in paying lip service to political trends and attitudes of the period. But its content rarely matched its rhetoric. Weekly, viewers were being programmed to laugh about poverty and social ills. Weekly, viewers were being asked to accept the fact that despite the problems, this Black family was all love and heart. Perhaps there was nothing inherently wrong with that idea. But in some respects, the series permitted the white critics and mainstream viewers a certain condescension toward the household. Why should anyone *seriously* fret about the problems of the Evanses when they themselves could still laugh and not be *profoundly* troubled? There was value, of course, in the fact that issues were being acknowledged in a Black situation comedy. But, shockingly, the issues were mostly fodder for one-liners, jokes, and gags.

Early on, *Good Times* also showed where its heart really lay by shifting its focus to the character J.J. Tall, beanpole skinny, given to mugging, clowning, and flashing his teeth, Jimmie Walker, when cast in *Good Times*, was a stand-up comic. Neither trained in nor aware of the technique and concentration required to create a rounded, dimensional character, Walker had little help from the writers, who exploited his character for laughs. Jimmie Walker's J.J. often dressed outlandishly—floppy hats, bright shirts, ill-fitting jackets—like the old-style coon figure and usually didn't seem to have a serious thought in his head. More often than not, he appeared most interested in razzing sister Thelma. One morning Thelma innocently asked, "You want some breakfast?" "Don't be fixing me nothin'," J.J. responded. "My stomach ain't insured against no food poisoning." On the series's second episode, J.J. uttered the line that became his trademark. Following a run-in with the police, he boasted, "They knew they were in trouble, once they realized they were dealing with Kid *Dyn-o-mite*." True, he uttered the line with a dopey panache. But often the fun of hearing it was that you wondered if J.J. could really say such a big word as dynamite. J.J. was a blatant caricature.

Jimmie Walker as J.J.

For a spell, J.J. became a pop hero and a favorite of kids around the country, who gleefully imitated him and bought J.J. T-shirts, belt buckles, and pajamas. They loved the Dyn-o-mite line, which was heard in schoolyards around the country. For children, he was as unreal as Saturday morning cartoons; they loved the exaggerations, the wild getups, the stylized movements.

For others, the character became an embarrassment. Here was television's most visible young African American male, and he was devoid of any signs of maturity or intelligence. To have given him any kind of challenging political consciousness seemed unthinkable to the writers, most of whom were white. Instead the only child in the Evans family with any political or historical awareness was the youngest child, Michael, who wrote essays on his "favorite people" such as Malcolm X and Jesse Jackson. Of course, his political utterings were acceptable—in TV terms—because they came from the mouth of an innocent Black kid, hardly someone who might be a threat to the political status quo.

When J.J.'s coonery was criticized, the writers sought to round him out. For some reason, they thought it would help if J.J. were turned into a ladies' man. But Walker always played the character in such a broad manner—with eye pops and facial contortions—that it was hard to believe any woman could ever take him seriously. The writers also attempted to deepen the character by making him an artist (with actual paintings done by the African American artist Ernie Barnes). But nothing about J.J. ever suggested he had any artistic impulse or temperament. Plain and simple, he just seemed jive, juvenile, and asinine. In time, viewers could anticipate Walker's every move and gesture. Built into the scripts was an element of self-mockery, but not for the character. Rather the scripts mocked and parodied Jimmie Walker's performing style, his looks, and his persona.

Eventually, other cast members became troubled by the J.J. character. "He's 18 and he doesn't work. He can't read and write. He doesn't think," Esther Rolle told *Ebony*. "Little by little—with the help of the artist [Walker], I suppose, because they couldn't do that to me—they have made him more stupid and enlarged the role." She added, "I resent the imagery that says to Black kids that you can make it by standing on the corner saying 'Dyn-o-mite!' "

Other problems flared up on *Good Times*. By now, John Amos was a seasoned pro, accustomed to the tough and competitive worlds of professional sports and network television. Having grown up in East Orange, New Jersey, he had won a football scholarship to Long Beach City College. Later he enrolled at Colorado State University. Afterward he played professional football with the United Football League. In the late 1960s, he began his television career, first as a writer for *The Leslie Uggams Show*, then as Gordy on *The Mary Tyler Moore Show*. Other roles followed in the film *Sweet Sweetback's BaadAsssss Song* and such television shows as *The President's Plane Is Missing*, *The Funny Side*, *The World's Greatest Athlete*, and *Maude*.

Within the industry, Amos became known as an uncompromising actor. Following a heated contractual dispute with Lear's Tandem Productions, John Amos was dropped from the series following the second season. Amos told the press that his only regret about leaving *Good Times* was that "it might mean the show would revert to the matriarchal thing—the fatherless Black family. TV is the most powerful medium we have, and there just are not enough Black male images—which I think James Evans is—on TV."

John Amos as James Evans and Esther Rolle as his wife, Florida, with their rambunctious son J.J. (Jimmie Walker), who seemed to cause problems for them on and off the set of Good Times

The series disposed of the character by having him go to Mississippi to work at a garage. There, he meets his demise in a car accident. *Good Times* tried to handle the death of James with a degree of seriousness within its gag-a-minute format. But the episode seemed forced and fake. Organizations like the National Black Media Coalition complained (just as Amos had predicted) that the series now fed into the familiar stereotype of a female-dominated Black family. The most serious and mature African American male on the weekly primetime series schedule had vanished, leaving a noticeable void. Afterward Florida was given a new husband, Carl Dixon (Moses Gunn). But even more emphasis was placed on J.J. as he became the technical head of the Evans household. Then, after the 1976–77 season, Esther Rolle quit the show.

The next season presented a special one-hour broadcast that introduced the little girl Penny Gordon, played by Janet Jackson. A victim of child abuse, she was adopted by the neighbor Willona. Here *Good Times* struggled again with the conflicting drives. On the one hand, it wanted to deal with an important issue. On the other hand, it felt compelled to keep viewers entertained with jokes. Though some critics lauded the effort, nothing about the child abuse episodes rang true.

Also introduced was the character Nathan Bookman (Johnny Brown), the hefty superintendent of the building where the Evanses resided. He seemed to be there mainly as the target of fat jokes. Thelma eventually married a football star, Keith Anderson (Ben Powers), who looked like a prince ready to lift her out of a world of poverty. But during the wedding ceremony—wouldn't you know it—J.J. accidentally trips the guy, causing an injury that puts his million-dollar career at stake. All ended well with Keith's recuperation—and the return of Esther Rolle. But *Good Times* had lost its steam and disappeared from the primetime schedule after five seasons.

Looking back on the series, viewers can easily understand why J.J. was criticized. The wonder is that he was popular for so long. But also glaring are the roles of the women on *Good Times*. While Esther Rolle's Florida can speak her mind and is fairly independent, she seems locked into a traditional nurturing box.

The most overlooked and perhaps saddest character was poor Thelma. Fortunately, she could exchange barbs but mainly her role was to react, not to initiate much action. Mostly, the scripts called for her to stand around, looking sweet and vaguely yearning for something else. The writers showed no interest in sensitively developing her as a young African American teenager on the brink of womanhood. Even her ideal marriage seems merely a plot device, a way of bringing in the deus ex machina for the family's happy ending.

The most interesting female character was Ja'net DuBois's Willona. DuBois had a racy, spicy way with the most banal of lines. "Make my coffee like I like my men," she said. "Hot. Black. And strong." Often viewers couldn't wait for her to enter the Evans apartment and relieve the tedium of life with J.J. With more attention and care from the writers, hers might have developed into an unusual portrait of a working woman. Willona didn't work because she wanted a fabulous career. She worked partly because she enjoyed it—partly because she *had* to. Away from work, she wanted a decent love life. But, independent and free-spirited, she was never so starved for male attention that she became a pushover or doormat. Of course, the series suggested that this kind of woman might never find a man. Actress DuBois, however, created a rounded character who could be nurturing (to Penny), domesticated, able to run her own household, and all the while hold on to a very sexy sexuality. Her single-parent adoption of Penny was one of the few serious "new" issues on the show handled with subtlety and a modicum of sensitivity.

Sometimes we looked at Willona and felt that beneath the snappy one-liners and the beautiful smile, her heart was breaking. In many un-expected ways, she was a precursor to the pop images of African American women that turned up in the 1990s in novels and films such as *Waiting to Exhale* and *How Stella Got Her Groove Back.* Yet ultimately the scriptwriters didn't take Willona far enough. DuBois herself admit-ted that her role paid the rent, "but there's got to be something that says more about the real me. I'm about love and I'm about feeling. Don't make me insensitive to life. Everything is not a joke."

Once *Good Times* ended, few of its stars stayed in the spotlight. Not much was heard from cast members BernNadette Stanis and Ralph Carter. Ja'net DuBois worked occasionally in such films as *A Piece of the Action* and *I'm Gonna Git You Sucka.* She also collaborated with Jeff Barry to create the song "Movin' On Up" for the series *The Jeffersons.* In the 1990s, she appeared on *The Wayans Bros.* and provided the voice for a character on the animated series *The PJs.*

Esther Rolle fared better than most of the performers. She walked off with an Emmy as Outstanding Supporting Actress in a Limited Se-ries or Special for her performance in *The Summer of My German Sol-dier.* But she often found herself relegated to roles beneath her in *To Dance with the White Dog* and *Message from Nam* and never worked as much as you might have hoped. John Amos kept his dignity in just about everything else he did, most notably in *Roots* and in films like *Coming to America* and *Die Hard 2.* He also was a cast member in such series as the short-lived *Future Cop, Hunter, 704 Hauser Street,* and *In the House.* Of course, *Good Times*'s latecomer, little Janet Jackson, went on to the series *Diff'rent Strokes* and *Fame* before becoming who else but Janet Jackson, pop superstar.

Badly hit, though, was Jimmie Walker. With his appearance in the

Sidney Poitier film *Let's Do It Again*, it looked as if a movie career might take off. But that didn't happen. Walker went into the 1980 series *B.A.D. Cats*—a cop show co-starring Michelle Pfeiffer and LaWanda Page—but it folded after only five telecasts. In March 1983, he starred in another series, *At Ease*—described as a 1980s version of the old Sgt. Bilko show, *You'll Never Get Rich*—but by July 1983 it was off the air. In the 1990s, he appeared in guest shots on such programs as David Letterman's *Late Show* and *Politically Incorrect*, on which he was weirdly fascinating to watch. Something about Jimmie Walker still seemed unreal and comic-strip-like. Though he continued to play clubs, Walker's career never regained its momentum. He was a prime example of one of those stars that TV ate up and then spat out.

Other programs quickly came and went, as TV producers and the networks tried to cash in on the appeal of the Black-cast sitcom. CBS brought on *Roll Out!* in the fall of 1973. Set in France during World War II, the series revolved around the adventures of the mostly Black 5050th Trucking Company, based on the real-life unit known as the Red Ball Express, which traveled through dangerous territory to get supplies to the troops on the front lines. The lead characters were Sweet (Stu Gilliam) and Jed (Hilly Hicks), two likable louts who, along with other soldiers, seemed to spend a lot of their free time at the nightclub of Madame Delacort (Penny Santon).

It's hard to imagine how anyone could think a weekly series about war was funny. But *Hogan's Heroes* had been successful. And in the early 1970s *M*A*S*H* had become a hit. *Roll Out!*—with a cast that included Mel Stewart, Darrow Igus, Garrett Morris, Theodore Wilson, Val Bisoglio, and Ed Begley Jr.—seemed like a "darkened" clone of that latter series. Despite some surprisingly lively moments and some good performances, *Roll Out!* wasn't a hit and went off the air after three months.

A slight and unformed show like *That's My Mama* (1974–75) starred Clifton Davis as Clifton Curtis, a young bachelor in Washington, D.C., who takes over the barbershop left to him by his deceased father. Mostly, Clifton Curtis liked to stand around and contentedly shoot the breeze with his cronies: the postman Earl (Theodore Wilson), the old-timers Wildcat and Josh (Jester Hairston and DeForest

Covan), and the streetwise philosopher Junior (Ted Lange). Everything might have been fine for poor Clifton had not Mama Eloise Curtis (Theresa Merritt) been around. She wanted her baby boy to settle down like his sister Tracy (Lynne Moody in the first season and Joan Pringle in the next).

Using a barbershop as a communal gathering place for African American males wasn't a bad idea at all. The scripts just failed to go anywhere with it. From the beginning, the episodes were thin. The first show centered on Clifton's dilemma when a young woman arrives carrying a baby, which she says he has fathered. *No way* is Clifton's response. Of course, he leaves it up to Mama to untangle everything, prove the child is not his, and set her sonny boy back on track. *That's My Mama* ran for a season and a half.

For Theresa Merritt, *That's My Mama* must have been a great professional disappointment. In selecting her to play the mother, the producers resorted to familiar typing. Merritt wasn't a bad actress. But large, fulsome, and brown-skinned, she fit the physical image of the acceptable, nurturing, seemingly sexless Black television mother. (The same was true of Esther Rolle on *Good Times.*) Her control over her dependent son was another portrait of a fundamentally weak Black man/strong Black woman. Yet again television was wasting an interesting talent. The role of jolly Eloise Curtis drew nothing out of Merritt. In fact, it made her look as if she had no talent. Merritt, however, must have assumed that, after having worked through long and lean years in show business, *That's My Mama* was the big break that would take her career in a new direction. Born in Emporia, Virginia, in 1922, Merritt had grown up in Philadelphia, where, after the death of her mother, she was reared by an aunt and uncle. With aspirations to become an opera singer, she sang in her church choir and studied at the Settlement School of Music in Philadelphia and later at Temple University and New York University. In 1943, she made her Broadway debut as Frascetta in *Carmen Jones*. Afterward she toured as a backup singer with Harry Belafonte and also with rhythm and blues sensation Jackie Wilson. She also appeared in the theatrical productions *Trumpets of the Lord, Mule Bone, Golden Boy,* and as the maid in *F. Jasmine Addams,* a musical based on *The Member of the Wedding*.

Once *That's My Mama* left the airways, Merritt found work in such movies as *The Goodbye Girl, The Great Santini, All That Jazz, The Best*

Little Whorehouse in Texas, and *The Serpent and the Rainbow*. On Broadway, she appeared in *The Wiz* and *Division Street*. Then Merritt had an unexpected success in 1984 when she played the title role in the Broadway production of August Wilson's *Ma Rainey's Black Bottom*. Here again was a large, brown-skinned African American woman who at first glance may have struck some as a traditional mammy figure. But Merritt's Ma Rainey had power and an unexpected sexuality; she created a sometimes difficult, even impossible, character calling the shots in her life and never taking crap from anyone.

On television, she turned up in episodes of such series as *Beekman Place*, *Police Story*, *The Love Boat*, *Cosby*, *Law & Order*, and *N.Y.P.D. Blue*. Sometimes the roles elicited something powerful out of her. Merritt won Emmy nominations for her special *All About Mrs. Merritt* and the PBS miniseries *Concealed Enemies*.

Few viewers could forget those moments in an episode of *Law & Order* when she suddenly appeared in a scene or two—and stopped you cold. As the wife of a man who has disappeared (and who she fears may now be murdered), Merritt quietly goes to the district attorney's office, where she speaks to Sam Waterston and Carey Lowell. She looks like an ordinary, soft-spoken woman, respectful of the gatekeepers of the law. But her mood and tone slowly change when she feels betrayed by the district attorney. She explains that another lawyer has said her husband could have been located the night before. Unable to understand why no action was taken, she continues, "My husband might be alive. Tied up somewhere. Wondering why nobody's coming to help him."

Waterston tries to placate her. "We're doing everything we can to find him," he says. "Mrs. Titus," says Lowell, "we understand how hard this is for you." But Merritt's anger has grown. "What if it were your husband?" she lashes out at Lowell. Then she turns to Waterston. "Or your wife. What are you people here for?" she says harshly. Then she walks out quickly. You want the script to tell you more about her character. Actually, you want the episode to focus mainly on her because Merritt has suggested an emotional power that tells a story of its own. But such moments remained few and far between for Theresa Merritt. She died in 1998 at the age of seventy-five.

MOVIN' ON UP: GEORGE, LOUISE, AND FLORENCE

Norman Lear hit the ratings (and longevity) jackpot with *The Jeffersons*, which debuted on CBS in 1975 and stayed on the air for the next ten years. This *All in the Family* spin-off centered on Archie's testy neighbor George Jefferson, whose successful dry-cleaning business enabled him to move out of Queens into the domain of his dreams, Manhattan's hoity-toity Upper East Side. As the theme song indicated, the Jeffersons were "movin' on up." Here was a sitcom celebrating African American upward mobility—and also celebrating a hero every bit as cantankerous and biased as Archie Bunker. In fact, George Jefferson had the dubious distinction of being referred to as the Black Archie.

The new series comically dramatized George's adjustment to and enjoyment of his new world of money and, so he hoped, privilege. Surrounding him were a familiar TV-style motley crew: his wife, Louise (again played by Isabel Sanford), and son Lionel (first played by Mike Evans, then Damon Evans [no relation], then Mike Evans again); his neighbors Tom and Helen Willis (Franklin Cover and Roxie Roker), an interracial married couple with a daughter named Jenny (Berlinda Tolbert) who later married Lionel; George's outspoken mother, Olivia Jefferson (Zara Cully); an eccentric English neighbor, Harry Bentley (Paul Benedict); and the Jeffersons' maid Florence Johnston (Marla Gibbs). Later in the run, there appeared Allan Willis (Jay Hammer), the "white" son of Tom and Helen, and a street kid named Marcus Garvey (Ernest Harden Jr.), who worked in one of George's cleaners, located in the lobby of his apartment building.

George Jefferson was hell-bent on living the good life. Snobbish, arrogant, petty, narrow-minded, and insensitive, he yapped and yelled at almost anyone, including the very balanced, levelheaded Louise, whom he called Weesie. Throughout the run of the series, George's blatant social climbing often made him the butt of jokes, especially when he committed some immediately recognizable faux pas. When a guest in his home commented, "Those are beautiful occasional tables," George responded, "Yes, but we're gonna use them all the time, not just occasionally."

Blatant in his displeasure about being around whites, he poked fun at them every chance he got. He once talked about a game called Pin the Tail on the Honky. He also loathed the presence of the interracial

Movin' on up and hootin' and hollerin' all the way:
George Jefferson (Sherman Hemsley) with wife Louise
(right, Isabel Sanford) and the servant he couldn't
abide, Florence (Marla Gibbs)

Willises. He called the white Tom Willis "Mr. Day" and the Black Helen Willis, "Mrs. Night." He later referred to the two of them as the Zebra. On one episode, he asked Tom Willis, "Want a drink? How about a white mule?" When Tom asked exactly what that was, George answered, "A honky donkey."

The one person who truly caused George grief was his Black maid Florence. The two couldn't stand each other. George never missed an opportunity to criticize, even when she wasn't around. "Are you sure you don't want any lunch?" Louise asked George. "Did Florence cook it?" he asked. "Yes," said Louise. "Then I'm sure I don't want any lunch!" he answered.

The Jeffersons aspired to be nothing more than old-fashioned entertainment. The last thing on its mind was social issues or the state of

Black America. That may explain why the critics didn't take to it. *TV Guide*'s Cleveland Amory wrote that "this show is not good, pretty good or even fairly good. At best, it's not bad." *Ebony* commented that for "those who may still be looking for a deep and satisfying social significance in black shows on television, the wait goes on. Although *The Jeffersons* portrays blacks on a different socioeconomic level than other Black TV shows, it is nevertheless, like the others, broad comedy and has to be accepted as such."

At first glance, *The Jeffersons* was nothing more than a collection of jolly stereotypes. Sherman Hemsley hopped and bopped and carried on in such a stylized, hyperfrenetic manner that his character—though he wasn't lazy and he wasn't shuffling—seemed an update of the exaggerated comic coon. As for Louise, one only had to take a quick look at the large, browner Isabel Sanford to realize that she was meant to be but one more strong nurturing Black woman dealing with an irrational Black male. Often she seemed more motherly than wifely to childish George. Marla Gibbs's Florence fell in the tradition established by Hattie McDaniel: the comic, audacious, sometimes lazy Black maid.

The direction and writing of the series, which strove to be something of a 1970s-style farce with jokes flying fast and furious, succeeded in making the whole concoction work on *that* level. *The Jeffersons* was probably the liveliest and the most entertaining of the 1970s Black sitcoms. And with the exception of Redd Foxx in *Sanford and Son*, no sitcom stars of the era appealed to the African American audience in as intensely a personal way as those on *The Jeffersons*.

Ultimately, the Black audience liked George Jefferson, despite his contradictions or perhaps because of them. While on a maddening climb to "make it," he yearned for white signs and symbols of success and acceptance, and he lived by traditional capitalistic American values. Yet, paradoxically, George never wanted to be white. For the African American audience, it was refreshing to see a middle-class Black man who asserted himself and his racial identity at every opportunity.

Yet had the social climate in America not changed, *The Jeffersons* would never have succeeded. Its popularity in the mid-1970s to the early years of the Reagan era indicated the race problem was no longer a great priority for many Americans. Instead, the big issue was one of economics. In the early seasons of *All in the Family*, George Jefferson was mentioned but not seen. He had such an animosity for Archie (and white people) that he refused to set foot inside the home of this bigot. "There were no pallid racial jokes back then," wrote Bonnie Allen in *Essence*. "George was venomous, even in absentia. While his wife, brother-in-law and son played foil for Archie's racial epithets, George was busy turning his small business into a chain of dry cleaners. He was too committed to his Blackness to find a racist either entertaining or tolerable. He was also too committed to moving out of a blue-collar white neighborhood where he felt he outclassed the people both financially and intellectually."

Once he made it to the East Side, George held on to his longstanding attitudes about race. But, perhaps surprisingly, his racial one-liners could be dismissed too. His use of the word *honky* didn't seem to faze or upset white viewers because George's behavior was too funny to be considered rooted in deep-seated racial anger. For mainstream viewers, George was amusing because he was behind the times. No one used words like honky anymore. George's "dated" politics became a source of humor.

Yet Black viewers responded to something else about George. His language and attitudes always appeared liberating in the world of the sitcom. He was also in control of his own destiny. They might have laughed at his pretenses "but nobody laughs at his ability to pay the note on the dee-luxe apartment in the sky-y-y," wrote *Essence*. "The fact that the show has avoided turning Black success into the brunt of the humor, that the story lines have not evolved into George's buying Cadillacs and mismanaging his business to the point where Louise has to fire Florence and apply for welfare, is a fear all by itself—and an indication of how we've come to dispelling certain stereotypes." *The Jeffersons* touched on another reality. "If one of the goals of the Civil Rights Movement was to gain equal rights that would form a basis for equal opportunity, then George Jefferson doesn't really contradict what black people have said we always wanted: he finally got a piece of the pie."

Without posing and posturing or any pretense about presenting something new, *The Jeffersons* actually introduced—through the Willises—the first married interracial couple to series TV. Though George picked at them, the two seemed well adjusted and didn't fret and frown over any tragic racial dilemma.

In time, the outrageous George was softened. He was revealed to be an insecure man whose braggadocio was a mask for his fears. The series also kept up with the times and probably best charts the changes that came over Black sitcoms from the mid-1970s to the early 1980s—changes brought about by new attitudes and trends in American society. In time, some observers believed that the series, which then lasted longer than any other Black sitcom in television history and had a longer run than most television series in general, became an interracial show rather than a Black one. Its weekly themes and situations were not racial ones. George and Louise appeared very much a part of traditional American society. Neither was fighting from the outside to overhaul the system. Of course, everyone might have hoped that *The Jeffersons* had pushed farther, dug deeper. But as a piece of surprisingly durable farcical entertainment, it succeeded exceedingly well. At its peak, it was seen by 33 million people.

The Jeffersons, like *Amos 'n' Andy*, owed much of its success to its cast. Sherman Hemsley infused George Jefferson with his own drive and restlessness. A native of Philadelphia who had been shy as a child, Hemsley came to acting late. After four years in the air force, he had worked in the post office but also studied at Philadelphia's Academy of Dramatic Arts. When African American actor Robert Hooks saw Hemsley in a local production, he suggested that the performer move to New York. Afterward Hemsley found work off-Broadway in a Black production of *Alice in Wonderland* and on Broadway in *Purlie Victorious*. A short time later came *All in the Family*. Once cast in *The Jeffersons*, he looked determined to make every line count and every joke zing and to perfectly coordinate every movement in his rambunctious jerky style. His bouncy, brotherlike bop as he entered the lobby of his apartment building—during the opening credits—was Hemsley's way of cueing Black viewers into the fact that George hadn't lost his soulfulness.

Hemsley later created another (dubiously) memorable character in the series *Amen*. He also appeared in the series *Goode Behavior* in 1996. The secret of his success, of course, was that, like Redd Foxx, he played himself time and time again. Part of his appeal also resided in his size. Short, slight, and never a physical threat, he was always the brash, energetic, loudmouthed little guy who won't ever back down from his opinions, no matter how misguided they might be. He was imposing only when he spoke.

The other cast members had also been struggling to get a foothold in show business. After having appeared in such New York stage productions as *The Blacks, The Amen Corner,* and *Purlie Victorious,* Isabel Sanford had boarded a Greyhound bus in New York with her three children and headed for Los Angeles. She appeared in such films as *Guess Who's Coming to Dinner, The Comic,* and *Soul Soldier* as well as such TV shows as *Bewitched, The Mod Squad,* and *The Interns.* But for years, her primary income had come from her job as a keypunch operator. In *The Jeffersons,* she perfected the part of the comic foil for both George and Florence. Yet part of the fun of watching Sanford was seeing her in those moments when she turned them into *her* comic foils.

Marla Gibbs also came to acting late. Born and reared in Chicago, she was the child of divorced parents. Her mother traveled and became known as singer Ophelia Kemp on radio and as a spiritualist and pastor in the Midwest. Often lonely and feeling rejected, Marla was left in the care of her father. She married and worked as an airline clerk and telephone solicitor. But after seventeen years and three children, she divorced her husband, packed her bags, and moved to Los Angeles, hoping for a career as an actress. By then, she was in her late thirties. She found parts in little theater and then on television's *Barney Miller* and *Doc* and in the films *Black Belt Jones* and *Sweet Jesus, Preacher Man.* But nothing clicked until *The Jeffersons.*

Originally, Florence was not written as a regular character. But on the series's first episode, as Gibbs used her expert timing and panache to walk away with her scenes, the television audience *discovered* Marla Gibbs and wanted to see more of her. Who could forget Florence's signature line on that first episode? A bit amazed by this heady new lifestyle she was being exposed to, Florence asked the Jeffersons and Willises if they all really lived in this fabulous high-rise apartment building. When they answered yes, Florence said, "How come we overcame and nobody told me?" That line explained the state of her life. It made audiences immediately identify with her.

Occasionally, Florence went off on wild flights of fancy. On one episode, she fell for a psychiatrist and pretended to be mentally disturbed. Thinking she was schizophrenic, he tried to commit her. Then Florence had to finagle her way out of the situation. On another, she went gaga when she finally got to meet her dream man, actor Billy Dee Williams. But for the most part, Gibbs never let Florence be condescended to. Gibbs created an assured, shrewd, quick-witted character with a common sense that shot through the pretensions of the other characters.

She also could never take master/servant roles seriously. When the doorbell rings, Florence says to Louise, "Get that for me." She matched wits perfectly with George, whom she called Shorty. "Get away from that mirror," he once told Florence. "You don't need any more bad luck!" "I know," she answered. "I already got you." Most importantly, Florence was always able to slap the highfalutin George back into place, anchoring him in a realism he might otherwise have denied. In one episode, George, who has fired Florence, has to rehire her. "This is my big chance," he tells Louise. "To make her crawl." He explains, "Look, you don't understand, Weesie. Florence has got some kind of power over me. In the seven years that I've known her, I've never once beaten her at anything." Part of the delirious anticipatory fun for viewers was their knowledge that George would still never beat her. It was now simply a matter of watching Florence outfox him. They weren't disappointed. Florence needs her job. But even so, she ends up making George crawl *for her.*

"I could be persuaded to hire you back," he tells her, "if you agree to wash all the windows every single day."

"Not a chance," she says without a second of hesitation.

"Every other day," says George.

"Nope," Florence says.

"Scrub the counter once a month," he tells her.

"Maybe," says Florence.

"The only way I'll hire you back is if you get down on both knees and beg me to."

"Forget it, Mr. Jefferson."

"One knee," says George.

She shakes her head no.

"Sitting down," says George.

"No."

"Just say please," he implores her.

"Well," says Florence.

"Oh, *please,* Florence," he says.

"Does it mean that much to you, Mr. Jefferson?"

"Yeah, I'd do anything."

Florence ends up letting herself be rehired *but* at a 20 percent raise *and* with a month's vacation.

Florence fell in line with classic manipulative servants dating back to McDaniel and Anderson's Rochester (and going back even further to *Volpone*'s Mosca). Viewers loved the fact that she didn't bite her tongue, that little impressed her (except perhaps a good-looking guy), and that she walked through life to her own beat. Gibbs herself didn't fall by the wayside after *The Jeffersons* folded. She would star in *227*, another successful series, in the next decade.

WHAT'S HAPPENING!!: HIGH SCHOOL HIGH JINKS

Not long after *The Jeffersons* appeared, *What's Happening!!* aired on ABC, first as a summer replacement in August 1976, then as a regular program on the fall lineup. Inspired by the hit movie *Cooley High*, the most youth-oriented of the Black sitcoms revolved around three urban teenagers: Roger or Raj (Ernest Thomas), serious and studious with aspirations to become a writer; Rerun (Fred Berry), overweight and full of fun; and Dwayne (Haywood Nelson), shy but trying to be hip. Most of their spare time was spent at the local soda fountain, Rob's, where they were served by a hefty, wisecracking waitress named Shirley (Shirley Hemphill). Other times, the three hung out at Raj's home, where his hefty mother, Mrs. Thomas (Mabel King), who worked as a maid, was always good for laughs. The same was true of Raj's outspoken kid sister Dee (Danielle Spencer).

The humor on *What's Happening!!* was usually obvious and embarrassing. "You could throw yourself on the mercy of the court," Dee tells chunky Rerun, "and smother the jury." There seemed no end to the fat jokes that could be told at the expense of poor Rerun. Then there were other just plain dumb jokes. "Mama, Raj ain't done his homework yet," Dee says. "Shut up, Dee," Roger says. "Don't say shut up to your sister," Mrs. Thomas says. "That's tellin' 'im, Mama," Dee says. "Shut up, Dee," says Mama. On another occasion, budding writer Raj tells his mother, "Everybody says I really write good." "*Well*," Mama Thomas replies. "Everybody says you really write well." Roger then says, "Thank you, Mama. I always knew it."

The images were as tired and trite as the jokes. The women were the most cartoonish of the characters with the camera angles spotlighting their weight and the dialogue emphasizing their sassiness. Weighing well over two hundred pounds and depicted as a no-nonsense matriarch, Mabel King's Mama Thomas was one more slightly updated overstuffed mammy. The same was true of the foul-tongued waitress Shirley, who looked ever ready for a fight. All you had to do was take a quick look at Shirley and you'd know it was best to stay out of this *sista's* way. Even daughter Dee, with her precocious sassiness, seemed as if she was a young mammy in waiting.

What's Happening!! made female assertiveness and independence look like something out of a nightmare. The women were horrific harridans—ball-busting control freaks—to be avoided at all costs. You might feel that poor Mrs. Thomas had to repeatedly assert herself in order to survive. But despite actress Mabel King's sweetness at times, the scripts kept her in a blatant comic-strip context; desexing her at one point or then exploiting signs of sexuality for the worst type of humor.

As might be expected, Mrs. Thomas and her husband were divorced; so it wasn't a surprise that this father was rarely around. But on those occasions when Mr. Thomas (Thalmus Rasulala) did appear (or was referred to by Mama Thomas), he was an undependable, triflin' lout. At least, George Jefferson had climbed up in the world, and even Fred Sanford had managed to make a place for himself. But the father on *What's Happening!!* made it look as if television's images of African American men hadn't progressed at all.

What's Happening!!'s real appeal belonged to the three youthful leads, whom teenage viewers (African American and white) could identify with. As with the teens on such general white-oriented programs as *Happy Days*, their exploits were puerile enough not to be offensive.

The show ran until August 1979. Then it resurfaced six years later as a syndicated series called *What's Happening Now!!* Most of the original cast appeared. Raj and Rerun were now roommates in their own apartment. Raj studied in college. Rerun worked. Later Raj and Shirley ran the fountain shop, Rob's, and Raj took a bride, played by Anne-Marie Johnson. Also appearing as a student named Maurice was a newcomer, Martin Lawrence. Though the original characters were older, the new series hadn't matured much.

The problem with the new shows was partly that they were all comedies, partly that the images still seemed locked in the past. For all his appeal, George Jefferson still didn't represent a mature African American male. The writers weren't able to develop a character that could be funny but without the familiar exaggerations. Because sitcoms like *Good Times, The Jeffersons,* and *What's Happening!!* had long runs, as did *Sanford and Son* in its various guises, they dominated the view of African Americans on weekly television in the 1970s.

Important African American characters also appeared on non-Black sitcoms during the era. Both *Welcome Back, Kotter* and *Barney Miller* looked like World War II bomber crew programs with characters representing various ethnic groups: Italian-American, Jewish, Asian-American, and African American. Though the 1970s seemed to welcome the idea of cultural diversity, the new characters sometimes conformed to set notions about ethnicity. As with those ethnic characters on sitcoms of the 1950s, the Ethnic Other was still the basis for a good joke or two that might be carried on all season.

Nonetheless, Lawrence-Hilton Jacobs, a good intense actor in a film like *Claudine,* played the hip "sweathog" Freddie "Boom-Boom" Washington in the high school sitcom *Welcome Back, Kotter.* It was a case of an intelligent actor being directed to give a conventional but likable characterization. With the help of some clever scripts, actor Ron Glass went against the grain of ethnic typing as the Black detective Ron Harris in the cop comedy *Barney Miller.* Glass created an ambitious, bright character that was the antithesis of what viewers had been conditioned to expect from Black males; something of a Black WASP, as the critic for *Saturday Review* commented, adding that actor Glass "displays the slyest wit on commercial television."

COP LAND

In the early and mid-1970s, a few Black-oriented dramatic series like *Get Christie Love!, Shaft,* and *Tenafly* appeared. All were short-lived action shows centered on a detective/cop protagonist. Former *Laugh-In* star Teresa Graves appeared as the sexy detective Christie Love—described as the *girl* with "beauty, brains, and a badge"—of the Special Division of the Los Angeles Police Department. Not only was *Get Christie Love!* the first series to feature a Black female cop but it was also the first hour-long dramatic series to star an African American woman. Originally, Cicely Tyson was set to play Christie but she *officially* bowed out at the last minute after suffering a foot injury. Actually, she ended up starring instead in *The Autobiography of Miss Jane Pittman*, which was not a bad career move at all. One only wonders what Tyson might have done with the role. No doubt in this era of the woman's movement, Tyson would have invested the character with more drive and independence, even when she had to utter Christie's signature line, "You're under arrest, sugah!"

As Graves played Christie, the character was a descendant of the movie heroines of Pam Grier and Tamara Dobson (*Coffy*, *Foxy Brown*, and *Cleopatra Jones*), but without any of Grier's raunchy high style or Dobson's sleek fashion model hauteur. Instead girlish and sweet-tempered, Graves—a Jehovah's Witness who had an agreement with the producers that she would be released at 5 p.m. once a week to study the Bible—didn't seem comfortable with the sexy part. Still, her leg kicks and fisticuffs could put any male cop to shame. *Get Christie Love!* folded after its first season.

As part of a rotating series that alternated with *Hawkins* and *The New CBS Tuesday Night Movies*, the television version of *Shaft* was a ninety-minute-long drama in which Richard Roundtree reprised his movie role as that smooth detective John Shaft. *Shaft* might have been developed into a hard-hitting, gritty urban tale with a strong African American hero. But the TV material was too tame, the scripts too weak. John Shaft's striking cultural context had disappeared. The great thing about the *Shaft* movies was seeing this brother talk back to the man and walk down those mean streets—in his leather jacket to the beat of Isaac Hayes's Oscar-winning theme song—with his cultural identity intact. Though he could operate in a white world, he was grounded in a Black one. Gone was Shaft's upfront sexuality, which had helped make him such an original Black movie hero. Gone too was his cool toughness. "The fans of the Shaft movies have to realize that you can't put *that* Shaft on TV," actor Roundtree defensively told the press. "If you edited any of those three movies for television, you'd wind up with maybe 15 minutes of usable stuff." True. But a Shaft who looked as if he had Listerine poured over him wasn't a Shaft most viewers cared to see. You couldn't have asked for a more antiseptic hero. The series premiered in October 1973 and went off the air in August 1974.

Debuting—and expiring—at the same time as *Shaft* was *Tenafly*, another ninety-minute Black detective series. It was one of four rotating series on the *NBC Mystery Movie.* Created by Richard Levinson and William Link, who had scored with the series *Mannix* and *Columbo, Tenafly* sounded promising. Its hero, Harry Tenafly (James McEachin), was a happily married family man with a darling wife, Ruth (Lillian Lehman), and two children. He was the polar opposite of John Shaft. On one episode, he even stumbles as he gets out of his car so we'll know for sure that he's not any larger-than-life superhero. Solving crimes to pay the rent, he's just an average middle-class Joe (with some color, of course), not very glamorous or sexy, trying to do his job while struggling for time at home.

Like *Shaft, Tenafly* bombed for a number of reasons. Neither appeared often enough to really develop a viewership—and also to better develop their characters and the story lines. The fact that both were parts of rotating series rather than weekly dramas indicated the networks' fear that the mainstream audience still wouldn't accept weekly dramatic Black programs. *Tenafly* also left its hero floundering in a cultural void, with the subject of race only occasionally surfacing. "I didn't know you were Black," a new client tells Tenafly, who calmly answers, "It's all right. I didn't know you were white." Not a bad moment, but Tenafly, having been made too middle-class, too suburban, was also deracialized.

"Whether at home or in the office—in a large detective agency— Harry Tenafly's color was, with one or two exceptions, rigorously ignored. His white neighbor couldn't have been more friendly. His white friend on the police force couldn't have been more accommodating," wrote John J. O'Connor in *The New York Times.* "Harry is, in other words, Columbo in blackface."

Other dramatic series featured African American supporting characters. The cop drama *Starsky and Hutch,* centering on actors David Soul and Paul Michael Glaser as two hip white cops in a violent urban setting, cast Black actor Bernie Hamilton as the stern police captain Dobey. It was an interesting piece of casting. Dobey represents the status quo; he was a traditional by-the-book police officer. Unlike the heroes, he's not aware that the system's rules have to be bent in this new era. At the same time, such good Black cops as Dobey (or Ed Bernard, the partner of Pepper, on *Police Woman* or Tony King on *Bronk* or even

Georg Stanford Brown's sturdy character on *The Rookies*) appear to be there to counter any complaints about all the Black criminals that proliferated on cop shows then and later.

Also on *Starsky and Hutch* was Antonio Fargas, who played Huggy Bear, an informant for the cops. Though Fargas was almost outrageously clever and quick-witted, giving the kind of highly kinetic performances rarely seen on television, the character Huggy Bear seemed an amalgam of old images: the once threatening buck coupled with the cartoonish coon. As such, he pointed the way to a new type of TV character. The violent buck of the past would now evolve into the *baad street nigga* whose threat was neutralized in one of two ways. If the buck/*street nigga* reformed, he'd use all his street smarts and his physical strength to help a white buddy. Huggy Bear was just such a figure. Still later there was Hawk on *Spenser: For Hire*.

If the buck/*street nigga* proved too menacing and unwilling to conform, he'd end up dead—or apprehended. All those pimps and thugs that reared their ugly heads on cop shows throughout this era and into the next would usually conform to this stereotype.

One of the more interesting of such figures was played by former football star (and Julia's onetime boyfriend) Fred Williamson on *The Dangerous Game* episode of *Police Story*. His character, Snake, was a high-flung dope pusher and pimp who's described by a cop as probably being "responsible for half the cocaine in the state. He's bad people. He's into everything. Dope. Girls. Stolen property. Extortion."

Worse, Snake's got a stable of white women at his personal beck and call. In one scene, Snake's joined in a hot tub by a young nubile white lass, looking ever ready to accommodate whatever request he might make. In another, he threatens a white woman who has betrayed him. "Remember the last time you made Daddy mad, baby," he says. "Now you don't want that to happen again, do you, baby?" Later he has her violently beaten. But his brutality also crosses racial lines. When a young Black woman plans to testify against him in court, he wants her scarred but not in front of her children. As it turns out, she is his wife.

A better actor than he was ever given credit for being, Williamson plays Snake with a confident, adroit, elegant street sophistication. Maybe he's not as sexy as he thinks, but he's plenty sexual for the medium. He's also far smoother than the undercover white cop opponent out to get him. "I ain't no highly educated guy," says Snake at one point. "I ain't no athlete. No musician. So you don't let me in your square world unless I entertain you. Well, I entertain you, baby. My employees entertain you. So I am therefore a public servant." He adds, "They don't let me play their game. So I play my game." Williamson delivers the dialogue almost gleefully, and this looks like daring stuff for television of the 1970s. But the problem was that this type of Black male sexuality and confidence was only shown on television when it could be neutralized—when it was also depicted as aberrant/deviant behavior. Ultimately, *The Dangerous Game* was a very calculated morality tale, commenting not only on men who abuse women but on Black men who abuse white women—and who also dare to assert themselves. How does Snake end up? Naturally, he's outwitted by the white cop hero and ends up behind bars. So much for any mainstream viewers' fears about an unrepentant *street nigga.*

DIFF'RENT STROKES: LIVIN' LARGE WITH A GREAT WHITE FATHER FIGURE

As the nation's conservatism grew during the Carter years, the Black-cast sitcoms were beginning to look passé. American movies had already undergone a change that would soon affect television's African American images. The Black-oriented movies of the early 1970s, which had been produced for the Black moviegoing public, had been replaced—as the era was drawing to a close—by new *crossover movies.* Hollywood believed films with African Americans had to appeal to white audiences in order to succeed at the box office. Soon the industry released films like *Silver Streak,* which featured Richard Pryor with white actors and actresses in a white cultural setting.

The same became true of the weekly primetime series in the late 1970s. Now whenever important Black characters appeared, they were plucked out of the African American community and dropped into a white environment, be it a family or work situation: basically a nonethnic cultural setting which the vast white audience could readily identify with. Some might argue that the new programs were interracial series. But the Black characters were so vivid and central a presence that African American viewers yearned to see them in an African American cultural context, rather than in worlds in which they often seemed the Comic Other yet again.

The best example was the hit *Diff'rent Strokes*, which appeared in 1978. Gary Coleman and Todd Bridges starred as Arnold and Willis Jackson, two orphaned Harlem lads sent to live in the Park Avenue home of Philip Drummond, a white millionaire. We're told that the boys' dying mother, who worked as a housekeeper for Drummond, made him promise to look out for her sons. Had this been an early 1970s series, the boys would have moved in with Black relatives. They probably would have roomed with J.J. and Michael in that tenement on

Life on Park Avenue with a great white father figure: Diff'rent Strokes *with Todd Bridges, Conrad Bain, Dana Plato, and the era's most popular child star, Gary Coleman*

Good Times. Diff'rent Strokes suggests that there are no Black relatives or a Black community to care for the children. For the late 1970s/early 1980s audience, the millionaire Drummond becomes a *great white father figure*, able to provide the material comforts (as well as the subliminal emotional ones) and the cultural milieu that the Black community supposedly could never hope to match. We are to believe he is the best person to bring the boys to maturity.

The early episodes of *Diff'rent Strokes* had some funny and occasionally telling moments. The twelve-year-old Willis remembered his past life (his cultural roots) and yearned for Harlem. But the younger Arnold, like a pint-sized potentate, loved the Park Avenue perks and privileges and luxuriated in his heady new lifestyle. "I think we died and went to heaven," said Arnold. Part of the fun of the early episodes involved the double takes people did at seeing Drummond and sons. When Drummond's snobbish mother paid a visit, she took one look at the boys and fainted. "She fainted because we're Black," Willis said. "Well," said Arnold, "it's nice to be noticed." Throughout, Arnold strutted around like he owned the world, delighting in the stares and in the setting.

Though it acknowledged race and cultural distinctions, *Diff'rent Strokes* enjoyed poking fun at racial attitudes rather than at racism. Whenever an outright bigot appeared, the series tried to hit hard. But rather than depicting racism as a national sickness, *Diff'rent Strokes* viewed it as so much nonsense. The series seemed to say, *Let's just let Arnold speak his mind to these silly bigots—and then have fun.* Much like Michael on *Good Times*, Arnold's age—and his size—contributed to his effects. Viewers could accept this precocious child speaking his mind and raising Cain. Out of the mouths of babes came racial pearls of wisdom. But *only* out of the mouths of babes.

Also in the Drummond house were his teenage daughter Kimberly (Dana Plato), and the housekeeper, Mrs. Garrett (Charlotte Rae). Ultimately, *Diff'rent Strokes* presented a portrait of an ideal integrated society; a portrait, of course, that was patently false. Race became less important as the series moved along. There were only so many jokes that could be made about the surprise of people upon learning that Drummond was the "father" of Arnold and Willis. When *Diff'rent Strokes* lost its racial comment, it became unrelentingly boring.

The heart of *Diff'rent Strokes*—and the reason for its popularity—

was Gary Coleman, who became a major child star, but, like our friend Beulah, only by showing up in a white home. He was, however, an American original. No African American child (and few white ones) had ever had such a cultural impact. Coleman had been performing since he was five. Born in Zion, Illinois, he had first modeled for the department store Montgomery Ward. An appearance in a local McDonald's commercial made him well known in the Chicago area. When Norman Lear's Tandem Productions planned a remake of the old *Our Gang* series, Coleman auditioned. The series was never made. But Lear remembered Coleman's performance on the pilot. So too did ABC's Fred Silverman, who asked Lear to develop a series around Coleman. Coleman kept working on such shows as *Good Times* and *America 2Night*. He also did a showstopping bit on *The Jeffersons*. Playing George's precocious, recalcitrant nephew from out of town, Coleman was quick with his lines, a fearless master of timing and double takes, who was able to match wits with George as confidently as Florence. Watching him, you ask yourself, "Where did this kid come from?" This episode alone proved he was born to be a star. But still his career hadn't taken off. No series had yet been created for him. When Fred Silverman left ABC for NBC, he called Lear and asked, "What about the kid?"

Later Silverman had Coleman do a reading of a five-page scene for a group of NBC programmers at the network's Burbank offices. Coleman won them over. Afterward *Diff'rent Strokes* was created specifically to showcase him. Silverman then devised a clever promotional campaign to introduce him to the American public. During NBC's coverage of the World Series, ten-second cameos were aired with Coleman tossing off one-liners. "Mr. Gary Coleman speaks out on marriage," said an announcer. Thereafter Coleman commented, "One thing at a time. I ain't even had a dog yet." Then the announcer added, "Watch for the new Gary Coleman show." Rival network ABC was so nervous about the competition that, at various times, it aired the already established hits *Happy Days* and *The Love Boat* opposite the Coleman comedy. But *Diff'rent Strokes* survived.

Viewers took to Coleman almost immediately. An appearance on *The Tonight Show* also helped him win a larger following. As he traded quips with host Johnny Carson or spoke about nuclear power, Coleman was bright, witty, literate—way beyond his years. When Carson asked if he knew about the birds and bees, Coleman told him, "No. And

I don't want to." As the series became even more popular, the nation grew openly fascinated with him. Often compared to Shirley Temple, Coleman became one of America's most famous child stars and appeared on the covers of *Newsweek, Jet, People,* and *The National Enquirer.* He starred in such feature films as *On the Right Track* and *Jimmy the Kid* and such television movies as *The Kid with the Broken Halo, Scout's Honor, The Fantastic World of D. C. Collins,* and *Playing with Fire.*

His well-publicized medical problems also drew the public to him. Having been born with a kidney problem, Coleman had three major operations before he turned five, including a kidney transplant. The steroid medication he took caused the puffy chipmunk cheeks that audiences loved. It also stunted his growth. Although ten years old when he first appeared on *Diff'rent Strokes,* Coleman was the size of a five-year-old, a little over three feet and seven inches tall and weighing fifty pounds.

Diff'rent Strokes ran for eight seasons, moving from NBC to ABC in 1985. Various cast changes came about. Housekeeper Mrs. Garrett left to become a housemother at a girls' boarding school in the series *Facts of Life.* Drummond remarried. An adolescent Willis found a girlfriend, Charlene, played by Janet Jackson. Kimberly finished high school and went off to study in Paris. Arnold remained at the center of the show. But the strain showed. As Coleman became older, he grew no taller, and the writers had problems developing realistic situations for him, especially the expected romantic ones for a teenager. Worse, Coleman often didn't look well.

Once the series went off the air, Coleman surfaced in newspaper headlines because of his battles with his parents over his past earnings. Accusing them of having mismanaged and misspent millions of dollars, he discovered himself broke. Later he took a job as a security guard. But new problems and tabloid headlines arose in 1998 when he was sued for having struck a young woman where he worked. She said she had simply asked for an autograph when a foul-tempered Coleman lashed out at her. The other child stars of *Diff'rent Strokes* also became fodder for the tabloids. Todd Bridges had numerous brushes with the law, including charges of drug possession. He was arrested in 1989 for the attempted murder of a drug dealer. With the help of his attorney, Johnnie Cochran, he was acquitted. Dana Plato was arrested for the armed robbery of a video store. She died at the age of thirty-four in 1999 from an overdose of a prescribed medication.

But the public remained most curious about Coleman, who made an appearance on ABC's *20/20* to discuss his financial problems. He was clearheaded, perceptive, and moving. Also surprisingly mature, Coleman appeared to have grown up in a world that had no place for him. Coleman made sporadic appearances on such shows as *Politically Incorrect* and *Shasta McNasty*. But like Jimmie Walker and so many other popular stars of TV series, he could never duplicate his early success.

THE WHITE SHADOW:
YOUTHFUL YEARNINGS, YOUTHFUL DILEMMAS

The dramatic series *The White Shadow* also focused on young African American males coming of age—but again being guided to maturity by an older white male. The program starred white actor Ken Howard as a former professional basketball player who, sidelined by an injury, becomes a coach at the fictional inner-city Carver High in Los Angeles. The students were an interracial mix but mostly African American.

Weekly, viewers watched as Howard taught the kids the rules of the game *and* also helped them work through their personal problems. In some respects, Howard's character, Ken Reeves, was another *great white father figure* to African American adolescents in distress. Would it not have been more interesting (also more realistic and encouraging) to see a Black coach (perhaps a new version of Pete Dixon from *Room 222*) exchange his experiences and insights with this group of mostly young Black athletes? But the series took an easy *crossover* route out, providing the large white television audience with a white lead character it could more readily identify with. Consequently, the idea prevailed that white supervision and advice would see us all through our bad days.

But aware of what the series suggested, the creators shrewdly tried working their way around the *great white father syndrome*. Often the coach was made to question his values and perspective. "Don't come in here like the White Knight," Carver High's attractive young Black assistant principal Sybil Buchanon (Joan Pringle) told Reeves on the premiere episode. After a big game, Reeves promises his players, "I'll be behind you every step of the way." One player responds kiddingly,

"Yeah, like a white shadow." Hence the title. For the most part, *The White Shadow* was a fine series that attempted to deal thoughtfully with conflicts confronting the urban young. Tackling such issues as drugs, teenage drinking, teen pregnancies, and police brutality, the series was not afraid of examining aspects of American racism.

Throughout, Reeves respected his players—and the culture they grew up in. He was willing to learn from them and to admit when he was wrong. The students themselves were beautifully drawn. During the first season, the actors—Kevin Hooks as Thorpe, Thomas Carter as Hayward, Byron Stewart as Coolidge, and Timothy Van Patten as the Italian character Salami—were a refreshing new breed. Later Larry Flash Jenkins, Stoney Jackson, Wolfe Perry, Ken Michelman, and John Laughlin joined the cast.

Race often came up, but without any heavy hammering of messages. Reeves might—with a vague suggestion of condescension—extend a courtesy to a player, who would thank him saying, "Gee, that's mighty white of you." (Of course, he echoes Otis Young saying a similar line in *The Outcasts*.)

The series was also willing to confront matters close to home. One episode touched on the subject of racism within the entertainment industry. When the character Coolidge is hired to play a small role in a film, his "success" goes to his head, and he's soon lording it over his classmates, excited by Hollywood parties and limos. But the other students remind him of the compromises that will be expected of him. Coolidge doesn't pay them much mind until a crucial sequence when the film's director has him play a shoeshine boy, going through the requisite stereotyped language and antics. Unable to take it, he explodes and shoves his white co-star off the shoeshine stand.

The White Shadow also encapsulated some of the pangs and frustrations of adolescence as well as the underlying connective cultural tissue that bonded these students. Ironically, the Black characters of this truly interracial series were better drawn and developed than those that appeared on the all-Black programs; the glimpses of African American culture were also more sensitively dramatized. Today *The White Shadow*, which never had great ratings and which lasted only three seasons, looks almost revolutionary when one compares it to what followed.

Some of its actors went on to very successful careers. Thomas Carter became an important television director and executive producer, who, like Ivan Dixon, directed both Black and non-Black dramas. Kevin Hooks, who had previously appeared in the film *Sounder* and was the son of actor Robert Hooks, later directed the feature films *Passenger 57* and *Fled* as well as episodes of *China Beach, 21 Jump Street, Profiler,* and *Homicide: Life on the Street* and such television dramas as *Heat Wave* and *Murder Without Motive: The Edmund Perry Story.* Timothy Van Patten also became a successful television director.

BENSON: FOREVER YOURS, THE CLEVER, RESOURCEFUL SERVANT

Benson, the series that closed the decade, also lifted its title African American character out of an African American cultural setting. When he first appeared on the sitcom *Soap* in 1977, Benson (Robert Guillaume)—the clever, outspoken butler for the eccentric Tate family—always struck viewers as the household's sanest character. With a line or two, he could shatter the pretensions of the family. He also seemed to feel that he was doing these poor dim-witted white folks a favor by working for them. Eventually, Guillaume, who won an Emmy for his performance, left the series, replaced by Roscoe Lee Browne.

As the star of his own series, Benson, played again by Robert Guillaume, went to work for former employer Jessica Tate's cousin, the dippy Governor Gatling (James Noble), in yet another dysfunctional household. But Gatling and his crowd had none of the zany originality of the *Soap* characters. Though still feisty, Benson himself had lost some of his spark and part of what had made him appealing. He had always maintained a certain distance from the Tates. Guillaume really gave the impression that his character had another life away from his job—a life he couldn't wait to get to and which he wasn't interested in sharing with his employers.

On the new show, we saw that other life. Unfortunately, it wasn't an especially interesting sight. Our imaginations had done a far better job of defining Benson. Now he was constantly at odds with the governor's aide, Clayton, and with the German housekeeper, Gretchen. But he seemed too eager to bond with the Gatlings, going so far as to help raise the governor's daughter Katie. And aware that Gatling was naive and foolish, Benson came to his aid and defense, even advising the governor on important political decisions. Talk about your clever, resourceful servants. Benson was but another descendant of Eddie Anderson's Rochester. But that wasn't exactly the kind of character we were pining for in the 1980s.

Later in the series, the writers had Benson become the state budget director, which seemed to be stretching matters. In 1984, Benson became lieutenant governor. Then, in the last season, he ran for governor—against Gatling. Benson's political aspirations indicated an important shift in images in the 1980s (that corresponded with new attitudes within the African American community): rather than rebelling or questioning the system as a program like *Good Times* wanted to do, Black Americans (as was now the case with *The Jeffersons*) were depicted as being ready to embrace that system, enter it, and perhaps make changes. Benson also had a fiancée, Diane (Donna LaBrie), who managed his campaign. It appeared as if the character might be ready to start a life independent of the Gatling family, which meant that there would no longer be a series.

Benson's closing episode had the two men, after a contentious political campaign, seated together, reconciled as they watched the election returns. It ended without revealing the winner. But the point had been made about Benson. Having been both politicized *and* softened and sentimentalized (through most of the run of the series), he remained by his good white friend's side. Guillaume won another Emmy for his work on this series in the 1984–85 season.

In the latter years of the decade, other Black characters appeared on white series. The hit melodrama *The Love Boat* featured Ted Lange as the likable, rather hapless bartender Isaac, who mostly was around to add some color to the white cruise liner and to provide a few laughs. The "race comedy" *Carter Country* featured white actor Victor French and Black actor Kene Holliday as a redneck sheriff and his shrewd Black deputy. The series *The Facts of Life* prominently featured Kim Fields as Dorothy "Tootie" Ramsey, the only Black student at the prestigious Eastland school for girls.

In the last year of the decade, three new series centered on more serious African American characters. The medical drama *The Lazarus Syn-*

drome starred Louis Gossett Jr. as the chief of cardiology at a metropolitan hospital, who was often at odds with the chief white administrator at the hospital. Basically, the series was intended as another study in interracial male bonding, but Gossett was such a striking solid presence that the series showed promise. However, after about a month, its low ratings led to its cancellation from the ABC lineup.

A similar fate awaited the Black-oriented drama *Harris and Company*. Bernie Casey starred as Detroit assembly-line worker Mike Harris, who, having lost his wife, moves with his five children to Los Angeles. There he runs a garage with a white friend. (Again—that old bonding theme.) But mainly it was a Black family story. Strong, eventempered, and sensitive about matters pertaining to his children, Harris showed signs of growing into a well-developed TV character. The children, especially David Hubbard as son David, were not television's typical cute youngsters. (Hubbard was also impressive as the teenage friend of the title character in the series *James at 15*.) There were convincing tender sequences for the kids and their father, who insisted that all family issues be put to a vote. Debuting on March 15, 1979, *Harris and Company* failed to pull in a large viewership and went off the air on April 5, 1979. So much for a serious Black family drama.

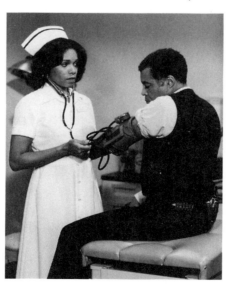

James Earl Jones and Lee Chamberlain in
Paris, an early weekly dramatic series with
African American stars

Finally, there was *Paris*. Created by Steven Bochco (later the co-creator of *Hill Street Blues*), it starred James Earl Jones as an erudite police captain, Woody Paris. In the evenings, he taught a class on criminology at a nearby college. His time at home was spent with his attractive wife (Lee Chamberlain). At work, he headed a Metro Unit that worked on tough, unusual cases. Though the series met with favorable reviews, *Paris* never clicked with audiences. One critic wrote that Jones "strutted through this role speaking in booming, stentorian tones, as if it were *Richard III*." Yet *Paris*, which had some warm, homey moments, might have succeeded had the network given it more time to find an audience. When CBS dropped the series after four months, there didn't seem to be much hope for a strong, dramatic African American lead on the weekly primetime schedule.

TV Movies

High-voltage dramatic Black characters—and high-voltage Black dramas—still seemed acceptable and successful only when they were presented and packaged as special events. In the 1970s, the rise of the made-for-TV movie and the miniseries afforded Black performers their best chance for serious roles. Early in the decade, Lamont Johnson's unusual and edgy *My Sweet Charlie* starred Al Freeman Jr. as a New York lawyer and Patty Duke as a young unwed mother who are both temporarily trapped in an abandoned house in rural Texas. Sparks fly as the two—each suspicious of the other—challenge one another on issues of race and class.

Not long afterward came Buzz Kuliz's *Brian's Song*. Based on a true story, this two-hour drama starred actors Billy Dee Williams and James Caan as professional football players Gale Sayers and Brian Piccolo. When Piccolo learns that he has cancer, his good friend Sayers remains by his side. Often sentimental and culturally evasive, the drama never gets at the root of the differences that might alienate one man from another yet which ultimately draw them together and cement their friendship. Dramatically and psychologically, everything seems done in soft focus. Yet after the social upheavals of the 1960s, mainstream viewers responded to *Brian's Song*'s idealized white male/Black male relationship. Its reassuring subtext said everything again was racially well and ordered in America. *Brian's Song* shot to the top of the ratings.

Both Williams (who had been working in television since the 1960s) and Caan found themselves one step closer to stardom—ironically enough, in the movies. Caan appeared in *The Godfather*, and Williams emerged as a romantic leading man—Mr. Black Prince Charming—in *Lady Sings the Blues*. Williams also appeared in such TV movies as *Scott Joplin* and *Christmas Lilies of the Field*. But even *Brian's Song*'s success dimmed next to two of the most important television dramatic presentations of the era that were also Black special events: *The Autobiography of Miss Jane Pittman* and *Roots*.

Ideal buddies in a racially ideal fantasy world:
Billy Dee Williams and James Caan in Brian's Song

MISS JANE GOES TO THE FOUNTAIN
AND CICELY TYSON RISES TO STARDOM

Based on the novel by African American writer Ernest Gaines, *The Autobiography of Miss Jane Pittman* marked a new maturity for the TV movie. This two-hour drama followed the life of a Black heroine from the end of the Civil War to the rise of the civil rights era in 1962.

Throughout, the character Jane Pittman tells the story, moving the viewer with her insights, humor, and, eventually, her wisdom. When first seen, Jane is a girl who watches the Union soldiers arrive victorious in the South. Afterward, as she lives, works, marries, and loses a husband, she is a witness to the great historical events and social changes of the twentieth century.

Always a keen observer rather than a participant and never a fighter, Jane is an ordinary woman trying merely to hold on to the pieces of her life with dignity and sanity. Only as an old woman at the age of 110 does Jane make a decisive move. Roused by the dawning civil rights movement, she walks to a fountain—reserved for Whites Only—and despite the warnings of the police, takes a drink. It is a triumphant moment for her and the African American community—and also for American television.

Directed by John Korty with a script by Tracy Keenan Wynn, *The Autobiography of Miss Jane Pittman* was an emotionally powerful and daring drama. Through Jane's narrative, history unfolded from an African American point of view; a first for television. It also gave a number of Black actors and actresses an opportunity to work on significant material. Its cast included Rod Perry, Odetta, Joel Fluellen, Thalmus Rasulala, Josephine Premice, and Valerie O'Dell (as the young Jane). Cicely Tyson as Jane towered above them all.

In the hands of a lesser actress, Jane might have receded into the background of the historical pageant presented. But, like Ethel Waters, Tyson had an intuitive understanding of television's (and film's) demands. Her tour de force performance may not have the theatrical embellishments of the great Waters—who could do just about anything on-screen, but always soared into another stratosphere when she spoke, often in righteous indignation. Tyson, however, let her eyes—quick, intense, intelligent—do much of the work. Her thoughts defined her character as much as her dialogue. As different as she and Waters were, Tyson was still the single television actress who best followed in Waters's footsteps, creating a character that was naturalistically drawn yet larger than life; one of the medium's greatest African American archetypes.

The Autobiography of Miss Jane Pittman was not without its compromises. Its weakest section dealt with a white reporter (Michael Murphy), who comes to record Miss Jane's story. No such white character

Miss Jane goes to the fountain: Cicely Tyson in her Emmy Award–winning role in
The Autobiography of Miss Jane Pittman

appeared in the Gaines novel. If anything, the reporter looked like a plot device employed to absolve the mainstream viewer of some guilt feelings about America's past history. Television appeared to be reassuring its white audience that there were *good white people* who, realizing the importance of Jane's story, had recorded it.

The drama, however, made television history. Reviewers who usually didn't write about television praised the production and Cicely Tyson's performance. *The New Yorker*'s film critic Pauline Kael called the drama "quite possibly the finest movie ever made for American television." She added that Tyson "has the haughtiness of the enormously gifted—of those determined to do everything the most difficult way, because they know they can. Her refusal to melt us with her smile is like Streisand's refusal to sing; there's some foolishness in these refusals, but also hard-won pride . . . She's an actress, all right, and as tough-minded and honorable in her methods as any we've got." John J. O'Connor wrote that "Cicely Tyson transforms the role into the kind of event for which awards are made. . . . Following the film *Sounder, The Autobiography of Miss Jane Pittman* firmly establishes Cicely Tyson as a major American Actress."

Originally, none of the three commercial networks thought the series could win an audience. But *The Autobiography of Miss Jane Pittman* was viewed by 42 million people (47 percent of the television audience) and won nine Emmys, including Best Special Program of the Year and Cicely Tyson as Outstanding Actress in a Drama. Tyson also picked up an additional Emmy as Outstanding Actress of the Year in a Special.

Afterward, Tyson became a "bankable" TV star—the first African American actress since Waters to emerge as such. For a spell, Tyson was one of America's most famous actresses. Her success had been a long time in coming. Born in New York, she had worked as a secretary at the Red Cross. One day she pulled herself up from her desk. "I'm sure God didn't intend me to sit at a typewriter," she said. Thereafter she studied acting and hit the pavement in search of work as a model and actress. Off-Broadway theatergoers came to know her for her award-winning performances in such dramas as *Moon on a Rainbow Shawl* and as Virtue in the celebrated off-Broadway production of Genet's *The Blacks*. But theater work was not easy to find even for this talented actress. She turned to television, where she appeared in *Brown Girl, Brown Stones, Naked City*, and *The Nurses*. After *East Side, West Side,* she won roles, usually as the girlfriend or wife: of Ivan Dixon (in *I Spy*), of Billy Dee Williams (*The F.B.I.*), of Robert Hooks (*The F.B.I.*), of Al Freeman Jr. (*The F.B.I.*), of Yaphet Kotto (*Gunsmoke*), and of Bill Cosby (on both *I Spy* and *The Bill Cosby Show*). Rarely at the center of the action, Tyson's characters were usually defined by their relationships with their men. Yet Tyson—still a striking visual presence who totally went against the grain of Hollywood's definition of beauty—always exuded that burning sense of commitment and integrity. Even when her roles might seem slight, viewers could not take her lightly. And surprisingly, the characters themselves were often enough written to stand for what was decent and honorable. Tyson might have made a great romantic heroine. You can see that with her warm touch and her regal appearance as an African princess opposite Ivan Dixon in the premiere episode of *I Spy*. Tyson, however, went for years without a great role to play. Her frustrations grew. When she felt it was pointless to continue scrambling about for acting parts, both Sidney Poitier and Sammy Davis Jr. urged her not to give up her career. Finally, her pre-Jane performance in the film *Sounder* won her critical raves and an Academy Award Best Actress nomination in 1972. Following *Jane Pittman*, she appeared in the films *The River Niger* and *The Blue Bird*. Her face graced the covers of *Ms., People, Ebony*, and *Jet*. For the woman who as a little girl had sold papers in Harlem and who had struggled to find work since the days of *East Side, West Side*, it looked as if her place as an American star was assured.

But no producers broke down her door with great parts for her to play. In 1976, she returned to television in the Melvin Van Peebles-scripted melodrama *Just an Old Sweet Song*, giving a charming performance in an unchallenging part. In the late 1970s, she played supporting roles in such television dramas as *Wilma, King*, and *Roots*. Eventually, she initiated her own projects, the first of which was the 1978 *A Woman Called Moses*, in which she gave another acclaimed performance as Harriet Tubman. Written by African American writer Lonne Elder III and directed by Paul Wendkos with a narration by Orson Welles, *A Woman Called Moses* also featured Hari Rhodes, Robert Hooks, Will Geer, Jason Bernard, and Dick Anthony Williams. In the next decade, Tyson would have another great success in the title role of the schoolteacher in *The Marva Collins Story*. By all rights, Tyson should have had the steady flow of important roles that were offered to dramatic film stars like Jane Fonda and later Meryl Streep. But there still didn't seem to be a real place for her as a star in films and on television. To her credit, Tyson would endure and ultimately remain one of television's finest dramatic actresses.

Emerging as a full-fledged television star, Tyson later appeared in **The Marva Collins Story**

POP HISTORY ON AN EPIC SCALE: *ROOTS*

Epic, sweeping, and larger than life, the twelve-hour, six-million-dollar miniseries *Roots* also told American history from an African American perspective. Based on Alex Haley's famous 1976 book, the drama traced the struggles of the author's family from its life in Africa to its enslavement and ultimate "freedom" in America. At first, *Roots* looked downright hokey. The initial episode opened in 1750 with the birth of the Haley forefather, the young Kunta Kinte (LeVar Burton), the son of two loving parents, Binta (Cicely Tyson) and Omoro (Thalmus Rasulala). Often the idealized portrait of life in Gambia seemed more Holly-wood than West African, with a sequence in which young Kunta under-went tribal manhood rites that looked much like the activities of college pledges during a fraternity initiation.

But *Roots* grew forceful and urgent once Kunta Kinte was captured by white slave traders and sent across the sea on a slave ship. Proud and confident, he rebels once put into slavery in America, attempting to es-cape (and losing part of a foot because of it) and refusing to let the slaveholders give him the name Toby. It is the older slave Fiddler (Louis Gossett Jr.), known on the plantation for his mastery of the fiddle, who teaches the boy the techniques of survival in America—and also the game of masks that any slave must learn to play. Around whites, Fiddler plays his fiddle, grins, and cavorts; the real man hides behind the self-imposed mask of a contented, happy darky who delights his slave own-ers. But away from the white master, Fiddler is his own man, dignified and assured. Kunta learns to respond to the name Toby. But from Fid-dler, he understands that in his heart and his head he will always be Kunta Kinte. He learns to preserve the customs and traditions of the culture from whence he has come.

Roots followed Kunta into adulthood (the role then played by John Amos) through his marriage to Bell (Madge Sinclair) and the loss of his only child, Kizzy, who is sold by a "good" master to a brutal slave-holder on another plantation. From there, the drama traced Kizzy's ex-periences—her rape by her new master, the birth of her son, and the hope always of freedom. The last episode of *Roots* followed the life of Kizzy's son Chicken George and her grandson Tom, who finally, follow-ing the Civil War, see the freedom their ancestors always dreamed of.

During the eight consecutive nights the series aired, *Roots* became one of the most watched television programs in the history of the medium. It was also the topic of conversation throughout the nation: in classrooms, dormitories, offices, elevators—and on the streets. It was a great shared national experience; its concluding episode was seen by approximately 130 million viewers, nearly half the nation's population. Later *Newsweek* reported that the drama had inspired hundreds of col-leges to start *Roots* courses and that the National Archives in Washing-ton, D.C., was flooded with requests by citizens seeking information on how to trace their family genealogies.

Though *Roots* became the type of cultural phenomenon that might

History from a new pop perspective: Roots *with LeVar Burton as the young Kunta Kinte. And Madge Sinclair, John Amos, and Leslie Uggams*

never be duplicated, it almost wasn't produced. Network executives had not expected such an extraordinary response and even initially feared that white viewers might not watch it. As early as 1974, producer David Wolper had approached ABC about a series to be based on the book that Alex Haley had not yet completed. ABC, however, was lukewarm to the idea because *Roots* "violated two long-standing truisms of network television," reported television journalist Sally Bedell Smith. First, historical dramas were thought to put viewers to sleep. Second, of course, was the belief that "dramatic portrayals of nonwhites held little appeal for most viewers." But then came the remarkable success of *The Autobiography of Miss Jane Pittman*. ABC fed Wolper $50,000 for development of a miniseries that might run three to four hours. Once Wolper submitted some scripts to ABC, he was given a budget of $6 million to do the entire miniseries.

Still, all types of safeguards were taken by the network to ensure that *Roots* would not be a TV debacle. Foremost, ABC had approval of the cast. At first, one executive, said Sally Bedell Smith, balked at using drama student LeVar Burton for the young Kunta "because his lips were too thick." Others at ABC argued, however, that Burton had a sensitive look that would make him sympathetic. To help draw a large white viewership, ABC insisted that white actors be prominently cast in the drama. Such recognizable white television performers as Ed Asner, Sandy Duncan, Robert Reed, Chuck Connors, Lorne Greene, and Lynda Day George were hired for the production.

David Wolper's team of writers also made changes from the Haley book that gave the series more of an emphasis on sex and violence. The sexy character Fanta, whom the young Kunta Kinte beds, was nowhere to be found in the book. The creation of a guilt-ridden slave-ship captain (Ed Asner) seemed a plot device to comfort mainstream viewers, assuring them that indeed there were sensitive whites trapped in the inhumanity of the slave system as much as the African captives. Haley had not written of such a character. In the African segment, women were seen bare-breasted but were shot from a distance without any close-ups.

The writers for the eight episodes of *Roots* were all white. Many of the episodes were directed as rather routine television melodrama, the result being that the actors looked as if they were heroically and triumphantly directing themselves. The directors, however, had sense enough not to pull back from the actors' emotions. Only one of the series's directors was African American, Gilbert Moses, who directed the sixth and seventh episodes. Originally, the network would approve only Black directors Gordon Parks Sr. and Michael Schultz, neither of whom was available. Producer Stan Margulies felt that at first Moses (originally a stage director) was not familiar with film. But Moses learned quickly and, said Margulies, "made a difference to the actors."

Roots was promoted as an elaborate piece of entertainment; twelve hours of glorious, high-flung soap opera. ABC did not want the miniseries to be perceived as *only* a recounting of Black history. "Our concern," said network executive Larry Sullivan, "was to put a lot of white people in the promos. Otherwise we felt the program would be a turnoff." "I think we fooled the audience," ABC executive Lou Rudolph said later. "Because the white stories in most cases were irrelevant, it was a matter of having some white faces particularly in the opening episodes."

Originally, the network planned to air the program over eight weeks in eight installments, as it had done with the miniseries *Rich Man, Poor Man*. But Fred Silverman, then a top ABC executive, took the episodes home to view with his wife, Cathy, over eight consecutive nights. Both were overwhelmed and moved. Silverman realized, "To spread it out would have dissipated the impact." He decided it should air nightly. ABC executives didn't argue. They decided by airing it in one week they'd dispose of it quickly. Should it bomb, the ABC brass felt, "they would only lose a single week of the ratings competition instead of dragging down their average over two months." Fred Silverman decided to air *Roots* in January rather than during the important February sweeps because, he admitted, "I did not have enough faith in it."

But, concessions, compromises, and campaign strategies aside, *Roots* was a powerful viewing experience. It told the flip side of the story of *Gone With the Wind*, revealing the horrors and tragedy of slavery, taking viewers away from the mist and magnolia to the slave quarters, the family separations, the beatings, the wholesale trading of Black lives. The miniseries form permitted the writers to develop stronger characters than generally seen on television.

Roots was also distinguished by first-rate performances from a gallery of talented African American actors and actresses: Madge Sinclair, Ben Vereen, Olivia Cole, LeVar Burton, Leslie Uggams, Georg

Stanford Brown, Moses Gunn, Hari Rhodes, Beverly Todd, Ren Woods, Scatman Crothers, Lawrence-Hilton Jacobs, Richard Roundtree, Hilly Hicks, and Lynne Moody. After all his troubles on *Good Times*, John Amos looked as if he finally had a part he could identify with: a strong, rebellious, unyielding older Kunta Kinte. His performance was complemented by that of Madge Sinclair as his wife Bell. Sinclair delineated a complicated woman, who has foolishly taken her master at his word and tragically made the mistake of actually believing in his goodness. When her daughter is sold, Sinclair's Bell falls on her knees, pleading with him in a sequence that was both shocking and moving. Later she turns her blind anger toward her husband, Kunta. Every movement of her body, every twitch or blink of her eyes, every sound of ache and desperation in her voice were all perfectly modulated and coordinated to create a wholly believable human being; a woman who knows she is dying at the very moment she is begging for her child's life—and in essence, her own.

Louis Gossett Jr. (billed as such for the first time), who won an Emmy for his portrayal of Fiddler, gave perhaps the most dazzling performance; perfectly illustrating a slave's awareness of his fate as well as his crafty maneuvers to make the system work to his advantage. Yet ultimately even Fiddler ends a heartbroken man, betrayed by the master he has so shrewdly served.

Perhaps most moving was the graveyard sequence with Leslie Uggams as Kizzy. Returning as an adult woman to the plantation where she had grown up, Uggams's Kizzy kneels before her father's tombstone, which is marked Toby. Having suffered and endured, she fully understands how her father's pride has sustained and strengthened her. She speaks in front of the gravesite, letting her dead father know of her new life, of her son George, and of her vow never to forget what her father taught her. She ends by scratching out the name Toby, replacing it with the name Kunta Kinte.

Watching Uggams in the sequence was one of those moments when a viewer responds as much to the person on-screen as to the character being portrayed. *Roots* helped Leslie Uggams find herself as performer. Having been in show business since her childhood, she had appeared on *Beulah* and served a young apprenticeship, singing on a host of variety programs: *The Ed Sullivan Show, The Jack Paar Show, The Arthur Godfrey Show,* and *The Garry Moore Show*. Finally, she arrived at early stardom as a singer on Mitch Miller's weekly program *Sing Along with Mitch.* Afterward she won a Tony for her performance in the Broadway show *Hallelujah, Baby!* and then had her own short-lived variety program, *The Leslie Uggams Show,* in 1969.

Every time a viewer saw her in this earlier phase of her career, Leslie Uggams looked like a well-mannered girl—really a windup doll—doing everything exactly as she had been taught; smiling, pleasing, singing on cue. She seemed bland without a single idiosyncrasy that might have made her distinct or interesting. One wondered what was underneath the plastic smile; if, indeed, there was a person inside this show business creation. But in her key scenes in *Roots,* she attained a newfound maturity, washing away any signs of the eager-to-please child star, going all the way emotionally to indicate she fully understood her Kizzy's torment. Knowing something about Leslie Uggams's past made her performance all the more moving. Here was a real woman suddenly come to life.

Most of the performers in *Roots* had spent years playing trivial or trashy roles. Some would return to such parts afterward, but in *Roots* they seemed invigorated by doing something of worth and meaning. They proved that the theory about television acting—the idea that performers had to play "tiny" rather than grand; that the little tube still wasn't comfortable with big, searing emotions—simply wasn't true. Even though the medium still was best at showcasing ordinary lives, *Roots* proved that larger-than-life experiences could engross an audience.

Roots altered television history. Not only did its success elevate the miniseries's stature (indicating that audiences would stay home night after night to follow a drama) but it also proved the popularity of a family saga that spanned many generations. Many *white-cast* imitations followed. Nominated for thirty-seven Emmy Awards, *Roots* won nine. (Some of the actors canceled each other out for awards. In the category of Outstanding Actor for a Single Performance in a Drama or Comedy Series, all the nominees—LeVar Burton, John Amos, Ben Vereen, and Louis Gossett Jr., who won—were in *Roots.*) Olivia Cole won the Emmy for Outstanding Single Performance by a Supporting Actress in a Comedy or Drama Series. Ed Asner won the same award in the actor category. Quincy Jones was awarded the Emmy for Outstanding Music Composition for a series. *Roots* also won the Emmy as Outstanding Limited Series.

Most important, both *The Autobiography of Miss Jane Pittman* and *Roots* indicated that the race question—indeed the race drama—was still, despite the beliefs of network executives, very much on the minds of the American public. Intelligent African American dramatic presentations could be mainstream hits. Yet, sadly, neither program had a lasting effect on Black television programming. One might have assumed a flock of similar serious Black dramas would have paraded across the airways. But no such thing happened. Nonetheless, some unusual Black specials did appear.

Two years after *The Autobiography of Miss Jane Pittman*, ABC broadcast a two-hour adaptation of African American playwright Lonne Elder III's *Ceremonies in Dark Old Men*. Under the direction of Black director Michael Schultz, this drama—set in Harlem in 1958—depicted a Black family in conflict with itself and a new set of values in an increasingly violent culture. Though tied more to theater than film, the production nonetheless had some fine moments and exciting performances by Douglas Turner Ward, Godfrey Cambridge, Robert Hooks (as the cool, sinister gangster Blue Haven), and Rosalind Cash. It also marked the television debut of the Negro Ensemble theater company. In 1974, the theme of interracial love was explored in fairly serious terms in *The Wedding Band* with Ruby Dee and James Broderick.

The two-hour TV movie *Green Eyes* starred Paul Winfield as an embittered war veteran who returns to Vietnam in search of the son he fathered with a Vietnamese prostitute. The story of Olympic runner Wilma Rudolph was dramatized in *Wilma*, which starred newcomer Shirley Jo Finney as Rudolph and Cicely Tyson as her mother. Maya Angelou's moving memoir *I Know Why the Caged Bird Sings* was also adapted—unfortunately, disappointingly so—as a two-hour TV movie with Diahann Carroll, Esther Rolle, and Roger Mosley. LeVar Burton also starred in such TV movies as *Dummy* and *Billy: Portrait of a Street Kid*.

An unusual telecast was *The Minstrel Man*, a somber glimpse into the world of the African American minstrel show that told the story of two brothers struggling to maintain their dignity while pursuing careers as blackface entertainers—even though they themselves are Black. The all-star presentation *Freedom Road* featured Muhammad Ali as a former slave who becomes a United States senator.

The lavishly mounted six-hour miniseries *King* dramatized the life of Dr. Martin Luther King Jr. Directed and written by Abby Mann, it featured Cicely Tyson (as Coretta Scott King) and Paul Winfield in the title role. Giving a stirring performance, Winfield managed to do the impossible: he vividly re-created King's legendary speeches without sounding like a parody. Yet King's lieutenant, Dr. Ralph Abernathy, complained that the role of a white adviser to King was overstated— and a distortion of history that made it appear that even the most successful African Americans relied on guidance and help from whites.

The Killing Affair dramatized the interracial affair of a white female police officer (Elizabeth Montgomery) and her African American partner (O. J. Simpson), who are drawn together as they pursue a psychopathic killer. Though *The Killing Affair* was—for 1977—strong television material (willing to acknowledge sexism and racism on a big-city police force), it was often predictably clichéd. Montgomery, however, gave a convincing performance while Simpson glided along on his charm surprisingly well. Perhaps the most interesting character was the Black cop's wife, played by Rosalind Cash. When she realizes her husband is involved with a white woman, Cash's intensity makes the drama searingly *real.* One almost wishes *The Killing Affair* was about her. As for Simpson, the part led the way to starring roles in such other TV dramas as *Goldie and the Boxer* and the sequel *Goldie and the Boxer Go to Hollywood* (in which he played the good-hearted protector of a sweet little white girl). Then came the famous Hertz rent-a-car commercials and, finally, his starring role in the most riveting TV of the 1990s, his trial for the murder of his former wife, Nicole Brown Simpson.

The Depression-era Black family drama *Roll of Thunder, Hear My Cry* also appeared in 1978. An unusual—and uneven—drama was *The Hollow Image,* the tale of a young African American woman (Saundra Sharp) struggling with conflicts over her career and her life in Harlem.

But the best of the post-*Roots* TV dramas were *Backstairs at the White House* (1979) and the sequel *Roots: The Next Generations.* The beautifully made nine-hour *Backstairs at the White House* seemed a mix of *Roots* and the PBS British import *Upstairs, Downstairs.* Based on a 1961 book and broadcast over four consecutive Monday nights, *Backstairs at the White House* chronicled the experiences of a real-life African American mother and daughter—Maggie (Olivia Cole) and Lillian (Leslie Uggams) Rogers, who worked as domestics in the White

Black women front and center: Leslie Uggams and Olivia Cole as daughter and mother in
Backstairs at the White House

House from the Taft administration on through the presidencies of Wilson, Harding, Coolidge, Hoover, Roosevelt, Truman, and Eisenhower. Here again American history was seen from another perspective. *Backstairs at the White House* also dramatized the conflict between a stern mother and a sensitive, insecure daughter. The production was strengthened by a powerful performance by Olivia Cole, who looked as if she might follow in the heels of Cicely Tyson. Also cast were Louis Gossett Jr., Robert Hooks, Eileen Heckart, Claire Bloom, George Kennedy, and Cloris Leachman.

Roots: The Next Generations was a real surprise: a sequel almost as good (in a very different way) as the original. This fourteen-hour, seven-part production traced the lives of four generations of Alex Haley's ancestors: opening with Tom Harvey (Georg Stanford Brown), the great-grandson of Kunta Kinte, and ending with Alex Haley himself on his trip to Africa to trace his family's roots. Throughout, the family members witness important times in American history: the Reconstruction era, the rise of Jim Crow laws and the Ku Klux Klan, segregation in the modern South and de facto segregation in the modern North, World Wars I and II, race riots, and the civil rights era.

Though the characters in the sequel had none of the pop tragic grandeur of the earlier characters—and though it was more soap-opera-ish—*Roots: The Next Generations* still engaged viewers. Perhaps the most unexpectedly moving sequence occurred when Beah Richards as Cyntha Harvey Palmer took her grandson, the young Alex (Christoff St. John), aside and explained the family history. Richards performed so simply yet with such a felt and credible intensity—not an actorish performance, just a *supremely* real one—that a viewer could be saddened by a dawning awareness of who Beah Richards herself was: yet another immensely talented African American performer who rarely got the parts she deserved. Yet she couldn't utter a line of dialogue without making it a thing of truth and beauty. Equally impressive was Al Freeman Jr., who played Malcolm X.

Also in the cast of this $16 million production (nearly three times the cost of the original) were: Dorian Harewood, Irene Cara, Stan Shaw, Bernie Casey, Debbie Allen, Brock Peters, Ossie Davis, Diahann Carroll, James Earl Jones (giving one of the few *un*convincing performances as Alex Haley), Fay Hauser, Lynne Moody, Debbi Morgan, Bever-Leigh Banfield, Henry Fonda, Ruby Dee, Olivia de Havilland,

Avon Long, Roger Mosley, Rosey Grier, and Lynn Hamilton. Making his television debut was Marlon Brando as the American Nazi leader George Lincoln Rockwell. This time around David Wolper's production company also employed African American directors like Lloyd Richards and Georg Stanford Brown and Black writer Thad Mumford.

And so the 1970s ended with the very look of the primetime schedule having been radically altered. Not only had more Black-oriented programs appeared than ever before in the medium's history but some—*Sanford and Son, The Jeffersons, The Autobiography of Miss Jane Pittman, Roots*, and *Roots: The Next Generations*—had been among the era's most successful broadcasts. African American performers—Cicely Tyson, Redd Foxx, Flip Wilson, Sherman Hemsley—were now also among the medium's great stars.

But still African American viewers often felt conflicted about the images. On one level, the weekly series succeeded in introducing the television viewer to homes and lives in America different from those presented on such shows as *Father Knows Best* in the 1950s or *The Brady Bunch* in the late 1960s. America now acknowledged its Black population. Yet many of the new Black sitcoms had been weak and pallid, their basic situations and family relationships having been defined by people—white writers, directors, producers—from an entirely different cultural experience and perspective. Seldom presenting a sensitive, intimate portrait of Black life, the shows had also been littered with stereotypes and clichéd images. Serious weekly dramatic African American programs were still missing from the airwaves. Thus with all the advances for African Americans in television in the 1970s, one still had the nagging feeling that the more things changed, the more they hadn't changed enough.

4. THE 1980s: SUPERSTARS

Perhaps few decades had such an array of incongruities and contradictions as the glamorous and glitzy 1980s. On the one hand, the era was marked by the political conservatism of the Reagan administration. On the other, the emergence of a political figure like Jesse Jackson, who audaciously announced his candidacy for President of the United States, indicated that traditional liberalism lived on—but with some new twists. The 1980s was also a time of yuppies and buppies; of greed on Wall Street and of scandals there too; of widespread drug use and of the rise of the Moral Majority; of the emergence of a new Black middle class and of demands for an end to quotas and affirmative action; of extraordinary wealth among less than 1 percent of the nation's population and of debilitating poverty for others. The 1980s were the decade of Trump Tower on Fifth Avenue and of waves of the homeless on city streets throughout America; of a nation seemingly untroubled by its growing indifference to social and racial problems; and of a nation soon shaken by a devastating new disease known as AIDS.

Television programming would eventually reflect these incongruities and disparities. The networks would air fewer Black-cast series than in the previous decade. Yet in time, television would have to comment on the familiar, long-standing social problems affecting Black and white. Some new shows like *Miami Vice*, with its ruthless drug czars and dealers and its morally ambivalent cop heroes, would serve as comments on the era's flagrant greed, and the corruption that grew out of it. A new series like *Hill Street Blues* would express the belief that liberal ideologies no longer worked for resolving the old tensions and problems—reflecting the era's resulting political conservatism. And a hit series like *The Cosby Show*—which occasionally would be criticized for ignoring the problems of the less fortunate, the people who couldn't live comfortably cushioned in a Brooklyn brownstone like its protagonists—would nonetheless give voice to the new African American middle class.

But television programming in the 1980s would also reflect changes in the medium itself. The once all-powerful three major networks soon discovered that their viewership was eroding, now that families had new viewing options in their homes. In 1980, only 1 percent of American homes had VCRs. By 1988, the number would rise to 58 percent. Viewers could now tape special programs. Or watch movies on cassette. Or they could skip television programs altogether and instead use their sets for playing video games. The proliferation of cable in American households would offer viewers the opportunity for more adult dramas that would cover subjects and use language that had long been taboo for television. Soon the networks would look more closely at the demographics for their shows. If they couldn't pull in the huge audience of the past, employing the old "lowest common denominator" strategy, then it was now important to attract the younger, more educated, and more financially secure viewers that advertisers favored. That, of course, meant a different type of product.

Demographics might explain the appeal of the medium's new Black stars (most of whom surprisingly were men) such as Michael Warren, Denzel Washington, Philip Michael Thomas, and Alfre Woodard, who created well-defined, sometimes complicated characters. A previously unthinkable new sensibility and sometimes a new sexuality were introduced. Yet demographics aside, TV habits died hard, and some of the roles of the era's other new stars, those garnering wide coverage and publicity, like Nell Carter and Mr. T, harked back to the past.

At the same time, those grand, now established stars like Cicely Tyson, Louis Gossett Jr., Billy Dee Williams, Ossie Davis, and Ruby Dee still worked. But some seemed in search of roles to revitalize their careers. Most ironically, though, with all of the Reagan era's evasions about race and racism, two of television's biggest stars and money-makers—by decade's end—would be African Americans.

But *that* came later.

At the start of the 1980s, it was business as usual.

The era opened on a rather glum note with new series—like *One in a Million, Sanford,* and *The New Odd Couple*—that not only failed to win audiences but often appeared as lackluster replays of the recent past. Formerly cast as the comically caustic waitress Shirley Simmons on *What's Happening!!,* Shirley Hemphill was the star of the sitcom *One in a Million.* Now cast as a cabdriver named Shirley, Hemphill inherits a multimillion-dollar conglomerate from one of her customers. Thereafter, Shirley teaches the company bigwigs to show some compassion for the Common Man/Woman. Shirley finds support from her parents, played by Mel Stewart and Ann Weldon. *One in a Million* was the familiar fish-out-of-water concept, meekly racialized by the mere fact that now we have an African American woman trying to alter the attitudes and values of a fundamentally white male corporate culture. It was a fairly appealing premise, but the jokes and situations on *One in a Million* were tired. Hemphill herself occasionally had a sweet, warm quality that the series failed to tap. After six months, the series was dropped from ABC's primetime schedule. NBC's *Sanford*—Fred Sanford on his own without son Lamont by his side—didn't fare much better. Premiering in March 1980, it left the airways in July 1981. And when ABC tried injecting ethnic juices into a familiar Neil Simon comedy by starring Demond Wilson and Ron Glass as Oscar and Felix in *The New Odd Couple,* the results were almost as dismal as NBC's attempts at a Black version of *Barefoot in the Park* in the late 1960s.

MIXED COMBOS FOR A CONSERVATIVE AGE

Amidst the new political conservatism, the networks assumed that viewers of the early 1980s, like those of the late 1970s, were no longer interested in programs set in an African American community—with a distinct set of cultural signs. Soon, those few African American performers who were prominently featured in primetime series found themselves, more often than not, starring or co-starring in what were essentially white shows. It was a continuation of the late 1970s mixed-combo concept in which Black and white characters, rather than being openly suspicious of each other, were living and working together harmoniously in a 1950s-style world. Of course, 1950s America, rather than being an integrated society, was in the process of being desegregated. But the new shows incorporated the 1950s TV concept of ordered worlds where, even when Black characters appeared, there were no serious racial problems. No social ills. No political tensions. All was fine and dandy between Black and white in America.

Sometimes that could lead to a reversion to the worst of the old stereotypes. Such was the case with the 1983 sitcom *Just Our Luck*. It told the story of a TV weatherman (Richard Gilliland), desperately in need of help with his weather reports—and fearing for his job. Who should come into his life but an ancient Black genie named Shabu (T. K. Carter), who could cast spells and work wonders. Having served the likes of Cleopatra and Napoleon in the past, Shabu clearly found his new master a comedown. Regardless, he kept the weatherman's life and job in order. Unlike Samantha on the old *Bewitched* series—who might use her magical powers to zip through mundane housework so she would have time for more pressing matters, and who was surrounded by relatives like her mother who understood her powers— poor Shabu was cut off from a cultural base. Moreover, throughout, viewers were being reassured that a Black man with power was not to be feared. Shabu, the magical Black man, used his skills in the service of his new white buddy. Worse, actor Carter didn't seem to have any idea what to do with the character. With his eyes popping and his jaw dropping, Carter's Shabu came across as an unabashed coon character. Somehow Carter survived this role and later gave a searing performance in the HBO drama *The Corner*. It was hard to believe you were seeing the same actor.

Other series tried a different approach. *Tenspeed and Brown Shoe* starred Ben Vereen and Jeff Goldblum as an oddball pair of private eyes working off Sunset Boulevard in Los Angeles. Vereen's Tenspeed was a crafty hustler who, in order to meet his parole requirements, had to help the straitlaced Brown Shoe track down various scam artists. In this bonding tale, the Black man's skills are still dubious ones. The series could have worked just as well had Tenspeed been depicted as a brainy schoolteacher out to put some zing into his life rather than a familiar Black con. What elevated *Tenspeed and Brown Shoe* were the playful, iconoclastic performances of Vereen—energetic, quick on his feet, smooth, and perceptive—and Goldblum—goofy and spacey but charming and game for fun. But this Stephen J. Cannell production couldn't sustain its early momentum and was off the air within six months.

Palmerstown U.S.A. was another mixed-combo-style series with a pair of pint-sized interracial buddies bonding like crazy. Based on an idea by Alex Haley (who, along with Norman Lear, was one of its executive producers), the hour-long dramatic series focused on the close relationship of two schoolkids—a Black boy named Booker T. (Jermain Hodge Johnson) and a white boy, David (Brian Godfrey Wilson)—growing up in the South during the Depression. Though *Palmerstown U.S.A.* sprang from Haley's boyhood experiences in the 1930s, the series, in many respects, looked like revisionist history. Racism was acknowledged, but it was racism of the past, something America, so we are to believe, outgrew long ago. As Booker T.'s mother, actress Jonelle Allen was singled out by the critics for "a performance of wide emotional scope that was kept in fine control at all times." But many of the other actors, especially the two unknowns playing the crucial leads, weren't strong enough to keep viewers watching. Also cast (as the father of Booker T.) was African American film/TV director Bill Duke. *Palmerstown U.S.A.* was off the air in a matter of months.

No doubt the quintessential early 1980s mixed-combo series was *Gimme a Break!*, which starred Nell Carter as Nell Harper, a familiar character: the hefty (almost two hundred pounds), all-knowing, all-seeing, all-comforting Black woman. This time around she's the housekeeper for a widowed white police officer, Chief Carl Kanisky, his three daughters, and a genial grandfather. Sassy and independent but also supposedly warmhearted and, naturally, lovable, Nell gleefully traded barbs and quips with Kanisky and the rest of the family. Their welfare, of course, always was her uppermost concern.

In one episode, when she learns of inheriting money from her deceased grandmother, Nell has nothing better to do with it (not very much, we should add) than to divide it among those in the Kanisky household and her friend Addy. On another episode, after a fellow has proposed to her, rather than jump at the chance for a new life for herself, Nell wonders—of all things—how leaving would affect these white folks she has worked for. Needless to say, she doesn't marry the guy. Later in the series, when Chief Kanisky died (following the real-life death of actor Dolph Sweet, who played the role), Nell becomes both mother and father to the girls and their friends. Then, perhaps most shockingly, in an episode when a Kanisky relative wants custody of the girls, Nell wages a battle to keep her babies. In a courtroom scene, she tells the judge she has made a promise to always care for the children. Finally, she falls on her knees and begs him to let her keep them!

A little nurturing still goes a long way: Nell Carter with Telma Hopkins in **Gimme a Break!**

Once the Kanisky children grew up, the writers devised a new plot turn to keep Nell's nurturing skills on display. So devoted does Nell become to an orphaned white kid named Joey (Joey Lawrence) that she moves to New York City with her friend Addy, Grandpa Kanisky, *and* little Joey. There Nell works at a publishing house. But she also meets Joey's father—and Joey's younger brother Matthew. Once the father skips town, Nell, as should be expected, cares for little Matthew too.

Interestingly, in a *Gimme a Break!* episode that served as a spin-off pilot for a new series, Don Rickles played a deli owner, who catches a little Black girl (La Shana Dendy) shoplifting. It's revealed that she's an orphan who has been living on the streets for three weeks since the death of her grandmother. He wants the girl sent to jail. But good-hearted Nell intervenes and persuades him to take the child into his home. Of course, here was yet another Black kid with no family or community to care for her. Surprisingly, it never crosses Nell's mind that she might take this Black child into her home; the writers keep her too busy with her white charges.

For African American viewers, *Gimme a Break!* was little more than a remake of *Beulah.* For some semblance of a Black community, *Gimme a Break* trotted out Addy as a chum for Nell, similar, of course, to Beulah's old friend Oriole. Later the series brought on Rosetta LeNoire as Nell's mother, Maybelle.

The most interesting aspect of the Nell character was the mean-spirited edge that Carter brought to the role. Though Carter shrewdly understood how to time and punch a line for maximum laughs, on those occasions when she tried to play Nell as lovable and warm, she sometimes looked like a blatant phony, both calculating and straining for effect. But when she had to be bossy and cutting, her anger seemed genuine, although you never understood its source. One might read into all of this a latent hostility for her job and the whole Kanisky family. (But, then, Nell also frequently insulted and shouted at her friend Addy.) Here, though, Nell often looked like Sapphire with an edge. And when she and Chief Kanisky bickered and berated one another, they were a rowdy married couple. Sort of an interracial Kingfish and Sapphire. But no matter how much Carter the actress might bark, the script made sure that Nell the character never bit.

Gimme a Break! never permitted Nell's vulnerability to fully surface. The creators couldn't imagine that a reputable guy might really like Nell—and take her seriously. Or that Nell might take herself seriously enough to form an important relationship. Her romantic encounters were used for quick, cheap laughs. *Gimme a Break!* rather cruelly delighted in exhibiting the hefty Nell (in unflattering camera angles) going gaga over some handsome hunk.

Nell Carter was quick to defend herself against the criticism that flared up around the show. "Instead of writing letters demanding that images be upgraded," she told *Essence* "many Black people still criticize me personally. I'm called Mammy and everything else. Why can't anyone say, 'Look, there's a Black gal that's got her own show!' " She also explained to *People*, "So blacks don't want to be represented as having menial jobs. I think anyone, black or white, who looks down on a person because she's a maid or a waitress is a real butt-face." But the point was never merely that she played a maid, but rather that the maid was defined in the same, tired simplistic way.

For Nell Carter, *Gimme a Break!*'s success was a mixed blessing. Certainly, the show took her career in a new direction and brought her wider attention, which she clearly deserved. Her life had already been marked by a series of dramatic peaks and valleys, which Carter shared with her public. Born in Birmingham in 1949, the fifth of nine children—her mother a homemaker and her father an army sergeant—she survived a difficult childhood. At nineteen, she went to New York to break into show business. Her stage debut came in the 1970 production *Soon* with such other new performers as Richard Gere, Barry Bostwick, and Peter Allen. Later she appeared in *Jesus Christ Superstar* and then became a star in Broadway's *Ain't Misbehavin'*, winning a Tony for her performance in 1978 and later winning an Emmy for the same role in NBC's 1982 television version. In the late 1970s, she appeared on the daytime soap *Ryan's Hope*. But when she made it to primetime series television, she was shoved quickly into the sassy quasi-mean-mammy slot in the series *Lobo*. Here she played the loudmouth police officer Sergeant Hildy Jones.

During and after the run of *Gimme a Break!*, Carter's personal problems continued. She had two unsuccessful marriages, suffered three miscarriages, battled obesity and diabetes, lost her brother to AIDS, and struggled with an addiction to alcohol and drugs. "I did coke all night, then drank at about 3 in the morning to get to sleep so I could get up for a 6 o'clock call at the studio," she told *People*. Hearing that, maybe it's not so difficult to understand why she appeared so angry on the series. In 1992, she underwent brain surgery for a double aneurysm that almost took her life. In personal interviews, she emerged as a woman whose sufferings had obviously deepened and saddened her. It was surprising to discover just how intelligent she was. Yet for all her personal insights and her talent, Carter seemed trapped professionally. Her later roles in series like *Morton's by the Bay* and *Hangin' with Mr.*

Cooper looked like little more than variants on the Nell Harper character.

WEBSTER: AND A CHILD SHALL LEAD THEM

Webster was another series in which the central character, an orphaned Black boy, was lifted out of an African American cultural context and plopped into a white environment. After his parents were killed in a car crash, young Webster (Emmanuel Lewis) went to live with a white couple, George and Katherine Papadopolis. A former football player who was a teammate of Webster's father, Travis, George had promised that should anything happen to Travis and his wife, Gert, he would take care of his friend's child. The series did not seriously question why Webster had no relatives to care for him.

Emmanuel Lewis as Webster, another precocious kid living an all-American dream, with the help, of course, of his white surrogate parents

Unlike *Diff'rent Strokes*, on which jokes were made about race and culture, *Webster*, in tune with the conservative 1980s, did all it could to ignore such subjects. Race problems, we're to assume, have vanished from the land. So too have cultural differences. Little Webster had no major problems adjusting to his new life in the Papadopolis household. On one episode, Webster takes a new white friend home to meet his family. The kid registers no surprise at seeing that his Black friend has white parents. That was the perspective of the series itself. If anyone has to adjust, it is Webster's new stepmother, Katherine, a socialite/ombudswoman (later a psychologist), who knows so little about parenting.

During the second season, Webster's Uncle Phillip (Ben Vereen) suddenly appeared and wanted custody of the child. But, of course, if Webster left to live with a Black family, there would have been no series. So Uncle Phillip eventually decides to go to Hollywood to pursue a career in show business, and now little Webster is free to remain blissfully secure with his white buddies.

Sometimes *Webster* attempted to focus on serious social issues. In one episode, Webster learned that a classmate—a little white girl he has befriended—was being molested by a teacher. On other episodes, Webster befriended a child suffering from leukemia; confronted a school bully; and—perhaps the most emotionally affecting of all—had to deal with his own size. At the start of the series, twelve-year-old star Lewis stood about forty inches tall. As the series continued, Lewis appeared not to grow at all. Thus, the writers addressed the questions which they no doubt felt television viewers were asking. Of course, it ended on an optimistic note. After a consultation with an endocrinologist, Webster learns he has the potential to grow in the future. In actuality, by the time he was a young adult, Emmanuel Lewis, like Gary Coleman, hadn't grown much taller.

Nonetheless, beneath the sugarcoated, fake exterior of *Webster*, comments about race unintentionally surfaced. Webster always addressed his adopted mother as *Ma'am* " 'cause it kinda sounds like *Mom*." This made him sound all the more like the little pickaninny finally allowed inside the master's home.

While Black audiences often considered Emmanuel Lewis skilled and talented—he really was an adorable kid—Black parents complained that the series sent a poor message to Black children: that whenever advice and comfort were needed, both would be dispensed by knowledgeable whites. Like *Diff'rent Strokes* and that ill-fated spin-off of *Gimme a Break!*, the subtext was that there was no Black community to nourish these kids. The Black father had long been absent from TV. Now the Black mother was disappearing too—unless, of course, there were darling white kids around in need of some lovin'.

Though it wouldn't qualify as a major hit, *Webster*, with a strong lead-in from *Benson*, won its time slot on Friday nights and stayed on the air for four seasons. It also briefly made Emmanuel Lewis a household name. Born in Brooklyn, he was already a veteran of forty commercials when he caught the eye of an ABC executive who saw him in a Burger King spot. Afterward, in hopes of duplicating Gary Coleman's success in *Diff'rent Strokes*, ABC developed the series around him. A People's Choice Award named *Webster* the Best New Comedy Series. Landing on magazine covers, including *TV Guide*, Lewis appeared on such other television programs as *Mr. T and Emmanuel Lewis in A Christmas Dream, Lost in London* (a TV movie with Ben Vereen and Lynne Moody), and *All-Star Party for "Dutch" Reagan*, hosted by Frank Sinatra. He had his own production company, Emmanuel Lewis Entertainment Enterprises, and the tabloids reported on his friendship with Michael Jackson.

But most intriguing was the reaction to Lewis in Japan, where he was looked upon as something of a deity. His mother Margaret informed the press that during the postwar years American GIs had handed out thousands of dolls, which Japanese families kept in their homes as a sign of good luck. "When people see me in Japan, they touch me for luck, they want to feel me to see if I'm for real," Lewis himself said. "Everyone thinks it's this doll come to life, women break down and start crying, they go crazy and charge the stage," Margaret Lewis said. Lewis made several trips to Japan, where he also made records and performed.

But much like Gary Coleman, Lewis discovered himself a commodity for which there was little use once the series left the airwaves. Occasionally, a program like *Entertainment Tonight* reported on him. Enrolling in television and film studies at Clark Atlanta University, he had hopes of producing and starring in a martial-arts film in Thailand. But by 1994, *People* included Lewis, at age twenty-three, in its roundup of "Where Are They Now?" stars.

THE NIGHTTIME SOAPS: A LITTLE COLOR DOESN'T HURT

Of course, placing African American characters in a white cultural context took on a whole other meaning in 1984 with the arrival of Diahann Carroll on Aaron Spelling's top-rated *Dynasty*. Like such other popular nighttime soaps of the Reagan years as *Dallas, Falcon Crest,* and *Flamingo Road, Dynasty* explored a seductively melodramatic world of wealth, privilege, and power. Beautiful women. Dashing men. Luxurious clothes. Plush settings. And endless manipulations and betrayals. It was also just about exclusively a white world. Though some African Americans like Georg Stanford Brown, Bill Duke, Stan Lathan, and Roy Campanella Jr. directed episodes of the nighttime soaps, generally the series were so tightly controlled by their executive producers and production companies that there wasn't much leeway for individual expression. For too long there were also no significant African American characters.

Diahann Carroll's character, Dominique Deveraux, changed that. Having watched the soaps, Carroll aggressively had her manager suggest to various producers that they add her to their primetime dramas. The manager, Roy Gerber, recalled that "the first one we called, the producer told me: 'We do not envision a Black person on our show.' And they were not talking about just Diahann. They were talking about all Black people." *Dynasty*'s co-creator, Esther Shapiro, however, had already considered the idea. "A lot of people suggested a Black maid—to do a sort of *Upstairs, Downstairs* kind of thing. I just hated that idea," she said. "I was leaning more to a beautiful, glamorous, active Black woman who was smart and had an interesting life of her own." Finally, Shapiro decided to create a role "where a Black could be on the same social and economic level as the other characters. The one thing we wouldn't do is put on a Black woman as a victim."

Carroll was signed to play Dominique Deveraux, an internationally famous singer and the half sister of series hero Blake Carrington (her mother and Blake's father had been lovers). She returns to Denver to demand her place in the Carrington empire. Haughty, outspoken, glamorous as all get-out, the Black woman was now depicted as a formidable combatant in a tough, competitive, dog-eat-dog, mink-lined world. Her initial appearance was like something out of classic 1930s/1940s Hollywood. Dominique enters a posh hotel dressed to the nines, wearing a lynx coat and $350,000 worth of jewels with a matched set of Cartier luggage. When a clerk at the hotel tells her that he has a junior suite for her, she replies, "I don't sleep in my clothes, and I don't sleep with my clothes. I need a bedroom for me and a bedroom for my clothes."

The press covered her appearance as a major television event with cover stories in *TV Guide, Ebony, Jet,* and *Essence* as well as features in other publications. *People* called her appearance "a blow against one of TV's last WASP bastions: the primetime soap." *Ebony* also reported that with Carroll's initial appearance, "the show's ratings zoomed in Chicago, Detroit, New York, and other cities with large Black populations. The average number of viewers rose from 34 million to 41 million." The press proclaimed that television now had its "first Black bitch."

But after all this fanfare, the excitement quickly died down. Despite her charisma, the writers did not know what to do with the character. Dominique was depicted as just another glamorous, high-powered character. Nothing wrong with that, on one level. Certainly, Carroll's very presence proved that glamour and swank allure were not the province of white women only. But without some cultural signs, the character turned flat and implausible. In one sequence, after having won acceptance by the Carringtons, Dominique, at an elegant dinner with the clan, announced that it had long been her dream to be reunited with her family. For African American viewers, the sequence seemed simpleminded and laughable. What about Dominique's Black mother and her other Black relatives or friends? Did they not mean anything to her? Poor Dominique often appeared to be an old-style tragic mulatto, simply grateful to be seated in the Big House. Never did the scripts endow Dominique with any type of Black sensibility. Or, dare it be said, anger, both social and racial. It's as if one were to tell the story of Josephine Baker's extraordinary career in France without ever mentioning race—or what drove her abroad in the first place.

Billy Dee Williams also joined the cast as Carroll's Berry Gordy-style record mogul husband, which was a good touch. But still nothing really differentiated them culturally from the rest of the cast. Later Dominique's daughter (Troy Beyer) by a white attorney showed up, coming across as merely a second-generation tragic mulatto or, to use the old terminology, a tragic quadroon (one-fourth Black blood). Certainly, no one would want to be knocked over the head with a race theme on every episode of a series like *Dynasty*. But a little racial juice here and there would have added to this pop soufflé. After only two seasons, Dominique disappeared from the show. Ironically, later Robert Townsend's *The Bold, the Black, and the Beautiful* for HBO spoofed the various cultural signs and symbols that *Dynasty* was too timid to assign to Black characters.

Occasionally, Black characters turned up on other nighttime soaps. Raymond St. Jacques played a doctor for a season on the soap *Falcon Crest*; later that polished stylist Roscoe Lee Browne appeared in the series. During the 1988 season of *Knots Landing*, Lynne Moody and Larry Riley joined the cast, playing Patricia and Frank Williams, who were living undercover in Knots Landing in the Federal Witness Protection Program. What a place for a Black couple to hide out and hope to be inconspicuous—a white suburban community. Saundra Sharp also appeared in episodes while Halle Berry joined the cast as Debbie Porter during the 1991–92 season. Apparently, their roles drew in Black viewers. A 1986 study conducted by BBDO Worldwide, one of the nation's largest advertising concerns, indicated that African American audiences—watching certain programs like *Knots Landing* in a block—boosted ratings and saved such shows from being canceled.

Generally, African Americans comprised about 14 percent of the total audience "between 8 p.m. and 9 p.m. and greater percentages after 11 p.m.," said David Poltrack, vice president of research at CBS. "You are not going to have a hit show if you only appeal to Blacks. However, if you can take a show that has appeal among all segments but particular appeal among Black families, that's a very good candidate for an 8 p.m. show. The size of the Black audience is certainly something that we take into consideration." NBC's vice president of research projects, Gerald Jaffe, added that about one out of every eight viewers was Black. "They can make the difference between a marginal program," he said, "and a program that is not." Black viewers could add one to two and a half ratings points, from 8 p.m. to 11 p.m. A show like *Knots Landing* had a total rating of 19.4. But because African American households gave the show a 28.8 rating, the total rating was up by 2.1 rating points. The study also revealed that while African American viewers were loyal to programs featuring Black actors and actresses, they also viewed certain programs without Black performers, such as action series (like *Amazing Stories*, which during its 1985–86 season had a 16.5 rating; among non-Black households, its rating was 15.2; among African American homes, it had a 20.7 rating).

Other series, such as *Strike Force, Trauma Center, Ryan's Four, Bay City Blues, The Mississippi, For Love and Honor,* and *Hotel,* featured (as supporting players or as part of an ensemble cast) such African American actors as Dorian Harewood, Albert Hall, Bernie Casey, Mykel T. (Mykelti) Williamson, Stan Shaw, Yaphet Kotto, Keenen Ivory Wayans, Shari Belafonte, and Nathan Cook. Most of the shows (with the exception of the hit *Hotel*) quickly disappeared.

On some of the new series, you felt embarrassed to see talented performers wasted on such shlock material. Alfre Woodard played a secretary on *Tucker's Witch*. Scatman Crothers was the dependable Sam in another revamping of a *Casablanca* series. And after Louis Gossett Jr.'s moving Emmy-winning performance as Fiddler in *Roots*, the primetime series couldn't come up with anything better for him than a role as the mentor/guardian to a boy who is an alien from another planet in *The Powers of Matthew Star*.

Most of these programs painted a portrait of an integrated culture in which African Americans were an important part of the workforce. Cast as top-notch professionals, their race and culture often were inconsequential, and if such an aberration as a workplace race problem flared, it was promptly defused.

Some series used their African American characters to present some revisionist history. Moses Gunn appeared as the coal miner buddy of a frontier hero in the Dakota Territory during the 1870s on *Father Murphy*. Gunn also made appearances along with cast regular Ketty Lester on another frontier saga, *Little House on the Prairie*. It wasn't that Black Americans didn't live in such communities at this point in history. But the dramas failed to accurately delineate the racial lines that then were so tightly drawn. Instead they presented noble white heroes of the past who had no racial hang-ups or biases. These self-congratulatory tales suggested that past racism had resided mainly in the minds and hearts of evil, deranged people. The good common folk could be misled by such critters. But ultimately they were always guided by their better instincts. The same would be true later, in the 1990s, with a frontier series like *Dr. Quinn, Medicine Woman.*

Other Black characters played a more significant role in contributing to the tone, indeed the psychology, definition, and *attitude* of certain series. Carl Lumbly's intense (actually, rather grim) presence as a police detective added to the urban realism of the police drama *Cagney & Lacey.* Charlie Robinson and Marsha Warfield injected some comic cynicism into the courtroom comedy *Night Court.* Roger E. Mosley contributed to the breezy mood of *Magnum, P.I.* Cast as a former Vietnam buddy of the central character, private investigator Thomas Magnum, and the owner and pilot of his own helicopter, T.C. often helped his friend on various cases. Hip and handsome, Magnum was surrounded by offbeat buddies, which made him look all the more like a rugged individualist. T.C. was cool, loose, and basically realistic, his racial identity seeming to qualify him as an offbeat friend of the hero. Occasionally, the series also commented on T.C.'s life away from Magnum. Tim Reid added flavor and comedy to the dramatic series *Simon & Simon.*

OFFBEAT CASTING, UNUSUAL ACTORS

Brian Mitchell also appeared as Dr. Justin "Jackpot" Jackson on *Trapper John, M.D.*, which premiered in September 1979 but ran for six additional seasons in the 1980s. Mitchell was an interesting figure on primetime: he was a light-skinned actor with sharp features and curly hair. His first important role made use of his appearance: as the young suitor of the great-granddaughter of Kunte Kinte in *Roots: The Next Generations*, he was rejected by the girl's father because he was too white-looking. The second *Roots* explored the Black community's color caste system; a system that also seemed to exist among Hollywood producers, who frequently didn't know how to handle actors who didn't fit preconceived notions of the way African Americans should look. Usually, such light actors (like Hilda Simms and Ellen Holly) had problems finding work, unless, of course, like Frank Silvera, they were lucky enough to play other ethnics. When television uses a Black actor, it wants the audience to know he/she is Black.

Trapper John, M.D.'s interracial lineup: Madge Sinclair,
Pernell Roberts, Gregory Harrison, and Brian Mitchell

Briefly, Mitchell (who was later billed as Brian Stokes Mitchell) proved an exception to the rule. He came to *Trapper John, M.D.* after his appearance in the musical *Festival* with Gregory Harrison. The series producers liked the chemistry between the two and hired them both, using Harrison, of course, as one of the stars. Though Mitchell may have been mistaken for white by some, Black viewers knew exactly what he was. Mitchell came across—refreshingly—as a good-natured, clean-cut middle-class educated young African American. After *Trapper John, M.D.*, Mitchell appeared briefly as a police sergeant on the series *Houston Knights.* Following a major success as the lead in the Broadway musical *Ragtime*, Mitchell appeared as the Hawaiian lover of Doris Duke in the TV movie *Too Rich: The Secret Life of Doris Duke* and as the embittered former husband of Diana Ross in the TV movie *Double Platinum.* But otherwise he didn't find much television work.

Madge Sinclair joined *Trapper John, M.D.* in its second season as Nurse Ernestine Shoop. While important in sustaining Sinclair's career, her role didn't amount to much. It was another of TV's stern, fussy, but endearing wanna-be matriarchs. Somehow Sinclair managed to keep her dignity, refusing to let her performance lapse into standard TV cute and maintaining her composure and assurance no matter what the script imposed on her. Were it "not for her magnetic appearance," *TV Guide* wrote, "she might pass unnoticed among the others in small roles, among the guest stars." Her weekly appearance was a sign of how a talented actress could make the best of anything. Sinclair might well have become a great actress of film and television had she been able to play great roles.

Sinclair had come to acting late. Born in Kingston, Jamaica, she had married a Jamaican policeman, given birth to two sons, and looked as if she had settled into a quiet, conventional life. For six years, she taught school. But, restless and ambitious, she studied speech and drama and also appeared in local theater productions. In 1968, when her sons were three and five, Sinclair packed her bags and moved to New York City to pursue an acting career. She arrived in the States with only twenty-five dollars to her name. Sinclair worked with African American actor Albert Hall to lose her island sound and speak with a "Black American accent." During this time, her great inspiration was Cicely Tyson, whom she saw perform on stage.

Tall, brown-skinned, with high cheekbones and dark eyes, Sinclair was a proud, unconventional beauty who looked like she was born to play royalty. That's precisely what she did when cast as Clytemnestra in the New York Shakespeare Festival production of *The Wedding of Iphigenia* in 1971. Other theater roles followed. So did movie roles in *Conrack* and *Leadbelly*, which led her to eventually settle in Los Angeles. Known for exacting and unyielding characters, Sinclair exuded confidence and a shrewd intelligence. Determined to audition for any kind of role, even if the script didn't specify a Black performer, she read so well for the part of a lady truck driver in Sam Peckinpah's film *Convoy* that he hired her almost on the spot. Then came small roles in such television movies as *The Autobiography of Miss Jane Pittman* and *I Know Why the Caged Bird Sings*.

Sinclair always seemed too big—in passion, in anger—for television. That explains why she worked so well on such unusual (from an actor's point of view) dramas as *Roots* and *Jimmie B. and Andre*. But despite the fact that Sinclair was well respected in the industry and eventually walked off with five Emmy nominations, many realized her talents were wasted. "Why isn't she famous?" *TV Guide* asked. "On 50 magazine covers? In commercials? Signing pacts with networks for trillion-dollar deals? Maybe because Madge Sinclair is black."

Sinclair herself was one of the few television stars to address racism in the industry. "If I were a white actress who's done what I've done, I would have been asked to do substantial roles," she said. "But the climate isn't right for it." She admitted feeling fortunate in being able to escape playing maids and instead to be cast as teachers or judges. But she also said with a note of resignation, "Maybe my roles weren't important enough for producers or casting people to care if I was Black."

Madge Sinclair worked throughout the late 1970s and 1980s, usually in such other unchallenging material as the sitcoms *Grandpa Goes to Washington, Ohara, Look Out,* and *Me and the Boys.* She also appeared in such TV movies as *High Ice* with David Janssen and Dorian Harewood. The real exceptions for Sinclair were *Guyana Tragedy: The Jim Jones Story,* in which, along with that other misused Black actress of the era, Rosalind Cash, she gave a ferociously rousing performance as a follower of cult leader Jim Jones, and later the series *Gabriel's Fire,* for which she won an Emmy in 1991 as Outstanding Actress in a Dramatic Series. Sinclair was one of those performers that Black viewers felt a special connection to, no doubt intuitively aware of the actress's professional standards and struggles, which made it all the more surprising and sad when Sinclair suddenly died in 1995—at age fifty-seven—from leukemia.

MR. T: BEEFING UP THE A-TEAM

At the same time, the action series *The A-Team,* which starred George Peppard, Dirk Benedict, and Dwight Schultz, brought newcomer Mr. T to unexpected stardom in the role of Bosco B. A. Baracus. (The B.A., so the team thought, stood for Bad Attitude, a euphemism, of course, for Bad Ass.) In some ways a reworking of the *Mission: Impossible* formula, the series revolved around the exploits of a group of soldiers of fortune. Previously serving together in Vietnam, the men had been unjustly imprisoned by their own government. Having escaped, they now traversed the country (and abroad) trying to right wrongs. *The A-Team* became a big hit for NBC, and Mr. T clearly contributed to its success.

The buck stops here: Mr. T as B. A. Baracus on
The A-Team

T's rise in show business had been fairly quick. Born Lawrence Tureaud, the tenth of twelve children, he'd grown up in Chicago and attended Prairie View University in Texas on a football scholarship. Later he was a bodyguard for such celebrities as Michael Jackson and Muhammad Ali. His acting career began after an appearance on NBC's *Games People Play*. The big break came when he was cast in Sylvester Stallone's *Rocky III* as Rocky's boxing opponent, the menacing Clubber Lang, a great white American nightmare of a Black man if ever there was one. Naturally, the snarling, hissing Clubber had to be defeated by the stalwart Rocky.

With his gold chains, his exposed beefy biceps, his thundering growl, and his Mohawk-style haircut (actually, T stressed it was a Mandinka-inspired do), Mr. T's entire persona (on the series and off) was the old-style physically powerful and intimidating buck. T's B.A. was a buck domesticated for the small tube, his bold sexuality turned into a gaudy, nonthreatening joke. Seemingly uninterested in romance, B.A. usually just hung out with the fellas. Rather than reach some heated sexual climax, B.A. preferred to blow up a building. He delighted in showing his skill at creating military hardware. He could remake an old school bus into an armored truck. Or transform battered washing machines into machine guns. B.A. liked to warn, "You better watch out, sucker." Though he looked rough and tough, T's strength was always used as part of the team, never against it. Viewers could also chuckle at this brawny guy who was terrified of flying in a plane when his cohort, the crazed character Howling Mad, was in the pilot's seat.

Much like Jimmie Walker in *Good Times*, Mr. T was a cartoon creation that became a favorite of younger viewers and the media. He starred in the TV movies *The Toughest Man in the World* and *A Christmas Dream* as well as episodes of *Diff'rent Strokes* and *Silver Spoons*. His tough guy face graced the covers of *People*, *Us*, *TV Guide*, and even *The Muppet Magazine*. A cereal was named after him. A cartoon show starring an animated Mr. T also aired. A Mr. T doll appeared. So did a book he authored titled *Mr. T: The Man with the Gold*. He even dressed as Santa Claus at a White House Christmas party, and who should sit on his lap and give him a kiss but First Lady Nancy Reagan herself. The photograph ran in papers around the world. His salary for *The A Team* was said to be close to a million dollars a year. For a time, America just didn't seem to be able to get enough of T. Later generations might wonder how anyone could ever have thought twice about him. But while T, the joke, went on to fame and fortune, serious actors like Paul Winfield, whose presence on the tube was needed, still scrambled for work.

HILL STREET BLUES AND ST. ELSEWHERE: BLACK HEROES, ENSEMBLE CASTS

During the early years of the decade, more realistic Black characters—and far more interesting African American actors—appeared on the dramatic series *Hill Street Blues* and *St. Elsewhere*. Created by Steven Bochco and Michael Kozoll, *Hill Street Blues* was a cop show set in a police precinct in an unnamed Eastern city. With its ensemble cast, it proved to be a television breakthrough, establishing the style and tone for other dramatic programs that followed, everything from *N.Y.P.D. Blue* to *ER*, *Chicago Hope*, and *Brooklyn South*.

Influenced by the social activism of the 1960s and the gritty style of movies of the 1970s/early 1980s, the series was known for its innovative use of overlapping dialogue, its cinema verité look (the handheld camera shots, the rapid edits, the fast pace), and its nonlinear approach to story and character development. With several story lines woven into each episode, there were some thirteen principal characters, most of whom were cops who, in some way or another, commented on political/social attitudes in America. Among them were: Frank Furillo (Daniel Travanti), the stoic captain of the precinct; Henry Goldblume (Joe Spano), the sensitive, die-hard liberal, struggling to hold on to his ideals in a rapidly changing and complex society; Howard Hunter (James Sikking), the head of the SWAT team, who was quick on the trigger and at heart racist; and the committed public defender Joyce Davenport (Veronica Hamel). Almost all the characters seemed tired, drained, and exasperated as they dealt with the depressing realities of urban life: rundown neighborhoods, drugs, prostitution, murder, violence of every type, and the unrelenting anger and frustration that infect so many of the people they see.

Hill Street Blues also presented serious African American characters like Bobby Hill (Michael Warren) and Neal Washington (Taurean Blacque), both members of the police department. With his beard and the leather jacket and cap he sometimes wore while on undercover assignments, Taurean Blacque had a gritty ethnic look and style. Bobby Hill—a clean-cut, young, middle-class African American—was sensitive and articulate. In the first season, he was one of the series's strongest assets.

Originally, Hill and his partner, a white urban cowboy cop named Andy Renko (Charles Haid), were to appear only on the premiere episode. At its conclusion, they were suddenly shot and left for dead. But when NBC tested the show, network executives discovered that while most viewers were confused by the episode and even hated it, the characters they liked best were Hill and Renko; this oddball pairing of sensitive Black and crude white. Together they seemed to indicate that, no matter how different two men might be, perhaps things could work out between the races. Of course, it helped that Hill was no firebrand, no loose cannon of a troublemaker but a good, patient Negro lad who could be depended on. Consequently, NBC's Brandon Tartikoff instructed the creators of *Hill Street Blues* to resurrect the two and include them as regulars on the show.

Throughout its run, *Hill Street Blues* determinedly explored issues of race (racism), class, and gender. Sometimes the series treated matters sensitively. Other times—for all its politically progressive intelligence when dealing with its central characters—*Hill Street Blues* fell into the trap of resorting to familiar and disturbing images of urban African Americans. Viewers saw that clearly on the premiere episode when Bobby and Renko were called to the home of a Black couple in the midst of a heated domestic dispute. The woman was threatening to kill the man after she learned that he had slept with her daughter. The levelheaded Bobby quickly assesses the situation. When the younger woman is introduced clad only in a towel, the scene suggests that she's invited the lustful eye of the man, that indeed a little modesty would help in this home. The older woman, too, Bobby learns, has been neglectful of the man. He works out a solution. "You break up this family, you got nothing," Bobby tells the older woman. "Mama, you got to make yourself available to William. All he wants is a little attention from his woman." By casting Black actors here, *Hill Street Blues*, while working hard to be realistic, had nonetheless presented a fixed image: that of a sexually overcharged Black man *and* an emotionally overcharged Black woman, prone to violence and a dysfunctional home life.

One has the same feeling about a later episode when again Hill and Renko arrive at the scene of a domestic crisis between another Black couple. "I want him out of here. I want his butt arrested and out of my apartment," says the woman, who is standing with her son in her arms. "Look like you forgetting who pay the freight around here," the man shouts to her. "Pay the freight?" she asks. "He hasn't paid the rent in maybe two months now. Besides, I got the lease in my name." She tells Hill and Renko, "Aside from hitting me in my face, he threatened me with that gun he's always playing with." Bobby asks her to come into the hallway with him while Renko talks to her husband. "We're not married," she says. A few minutes later, the man is depicted surprisingly sympathetically. He is a housing authority cop who has lost his job. "I went places you dudes wouldn't go," he says to Hill and Renko. "Got shot twice. Stabbed three times. All in the line of duty." But by the end of the episode, he has killed the woman. By this point, you may begin to wonder if there are *any* balanced African American couples around.

On the premiere episode, Hill and Renko were also shot after stumbling upon a group of junkies shooting up. Originally, it was assumed that the junkies would be Black. Creator Steven Bochco contended that "the criminal element at this particular precinct was almost 100 percent Black or Chicano." "We were not trying to make a specific comment about Blacks per se," said Bochco, "though there is a very high incidence of abandonment within the Black community in ghettos. There are certain sociological realities there." But Jerome Stanley, the head of NBC's West Coast Broadcast Standards office, well aware of the sequence with the Black couple in this same episode, feared offending people of color. "Our quarrel with them [the creators of the show], if you want to call it that," said Stanley, "was that they were simply going to have to fictionalize it to the extent of saying that all criminals weren't Black. There are some white Anglo-Saxon Protestant thieves and killers and pimps."

Therefore it was decided that there should be "a mixture of various ethnic types in the station" to avoid any "problems that we might be confronted with as broadcasters [with protesting groups] saying that all the bad guys are Chicanos or Blacks. And we were quickly pointing out that a lot of the [cops are] Blacks and Chicanos as well, so it's saying that there is good and bad in every group." Consequently, on that first episode, the junkies were neatly divided ethnically: one was Black; one, Hispanic; one white; and the fourth, "wholly unrecognizable." The one who actually pulled the trigger on Hill and Renko was white.

Steven Bochco felt the show was "unfashionably liberal," which in some respects it was. But as media critic Todd Gitlin has commented, for all its liberalism, the show clearly touched on some of the politically conservative racial attitudes of the era. That was certainly the case on an episode when the liberal Goldblume tries to save a young Black man who, unable to find work or to get into a vocational school, threatens to commit suicide. Ultimately, the young man leaps to his death. Afterward, saddened and guilt-ridden, Goldblume, on his way home, has to change a flat tire on his car. He is accosted by a group of rowdy Black teenagers. Trying—and failing—to reason with them, he finally pulls out his gun. They run off. Once he's back at the Hill Street station, Goldblume talks to a Black cop about the incident. "What's wrong with those people, Alf? Are we past fixing it up between us? I mean—if that's the way it is, what the hell's the sense?" One tends to agree with Todd Gitlin's comment about the sequence, that indeed "Goldblume, disillusioned yet hopeful, expressed the society's more widespread separation between political hopes and practical life." Yet though the episode was written in fairly complex terms and was well acted, the writers, in their attempt to present both sides of the racial story, to express the concerns of the liberals as well as the despair and "understandable" anger of the conservatives, seemed to undercut their initial point. The story of the suicide would have been far stronger had it stood on its own.

At times the series also used Hill and Renko in unappealing ways. The right-wing Renko was a figure we were supposed to laugh at; never were we to take his comments seriously for the racism inherent in them. And poor Hill, possibly the most likable character on the show (thanks to Michael Warren's relaxed, warm performance), remained such a diplomatic figure, coolly handling testy situations with Black characters, that he became at times too representative of *a sane Black voice*, even a *Good Negro* in some respects. That was apparent when Hill was urged to run for the vice presidency of the Black Officers Coalition. But when Hill began taking time off from his beat because of his involvement with the Coalition, Renko sulked. He felt his good friend and partner had turned his back on him. When Renko was slashed while on duty with another partner, Hill then felt guilty. At one point, Renko tells Bobby, "I don't really mind you fooling around with this Afro American political gig as long as you're loyal to auld lang syne." Ultimately, Bobby continues to support the organization but says he's not cut out to run it. Afterward he tells Renko that he had expected "understanding" about his involvement with the Coalition, but all he's heard has been self-centered moaning. "I guess I was afraid of losing you," says Renko. "I can't fill in for your family, cowboy," the sensitive Bobby tells him. "But as far as this friendship goes, I'd say there's a few miles left on it." The two then laugh. "In the end, loyalty to his partner," said Todd Gitlin, "mattered to him more than organizing for affirmative action. The private code prevailed."

For African American viewers, it was hard to imagine how the writers could have let this story line pass. Why make Bobby, in essence, choose between Black and white? And if he had to make such a choice, most Black viewers felt it should have been for the Coalition. If anything, the sequence reassured its white mainstream viewers, even the demographically treasured ones who were better educated and economically secure, that the Black man's priorities, rather than growing out of political activism, sprang instead from his friendship with the white man. Throughout, the series stressed this kind of Black/white buddy friendship. On one episode as Bobby and Renko sit in their patrol car, Renko confides that his father has cancer. He cries and falls onto Bobby's chest. Bobby holds him as the episode ends. Even the tougher Black character Neal Washington had moments when he proclaimed his loyalty to the white detective J. D. LaRue (Kiel Martin). When the alcoholic J.D. finds himself in trouble with the department, Neal says somberly, "Half the stuff I know about the undercover world I learned from J.D. Up until last year I felt lucky just to be teamed up with him." Later he puts in a good word for LaRue with Furillo. "He's straightened up his act, Captain. I think he really means it this time," says Neal. "I've heard that one before. And so have you," Furillo tells him. "Feels a little different to me this time, Captain," says Neal. "I guess what I mean to say is what do you think the chances are of his coming back?" Even on a realistic series like *Hill Street Blues*, a little Black nurturing—especially from strong, confident Black males who otherwise might be threatening—still doesn't hurt.

At times, *Hill Street Blues* came across as the work of a group of self-consciously smart white guys who thought they were knowing enough to be "familiar" with their Black characters and to say things that, if uttered by less liberal souls, might be construed as racist. Sometimes *Hill Street Blues*'s creators believed they were hip enough to play with stereotypes. Yet on occasion, they seemed to be feeding into stereotypes. Michael Warren himself was aware of the scripts' sometimes twisted hip white guy perspective. When one episode had Renko kid Hill about barbecues, Warren asked for a change in the dialogue. Why should Bobby Hill simply laugh at Renko's crude remarks? Warren understood that even in the best of Black/white friendships, there were lines that couldn't be crossed. He insisted other dialogue be changed on an episode when Renko referred to Hill as Beulah. "There's no way you're gonna call me Beulah," he told the producers. The line was dropped.

Still, *Hill Street Blues* was willing to walk into a 1980s no-man's-land: the ghetto itself, the place of the despairing and the disenfranchised. And when the writers didn't try to play it too hip, they came up with some telling vignettes on life in a segment of the African American community. Alfre Woodard gave a highly praised performance as the distraught mother of a seven-year-old boy accidentally killed by a police officer who thought the child's toy gun was a real weapon. You would assume that everyone would be sympathetic toward her. But Woodard's character finds herself treated like a criminal. She is grilled as to her whereabouts at the time of the killing. Why wasn't she at home with her son? She explains that she had to stand in line for a job interview and that she couldn't afford a baby-sitter. "My boy was hungry," she says, "and if I didn't get a job, he wasn't going to eat." Still, she is charged with negligence and abandonment for leaving the boy alone. "God, isn't there any common decency left in the world?" says public defender Joyce Davenport. Yet the woman does not lose her humanity. When the police officer who has killed her child approaches her in the precinct, she tells him, "The Lord is forgiveness. I know it wasn't in your heart to hurt my Johnny." In some respects, here she seems *too* humane and stoic. Woodard's work, however, earned her an Emmy as Outstanding Supporting Actress in a Drama Series during the 1983–84 season.

Perhaps most significant, the series didn't shy away from revealing racism in the workplace, sometimes in small, toss-away moments, sometimes in the way the series defined regular characters. On one episode, a police officer casually refers to Blacks as spades. You wonder if that's what you really heard. You soon realize you have heard right when Furillo stops the cop and tells him, "If I hear another racist crack out of you, I'm going to run your butt back to school patrol." On another episode, the white detective J. D. LaRue tells his friend Neal Washington of his feelings about the city's Black mayoral candidate, the former Black police officer Ozzie Cleveland. "Ozzie is a real nice guy," says LaRue. "I just don't see him as mayor of the city." Without missing a beat, Neal says, "White man's job, right?"

On that same episode, the white character Howard Hunter expresses his feelings about Black mayors. "The current fad of electing mayors with the last names of former generals and presidents in your major urban areas is one that causes me some distress," he tells the Hispanic lieutenant Ray Calletano (Rene Enriquez). "You've got Washington in Chicago. You've got Bradley out in the West. And now you've got Cleveland right here in our environment. I mean, they're usurpers. They're trading on the names of our great dead heroes."

"They didn't exactly usurp their names, Howard," says Calletano. "They had their real names stolen from them."

To its credit, *Hill Street Blues* wouldn't let up on the race issue. Ultimately, its exploration of attitudes about race helped make it one of the era's most thematically innovative series.

St. Elsewhere, another urban workplace drama striving for a note of realism, seemed tamer yet more idiosyncratic than *Hill Street Blues* with a deft admixture of drama and comedy. Set at St. Eligius, a hospital in a run-down section of Boston, it too had numerous principals, some of whom were African American. Like *Hill Street Blues, St. Elsewhere* seemed to announce that the workplace wasn't complete without Black faces, representing various classes and cultural attitudes. At times, the series seemed more inclined to show Black faces than to spend much time dramatizing their lives and conflicts.

Nonetheless, some interesting faces came and went. Saundra Sharp appeared as the nurse Peggy Shotwell. Alfre Woodard played a brisk and thoroughly professional obstetrician-gynecologist, Dr. Roxanne Turner. Also cast as an orderly was Byron Stewart, who reprised his role as Warren Coolidge from *The White Shadow*. For viewers familiar with that earlier series, it was intriguing to learn what had become of the former high school basketball star Coolidge, although many Black viewers would have preferred seeing the character taken in a different direction. (*St. Elsewhere* frequently made references to past TV shows and characters. On the hospital public-address system, one could hear a "Dr. Morton Chegley" being paged. Chegley was a character from the TV series *Julia.*) Most prominently featured was Eric Laneuville as Luther Hawkins, an orderly who often provided gentle comic relief.

But the Black character that viewers were most taken with was Denzel Washington's Dr. Philip Chandler, a resident at the hospital. Usually, he had little to do. But as late as 1982, his was still a fairly potent image for Black viewers: here was a handsome, articulate, well-educated African American male, functioning successfully in an integrated workplace. Though Chandler frequently seemed insecure and questioned his own skills, he got along not only with his colleagues but also with Luther. Washington's Chandler certainly wasn't the first such character. Dorian Harewood, Albert Hall, and Brian Mitchell had played doctors on the respective series *Trauma Center, Ryan's Four,* and *Trapper John, M.D.* But Washington seemed both loose and intense with a relaxed sex appeal that did not go unnoticed. In many respects, just the fact that he was *there* was important for Black viewers. It wasn't too different from the effect that Raymond St. Jacques, as a man of color in the Old West series *Rawhide*, had on viewers of the 1960s. Washington also appeared in such TV movies as *Wilma* and *The George McKenna Story* (directed by Eric Laneuville). But he soon left the little screen for work on the big one, where he became a major star.

MIAMI VICE: TEEN DREAM HEROES IN BLACK AND WHITE

The 1984–85 season proved to be a major breakthrough in the world of Black images—and also neatly divided the decade in half—with two new series, one white with an important Black co-star, the other Black: *Miami Vice* and *The Cosby Show*.

At heart, *Miami Vice* was a familiar staple of television, the cop show, but one made hip and contemporary by its use of music, its unusual look (odd camera angles, rapid editing, expressive lighting), and its casting. NBC's Brandon Tartikoff came up with the idea for the series with the succinct description "MTV Cops." At its center were actors Philip Michael Thomas and Don Johnson, as Miami police partners Ricardo Tubbs and Sonny Crockett. Later Edward James Olmos appeared as Lieutenant Castillo, a sullen, uncompromising, morally centered officer in charge of Crockett and Tubbs. African American actress Olivia Brown and Latina actress Saundra Santiago were cast as research computer analysts, who also went undercover, often enough as hookers. Their Miami, centered mostly in the South Beach district, then a rather seedy area, was a visual pleasure dome of striking Art Deco architecture and lush tropical pastel colors—pinks, blues, greens, fuchsias, and soft violets. (Executive producer Michael Mann had given the dictum that there would be no earth tones on the series.)

In contrast were the drug lords, gang leaders, smugglers, prostitutes, porn peddlers, and petty hangers-on that peopled this American-style Casablanca; glorious, *dark* sleaze amidst the *light* splendor. In this Miami, everyone seemed on the make and on the take, ready to do anything to get some big bucks and to live in high capitalist style. (Ironically, because of the city's high percentage of Cuban and Central American immigrants and because the series focused so much on the

underworld, it looked as if Miami's problems were often Latin ones.) Even Tubbs and Crockett, as they went undercover, seemed morally ambivalent. They had no problem fitting into the crime and drug culture, obviously enjoying the clothes, the women, the cars, the speedboats, the automatic weapons, and the pace of a city where everything moved at breakneck speed. *Miami Vice* and its cop heroes appeared very much in sync not only with the rhythm of a decade known for its avarice and rampant materialism but also with a world in which drugs had become a fact of life for many Americans. The series may well have represented, as *The New York Times* pointed out, "the culmination in popular culture of America's decade-long romance with cocaine, a drug that stimulates the central nervous system, is an anesthetic, and costs a bundle."

The two-hour pilot for *Miami Vice*, which set the tone for the series,

Bonded buddies never die, they just go from one series to another: Miami Vice's *teen dream heroes Don Johnson and Philip Michael Thomas. Michael Warren and Charles Haid's grittier duo on* Hill Street Blues. *Avery Brooks and Robert Urich as the unlikely team of Hawk and Spenser on* Spenser: For Hire. *Howard Rollins and Carroll O'Connor as old-style officers Tibbs and Gillespie in* The Heat of the Night. *Robert Guillaume and James Noble as onetime butler and boss on* Benson

was written by Anthony Yerkovich, previously a writer and producer for *Hill Street Blues*, and directed by African American Thomas Carter. Not only did Carter devise a fast-moving method of storytelling but through his use of music, he endowed *Miami Vice* with a soulfully emotional core—and a very hip and knowing edge. "What I wanted to do was not to use music as just background," said Carter, "but as psychological subtext, if you will." Throughout the run of the series, there was always a pulsating soundtrack of various pop idioms, representing diverse urban cultures, by stars like Tina Turner, Glenn Frey, Chaka Khan, Lionel Richie, U2, Phil Collins, Run DMC, Cyndi Lauper, and the jazz/rock keyboardist Jan Hammer. The music established the mood for scenes and sometimes filled in the holes of the scripts. The setting and the soundtrack were often more important than the dialogue and story lines (which could be confusing).

Miami Vice didn't immediately rise to the top of the ratings. But everything about it seemed daring and new. The dialogue was often street-smart, tough, and cool. And part of the excitement was that in the midst of the pretty pictures, colors, and dreamy leads, violence, like real contemporary urban violence, could come quickly and unexpectedly. A postmodern wonder, the show caught the eyes of the critics and younger audiences. *Miami Vice* became the show that people stayed at home on Friday nights to watch.

Younger audiences gravitated to the interracial pairing of the leads, which gave the show its kick, making it seem more contemporary than past white-boy pairings like *Starsky and Hutch*. The two were then a startling combo (as much so for their era as the *Mod Squad* trio had been for theirs): each Hollywood-handsome, each dressed to the hilt in designer duds (Versace, Hugo Boss, Vittorio Ricci), each soulfully concerned about the other's welfare. Indeed, in a TV age of rather ordinary cops or sleuths, part of the appeal of Thomas and Johnson was that they were anything *but* ordinary guys. Their very glamour made them seem, in television terms, larger than life.

Of course, this 1980s-style theme of interracial male bonding wasn't too different from such couplings in the past. As in *I Spy*, racial differences seldom emerged between the two. Nor was there any serious comment on the varied cultural backgrounds of the two men. Ironically, in the pilot, despite the look of hip egalitarianism, Yerkovich's script told us more about the white Crockett than the tan Tubbs. Thomas's Tubbs, a New York City cop, goes to Miami to track down the Colombian drug lord named Calderone who is responsible for his brother's death. There he meets Crockett, a Miami undercover cop in search of the same man. But Sonny Crockett was given a colorful backstory. A former football player who was being sued for divorce by his wife, Sonny was something of a dashing loner, living on a houseboat with a pet alligator named Elvis. Still, the first episode—and the first season—attempted to present Tubbs and Crockett as true partners. The underlying idea was that the two cops had one important thing in common: they needed each other to survive.

What excited African American viewers was, simply stated, Philip Michael Thomas. Though he was new to most of the television audience, many Black viewers knew him already. Thomas had been on the scene for a decade. Born in Columbus, Ohio, and growing up in Southern California, he had briefly attended Berkeley and also studied religion for a year at an Alabama educational institution. After a role in a production of *Hair* in 1968, he had appeared in such Black-oriented films of the 1970s as *Sparkle*, *Stigma*, *Black Fist*, and *Book of Numbers*. He also appeared on television. Now, on *Miami Vice*, he was a cool Black lead on a major dramatic primetime series who wasn't relegated to the comic sidelines like Huggy Bear. With his expensive double-breasted suits, silk shirts and ties, and with a camera that came in close to record his wounds and longings, Thomas's Tubbs, more so than an actor like Denzel Washington on *St. Elsewhere*, seemed to be the embodiment of what past African American viewers may have felt that actors Greg Morris and Hari Rhodes should have been: a bona fide old-style matinee idol and a full-fledged action hero.

Thomas's sexuality on *Miami Vice* was more explicitly drawn than that of television's previous Black leading men. Thomas, who clearly relished his lover boy status, also enjoyed depicting himself as pan-racial. He once informed *Time* that he was part Irish, German, American Indian, and oh, yes, Black. "I'm American gumbo," he said. Perhaps white viewers, who didn't seem to have a problem accepting Thomas as a hero and quasi lead, viewed him in that way. Like Lena Horne and Dorothy Dandridge in an earlier time, Thomas, with his dark olive coloring, his curly hair, and his keen features, had an acceptable look—as much Latin as traditional Black—which in the eyes of some may have qualified him to be something of a sex symbol.

Some episodes shrewdly mixed in some soulful vulnerability, which always made the sexuality seem more mature. During episodes of the first and second seasons, he was paired with that goddess of Blaxploitation cinema, Pam Grier. Thomas brooded beautifully over his troubled relationship with Grier—and over those with other women as well. An episode like *Walk Alone* opened with a love scene between Tubbs and a beautiful young woman. When she is killed, a bruised Tubbs is determined to avenge her death as well as to dull his emotional pain. He goes undercover as an inmate on a dangerous mission inside a prison where he's physically assaulted. All of this in the name of love.

Thomas, however, never came off as the one-dimensional old-style buck. His sensitivity always saved him. But, of course, mainstream audiences didn't have to fret about Tubbs and his women because it was clear that Tubbs's most important relationship was with Crockett. In *Walk Alone*, after the death of his lady, Tubbs is consoled by Crockett. "Hey, buddy," Sonny says softly. "Listen, why don't you take a couple days off, buddy, and deal with what's happened."

Occasionally, episodes attempted to comment on Tubbs's personal history, to explain and explore his goals and drives and the dark fears and dreams that possessed him. Yet those episodes seemed to sell Tubbs short, to deny him a certain moral complexity. *Calderone's Demise* found Tubbs, while still in pursuit of the drug lord Calderone, falling for a beautiful young Latina named Angelina. At first, he believes she is one of Calderone's women but, after a tender lovemaking session with her, he learns differently. "The problem is," Tubbs confides to Crockett, "Angelina is Calderone's daughter." Tubbs discovers himself in a moral/emotional bind. How can he avenge his brother's death without destroying his relationship with this woman? What will his feelings be when he actually has to kill Calderone?

"I'm going to get him," Tubbs says at one point. But when Calderone was finally surrounded, it was Sonny—just as Calderone was about to shoot Tubbs—who pulled the trigger. The episode robbed Tubbs of a key moment of self-assertion and self-definition. Instead it trumpeted the heroics of Crockett, the good white friend who remains in charge and in control of Tubbs's destiny. The sequence was reminiscent of the climax of *48HRS.*, when Eddie Murphy was saved by Nick Nolte, who also kills the villain about to shoot Murphy. Yet unlike Sidney Poitier in such dramas as *The Defiant Ones* and *A Man Is Ten Feet Tall*, in which the Black star, in coming to the aid of a white friend, sacrifices himself, the white star isn't made to sacrifice himself in any way.

Calderone's Demise ends with Tubbs trying to explain to Angelina what has happened. But to no avail. A saddened Angelina drives off alone in her car. Afterward Sonny puts his arm around his buddy. "Come on, Tubbs. Let's go home." They walk off together.

Nonetheless, the excitement initially generated by Thomas didn't last long. In a short period of time, most viewers realized that Johnson's Crockett was the leader and Johnson was the real star. Usually, the series focused on Sonny the ladies' man and Sonny the alienated loner trying to sort things out. Too many episodes seemed devoted to Sonny's drives and dilemmas. Always *Miami Vice* wanted us to think of the men as ideal buddies, quick to nurture one another, and they were that, as long as the familiar racial lines were drawn.

By later episodes, the two men seemed to have less emotional rapport, and Thomas looked as if he might end up as simply a deluxe sidekick. It was amusing to note the sequences when Tubbs literally appeared to be following Johnson around. Sonny would enter a room first. Tubbs promptly followed three steps behind. "The relationship of Crockett and Tubbs seems to pivot mostly on whose car they decide to take," *TV Guide* commented, adding, "and just once, couldn't Sonny flip the keys to Tubbs and let *him* drive the Ferrari?"

Off the *Miami Vice* set, things weren't any better. Don Johnson's face graced the covers of magazines. Newspaper items recorded everything from his salary demands to his romances with Barbra Streisand and his former wife Melanie Griffith. Well aware that he garnered far more attention than his co-star, Johnson let it be known that now that *his* day had come, he was taking it.

Eventually, the critics took note. "The Tubbs character is supposed to be half the team, and after two and a half seasons," *Us* magazine commented, "we don't even know such basics about him as where he lives." *Miami Vice*'s reign at the top of the ratings, when it beat out competition like *Matt Houston* and then *Falcon Crest*, proved short-lived. Critics griped that it was all style over substance; that it made violence attractive; that its story lines had become incoherent. By its third season, when its color scheme had changed (now those earth tones were in), the series was considered passé. By the time *Miami Vice* finally left the airways in 1989, no one seemed very much interested in it. The *New York Post* complained, "What had been an equal partnership in the first season degenerated into 'The Don Johnson Show' for months on end, thus robbing *Miami Vice* of one of its key ingredients." The reduced exposure of Thomas was, the paper concluded, "a fiasco that damaged the show."

Afterward Philip Michael Thomas's future as a leading man looked dim. "Philip Michael Thomas: Is There Life After *Miami Vice*?" read a headline on *TV Guide*'s October 21, 1989 cover. Of course, Thomas's career wasn't helped by the media depiction of him as something of an egotistical flake. In interviews, he contributed to that image, seemingly unaware of the way in which his comments could be used against him. "I realize how important it is to stand for something positive," he proudly told *TV Guide* as he explained that his initials PMT stood for Perfect Moment of Truth. He also announced, "I have a game plan in my mind called EGOT. It stands for *Emmy, Grammy, Oscar and Tony*, and I plan on winning or being nominated for all four." *Rolling Stone* reported that Thomas had "put a lot of people off with some of his outrageous statements," and asked the question: "Is this guy for real or what?"

For a brief spell, though, Thomas—who clearly had the presence to become a television mainstay like such other TV hunks as Robert Urich and Tom Selleck—looked as if he might be able to sustain his stardom. Wisely, while still appearing on *Miami Vice*, he starred opposite Lesley Ann Warren in a TV movie, *A Fight for Jenny*, a tale of an interracial love affair. It did well in the ratings, indicating that viewers were willing to watch him in a serious drama. He also co-starred with Phylicia Rashad in a crime story, *False Witness*.

But ultimately, television didn't seem ready for this kind of glamorous, sexy Black leading man, and his fate was similar to that of Billy Dee Williams in the movies. After *Miami Vice*, Thomas, whether because of personal problems or attitudes within the industry, made only rare appearances in such fare as *Perry Mason: The Case of the Ruthless Reporter* and then in a 1997 guest appearance on Don Johnson's new series, *Nash Bridges*. His private life, though, still drew the interest of the press.

THE COSBY SHOW: CULTURE AND CLASS IN A BROOKLYN BROWNSTONE

Interestingly, the most successful 1980s primetime Black-oriented series, *The Cosby Show*, completely abandoned the mixed-combo format. This groundbreaking Black family sitcom seemed to pop up out of nowhere. No one in the television industry could have predicted its extraordinary (and rapid-fire) success *and* cultural impact.

By the time of *The Cosby Show*'s appearance, its star, Bill Cosby, had been around the series block *many* times. Clearly, he was a TV fixture and perhaps something of an oddball icon but not yet a true megastar. Many viewers had followed his career since *I Spy*. Yet he had varying degrees of success. *The Bill Cosby Show* lasted only two seasons. Then Cosby tried his hand at hosting variety shows. His first, *The New Bill Cosby Show*, died after one season. His second, *Cos*, lasted less than two months. His luck was better with the daytime animated series *Fat Albert and the Cosby Kids*, which was based on his childhood experiences in Philadelphia. Innocuous and devoid of any racial comment, that series featured a gallery of funny characters—such as Fat Albert and Mush Mouth—that brought pleasure to many viewers, Black and white. Still, it wasn't that great primetime hit that every TV star needs.

Cosby also worked in movies, again with varying degrees of success.

Some films like *Mother, Jugs & Speed* and *The Devil and Max Devlin* were forgettable. Another like *Hickey & Boggs*, which reteamed him with Robert Culp, had a certain nostalgic appeal (even at this early date in his career). Another like *California Suite* had him match wits and some physical comedy with Richard Pryor. Still another like the Western *Man and Boy*—a tale of a father and son in the Old West—afforded Cosby the opportunity to hone his persona as a concerned father, sensitively leading his son to the brink of manhood. Yet another like *Bill Cosby Himself* presented an unfiltered Cosby in concert, talking about family life—his marriage and kids and the attendant hassles.

Where he shone brightest on-screen was in his co-starring vehicles with Sidney Poitier: the 1970s trio of Black-cast comedies *Uptown Saturday Night, Let's Do It Again*, and *A Piece of the Action*. Watching Cosby in these films was seeing an expert comic technician in top form. While he didn't appear particularly spontaneous, he was wholly natural with a timing so precise and proficient that he never missed a beat. In an era that saw a proliferation of Black bucks in the movies, Cosby, without resorting to any of the old typing, sensitively presented the image of a relaxed working-class African American male. No dialect. No broken English. No outlandish exaggerations. No mugging. Nor did he ever let himself become desexed. He could casually eye a woman, without projecting an image of some oversexed adolescent. Instead, working beautifully with an actress like Denise Nicholas, he cued us in to his connoisseur's appreciation of the "fairer sex." He also blended in perfectly with an ensemble troupe of dazzling Black stars: Poitier, Richard Pryor, Flip Wilson, Rosalind Cash, Harry Belafonte, James Earl Jones. Yet as important as he was to the films, these were never Bill Cosby star vehicles.

Cosby also appeared on his own specials and even guest-hosted that all-American institution *The Tonight Show*. But during these years Cosby proved himself a television and entertainment phenomenon in a series of highly effective TV commercials. Television sponsors had long been resistant to using Black Americans to promote products, for fear that the African American's association with that product might alienate the mass white audience. Millions of viewers, white and Black, saw advertisements hawking all the material acquisitions and comforts of middle-class life—from cars to refrigerators to shampoos to toothpastes—that Americans were encouraged to desire and which were available. But the subtext of commercials in the early years of television was that this brave new consumer world was exclusively white.

The first wave of change in the advertising world came about in Black publications like *Ebony*, which, aware that their readers had to see Black faces in order to identify with an ad, ran photos of the famous and not-so-famous promoting products. An African American model like the elegant Helen Williams and another like Hal de Windt appeared in advertisements in Black publications. Black celebrities like Dorothy Dandridge, boxer Floyd Patterson, comic Slappy White, and later Stevie Wonder were pictured endorsing products. But except for the images of African Americans as accommodating servile figures that had long been used in print logos and advertisements for such products as Aunt Jemima pancakes and Uncle Ben's rice, white periodicals still shied away from using African Americans in ads. The same was true of television and radio.

By the 1960s, Black actor P. Jay Sidney had practically led a one-man crusade to get African Americans fair representation in television programs *and* commercials. He testified in 1963 before a congressional committee investigating charges of discrimination in the television industry. Eventually, because of changes in the social/political climate, Sidney himself helped break ground with his voice-overs for commercials for such products as Anacin and Hazel Bishop lipstick. He also was on-camera for Ajax (he was featured as Waxin Jackson) and Cool Whip. By 1976, once African American actors finally worked more in TV commercials, Sidney complained that Madison Avenue was "reghettoizing" commercials. He pointed out that the major ad agencies asked him to audition only for "blurbs aimed specifically at blacks," what he called "the cullud beat." None of the major agencies asked him to audition for spots targeted for the general market. *Variety* reported that it was no problem for Sidney "to affect Negro accents" because "his natural speaking voice is lily-white, and few if any viewers could distinguish his race on blurbs [in voice-overs] for such clients as Hertz, Swissair, Anacin, and many others."

Cosby, however, opened the field, deghettoizing commercials; eventually becoming a pitchman for all types of products. His three consecutive Emmys for *I Spy* were a clear indication of audience and industry perceptions about him, that indeed he was acceptable *and* likable. Cosby then found himself in an unusual position for an African American star. Though the mainstream culture always considered him Black, he nonetheless was not perceived as being ethnic; he never had the heavy cultural baggage that might have made him seem like the Other. With his concerns about family and a bourgeois lifestyle, he seemed to be the embodiment of the cultural mainstream itself. Advertisers found him establishment enough to hire him as a pitchman not only in Black publications but in white ones as well and more significantly on network television. In time, he became a spokesman for cars and computers, and what may be the most American of products, Coca-Cola and Jell-O.

He proved ideal: playful, engaging, inventive, and reassuring; adroitly brushing aside any fears of Black male power and sexuality, yet again (paradoxically) without ever desexing himself. His imaginative appearances with children on the Jell-O commercials established him as something of a hip, big brother/father figure. The commercials were pivotal pit stops on Cosby's road to becoming a national icon and marked the real ascent of Cosby the megastar. His *TVQ* point rating, which was an annual national survey of a performer's popularity with viewers, eventually soared, giving him (by 1985) the highest recorded rating of anyone in more than a decade. It was higher than that of Clint Eastwood (who finished second) and that of Eddie Murphy (seventh). By the mid-1980s, Cosby had released twenty-two albums, made countless nightclub appearances, and was earning about $10 million a year. That meant he was also making a lot of money for the entertainment industry itself.

Throughout, Cosby held on to his dignity and integrity. Never considered a pushover or any kind of agreeable tom-like star, Cosby was known for being moody and prickly with the press. During those rare interviews he granted, he could be curt and dismissive. *Newsweek* reported that a *TV Guide* reporter left an interview saying Cosby had been "by turns combative, defensive, challenging, threatening, and hostile." *Newsweek* also commented, " 'Egomania' and 'arrogance' are the pejoratives that surface most frequently among Cosby's few detractors.' " Commenting on the press, Cosby once said that "too many of these people would rather find out when I was toilet-trained than learn what I'm trying to do on a stage or TV." For the rare print interviews that he granted, he set the ground rules. There were to be no questions about his family life. "I hate it when writers try to psychoanalyze my life," he said. "I mean how many of them have degrees in psychology." But Cosby became one of the most respected men in the entertainment industry—by those controlling the industry, who understood that he could not be messed with. Yet in early 1984, Cosby hadn't been seen regularly on a TV series in eight years. Many wondered if he could ever come up with a real TV hit.

Late one night when NBC programming executive Brandon Tartikoff was unable to sleep (his newborn infant was crying), he turned on the television set and saw Cosby hosting *The Tonight Show*. It didn't take him long to realize that the time might be right for a Cosby series. All that political fallout from the 1960s had evaporated. All those ethnic hoot-and-holler Black series from the 1970s had faded away. Now, in an era with an emerging new African American middle class and a baby boomer television audience that had grown up with Cosby, perhaps all Cosby needed for a hit was the right vehicle.

Though Tartikoff met with some resistance at NBC to the idea of a Cosby series, talks began with Cosby. Various concepts were tossed about. Cosby also approached ABC with the idea of a show about Black family life. But ABC rejected the series. "Anyone hearing that the sitcom was supposed to be dead, and suddenly, man, here's Bill Cosby wanting to do one with an *all-black* cast," Cosby later said, "had to say: 'Wrong time, wrong color.' It was all against us on paper."

Working with the production company Carsey-Werner, Cosby came up with an idea that Tartikoff liked and which he got through at NBC.

Initially, Cosby planned to make the father a chauffeur. But his real-life wife, Camille, nixed that idea. Now was the time to go all the way with the type of middle-class African American experience that Cosby had toyed with in *The Bill Cosby Show*. This would not be a single-parent household like that of *Julia*. Nor would it present a fake cutesy couple as in *Barefoot in the Park*. Instead *The Cosby Show* would mark television's first full-fledged depiction of African American upper-middle-class life. Cosby would be Heathcliff Huxtable, a doctor (at first, a gynecologist; later an obstetrician) married to an attorney, Clair (Phylicia Ayers-Allen, who later became Phylicia Rashad). Living comfortably in a Brooklyn brownstone, the couple would have four children (later five): a trio of daughters (later a quartet). After a talent search, the children—Denise, Vanessa, Rudy, Theo, and Sondra—

The last series that almost all of America watched: The Cosby Show's original family members included (clockwise) Sabrina LeBeauf, Tempestt Bledsoe, Bill Cosby, Keshia Knight Pulliam, Malcolm-Jamal Warner, Phylicia Rashad, and Lisa Bonet

would be played by Lisa Bonet, Tempestt Bledsoe, Keshia Knight Pulliam, Malcolm-Jamal Warner, and Sabrina LeBeauf. Inevitable comparisons would be drawn between Cosby's real-life family (four daughters, one son) and his TV counterpart. All of this would blur the lines between Cosby the star and Cosby the man, which worked splendidly to Cosby's advantage.

Much of the credit for the show's success would go to Cosby himself. In the past, a star like Flip Wilson had exerted an important degree of control on his series. But not until the advent of Cosby's series was there a program in which the governing sensibility—the absolute first and last word on just about every detail—lay in black hands. Cosby would be not only the lead actor but also the show's co-creator, co-producer, and executive consultant. No script got by without his approval. Jay Sandrich (who directed most episodes in the early seasons) understood that the show had to meet Cosby's standards and approval. Later Cosby gave such young African American directors as Neema Barnette, Regge Life, and Tony Singletary a chance to work on the series. To avoid negative images, Cosby hired the African American psychiatrist Alvin Poussaint as a consultant to read every script. If Poussaint ever found something he thought a less than positive comment on African American life, Cosby had the material either changed or dropped altogether. Cosby also co-wrote the show's theme song and even helped design the set for the series. He also insisted that it be taped in New York, not Hollywood.

The premiere episode—September 20, 1984—introduced the family. Here the focus was primarily on the son, Theo, whose poor grades disturb his parents. Throughout, there were wry observations on family life. As Cliff enters Theo's room, he maneuvers his way around the clothes and clutter that lie about. "Hard to find good help, isn't it?" he says to his son. Then Cliff proceeds to actually *talk* to his son about school. Throughout, the scenes with the children were warm and perceptive, and, though idealized, emotionally true.

Yet in that first episode, Cliff the parent also revealed his exasperation with his children, and he never hesitated to exert his parental authority. "I am your father," he says at one point, "I brought you into the world and I'll take you out!" Cliff also tells wife Clair, "I just hope they get out of the house before we die." Kids were wonderful, the series announced, but, as *Newsweek* commented, family life in the Huxtable

household was something of a domestic war zone, "a source of unconcealed adult resentments."

Other episodes focused on other seemingly small or inconsequential events in a family's life: sibling rivalries; a daughter's romance; a
son's problems working on a history paper. In time, the series also dealt
with issues the sitcom still did not always feel comfortable with: Clair's
menopause, Rudy's first period, and Theo's dyslexia. Throughout,
Cosby refused to depict the standard raucous (ghetto) Black television
family that cracks jokes or whose members sound off on one another.
Instead, rather than relying on gags to propel the action as sitcoms generally did, *The Cosby Show* concentrated on life's seemingly small incidents. Said Cosby: "My one rule is to be true rather than funny."

For television viewers, here was a richly humorous depiction of
Black life, a portrayal of people—the Huxtables—who, in so many respects, were no different from white America, yet, in other very specific
and subtle ways, were *quite* different. Ultimately, Cosby's series revealed
the connective tissue between two separate cultural experiences in
America.

Newsweek called *The Cosby Show* an "irresistibly charming, flawlessly executed sitcom." *People* called it "a supersitcom, funny, fast-
paced, loveable and real." Later the *New York Times* critic John J.
O'Connor raved, "*The Cosby Show* is that rare commodity—a truly
nice development in a medium that seems increasingly preoccupied
with trash. . . . At a time when blacks were once again being considered
ratings liabilities by benighted television executives, the middle-class
Huxtables have become the most popular family in the United States.
And at a time when so many comedians are toppling into a kind of
smutty permissiveness, Mr. Cosby is making the nation laugh by paring
ordinary life to its extraordinary essentials. It is indeed a truly nice development."

To the surprise of NBC executives, the premiere episode jumped
into Nielsen's Top Ten and soon afterward the series hit number one,
becoming the most successful new series on the new fall lineup as well
as the highest-rated new series on *any* network since the 1978–79 season. From 1985 to 1989, *The Cosby Show* would remain number one,
with some 63 million viewers tuning in at its peak. For a time, the series
was even number one during its summer reruns. Eventually, it kicked
off NBC's strong Thursday night lineup, the lead-in to such shows as *A*

Different World and *Cheers. The Cosby Show* also enabled a troubled NBC to reestablish its prestige and become the number one network. At one point, advertisers paid $380,000 for a thirty-second spot on the show. Later the series was sold to syndication for a record deal of $800 million. Significantly, too, it would always be a favorite with African American viewers. At one time when the show won a 34.9 general rating, it had an even higher 48.7 rating among African Americans.

The Cosby Show, as should be expected, also had its critics, who complained that the series was too soft and safe. By depicting this model affluent Black family, some argued, the show ignored the effects of institutionalized racism and alleviated white fears and guilt about social and political problems facing many African Americans. Two professors at the University of Massachusetts published a two-hundred-page study on the social effects of *The Cosby Show*. "If black people fail, then white people can look at the successful black people on *The Cosby Show* and say they only have themselves to blame," they said. "The presence of the Huxtables and their spinoffs really seems to send a message to white people that black people can make it if they try." In essence, the report said that the show had desensitized viewers to some very real racial inequities in the Reagan 1980s. (Ironically, a $16,500 grant from Cosby—who by then held a doctorate in education from the University of Massachusetts—had helped subsidize the study.)

Complaints also shot up that the series failed to challenge patriarchal traditions. One critic noted that at Thanksgiving, Theo carves the turkey. Some argued that Cliff paid more attention to the problems of Theo than to those of his daughters. Others complained that all the Huxtable kids were too idealized, not at all like the rebellious adolescents that parents had to contend with daily.

Others griped that *The Cosby Show* wasn't Black enough. *New York* called the show "*Leave It to Beaver* in blackface." In *The Village Voice*, critic Tom Carson wrote that Cosby "subscribes too readily to the television dictum that you can do whatever you want, so long as the form in which you do it remains benign; you can even be a bastard, so long as your bastardliness is presented as a personality quirk, and not something that seriously challenges the audience's perceptions of any larger status quo." But perhaps most stinging was *The Village Voice*'s comment that some "white liberals and the few blacks who care may think of Cosby as a sellout, but the truth is that he's rigged the game so solipsistically that he no longer qualifies as black enough to be an Uncle Tom. The niche he carved out has also so little applicability to anyone's priorities or realities outside his own that he's more like a brother from another planet."

All the criticism partly revealed that no one television show can answer everyone's needs. Because viewers still had little choice in selecting African American images, Cosby came to represent all things to all people, and consequently there were bound to be disappointments and complaints. Still, some of the criticism was valid.

One episode did focus on Theo's having tucked a marijuana joint into a math book. But with rare exceptions, the brownstone in Brooklyn seemed removed from such contemporary urban ills as homelessness, crime, drugs, violence, AIDS, marital conflicts, and deeply rooted parental tensions. It was also removed from such real-life events as the 1985 racial incident when a young black man was killed in New York City in the white working-class community of Howard Beach. In some respects, the Huxtables seemed to exist in a social/political vacuum.

Some may have longed for Theo just once to venture into the wrong neighborhood and encounter trouble from white toughs—and perhaps be roughed up. It would have been an extraordinary television moment to see Cliff deal with that. The Huxtables would have found their fundamental assumptions about life (and America) seriously challenged. And a segment of the Black audience might have had a stronger point of identification. Of course, we wouldn't want to see Theo attacked *every* week. But some major comment once in a while would have given the show another type of power and urgency.

Yet despite the series's acceptance of the system—and its subtext that America had gone beyond racial and cultural divisions—*The Cosby Show*'s achievements far outweighed everything else. The show was greater than its critics, who sometimes lost sight of what the show *said* to the audience, which loved and valued it for good reason. The audience understood that *The Cosby Show* was not about contemporary politics. Rather it was about culture. The Huxtable family members never had to discuss being Black in the fake way of *Good Times* because their Blackness was something so much at their core that they didn't have to dramatize it.

Throughout its run, the series was subtly and brilliantly contextualized with African American cultural signs and references. That could be something as casually presented as the T-shirts that Cliff loved to sport. One might have Morehouse College, the famous African American institution, stamped on it. On another might be a lesser-known Black college like Cheyney University in Pennsylvania. There were posters of Frederick Douglass and Martin Luther King Jr. Much was made of the artwork on the walls of the Huxtable homes, work done by African American Varnette Honeywood. The paintings were copies of those in Cosby's personal collection.

Even more explicitly, references were made to such Black writers as Richard Wright and Jamaica Kincaid. Or to any number of African American jazz artists. In fact, Cliff's passion for jazz was one of his distinguishing characteristics. He went wild for it and shared his enthusiasm with his kids. Cliff's father, Russell Huxtable (played by veteran actor Earle Hyman), was a former jazz musician. Cosby brought on such stars as Nancy Wilson, B. B. King, and Count Basie with his entire band. Jazz vocalist Joe Williams was also cast as Clair Huxtable's father.

But jazz wasn't the only type of African American music brought into the series. Posters of pop stars like Whitney Houston and Prince were in the children's rooms. Stevie Wonder and Sammy Davis Jr. made guest appearances. On one episode when Cliff had a chance to meet

*Cliff meets the goddess of his dreams: the Cosby family
with guest star Lena Horne*

a goddess of his dreams, who was it but Lena Horne, a potent pop cultural symbol for African Americans of the 1940s and 1950s. On another episode the entire family exuberantly lip-synched to the Ray Charles recording "The Night Time Is the Right Time."

Cosby deftly wove African American history into a number of memorable episodes. It's doubtful if anyone who saw it has ever forgotten the episode when pint-sized Rudy sat alone (later joined by the family) quietly spellbound as she watched a television replay of Martin Luther King Jr.'s "I Have a Dream" speech. Then there was the episode in which Theo struggled to write a paper for school. When his grandparents learned that his topic was the 1963 March on Washington, they were flooded with memories. Having attended the march themselves, they reminisced, and Theo experienced living history right there in the Huxtable living room.

The episode in which Clair and her school chums recalled their college experiences during the civil rights era was a wonderful television moment, beautifully felt and acted, and skillfully incorporating in the sitcom format a powerful dramatic historical experience that the African American audience could identify with in the most personal of ways. What other sitcom of this era brought in important Black cultural experiences? Would viewers have seen this on *Growing Pains* or *Family Ties* or *Who's the Boss?*

On other occasions, politics emerged in unexpected ways. The press reported that before the taping of one episode NBC censors wanted to remove a foot-long "Abolish Apartheid" sign that was pinned to Theo's bedroom door. When Cosby was informed that the network could not "appear to endorse controversial positions on which there are two sides," he was "seething." "There may be two sides to apartheid in Archie Bunker's house," said Cosby. "But it's impossible that the Huxtables would be on any side but one. That sign will stay on that door. And I've told NBC that if they still want it down, or if they try to edit it out, there will be no show." The sign was not removed. After Cosby had selected the names Nelson and Winnie—a tribute to South Africa's Mandelas—for his grandchildren on the series, there was some discussion that the names should be changed in light of emerging political controversies about Winnie Mandela. Cosby flatly refused.

Where Cosby succeeded brilliantly, though, was in the creation of a series that appealed to both the mainstream *and* the African American viewer. Often when a Black star has crossed over, he/she has lost some of his/her appeal to the Black audience. In music, there have always been complaints that the big crossover star has forsaken his/her ethnic roots for a bland mainstream style. The same has held true for certain Black actors and actresses, from the days of Sidney Poitier to those of Denzel Washington. That never happened with Cosby, perhaps partly because the style and subject matter that had originally brought him to attention was not rooted in a particular kind of ethnic experience.

But more important, on *The Cosby Show* he was able to incorporate African Americans into the type of fundamental experiences thought to be exclusively those of white America. Upon learning that Theo was going out for the football team, Cliff appeared almost overcome with joy and traditional fatherly expectations. "My boy. Play football. My son," he exclaimed. "Carry the ball for me. I sit in the stands. 'Is that your son?' Yes, my boy. See him running the touchdown with the name Huxtable on the back? I would have done it myself, but I'm too old now. So I gave him the business. Huxtable and Son . . . The circle will not be broken." As innocuous as this dialogue might sound, it nonetheless gave the lie to the image of the African American as the Other who is removed from archetypal American rites, customs, and traditions.

Yet, with a series of masterly strokes, Cosby also expressed the significance of a basic family experience in terms that both the general white audience and the specific African American one could identify with. On one episode, Theo arrived home wearing an earring, after having had his ear pierced in order to impress a girl. Cliff thought it was the funniest thing he'd ever seen, and later that evening when his parents came over, he was quick to tell them about Theo's folly. Then Cliff's father reminded him of the time Cliff had conked his hair in order to impress his girlfriend Clair. Now he laughed at Cliff's expense—until Cliff's mother reminded her husband of the time many years ago when he had gotten a tattoo to impress her. The episode ended with Theo, Cliff, and Cliff's father seated on the sofa, facing the audience, three generations of Huxtable males who had all employed various methods in the name of love or infatuation.

The episode worked splendidly. General white viewers could identify with the basic situation (a courtship ritual) *and* the earring and tattoo. But Cosby had shrewdly particularized the experience for African American viewers with the information that Cliff had conked his hair, something the white audience might not even have comprehended but which the Black audience understood immediately. In the Black viewer's mind, that sight of a Cliff Huxtable with a head full of slicked-back greasy hair was hilarious.

Even something seemingly as inconsequential as the choice of colleges for the Huxtable children served as a telling comment on a changing world for Black Americans. Eldest daughter Sondra attended Princeton, indicating a more open society in which African American children (mostly middle-class) could now study at Ivy League schools. (Of course, we never learned of any racial problems, subtle or overt, that Sondra might have encountered at this traditionally white institution.) Daughters Denise and Vanessa, however, chose historically Black colleges: the fictional Hillman and the very real Lincoln University in Pennsylvania. Later Theo attended New York University.

Cosby was quick to defend himself against his critics. "Some people have said our show is about a white family in blackface," he said. "What does that mean? Does it mean only white people have a lock on living together in a home where the father is a doctor and the mother a lawyer and the children are constantly being told to study by their parents?" But in time, Cosby also responded to some criticism with some subtle and significant changes. He focused more on his daughters' problems as well as (occasionally) on women's issues and attitudes. In an attempt to de-idealize the children, the writers created some very clear growing pains for Vanessa. Rudy also experienced the problems of sibling rivalry when another child came into the Huxtable home.

With the appearance of Theo's friend Cockroach (a deplorable name but a winning performance by Carl Anthony Payne Jr.), the series looked as if it might examine another kind of class system within the African American community. That didn't happen. But in the seventh season, with the introduction of the character Cousin Pam, a teenage relative of Clair's from the inner city (Bedford-Stuyvesant) who came to live with the Huxtables, *The Cosby Show* zeroed in on class distinctions. On the day she arrives at the Huxtable home, Pam enters quietly and deferentially, obviously nervous and a bit intimidated by the class differences within her own family. On her best behavior, she doesn't want to mess up. Or embarrass herself. You couldn't ask for a politer (or more inhibited) young woman. But once Cliff and Clair have left the house, Pam is shown alone speaking on the telephone with a friend from the old neighborhood. Her rhythm, language, and attitudes change immediately—she's looser, freer, obviously more herself—as she openly expresses her feelings about staying with these *bourgsee* folks.

At another point, Cliff opens the refrigerator to find food containers marked with Pam's name. In Pam's world, everyone has had to stake her claim on just about everything, including the nourishment that would go into her mouth. In a touching exchange, Cliff warmly explains that in Pam's new home with the Huxtables, everything is shared, there is enough to go around, and labels aren't necessary. It will take Pam a while to get over this intracultural clash and to feel truly at home.

Also appearing were Pam's friends: Slide (Mushond Lee), Charmaine (Karen Malina White), and Lance (Allen Payne). With the exception of Pam (beautifully portrayed by Erika Alexander), the ghetto kids were never as individualized as the Huxtable clan. The writers relied too much on familiar attitudes and images. But though the young actors sometimes fell into the familiar trap of overattitudinizing—with "rough" edges that were often too rough—for the most part they were appealing, and their characters never became caricatures.

Other changes came about in later seasons. Sondra married her college sweetheart Elvin, and soon Cliff and Clair were grandparents. After having left home to attend Hillman College only to have dropped out to work for a photographer in Africa, daughter Denise returned to the Brooklyn brownstone with a navy lieutenant husband (Joseph C. Phillips) and a cute stepdaughter (Raven Symone). Often the new characters, especially Pam and her friends, made *The Cosby Show* seem like an entirely different program.

But ultimately *The Cosby Show* altered the face of the Black sitcom. While other series, as diverse as *Sanford and Son* and even *Good Times*, had moments that expressed familial warmth and understanding, none went as far as *The Cosby Show*. Cliff's scenes with his children, listening to their problems, offering suggestions, and sometimes giving orders, without barking and biting, remain a television milestone. The children themselves were new: not some overly energetic, hopped-up TV-cute gagsters.

Perhaps the most subtle and (paradoxically) startling innovations were Denise and Theo. Representing the sweet girl next door who was also a space cadet, Lisa Bonet's Denise was poetic and dreamy, sometimes making mistakes on her way to maturity, sometimes taking splendidly adventurous turns. Black teenage girls weren't supposed to be able to make the kind of choices Denise did. Nor were they supposed to think as she did. Once when she balked at the wisdom of her parents, she composed a poem that expressed her view of life. "I'm an orphan of the darkness / A prisoner of my tears," she wrote. The scripts showed a remarkable respect for her individuality.

Theo was a marked departure from the typical ghetto youth of the TV past. All one has to do is compare him with Jimmie Walker's clownish J.J. to see the way in which Cosby's writers—and actor Malcolm-Jamal Warner—created a sensitive, intelligent, well-rounded young Black male. For Black kids around America, it was wonderful at last to have some kind of choice in images on TV.

Certainly, Clair Huxtable was also an invigorating portrait of a contemporary African American woman. Refusing to cast this wife/mother in the traditional mode—of a heavyset, browner or darker all-nurturing woman—Cosby selected Phylicia Rashad, who projected intelligence and wit combined with a mature, relaxed sensuality. Though she was not homebound like past Black sitcom mothers (who even when they worked seemed stuck in the kitchen), Clair's profession as an attorney was rarely dealt with, and viewers questioned how this working woman could keep such an immaculate house (without any signs of help). Regardless, audiences were reminded of her life outside her home; of the importance of her professional life.

Sexy sparks also were ignited between Cosby and Rashad, which was new to the sitcom. Viewers didn't expect to see a married couple like this one engage in a little under-the-covers foreplay. But often Cliff and Clair really looked as if they couldn't wait to have some time alone together. Rashad could also be firm with the children. If something displeased her, she could give some well-known (to the Black audience) race-specific gestures. It might be a neck roll or a roll of her eyes. Or there might be vocal inflections that indicated that she meant business.

Determined to make her own decisions, Clair was never hesitant about speaking her mind to Cliff. Or anyone else. On one episode, Sondra's then boyfriend, the rather bratty Elvin (Geoffrey Owens), asked Clair, with a note of condescension, if she minded "serving" her husband. Without missing a beat, Clair told Elvin that "serving" was what someone did in a restaurant. She, however, doesn't mind "doing for" someone as long as the gesture is reciprocated and there is mutual respect. Here Cosby was dealing with the issue of choice for women, and while the Clair/Elvin exchange might be viewed as upholding conventional male attitudes, the sequence nonetheless expressed the feelings of a certain generation of African American women.

Finally, just as he had done in films and past series, Cosby presented a very casual, refreshing view of Black masculinity. Though in some ways, his Cliff was a very traditional male figure, heading a household and happy to assume his fatherly/manly responsibilities, this type of Black male hadn't been seen regularly on television, which meant that Cosby's traditionalism was rather radical within America's color scheme. In other ways, though, Cliff was a new-style figure for the sitcom. He didn't have to stomp and scream to make a point. Nor was he threatened by intelligent, educated women. A wonderful aspect of Cliff was that he was always willing and eager to *listen* to Clair. Yet while Cliff could admit to being wrong about something, he was never a pushover. "Usually, the fathers in sitcoms were wimps," Brandon Tartikoff once said. "Sitcoms were watched by mostly female audiences, and so the most identifiable characters were shaped accordingly. Bill Cosby brought masculinity back to sitcoms." Significantly, at a time, too, when the sociologists and psychologists were telling us that there was no such thing as a Black father, that he was either missing from Black households or irresponsible, thanks to Cosby the most famous father in America was, in the mid and late 1980s, an African American one.

Gradually, *The Cosby Show* slipped in the ratings. By early 1988, the critic for *The New York Times* asked: Is Cosby "running out of steam? Has he peaked?" Believing that he'd accomplished all he wanted to do, Cosby announced that the 1991–92 season would be the last. The final episode ended with the family gathered for Theo's graduation from New York University.

Ultimately, *The Cosby Show* proved to be the last of its kind. As cable entered more American homes, providing more choices for viewers, individual television programs were gradually becoming less of a shared national experience. The days when the country, in extraordinary numbers, would tune in to see the birth of Lucy's baby or the trials of Kunta Kinte or the close of the MASH unit were disappearing.

Viewership—and the TV experience itself—became fragmented. The once mighty three networks found their audience numbers continuing to drop. As *Entertainment Weekly* pointed out: "Before the demographically divvied, zillion-channel cable universe arrived, *Cosby* was the last show everyone watched."

BONDED BUDDIES: THEY NEVER DIE

The Cosby Show and *Miami Vice* influenced other series that followed. Once *Miami Vice* made interracial bonding fashionable again, the theme turned up in such series as *The Insiders* (something of a *Vice* clone) and *Stir Crazy*. *The Equalizer*, starring Edward Woodward as a former espionage agent turned detective, brought in Steven Williams and then Ron O'Neal (formerly the star of *Superfly*) as men who aid him in his quest to help the people who have nowhere else to turn. Not a bonding series in the traditional sense but still one that depicted Black and white men working together for a common good.

Double Dare, however, had a more traditional approach. Billy Dee Williams starred as a dapper former thief who, rather than be incarcerated, agrees to a deal with the cops. He'll work undercover for them while they permit him to maintain his lavish lifestyle. He has one stipulation, though. His former cohort in crime, played by white actor Ken Wahl, has to be released from San Quentin to perform undercover duties with him. Debonair and suave as ever and even more of an engaging narcissist, Williams seemed primed to play an aging roué. Had the scripts been better, the series might have had some of the stylish appeal of *Hart to Hart*. *Double Dare* first aired in April 1985 and was off the network schedule the next month.

None of the male-bonder series wanted to admit that in actuality African American men rarely had intense friendships with white men. Instead, like so many of the white/Black buddy movies of the Reagan era, they were dreamy fantasies that once again promoted the notion that white men need not fear Black (male) dissent or resistance because now the Black man was a dependable, trusty, loyal friend with no societal gripes to grind.

The exception—and consequently one of the most interesting Black/white male relationships—was that of the white detective Spenser (Robert Urich) and his Black helpmate Hawk (Avery Brooks) on *Spenser: For Hire*. Talk about suspicion and hostility! Hawk has it in spades!

Based on characters in novels by Robert Parker, the series *Spenser: For Hire* revolved around a maverick Boston detective Spenser (no first name), who quit the police force because of its restrictions. An unusual tough guy, Spenser (who was also once a boxer) can readily flatten the bad guys. But he also has a sensitive side. He reads poetry and can quote Wordsworth or his namesake, the sixteenth-century bard Edmund Spenser, author of *The Faerie Queene*. As if that weren't enough to set him apart from most TV private eyes, Spenser's also a gourmet chef.

But what distinguished Spenser most was his friendship with the Black character Hawk, a magnum-toting man of the streets with ties to the underworld. Like Spenser, Hawk too is philosophical and poetic. The two met years earlier at a boxing gym. Now, as he helped Spenser solve crimes, Hawk's enigmatic presence individualized Spenser just as Scotty's had done for Kelly on *I Spy*. Yet the educated Scotty resided in a cultural world similar to Kelly's. But Spenser and the *dark, mysterious,* rather *exoticized* Hawk, at first glance at least, seemed worlds apart. With Hawk by his side, though, Spenser (like Magnum with T.C.) seemed even less a straight-up, conventional white guy and more a man with some soul.

Though Hawk and Spenser often viewed each other warily and though Hawk was quick to speak his mind when with Spenser, ultimately the primary reason for Hawk's acceptability to mainstream viewers was that his threat was always neutralized. Coming to Spenser's defense, Hawk became an enforcer of law and order. No matter what the situation, Hawk ultimately—despite any disputes—would never betray Spenser or be anything but loyal to his white friend. On the very first episode, Hawk double-crossed his boss in order to save Spenser's life. Episodes often seemed to present Hawk as a deus ex machina, arriving on the scene at the crucial moment to rescue Spenser.

In many respects, Hawk represented the *street nigga*, the bad dude who can't be played with; a brother familiar (even at home with) violence. He was a descendant of the buck, a type which had been revitalized in Blaxploitation films of the 1970s: a character with an exaggerated sexuality and masculinity and with great physical power.

The buck was always ready to wreak violence and vengeance on deserving whites.

Brooks, however, brought other dimensions to Hawk. Tall and muscular, with a deep bass-baritone voice, and often unyielding and supremely confident, Brooks—through language (his inflections and intonations), dress, and attitude—enlivened the Hawk character in ways that the African American audience could identify with. Hawk always moved and spoke with authority and in his own highly idiosyncratic manner. Never did he simply say *Spenser*. Instead, it was *Spensahr*. When asked a question, he might not give a simple *Yes* but an *Ah-firm-ma-tiff*. Hawk sported dark glasses (which added to his mystery and gave him a menacing appearance), dark leather jackets and pants, and a leather hat. When he walked, Hawk had a rhythmic *baad brother* strut. Whenever possible, he was quick to make some comment on race—even when Spenser did something as mundane as to offer him a cup of coffee. "Cream and sugar?" Spenser asked. "Black!" Hawk responded.

Certainly, African American viewers understood what Hawk's signature walk and attitude were all about. To survive on mean urban streets, African American men frequently adopted a rhythmic, defiant gait; it expressed their self-control and self-empowerment; it signaled that they were on their own turf. Already actors like Ron O'Neal and especially Richard Roundtree had done this in such films as *Superfly* and *Shaft*. Now Brooks brought this cultural sign to the small tube. In turn, Black audiences helped boost the ratings of the show. *Spenser: For Hire* had a rating of 13.0. Among non-Black households, it scored 11.9. But among African American homes, it had a rating of 19.8.

Before working on the series, Avery Brooks had already established an impressive set of professional credentials. After growing up in Gary, Indiana, the son of a mother who was among the first African American music graduates at Northwestern University and a father who was a member of the gospel choir Wings Over Jordan, Brooks graduated from Oberlin College in Ohio. Afterward he performed in productions at New York's Public Theatre, portrayed Paul Robeson in a one-man show, appeared as Malcolm X in the opera *X*, acted in such Shakespearean productions as *Othello* and *A Midsummer Night's Dream*, sang jazz at the Montreal International Jazz Festival, and starred in Gordon Parks's *Solomon Northrup's Odyssey* on PBS's *American Playhouse*. He also taught at Rutgers University. Consequently, he arrived on the *Spenser: For Hire* set with a sure sense of himself (some might have said *too* sure a sense)—and also an awareness of the way films and television had depicted African American male characters. On the set and off, he demanded respect, for himself and Hawk.

One of Brooks's associates on the series described him as a marvelous actor but "just a bit touchy, perhaps, about race." Incidents on the *Spenser* set may have given him no choice but to be touchy. *TV Guide* reported that on one occasion a young white messenger "tried (unsuccessfully) to mimic Hawk's dialect, and seemed bent on pulling Brooks out of standard English into the on-the-spot blackness he obviously expected." On another occasion, a stuntman's wife laughed as she passed Brooks and his stand-in. "I *still* can't tell you two apart," she said. "Aside from shaved heads," wrote *TV Guide*, "these two do not look alike."

Brooks sought to define and contextualize Hawk in a manner the writers might not have imagined. Comparing the Hawk of his novels with the Hawk created by Brooks, author Robert Parker said simply, "My Hawk is easier, less tightly wound." "In large measure, Avery has remained a man of mystery to me. He's as good as I've ever seen at playing his cards close to the vest," co-star Robert Urich once said of Brooks. "He gives you no more than you need to know about the character or the moment." "Hey! I am not Tonto. I am *not* his sidekick," Brooks once said of his character. "I trust Hawk to trust Spenser. There *are* people in this world you'll be there for. Hawk has his reasons." For Brooks, Hawk was a "blues hero." "You see them everywhere, in Stagger Lee [hero of the Black folk poem], in the slave narratives," the actor said. "I look at Hawk that way. He's not a sociopath. In the context of Afro-American people, you can see that *he* is not the one to fear."

Yet, oddly enough, Brooks delineated the character in such a stylized way—everything about him seemed based on something culturally authentic but also an exaggeration—that there was always something cartoonish about Hawk. He was not only the *street nigga* but also a parody and a caricature of that type. Hawk was a character to be both feared and laughed at. That may be another reason why mainstream viewers accepted Hawk sauntering into their homes.

The critics noticed Hawk immediately. "One of the neater devices in the plot," wrote John J. O'Connor, "is Spenser's wary relationship with a character named Hawk (Avery Brooks), a black man who has made it to posh Beacon Hill through his own distinctive methods of hustling. It's the kind of oddball twist that gives the series an edge for potential survival." O'Connor also commented, "Played to a spiffily wicked turn by Mr. Brooks, Hawk is an intriguing creation, whether working out with Spenser at the local gym or prowling around the city in his expensive clothes and luxury car. He always seems to know a little more than anyone else and he is apparently physically invincible. In fact, he almost steals the show."

Though *Spenser: For Hire* never sailed to the top of the ratings and left the airways after three seasons, the two leads became heroes, and the series achieved something close to cult status. Later cable's Lifetime Channel brought the pair back for a series of made-for-TV *Spenser: For Hire* movies.

ABC also developed a series built around Brooks's character titled *A Man Called Hawk*. Set in Washington, D.C., it dramatized Hawk's post-*Spenser* life—as a savior of the people. Anyone with a problem could come to Hawk, who used either legal or illegal means to help the community. Hawk cuts a dashing figure as he drives around town in his BMW while packing a silver .357 magnum. For an action series, *A Man Called Hawk* infused its hero with even more of a cultural and literary bent than Spenser. Hawk is a refined jazz pianist and a knowledgeable gastronome. Though as stiffly stylized as ever, Brooks's Hawk remained startlingly strong, one of television's most interesting symbols of Black masculinity. Even if the idea seemed to be that an African American male couldn't be truly virile unless he was somehow connected to crime and violence.

Still—a product of Avery Brooks Productions—the series had its moments. Hawk's one close friend is Old Man (Moses Gunn), a lofty philosophical soul whom Hawk skips off to see for advice and solace. In one wholly unexpected sequence, Gunn began reciting Langston Hughes's poem "The Negro Speaks of Rivers." As his recitation becomes all the more rhythmic and fluid, you assume the sequence will cut away to something else. But Gunn delivers the poem in its entirety, an astonishingly powerful and moving television moment. Throughout the run of the series, the writers juggled the demands of the basic format with those of a more personal, African American cultural point of view. On one episode alone, the characters spoke of Langston Hughes,

Zora Neale Hurston, and Sterling Brown. Black writer Calvin Hernton was the show's technical adviser and, on occasion, writer. If anything, though, the series may well have proved that mainstream viewers preferred Hawk by his white buddy's side rather than on his own, front and center. A midseason replacement, *A Man Called Hawk* debuted in late January 1989; it was off the primetime schedule by late August of the same year. Brooks kept working and later appeared as Benjamin Sisko, commander of a space station orbiting the planet Bajor on the syndicated spin-off *Star Trek: Deep Space Nine*.

OUTLANDISH CHARACTERS, COMMUNAL GATHERINGS

Following the success of *The Cosby Show*, the networks aired other sitcoms that focused on Black families with more of an emphasis on an African American middle-class experience. Many proved disappointing. A series like *Charlie & Co.*, starring Flip Wilson and pop songstress Gladys Knight as the parents of a brood of three outspoken children (including Jaleel White as the youngest), failed primarily because it lacked a fresh take on the African American middle-class experience. *Melba*, starring singer Melba Moore as a middle-class single mother rearing a young daughter, proved such an embarrassment that CBS pulled the series after its first week. Episodes that had already been filmed aired during the summer. A show like *He's the Mayor*, featuring former *White Shadow* star Kevin Hooks as a twenty-five-year-old mayor who appoints his father, a onetime janitor, as a member of his "kitchen cabinet," lasted a few months, then expired. *The Robert Guillaume Show* didn't fare much better. Here Guillaume was cast as a *divorced* marriage counselor—with a white girlfriend who was also his secretary. Viewers stayed away. Granted the concepts of these series were either tired or simpleminded, audiences also didn't seem particularly interested in these new-style representations of African American life. *The Cosby Show* remained the exception rather than the rule.

Shows like *227* and *Amen* fared better. Though we were to believe that their characters were middle-class, in values if not lifestyle, the programs seemed like sitcoms from another era. Frequently using the old types (especially of women), both also constantly relied on jokes to move the plots along. What saved them were their winning casts: such veterans as Marla Gibbs and Sherman Hemsley and such cunningly engaging newcomers as Jackee Harry (for a time billed simply as Jackée) and Anna Maria Horsford.

227 was the brainchild of Marla Gibbs. Having appeared in a play of the same title about a group of friends in a Washington, D.C., apartment building, Gibbs took the concept to NBC, where she landed herself a pretty good deal. She would not only be the series's star but also its creative consultant with a say over the story lines, characters, and dialogue. NBC hoped Gibbs would pull in big numbers. In this domestic comedy, she played Mary, the wife of Lester, a contractor (Hal Williams), and the mother of teenage Brenda (Regina King). Mary, however, spent much of her time with her neighbors: Pearl (Helen Martin), an older woman who usually sat perched in her window, spying on the neighborhood; Rose (Alaina Reed-Hall), the landlord of the building, who, as might be expected, had man problems; and Sandra Clark (Jackee Harry), a man-crazed voluptuary hoping to snag a guy with big bucks.

Life on and off the stoop: Marla Gibbs, Jackee Harry, and Alaina Reed-Hall in 227

227 didn't get off to a propitious start, and some thought its lead was miscast. "On *The Jeffersons* supporting actress Marla Gibbs stole the show from the stars," wrote *People*. "Unfortunately, Gibbs makes a better second banana than a centerpiece; it doesn't take long to over-dose on her wry cracks, *especially* when they're not all crackerjack . . . . *227* is barely above average."

Yet despite its shaky beginnings, the series found an audience, had good ratings, and stayed on the air for five seasons. Added to the cast in later seasons were: Stoney Jackson and Barry Sobel (as wacky room-mates in the building); Countess Vaughn (as child prodigy Alexandria); (briefly) Toukie Smith (as the ditzy Eva Rawley); and Paul Winfield (as Mary's new landlord).

As the one married female, Mary coped with some predictable ten-sions: the growing pains of her daughter; the stability of her relation-ship with her husband. But when Mary was with her women friends, things were far livelier. The series's view of the women—who spent a lot of time gossiping on the stoop—was a clichéd one. Yet Black audi-ences liked the various scrapes and shenanigans that Mary and friends experienced; they were sometimes reminiscent of those of Lucy and Ethel. On one episode the women comically battled it out as contes-tants on the game show *Wheel of Fortune*. On another the women went off to a spa where they got into a mud fight. Mary's various battles with Paul Winfield were similar to Lucy's encounters with Gale Gordon on the series *The Lucy Show*. In fact, *227* itself looked like something out of the 1950s. Its main appeal was that here were African Americans living together in an urban setting, one not seriously fraught with any social problems, and managing to enjoy life and each other.

Contrary to *People*'s comment, Gibbs also worked well. Though at first audiences missed her wickedly funny retorts from the past, she managed to become the show's voice of common sense, its moral core, and its emotional centerpiece, without always being center stage. In this ensemble group, Gibbs wisely gave some of the best lines to other per-formers, and shrewdly used her talents to showcase theirs, especially those of Jackée, who worked wonders with her character Sandra.

Was there any other television character of the 1980s as retro and as gender-typed as Sandra Clark? No one could be sure what she did pro-fessionally. Most of her time was spent on her mad search for a man. Sandra's typical behavior could be seen in an episode about an opera fund-raising benefit for her church. She is opposed to the event—that is, until she catches a glimpse of the good-looking conductor.

So much about Sandra seemed to be overdone parody. Often she spoke baby talk, like a little girl pleading with Mommy and Daddy for a lollipop. When she walked, she was the full-figured girl with the rotary hips, who worked them overtime. When she dressed, the tighter the sweater, the better. Of course, the women of *227* were usually shocked by Sandra's behavior, and they argued with her at just about every opportunity. Yet Sandra is a part of their supposedly diverse community, and they would no more expel her than they would adopt her habits. Besides, they all seem to agree with her that life would be a whole lot better if there were more men around. *Rolling Stone* declared that Harry's "temptress Sandra has shades of *Mary Tyler Moore*'s Sue Ann Nivens, Gibbs's Florence and *Newhart*'s Stephanie, but she's also a composite of other kinds of showbiz personalities: Bette Midler, Betty Boop, Little Richard, Pearl Bailey, R. Crumb's cartoon characters and any number of female impressionists. The strength of Harry's portrayal is that she's absorbed the exaggerated mannerisms of generations of minority-group comics and made them her own."

Jackée had been honing her distinct style for years. Born in North Carolina and raised in New York, she had first worked in theater (such productions as *Eubie, One Mo' Time, Adam,* and *I'm Getting My Act Together and Taking It on the Road*) and in bits in movies (*Moscow on the Hudson* and *The Cotton Club*). Her big break had come with the role of Lily Mason on the daytime soap *Another World*. While appearing on the latter program, she beat out eighty other candidates for the Sandra role, and for a spell worked on both shows, shuttling back and forth between New York and Los Angeles.

The real surprise was that Sandra was pretty hard not to like. Whenever you heard her call out "Maryyyyuuureeee" to Gibbs, you were bound to brush aside certain critical assessments and just let yourself be swept away by the sheer force of her personality. In many ways, she was similar to the ribald, naughty girl persona of the young Pearl Bailey, who also was mighty interested in the fellows and the birds and the bees.

As much as feminists might have deplored her (she is indeed the oldest of stereotypes; a blond bimbo turned bronze), perhaps she was the right kind of heroine for a postfeminist age. True, she would do anything to get a man, yet in an era when Madonna rattled feminist ideologies by stating emphatically that *she* was always in control, Sandra also always made her own choices. In a world where women had only so much power, Jackée's Sandra employed—to the max—that age-old notion of woman's sexuality as her source of empowerment. Some African American women identified with her body language and body definition. Whereas many television heroines were slim and girlish-looking, Sandra had full hips and breasts, which she proudly displayed for the perusal of any interested party. (In real life, Jackée at times must have felt she was *too* full-looking. Her diets were well publicized.) Part Bessie Smith and Mae West (women who didn't hesitate to make their sexual demands known) and part Marilyn Monroe (a brazen parody), Jackée was so playful about it, so joyously consumed with the pleasure of living, making love, and having fun, and never being seriously frazzled or depressed by anything, that she was perfect pop escapist entertainment.

Touching a nerve with African American audiences, Jackée's Sandra surely gave birth to the character Regine on *Living Single* in the 1990s, and the actress herself became a television star. In the 1986–87 season, she won an Emmy as Outstanding Supporting Actress in a Comedy Series for her portrayal of Sandra Clark. Though she was never able to extend her established television persona (it looked as if she were trying in *The Women of Brewster Place*) to the point where she could draw out the possible disappointments or even loneliness and desperation of such a woman as Sandra and though *227* will probably always be thought of as the high point of her career, Jackée kept working and later appeared in such series as *Designing Women* (briefly), *The Royal Family*, and *Sister, Sister* (which she also occasionally directed), and such TV movies as *Crash Course, Double Your Pleasure,* and *Ladybugs.*

Just as Gibbs was the anchor of *227*, that other *Jeffersons* alumnus Sherman Hemsley kept the ensemble group of *Amen* grounded. Set in Philadelphia, *Amen* centered on the activities of Deacon Ernest Frye (Hemsley), his daughter Thelma (Anna Maria Horsford), and their friends and associates at the First Community Church. There were the heavyset Hetebrink sisters (Barbara Montgomery and Roz Ryan), the young minister Reuben Gregory (Clifton Davis), (later) the teenage rapper Clarence (Bumper Robinson), and the elderly church board member Rolly (Jester Hairston, who years before had appeared in episodes of TV's *Amos 'n' Andy*).

Here too was a series—with a distinct sense of community—that harked back to a past era. By now, fathers on such programs as *Growing Pains, Family Ties,* and *The Cosby Show* represented contemporary, mature males grappling with new ways of rearing children and with the changing roles of their wives. But *Amen's* Deacon Frye appeared as if he had been out of the country—or out of his mind—during the

Thelma finally gets her man: Anna Maria Horsford,
Clifton Davis, and the irascible Sherman Hemsley

politically restless 1960s and the feminist 1970s. Frye was a lawyer. So you might assume that he's representative of a modern, sophisticated African American character. But as he bopped and hopped, as he shouted and threw tantrums, Frye looked as if he knew as much about the law (or had as much common sense) as Calhoun on *Amos 'n' Andy.* Together Calhoun and Frye made the idea of a seemingly educated African American male something of a slapstick joke. As he had done with George Jefferson, Hemsley created a little guy character, who was struggling to maintain his place in a big guy's world. Free of inhibitions and hardly politically correct, Hemsley's Frye was so outrageous that one kept watching to see what he'd do next.

Even more outrageous was his daughter Thelma, who, like Sandra

Clark, seemed to suffer from arrested development and was almost as man-hungry. But whereas Sandra at least seemed like a precocious adolescent, Thelma appeared infantile. Stuck living at home with her domineering father, Thelma whines, pines, frets, and cries. She can expect no sympathy from her father, who, whenever the opportunity arises, pokes fun at her. He makes as much a to-do about the fact that she can't cook as J.J. did with TV's other Thelma on *Good Times*. Thelma Frye has failed not only at her womanly responsibilities but at almost everything else. She can do nothing right. And at the start of the series, her greatest failure was that she couldn't get a man. Once she finds one—the handsome Gregory, whom she forever swoons over—the question is: Can she keep him?

Poor Thelma, too, was like Lucy, constantly getting herself into the most absurd of situations. At one point, Thelma inadvertently enlists in the army! At another point, she sets the house on fire! (That poor girl really *can't* cook!) And for the longest time, she looks as if she'll lose her mind if Gregory doesn't pay some attention to her. Finally, he does. The two eventually marry. But Thelma seems as ill equipped for that as she did for everything else. On the final episode of the series, Deacon Frye, at a benefit to save the church, does a wicked impersonation of James Brown on stage—only to be joined by the real Brown, singing "I Feel Good." Meanwhile, as Frye and Brown scream, wail, and moan, a pregnant Thelma does some moaning of her own backstage. Caught off guard, she ends up having her baby right there in the theater. Again, like Lucy, Thelma, throughout *Amen*, was hardly cut out for a domesticated, ordered middle-class existence, and always beneath the whiny exterior, as a sweet subtext, is the idea of a repressed woman struggling to break free and define herself.

Judging by the series, no one would have realized Horsford's range. For eleven years, she had worked as a producer for New York's PBS affiliate WNET. She also appeared in a daytime soap, worked in such movies as *St. Elmo's Fire* and *Heartburn* and in the stage production of *For Colored Girls Who Have Considered Suicide When the Rainbow Is Enuf.* "I was holding down three jobs—playing Clara Jones on *The Guiding Light* in the morning," she once said, "working at the [WNET] office in the afternoon and doing *Colored Girls* at night." Sometimes her television work was broad and theatrical. Yet at other times, notably in the film *Street Smart* with Morgan Freeman, she was luminously restrained and tough. Given the right roles, she could turn in first-rate performances.

Usually, though, there was a warm vulnerability in Horsford's work that ultimately made her Thelma so appealing. Viewers loved those moments when she told her father off, and they were touched by her bumbling attempts to win Reuben's affections. "As Thelma," wrote *Rolling Stone*, "Horsford plays that rarity, a victim with backbone. Less Billie Holiday than Judy Holliday, Horsford can tug on your heartstrings with a sigh and then make you cackle with pleasure."

Clearly, it was Anna Maria Horsford's performance that helped keep viewers tuning in to *Amen* each week, to the point where this old-style farce made its way into the Top Ten of the ratings. But the writers never gave the character the chance to express any realistic comment on issues pertaining to contemporary African American women.

Amen and *227* were alternatives to *The Cosby Show*. Whereas *The Cosby Show* remained a wonderful ideal, the other two offered *down*, grittier characters whose obvious ethnic juices were flowing like mad. Shrewdly, *Amen* made use of the Black church as a cultural anchor (or prop), mooring its episodes in a type of cultural-specific experience while at the same time avoiding any perceptive comment on that experience. Because of their repeated exaggerations, the sitcoms veered close to caricature, not in the very broad sense of *Amos 'n' Andy*, but still at a point where certain realities and specific questions about family, relationships, and culture were frequently lost in the melee.

Yet many Black viewers enjoyed these looser, more frantic, less responsible, and highly entertaining representations of African American life. Viewers didn't have to take any of it seriously. Nor did they have to feel guilty about liking this energetic trash. The shows, in some respects, were the essence of a disposable, giddy pop culture. Some episodes were well developed. Others were trite and clichéd, hobbling along on timeworn jokes. Clearly, though, both shows were the wave of the future and led the way to some of the popular series (with African American audiences, not white ones) that appeared in the next decade on those alternative networks: Fox, United Paramount Network (UPN), and The Warner Brothers Television Network.

DIFFERENT WORLDS, NEW PERSPECTIVES

Other series of the late 1980s, however, like *A Different World* and Tim Reid's *Frank's Place*, showed signs of originality with warmly developed characters and unusual story lines.

A spin-off of *The Cosby Show*, *A Different World* chronicled the adventures of Denise Huxtable once she had left home to attend the predominantly Black college Hillman. There she encountered a new group of friends: a dippy roommate, Maggie (Marisa Tomei), one of the few white students on campus; another roommate, the older (twenty-six-year-old) divorced Jaleesa (Dawnn Lewis); a self-styled ladies' man, Dwayne Wayne (Kadeem Hardison), who has a crush on Denise; his buddy, the jivey Ron Johnson (Darryl Bell); a sweet house-mother Stevie (Loretta Divine); and a haughty Black Southern belle of a coed, Whitley (Jasmine Guy), who became Denise's nemesis on campus.

*Starting over: Lisa Bonet as Denise on her own
at Hillman College with Marisa Tomei and
Dawnn Lewis*

The first season was fairly bumpy. The writers didn't seem to understand their characters, and the situations weren't specific enough about the experiences or feelings of African American college students. Too much about the series was trivial, silly, and inconsequential. On the initial episode, Denise was faced with a tough decision: whether or not to stick with her new college roommate Jaleesa. By the show's end, as should be expected, Jaleesa and Denise are well on their way to becoming the best of friends. On another episode, Denise and Dwayne steal the costume of a rival team's mascot. On another, Denise is punished for littering on campus and must wear a pig's mask. On yet another, Dwayne tutors Denise in calculus but loses track of the time and is caught leaving her dorm way past the curfew.

Rarely were the kids seen in a classroom. Rarely was there any attempt to uncover the ways students juggle personal and academic issues. Nor did it capture youthful tensions and angst. *A Different World* seemed the very antithesis of *The Cosby Show*: it was joke-oriented television in which the behavior of the characters often was forced and unrealistic with everything played too broadly without any subtlety.

Usually, the actors were left stranded. With his pop-up sunglasses, with his boasts to the world of his sexual prowess, and with his ever ready tendency to bug his eyes (as well as the unfortunate way he dressed), Kadeem Hardison's Dwayne looked as if headed for coonville. Ron also seemed like a super-hip little clown, a sexist, a chauvinist, a cipher without a thought in his head. At times, Marisa Tomei's struggle to give her empty-headed character Maggie some shape was rather touching. But when she was dropped after that first season, it wasn't hard to figure out why. (As it turned out, that was probably the best thing to happen to Tomei. She ended up working in the movies and winning a Best Supporting Actress Oscar for her performance in *My Cousin Vinny* in 1992.)

Most critics pounced on the show. Kay Gardella, who called it "a vulnerable 'Cosby' spinoff which could drive some viewers back to CBS," predicted that *A Different World* "will not be long for this world."

A different reaction, however, came from critic Marvin Kitman, who wrote, "I have a confession to make. I have been secretly watching *A Different World* . . . and enjoying it. I feel like a traitor. All the hip people I know want it to fail. . . . But what makes the show work is Lisa Bonet." Kitman was right. Even before *A Different World* had grown into itself, it was unique because of Denise—and another female character, Whitley.

The Cosby Show had already established Denise as an unusual, untyped African American character: dreamy, vulnerable, a lyrical individualist. With her punk hairdos and New Wave outfits, she was a self-styled New Age teen rebel. Clearly a child of privilege, Denise adopted rebellion as a trendy pose, a new style of dress and attitude. Hers was never a fight against social injustices or racial inequities, because in her sheltered world such things did not exist. Yet Denise never came across as a Black girl trying to play at being white; instead she was rooted in a Black family and an African American cultural context.

Viewers carried this awareness of Denise to *A Different World*. Watching her relate to more conventional or ethnically typed characters gave *A Different World* a certain perverse kick. Never did Denise wilt around these people, and Bonet always had a sweet twinkle in her eye that led one to believe she was knowingly floating through all this unreal Hollywood nonsense. Though Denise herself still might not know who she was or what she wanted, we always felt she was on a quest for self-realization. Viewers often wanted to shield her, although,

A new kind of TV character: Jasmine Guy as the hincty Southern belle Whitley

vulnerabilities aside, Denise seemed capable of taking care of herself. Fortunately, the writers respected the character (as she had been created on *The Cosby Show*) and never turned Denise into a clown.

On the other hand, Jasmine Guy's Whitley was a totally unexpected—and unprecedented—TV character. The world of Southern belles was assumed to be the terrain of white actresses only. How could any woman be vain, selfish, good-looking, sexy, demanding, and so confident that she felt superior to just about everyone around her—unless that woman were white? As the self-absorbed Whitley, who waltzed through campus life as if she were at a charity ball, Jasmine Guy overturned those old assumptions about what an African American woman could or could not be. Guy created that kind of assured, *hincty, highyeller* bitch goddess that African Americans were all too familiar with and which white viewers probably never knew existed. It was hard not to be curious about Whitley, hard not to want to see what lay beneath her arch air of superiority. That's probably why the episode on which Denise's baby sister Rudy visited Hillman was so memorable. To Denise's surprise, Rudy is fascinated by Whitley and wants to spend all her time with her.

That first season, the juxtaposition of Guy's Whitley and Bonet's Denise helped lift *A Different World* out of the realm of the ordinary TV series. Whitley was an apt representation of a social system television had never before acknowledged: she was a member of the old Southern Black aristocracy, those light-skinned, straight-haired African Americans who took pride in their accomplishments, their lineage, and their climb up the social ladder. That they could be ruthless snobs was one matter. That many worked to elevate the lives of African Americans—through their social clubs, their church work, their charities, their belief in education—was another.

What was so funny about Whitley (with her affected Southern accent and ladylike airs) was that should any white character even suggest that she was anything but superior to most of God's creatures, Whitley would not only plaster him/her with a flip, nasty retort but probably blast him/her out of the room. This is a young African American woman who sees herself as *nobody's* inferior. One felt the same about Denise: should she ever be confronted with racism, with being told that she could not do this or that because of her race, she would not so much be angered as amused.

Characters such as Denise and Whitley, to a certain extent even Jaleesa, may have accurately conveyed a point of view prevalent among a new generation of young Black Americans in the mid/late Reagan 1980s. These were people who had grown up in a middle-class system, had frequently attended integrated schools, had enjoyed many material and cultural "advantages," and had not been seriously stung by racism. Sometimes this new generation could appear hopelessly uninformed— so mainstream that we felt they had bought into the worst aspects of the American dream. This new breed would have been viewed as politically inert by the politically charged generation of the 1960s or early 1970s. Yet many had a greater sense of cultural identity than we might have thought at first. This was where *A Different World*, even in its unformed first season, succeeded best: its subtext was the story of this new generation, with its sometimes superficial goals and aspirations or mock traumas, that has also been blessed with a sense of security by an older generation.

Thanks in large part to Denise and Whitley and also to the fact that it followed *The Cosby Show*, *A Different World* made it quickly into the Top Ten of the ratings. In the second season when Denise disappeared, it looked as if *A Different World* had lost its heart. But shrewdly the writers concentrated on Whitley, giving fuller dimension to the character. Toned down and sensitized, Dwayne—in the following seasons— became a good foil for her, then the appropriate love interest. The original characters often seemed to be maturing—as kids their age at school would. New episodes took them into the classroom as the series tried dealing with more serious subjects such as the stigma of AIDS or the lessons of cultural history. Other characters appeared: the feisty cook Vernon (Lou Meyers), who runs the campus hangout The Pit; the coeds Freddie (Cree Summer) and Kim (Charnele Brown), both beautifully drawn and warmly acted. Eventually, *A Different World* could boast of giving exposure to such rising stars as Sinbad (who played Walter) and Jada Pinkett (who played the homegirl-style coed Lena).

Because the series had a long run (six seasons), stretching into the more race-conscious, neonationalist 1990s, even this new generation eventually had to experience the sting and shock of racism. In 1992, a two-part episode, *Honeymoon in L.A.: The Simi Side of Life*, focused on the Los Angeles uprisings of 1991. But, mainly, much like *The Cosby Show*, the series focused on cultural distinctions within the African

American community. A memorable episode featured a Step Show, an African American fraternity and sorority ritual in which students dance and perform in highly syncopated rhythms derived from African dance.

Still, some problems were always present. Too often the writers were unable to create full-blown Black men, young or old, without resorting to familiar exaggerations. Can't a guy pursue a girl without coming off like a hormonally overcharged adolescent? Funny as Lou Meyers was, the cook Vernon remained something of a fussy mammylike character. At times, even Sinbad's Walter Oakes seemed an exaggeration. The series, usually directed by Debbie Allen, always fared better with its female characters, who could be counted on to make all the intelligent decisions. It was also well served by its African American executive producer Susan Fales.

Director Debbie Allen

At odd moments, the series couldn't shake itself from traditional forms of casting. On a Thanksgiving episode, the mothers of Whitley and Dwayne arrive on campus to see their kids, who by now are hooked on one another. As should be expected, Whitley's mother is slender, glamorous, and sexy, played perfectly by Diahann Carroll. Dwayne's mother, who is determined to nurture, protect, smother, and literally feed him (her baby), was the darker, heavier Patti LaBelle. Without intending to, *A Different World* had divided its mothers into familiar roles, seemingly based on color and physicality: Carroll, the lighter mulatto type; LaBelle, the physically larger, quasi mammy.

Still, *A Different World* presented a new view on the African American young. In the past, Black series as diverse as *Amos 'n' Andy, Julia, Sanford and Son*, and *The Cosby Show* were geared for family viewing. But while families no doubt watched *A Different World*, young viewers were its most ardent fans, mainly because the series ultimately expressed their perspective without condescending to them. When about to launch itself as the fourth network, Fox Television sought just this type of young African American audience. So, too, did UPN and WB.

Frank's Place also carried African American images in a new direction. Created by Hugh Wilson (who had previously created *WKRP in*

Great promise but an early TV death: Tim Reid
and Daphne Maxwell Reid in the dramedy
Frank's Place

Cincinnati), it starred Tim Reid as a Black college professor, Frank Parrish, who leaves his home in Boston to go to New Orleans. There, he has inherited a restaurant, Chez Louisiane, from a father he has never known. At first Frank is anxious to sell the restaurant. But, of course, he doesn't. Soon he's as intrigued as we are by the city's rich culture: its food, its music, its social clubs, its jazzy seductiveness.

In many respects, *Frank's Place* was a mood piece, a dream play, its tone set at each week's opening with the voice of Louis Armstrong on the soundtrack singing "Do You Know What It Means to Miss New Orleans?" This melancholic, evocative song conjures up the New Orleans of our imagination: a city of lights and color, magic and Mardi Gras, mystery and romance. Shot on film with one camera (rather than on videotape with a three-camera setup as most television sitcoms were) and abandoning a laugh track, *Frank's Place* had a misty, hazy look, making it seem all the more like a story filtered through memory and dreams.

Mainly, *Frank's Place*—part comedy, part drama, tagged a *dramedy* by the critics—was an examination of culture and relationships. Its characters were unusual too. There is Big Arthur (Tony Burton), the feisty cook, who refuses to be called a chef; Anna-May (Francesca P. Roberts), the head waitress; Miss Marie (Frances E. Williams), the elderly "waitress emeritus," who won't wait on anyone who hasn't been her customer for at least twenty years; Reverend Deal (Lincoln Kilpatrick), a shady minister; Tiger (Charles Lampkin), the warmhearted bartender; Bubba (Robert Harper), the white attorney, who is a regular at the restaurant; and Hanna Griffin (Daphne Maxwell Reid), the mortician, who becomes Frank's love interest.

The characters related and reacted to one another without the standard round of gags, without the outlandish attitudinizing that viewers had come to expect. Though they were not without theatrical embellishments, there was a warm, low-key quality about them that seemed real yet also folkloric.

As Frank, Tim Reid, with his dry humor and charm, set the tone. Previously, when Reid had appeared as the disc jockey Venus Flytrap on Wilson's *WKRP in Cincinnati* and as Downtown Brown on *Simon & Simon*, he convincingly played offbeat characters that in other hands might have been merely rowdy, urban stereotypes. Occasionally, he could be pleasantly silly. But Reid always let his intelligence light up his characters. The important thing about Frank was that he was an educated, middle-class Black man whose ethnic roots shine through.

Most impressive was Virginia Capers as Hanna's mother, the unbearably proper funeral parlor directress, Mrs. Griffin-Lamour. A matriarch of the African American community, she maintains a rigid set of standards that she imposes on just about everyone else. Tall, dark-skinned, and full-figured, Capers—simply as a physical type—could easily fall into the old loud/tough/mean mammy category. Having worked in theater, films, and television for over twenty years, Capers had usually been consigned to traditional motherly roles. She had been nominated for an Emmy for her appearance in an episode of *Mannix* and had also played Diahann Carroll's mother in episodes of *Julia*. But in *Frank's Place*, she moved in a whole other direction, playing her character as an imperious grande dame. Always impeccably dressed (sometimes with dramatic hats) and coiffed, she was a social arbiter.

She is also a woman who has never let any aspect of life pass her by. In one episode, when it was suggested (by daughter Hanna) that she might have once had a relationship with Frank's father, Capers turned self-righteously indignant. How dare anyone think such a thing! Of course, we felt she was lying through her teeth. But this unshakable sense of pride and composure distinguishes her character. For African American viewers, she reminds us of countless Black female community leaders we've seen over the years: high-minded, unyielding women (perhaps a bit like Barbara Jordan) who took a backseat to no one yet who also knew what it meant to kick up one's heels and have some fun. She, too, represents the old Southern Black aristocracy. Yet by casting Capers the creators indicated that this class system was not exclusively the province of lighter African Americans, though in truth Black America's color caste system was very much tied into class distinctions.

Frank's Place tried to capture that sense of pride and wonder of Black Americans of the past about Black achievers who seemed larger than life—men and women whose very skills and exploits gave a lie to white America's notions about Black inferiority. Like great urban folklore, the series delighted in proclaiming the deeds and doings of Big Arthur and Reverend Deal and in pointing up Mrs. Griffin-Lamour's blazing self-assurance and assertiveness. So great a cook was Big Arthur that Frank's rival Pokie LaCarre tries stealing Arthur away. So proud was Arthur of his own reputation that he entered a boxing ring with another chef who had dared proclaim himself as New Orleans's best. And Reverend Deal was the perennial con man wheeler-dealer, whose large-scale schemes and dreams backfire on him—and are recounted with a sense of pleasure and awe by those who know him.

Within the Black community, particularly in the past, legend and myth occupied a unique place. Before the history books told us anything about Black men and women of amazing deeds or accomplishments, word of mouth—the Black oral tradition—within the African American community carried dazzling stories of remarkable people. A gifted cook or a talented seamstress or a visionary scientist would be known, appreciated, and saluted in one tale after another. "That woman could sew for days" or "That man could add and subtract and multiply without ever touching a pad" or "She could make a cabinet better than any man ever dreamed of doing." Public figures like Joe Louis, Jesse Owens, Jackie Robinson, and later Muhammad Ali all had stories spun about them. Those who saw Ali fight in his heyday still tell us there were moves and techniques the cameras never recorded.

The series spotlighted a healthy relationship between Frank and Hanna. Here were a Black man and a Black woman who were both a bit stubborn and each determined to hold on to his/her independence. In one episode, when Frank looked as if he might lose his restaurant, Hanna showed up with some much needed cash to save the place. In typical hardheaded male fashion, he refused her help. Finally, Hanna just threw the money at him and walked out the door.

Frank's Place tackled themes seldom explored on sitcoms: cancer, suicide, drunk driving, racism in America, and the color caste system within the African American community. Some of the folkloric quality may be attributed to Samm-Art Williams, who served as story editor for the series and also wrote various episodes. Williams had previously written the Broadway play *Home.* His work on *Frank's Place* was a far cry from some of what followed for him: a position as a producer and writer on *The Fresh Prince of Bel-Air* and then as executive producer of *Martin.*

The critics loved *Frank's Place,* which won nine Emmy nominations, including one as Best Comedy Series. Beah Richards won the Emmy for Outstanding Guest Performer in a Comedy Series while Hugh Wilson won the award for Outstanding Writing in a Comedy Series. It also won a prestigious 1988 Humanitas Prize (the award given to television programs that "affirm human dignity and probe the meaning of life").

Industry watchers paid close attention to this oddity of a show. When early research indicated that *Frank's Place* appealed "strongly to Blacks of all socioeconomic levels," CBS thought it might "have a crossover hit on its hands." But having premiered in September 1987, the series was in 45th place in the ratings by December. CBS changed its time slot to a half hour later on Mondays. Within a month, the network changed the time again.

Part of the show's problems obviously lay in the botched manner the network programmed it. But *Frank's Place* also proved confusing to viewers, partly because of the series's innovations. Abandoning a laugh track had been a valid creative decision. But this part-comic, part-dramatic series was so unusual that had it been taped before a live studio audience with spontaneous reactions (and appropriate laughter for the humor), viewers might have had a better communal sense of the episodes' moods. The actors too might have had a better sense, in terms of their timing, of those moments when the pace has to slow for there to be time for viewer laughter—and also when to speed things up. As it was, viewers didn't seem to know how to relate to the series.

By season's end in April, *Frank's Place* ranked 62nd among 105 primetime network shows. Then the show disappeared for a spell, only to resurface on Saturday evenings during the summer reruns. In the past, networks had stuck with some low-rated shows until the programs found their audiences (and became big hits). *Family Ties* was 56th in its first season. *Cheers* was 74th in its first year. Some held out hope for *Frank's Place*. Finally, CBS announced the series would not return in the fall. A grass roots lobbying organization called Viewers for Quality Television, which had persuaded CBS to renew *Cagney & Lacey* and *Designing Women*, urged that the show be kept on. The Beverly Hills/Hollywood branch of the NAACP waged a campaign to keep the show alive but to no avail. *Frank's Place*, which premiered in September 1987, went off the air in October 1988.

Frank's Place nonetheless gave Tim Reid's career a boost. Afterward he was considered a player in network television. CBS took a chance on another series starring him called *Snoops*. Striving for a sophisticated mystery program along the lines of the *Thin Man* movies and the television series *Hart to Hart*, Reid and his wife, Daphne Maxwell Reid, played a Washington, D.C., married couple turned sleuths. He was a criminology professor at Georgetown University. She was a State Department official. Also appearing were Tim Reid Jr. and Tracy Camilla Johns as Reid Sr.'s students. To succeed, *Snoops* had to have clever scripts, oozing a sleek elegance and witty banter; the series also had to appeal to the large general audience that was still unaccustomed to a program with Black stars that was not in some way race-centered. Though the two leads made a valiant effort, *Snoops* went the way of a previous attempt like *Paris*. It lasted only one season.

But Tim Reid kept working. Later he co-starred on the series *Sister, Sister*. He also produced and directed the film *Once Upon a Time . . . When We Were Colored*. Then, in the late 1990s, he returned with a *Frank's Place*-style series—for cable's Showtime—called *Linc's*, another Black workplace drama.

Similar to *Frank's Place* was the series *Gideon Oliver*, which starred Louis Gossett Jr. as a Columbia University professor of anthropology who was also an expert kickboxer—and a shrewd amateur sleuth. If anything, *Gideon Oliver* was a star vehicle, well mounted to showcase Gossett's talents. The actor delighted in scenes in which his character displayed his academic knowledge as well as those in which he could strut with great flair in his academic garb, beautifully tailored tweedy suits with vests (the very type few college professors could probably afford). Gossett pulled the role off, and it was a pleasure to watch him in action. But *Gideon Oliver* appeared only once a month or so, as part of the *ABC Monday Mystery Movie* series. Viewers never really had the chance to become familiar with Gideon's idiosyncrasies and his unusual skills. A midseason replacement, it ran only one season.

Other series like *Fortune Dane*, *Sonny Spoon*, and *In the Heat of the Night* also toyed with the idea of strong, assertive professional Black male leads. Again they were usually cops (or former cops and detectives), who could be counted on to preserve the system.

An unexpected success was the series *In the Heat of the Night* (March 1988 to July 1994). Based on the 1967 Academy Award-winning movie starring Sidney Poitier and Rod Steiger, the television version featured Carroll O'Connor as the Sparta, Mississippi, police chief Bill Gillespie and Howard Rollins as Virgil Tibbs, the upstart Philadelphia detective, who had been born in Sparta and was now returning to live there. Gillespie represented the past: a streetwise man bred on the ways of the South and familiar with the residents of his community. Tibbs—with his knowledge of the latest methods of scientifically ferreting out criminals—represented the police force of tomorrow. The two men were born to clash. The premiere episode centered on the death of a girl in the town. A young Black man, who was accused of the crime, was found hanged in his prison cell. Gillespie and Tibbs psychologically duke it out, and the conflicts are not merely over their methods of solving the crime, but of course their fundamental views of race relations. Eventually, the men learned to work together, and each came to respect the other.

Although the series appeared twenty-one years after the film, not much seemed to have changed, which partly explains the appeal of the series to older audiences. Crimes now involved drugs and incest, but this was still sleepy time down (a relatively rural redneck) South. Violence and sex were kept to a minimum. And the scripts, while smoothly written, seldom had the gnawing moral ambivalence of the postmodern cop dramas like *Hill Street Blues, Miami Vice,* and later *N.Y.P.D. Blue* and *Homicide.* The episodes were intelligently done; the characters—their motivations and aspirations—were easy to understand and enjoy.

The racial subtext of the weekly episodes, however, enhanced the tensions. Black viewers rarely considered the differences between Gillespie and Tibbs as merely professional ones. Rollins seemed edgy and defensive, aware and resentful that he still had to prove himself to this white man boss. O'Connor appeared suspicious of this Northerner (Negro) coming down to change the South's ways. Fortunately, the series was willing to focus on racism, as text and subtext. As *TV Guide*'s Merrill Panitt noted: "So far as entertainment is concerned, *Heat* scores a B-minus as cop show. As an exercise in tolerance and understanding between races, which all of us—black and white—can use, it warrants an A."

A nice twist was the introduction of the character Althea (Anne-Marie Johnson), the wife of Virgil. Though her purpose seemed to be to flesh out the character of Virgil, to set his tensions and conflicts in bold relief against a domestic backdrop, Althea eventually developed into a decent character. Of course, it was always amusing for African

American viewers to hear Gillespie deferentially address her as "Mrs. Tibbs."

Later in its run, *In the Heat of the Night* struck a note of a modern South through the character Harriet DeLong (Denise Nicholas)—a Black city councilwoman, who at first was a recurring character, then a regular. Nicholas's Harriet was not as pliable as Mrs. Tibbs. Just as she had done on *Room 222*, Nicholas skillfully pumped some bite and sarcasm into any dialogue that had the merest suggestion of annoyance or anger. Even Gillespie knew he had to watch himself with her. When viewers detected signs of Gillespie's budding romantic interest in DeLong, they no doubt brushed such thoughts aside at first. But the two became lovers, which raised eyebrows in Sparta and brought on some professional problems for Gillespie. In the last season, they married.

By then, unfortunately, *In the Heat of the Night* had lost its rhythm and appeal. Viewers didn't see as much of Gillespie (now working mainly in a nearby town), and Howard Rollins had left the cast. (His character, having had marital problems with Althea, was said to be pursuing a law degree.) Carl Weathers stepped in, portraying a former FBI agent who becomes Sparta's sheriff. But without the O'Connor/Rollins chemistry, viewers lost interest.

Sadly, *In the Heat of the Night* marked the end of Howard Rollins's career. Hollywood-handsome with dark eyes, a strong jawline, chiseled features, and a dark complexion, Rollins—born in 1950 in Baltimore—looked like he was created for the movies. In 1981, he had given an impressive performance as Coalhouse Walker in the film *Ragtime*, which won him a Best Supporting Actor Academy Award nomination. Afterward it should have been smooth sailing. But another important lead role didn't come until three years later in *A Soldier's Story*. Rollins was something of a displaced actor: the wrong performer at the wrong time. In the early 1980s, the few Black film stars who found success were the comedians Richard Pryor and Eddie Murphy. Leading dramatic film roles for African American actors remained a rarity. By the end of the era, the situation would change.

Rollins turned to work on television, appearing in *He's Fried, She's Fried*; *Johnnie Mae Gibson: FBI*; *With Murder in Mind*; and *For Us the Living: The Medgar Evers Story*. Though always professional, his performances were not always exciting. (An exception was his appearance in

The Children of Times Square.) Often he looked as if he had lost his spark. Then, as the actor's professional frustrations must have grown, his looks changed, the face becoming puffy, sometimes bloated; his body too turned slack. Rumors spread of drug problems. It must have been all the more frustrating for him when in the late 1980s and early 1990s actors like Denzel Washington and Wesley Snipes began to emerge as important dramatic leading men in the movies. Rollins's day had passed him by.

On the set of *In the Heat of the Night,* he became known for erratic behavior—and his scrapes with the law. When he checked himself into a rehab center, the tabloids were filled with stories about his medical problems, including reports that he had AIDS. Once he left the series, his health continued to deteriorate. Then, in 1996, Howard Rollins was found dead in his New York apartment—his body discovered by a friend. He was said to have died of a bacterial infection caused by complications of lymphoma. He was forty-six years old. Among his later performances were roles in an episode of *New York Undercover* and on the American Movie Classics Channel's *Remember WENN* series. His last TV appearance was in December 1996 in the PBS presentation *Harambee,* a program about the African American holiday Kwanza.

During the last year of the decade, the sitcom *Family Matters* aired on ABC. A spin-off of the series *Perfect Strangers* in which actress Jo Marie Payton-France played the sharp-tongued elevator operator Harriette Winslow, *Family Matters* was the story of Harriette, her police officer husband Carl, their three children, and their extended family—Harriette's cranky mother (Rosetta LeNoire), her young widowed sister Rachel (Telma Hopkins), and Rachel's infant son Richie, who all lived together in a Chicago suburb. Generally, the critics dismissed the series as bland, predictable, and little more than a watered-down, working-class version of *The Cosby Show.* Yet *Family Matters* found an audience of respectable size.

In the second season, its tone changed, and *Family Matters*'s ratings shot up, thanks to the arrival of a new character, Steve Urkel. As played by twelve-year-old Jaleel White, Urkel originally made guest appearances but was so popular with audiences that he was added to the cast.

A wholly new kind of African American character, he was a nerdy schoolboy who snorted when he laughed and who repeatedly whined in a nasal voice when he spoke. Usually, he was dressed in pants—held up by suspenders—that came up way over his skinny waist and wore oversized glasses that one critic said made him look like "a cross between Pee-wee Herman and Spike Lee." Weekly, audiences laughed at this rather pathetic-looking soul who had a crush on the Winslows' daughter Laura (Kellie Shanygne Williams). Doing everything he could to please her, he told corny jokes that made no one laugh. Urkel was also an inventor who created a vehicle called the Urk-

Jaleel White as a different kind of Black kid on the block, the nerdy Urkel on Family Matters

Pad that transported the Winslow family to Paris. With another invention—a time machine—he carried his comic foil, Carl Winslow, back to the eighteenth century. Capitalizing on his popularity—and the belief that viewers couldn't get enough of him—the writers had Urkel clone himself. Afterward there were Myrtle Urkel, his outrageous cousin, and Stefan Urquette, a debonair version of Steve. While Urkel yearned for Laura, another teenager, Myra, pined for him. That role was played by Michelle Thomas, who also became a favorite for viewers and later appeared on the daytime soap *The Young and the Restless*. Most were stunned when the young actress suddenly died of stomach cancer in 1998. Ugly reality intruded on viewers' perceptions of the fantasy world of a television series.

In the minds of some, what made Urkel unique for a Black teenage male character was that he was something of an intellectual. The president of the Beverly Hills/Hollywood NAACP found him refreshing because he revealed "the diversity within the African American community." Psychiatrist Alvin Poussaint commented, "He's not up on street talk, not a dancing, bopping kind of kid. The fact that he's a nerd and very bright may be a step forward—accepting that a Black kid can be bright and precocious and might end up in an Ivy League school." But while Urkel was obviously bright, he was also a buffoon with stooped shoulders and pursed lips.

In some respects, Urkel was deracialized; a clownish geek who wasn't depicted any differently from your generic bookworm. Yet because he was played by an African American performer, the character took on another meaning for some viewers. Critic John J. O'Connor went so far as to write that Urkel's "broadly caricatured antics uneasily smack of a modern Stepin Fetchit in the making."

Regardless, Urkel became something of a phenomenon. Much like Mr. T and Jimmie Walker's J.J., he was a walking cartoon, a rather creepy exaggeration that kids could not resist. His pat phrases became well known: "Did I do thaaaat?"; "No sweat, my pet"; "Snookums"; and "You got any cheese?" There were at one time an Urkel doll, trading cards, and a cereal, Urkel-Os. Actor White also hosted his own special: *Steve Urkel's Other Side: The Jaleel White Special*. With Urkel as its focal point, *Family Matters* became more like a Saturday afternoon cartoon than a traditional sitcom. But it ran for eight years on ABC and then was picked up for another season by CBS. Afterward Jaleel White made the transition to adult star in the late 1990s sitcom *Grown Ups*.

Other series featured interesting Black characters. On the medical drama *Heartbeat*, which was considered something of a feminist series with its focus on female physicians, Lynn Whitfield was cast as Cory Banks, a doctor and the mother of two. Here was another attempt, similar to *St. Elsewhere*, to depict African American professionals operating successfully in an integrated workplace. Set in a hospital and USO entertainment center in Da Nang in the 1960s, *China Beach* attempted to focus on the war in Vietnam from a woman's point of view. Dana Delany starred as a nurse at the hospital. African American actress Nancy Giles was cast as the deejay Frankie Bunsen, and Black actor Michael Boatman played a young private. Of course, it might have been just as interesting a premise had *China Beach* attempted to tell the story of the war from the perspective of its African American characters.

Airing on the new Fox network, the police drama *21 Jump Street* was specifically geared for young audiences. Looking like an update of *The Mod Squad*, it centered on four youthful undercover cops, who posed as high school students in order to help solve problems facing teens, such as gangs and drugs as well as murder and prostitution. As on *The Mod Squad*, its characters, though law enforcement officers, were hip and seemingly rebellious. Once again, the officers looked like a bomber crew from a World War II movie: clean-cut pretty boy Johnny Depp, Asian American actor Dustin Nguyen, wholesome Peter DeLuise, African American actress Holly Robinson (as Officer Judy Hoffs), and later Richard Grieco. Robinson's appearance may well have helped the show win young Black viewers. After three seasons, the series ran in syndication. But it clearly was a sign of the future—for Fox, UPN, and WB. Not only would these new networks specialize in series directly aimed at the young, but they would also develop programs for African American viewers.

L.A. LAW'S JONATHAN ROLLINS: THE BUPPIE COMES TO PRIMETIME

Then there was the slick and sexy *L.A. Law*, the highly rated hour-long dramatic series about smart, aggressive attorneys at the law firm McKenzie, Brackman, Chaney & Kuzak. Created by Steven Bochco and Terry Louise Fisher, *L.A. Law*'s debut episode focused on the dilemma facing young attorney Michael Kuzak in a case involving a Black rape victim (Alfre Woodard) who is dying of leukemia. Kuzak has no choice but to defend an obviously guilty young white assailant, the son of a wealthy client of the firm. Kuzak is advised by a colleague to delay the case until the woman "either quits or dies." During the courtroom testimony, the woman is put through a grueling—and, for viewers, moving—cross-examination. When she cries out in indignation at her treatment, the judge sternly warns her, "I'll hold you in contempt." "The feeling is mutual," she responds. But she is later made to apologize to the court. The episode raised questions that seemed to spring from the headlines: are the poor and disenfranchised further victimized by the judicial system? Of course, the writers played it safe by making Kuzak feel so torn. "I may not always believe in the client," he says, "but I have to believe in the system." Because of the casting of Woodard, race was very much on the minds of viewers. Woodard was again playing a rather defenseless victim (similar to her award-winning role on *Hill Street Blues*), but her performance graced the episode with an emotional depth it would have otherwise lacked. She won another Emmy as Outstanding Guest Performer in a Drama Series. The role helped Woodard to become a distinctive TV star of the 1980s. Nonetheless, though Black characters appeared in various episodes, race initially seemed something of an afterthought among the major characters of the series.

During *L.A. Law*'s first season, Mario Van Peebles appeared as a Black attorney who eventually resigned from the law firm because he did not want simply to be window dressing. And window dressing was precisely what his 1987 replacement, Blair Underwood, at first seemed to be. Cast as the Harvard-educated Black lawyer Jonathan Rollins, Underwood gave a convincing performance as a spoiled young hotshot. He's a buppie—a Black urban professional—who gleams and glows with the knowledge that he has the best of academic and social credentials. Of course, that's a twist that makes him perversely likable—even though at heart he's not a very warm or likable character in his early episodes. Confident and arrogant, Rollins would do anything to win a case. Nothing wrong with that aspect of his characterization. But *L.A. Law* carefully neutralized his ethnic background. We heard of Rollins's family but didn't see them. Nor for a long time did we see much of his private life. At one point, the series titillated viewers with a suggestion of a budding romance between Rollins and the white lawyer Abby as well as a relationship between Rollins and Diana, a young African American attorney in the office (played by Renee Jones). How he felt as a Black male at this white firm was a question the series avoided asking.

Blair Underwood as the buppie lawyer Jonathan Rollins in L.A. Law. Underwood with L.A. Law cast members Susan Ruttan (left) and Sheila Kelley

Initially, *L.A. Law* creator Steven Bochco decided that Rollins not be a civil rights crusader. "We didn't originally put a major Black character into the show," explained Bochco, "because, by and large, law firms tend to be lily-white. It's far more interesting to establish the fundamental whiteness of a work environment and then bring a Black into it." But Bochco seemed determined that race not be an issue in Rollins's life. "Victor Sifuentes doesn't function as a Chicano lawyer," Bochco said of another minority character on the show. "He's simply an attorney, and does it well. We'll do the same with our Black lawyer. We'll deracialize him."

Of course, no one wanted to see Rollins confronted with some racial dilemma every week. Nor could anyone be fundamentally opposed to color-blind casting. But when a series denied race—ignoring the presence of a major Black character's family or friends—then color is surely being used merely as part of a window display.

Certainly, African American viewers must have questioned an episode on which a young white woman—whom Rollins refers to as his "bestest friend" from law school—seeks his help in a legal matter. She is terminally ill and wants to be cryogenically preserved before death. Though the two are obviously close, matters were kept nonthreateningly ambiguous. It was hard to understand if theirs had ever really been a romantic relationship. As the episode drew to a close, the two were openly affectionate. "You remember the time we stayed up all night and talked about whether we should be a couple or not," the young woman tells Rollins. "And you said you didn't think we should because it would jeopardize our friendship," he responds. The dialogue was good enough, but you still may have wondered if—during this all-night conversation—the subject of race had ever entered their little heads; if it hadn't, the two appeared hopelessly naive. The episode ended with the two embracing and saying they still loved each other. Then she drove off and he stood alone. If any mainstream viewers worried about an interracial relationship between the two, they didn't have to fret for long. After all, she was driving off—to die sometime in the near future—and poor Rollins remained racially/culturally adrift.

One of *L.A. Law*'s best stories—dramatized over several episodes—centered on an African American college professor, Earl Williams (Carl Lumbly), wrongly convicted of having killed his research assistant, a young white woman. Proud, intelligent, aware of the culture in which he lives, Williams has tried to live without compromising himself. Yet he admits belatedly to having had an affair with the murdered young woman. The revelation stuns his wife (Vonetta McGee) and children, who sit in the courtroom. The episode suggests Williams is as much on trial for the taboo interracial affair as for murder. Later an eyewitness reveals that he saw another Black man—not Williams—leaving the woman's apartment on the day of the killing. But the judge will not allow the eyewitness's testimony in the trial. Defending Williams—and agonizing over the case—was again stalwart Michael Kuzak. It might have been far more interesting had Rollins handled the case, so the writers could deal more frankly with the young attorney's feelings about race in the workplace—and the judicial system.

On the fifth and next-to-last episode of the Earl Williams story (when his conviction was finally overturned), it appeared as if the writers, David E. Kelley and William M. Finkelstein, realized they had to have some comment from Rollins about race. A deracialized Rollins now looked hollow, as if cut off from—and ignorant of—fundamental realities of urban life. But it was too late to involve him in the Williams case. Instead, Rollins protests his firm's involvement with a client, Anderson Industries, which has ties to South Africa. Suddenly, he comes to a new awareness about race as a factor in his life. "I'm a rich boy, Leland, I had everything. Everything," he tells the head of the firm, Leland McKenzie. "It was easy to forget I was Black, and that's exactly what I did." Rollins also admits, "I'm not a very political person." He recalls, "When I was at Harvard, they had protests all the time over apartheid and divestitures. See, I was always too busy studying to take part." Surely, viewers liked seeing the Rollins character come to life. There had always been something about him that seemed to be missing. Now a racial consciousness made Rollins seem more real and contemporary. By commenting on the apartheid system in South Africa, *L.A. Law* could also be credited with addressing an important current social/racial issue.

Yet *L.A. Law*—adhering to television's fundamental conservatism—also felt compelled to present another point of view on apartheid. The writers used Rollins's love interest, the Black character Diana, for a counterstatement. When Rollins tells her that he couldn't stay at the firm with Anderson Industries as a client, Diana says in no uncertain terms that she is not quitting. "Do you think because we're Black we've got an exclusive on outrage?" she asks. "Did it ever occur to you that your quitting would accomplish nothing? Did it ever occur to you that by staying you could help influence Anderson Industries? Maybe even convince them to change?" She adds, "I don't want to lose my job. I can't afford to. I'm already about $20,000 in debt in student loans. This job is also my best career opportunity and I shouldn't have to give it up just because you're having a little spasm of Black guilt."

"If you don't want to quit," says Rollins, "don't quit. Stay here and represent racists."

"Maybe you're the racist. You're the one making assumptions on the basis of my skin color."

In essence, Diana's attitude was meant to be taken as the more mature and astute one. (The message was that if a clear-thinking, well educated, young African American had no deep qualms about working for a firm with a client with ties to South Africa, then why should anyone else have any qualms?) Rollins appeared rather petulant in his insistence on leaving the firm. It was also *his* racial attitudes that were being called into question—even though Diana's comment about him being a racist doesn't hold water in the context in which it's stated. In the end, though, the honorable firm McKenzie, Brackman, Chaney & Kuzak rejects Anderson Industries, and Rollins does not have to leave.

But afterward the Rollins character underwent more changes as he grappled with the issue of race in his life and profession. On the concluding episode of the Earl Williams story, he assisted Kuzak in the courtroom, although he didn't have much to do. But on a later episode, while jogging in the posh neighborhood near his home, he was stopped and brutalized by the police, who suspected him of being a mugger. He almost found himself charged with rape. But Rollins refused to back off from his complaint that he was a victim of racial profiling.

On another occasion—in a story line that ran over several episodes in the early 1990s—Rollins became involved in the case of a white police officer accused of having killed a young Black. At first, he expresses anger about his firm's defense of the cop, which has drawn great media coverage. During a staff meeting, Michael Kuzak says that the media coverage will go away. "Why shouldn't it?" counters a cynical Rollins. "It's just a Black kid who died." "It was an accident," says Kuzak. "Yeah, an accident by a white cop," says Rollins. As it turns out, the killing really was an accident, a case of involuntary manslaughter. The cop himself is a rather serious, sensitive fellow. By all rights, the case should be dropped without a trial. Even the prosecutor feels that way at first. But a hot-headed, rabble-rousing African American attorney named Derren Holloway (played by Paul Winfield) leads a protest movement, insisting that the cop be tried. "Don't cops give out special merit for executing niggers?" Holloway asks.

Eventually, justice appears to give way to politics. "If we don't prosecute, it'll mean another Bensonhurst," the District Attorney tells Kuzak. He is referring to the real-life racial tensions that erupted after sixteen-year-old Yusef Hawkins was killed by a gang of white youths in the Bensonhurst section of Brooklyn in 1990. Because the DA is up for reelection, he doesn't want any political backlash. Nor does the judge in the case who refuses to delay the trial. He also is up for reelection. No one wants to take the political risk of looking like a racist. Kuzak sees the corruption of the system—*and* of the protesting Black attorney. "Mr. Holloway," he says in court, "is representing the family of the victim in a civil litigation. And it is my belief that he is publicly promoting a criminal conviction here in order to bolster his own civil cause of action." Kuzak calls for Holloway to stop the "hysterical grandstanding," which has become a "sideshow." "Your honor," says Kuzak of Holloway, "he is inflaming the public and the media."

It indeed does look as if Holloway (who seems patterned after the Black activist New York attorney Vernon Mason)—and his Black followers who sit in the courtroom—are merely playing the race card, looking for racism in a case where it doesn't exist. Never does this particular episode take the anguish of the Black protesters seriously.

An unexpected plot twist occurs when Kuzak decides that Rollins should participate in the defense. "Why?" asks Rollins. "Because you're Black," says Kuzak. "Because the media and everyone else is making this into a race thing. And because I need some window dressing."

Rollins detests being used in this way. But again *L.A. Law* appeared to back off from giving his racial commitment a real validity. From the perspective of the writers, Rollins's initial attitudes and his anger were (again) not meant to be representative of those of a mature African American male. Viewers could see right away that Holloway was just a self-aggrandizing troublemaker. Viewers could also see immediately the innocence of the white cop. Why didn't Rollins? Once again, Rollins's love interest, Diana, served as a counterpoint, a spokesperson for more conservative (reasonable) values.

"I sit at the defense table, looking Black, letting myself be exploited," Rollins tells Diana as the two lie in bed together.

"You don't think Holloway's exploiting things?" she asks. "He offers up nothing but rage. It gives him a lot of cheers. But what does he accomplish?"

"Sometimes rage is a start," he says.

"And look at what it started. A public desperation for a conviction, no matter what. Innocent or guilty, there damn well has to be a conviction to keep the peace. That's what Holloway has started."

Here *L.A. Law* refused to make a politicized as well as racialized Rollins a full-fledged television hero. Instead he has to be taken down a few pegs. Though Rollins can rock the boat, ultimately he must regain his rational equilibrium and get back to the mainstream shore.

In the end, Rollins defends the cop with a newfound commitment. A new judge—played by Black actor John Hancock—is also put on the case. He, too, understands the problems Holloway has caused.

Yet to its credit, *L.A. Law* provided an unexpected twist to the Rollins/Holloway relationship. Privately, Rollins tells Holloway, "I want to say this just once for the record. There has been nobody, no lawyer anywhere, I've admired more than you, Mr. Holloway. I can't tell you how many times over the years I've looked in the mirror, wanting to see some reflection, some hint of what I've always seen in you." This comment seems contradictory when one remembers Rollins's earlier statement about not being a political person and not being involved in protests while a student at Harvard. If an activist Black lawyer had been his true hero, wouldn't it have affected his earlier life? Nonetheless, the writers use the encounter to present another view, partly of Rollins but mainly of Holloway.

"You talk about the system. You talk about the process," Rollins says. "Then you stand in front of the cameras and film crews and willingly pervert it."

"The perversion *is* the system," says Holloway. "The system was going to let that man walk without even a trial."

"If that kid was white, you wouldn't be here right now," says Rollins.

"Oh, man, where have you been? If the kid had been white, I

wouldn't *have* to be here," Holloway says. "But when that day comes—when society cries for Black children with the same passion that it does for whites—when the senseless death of an African American is just as unacceptable, then I'll stop. I'll stop. But the truth is, Mr. Rollins, that racism is going to outlive me. What sickens me is to think that someday my dream will one day rest in the hands of Black lawyers like you."

During the trial itself, Rollins accuses Holloway of being a racist. (Black characters seemed to love calling one another racists.) "If I'm a racist," says Holloway, "and you suppose I am, then it's by necessity, to combat a much larger white racism built into the framework—not only of society in general but specifically a judicial system which does not render fair treatment to Black Americans."

The jury finds the white policeman guilty. But then in yet another plot twist, the African American judge addresses the courtroom. He speaks of a previous trial (at which Rollins was present) that was "also a case of white America trampling Black America. And the hatred rose up and took that room. And I've seen that hatred in this room too. As a Black man, I understood that hatred. I grew up in a poor neighborhood. I've seen innocent Black people shot dead by white policemen. I've seen it. And every day as I sit up here, I carry that baggage. But first and foremost, I sit up here as judge. And as a judge, my job is not to affect race relations but to affect justice in this courtroom." The judge does not believe that a Black eyewitness's testimony against the cop is credible. "If my choice is between a riot and an unjust verdict," he says, "I have to opt for the riot." He then overturns the conviction.

Afterward in the courthouse parking lot, Rollins speaks to a subdued and reflective Holloway, who says he too realized the white cop's innocence once Rollins had cross-examined the Black witness. But Holloway knows his struggle must continue. "A couple of weeks from now, maybe sooner, another Black man will be dead by a white cop's gun. And I'll be there, making the same noise all over again," he says. "Making sure questions get asked."

"Maybe I'll meet you there," says Rollins.

"That would be my pleasure," Holloway responds.

Ultimately, Holloway came across as an honorable man. Rollins also rose in stature because he understood the importance of the attorney's activism and also the inequities in the judicial system itself. This multiple-episode storyline—like that of Earl Williams—proved

to be among *LA Law*'s most engrossing and thought-provoking dramatizations.

Later *L.A. Law* was fairly bold in dramatizing a steamy relationship
between Rollins and a white prosecutor, who was the former wife of a
colleague of his. Interestingly, he was far more sexual here than in his
earlier scenes with Diana. At this point, those grand masters of style
and technique, Robert Guillaume and Madge Sinclair, appeared as
Rollins's parents. He's a staunch Republican. She's a fiery civil rights
attorney who is openly opposed to her son's interracial relationship.
The two are so good—and the concept of this seemingly politically
mismatched Black couple is so intelligently developed—that you wish
there was a dramatic series about them. The series also examined another brand of racism, that of African Americans against their fellow
African Americans. Other episodes also touched on the race theme in
an adult, complex manner. Then the Rollins character developed in
other ways after the Los Angeles uprisings following the decision in the
case of police officers accused of beating Black motorist Rodney King.
In its seventh season premiere in 1992, the entire episode took place on
the day that the verdict in the King case was rendered. As lawyer Arnie
Becker represents a worker who has been fired from the Family Land
amusement park because he broke character by removing his Homer
Simpson costume head in order to throw up, Becker asks, "What didn't
we see? What are we missing?" He's referring to a camera-recorded tape
of the incident. But, of course, he's also referring to the police-beating
video in the King case—and the manner in which it was used in court.
Attorney Douglas Brackman was mistakenly arrested during the upheaval while he was en route to remarry his former wife.

But most important is the effect of the verdict on Rollins, who is
forced to reexamine his decision to run for the city council in South
Central L.A. He doesn't even live in the area. His boss, Leland McKenzie, reminisces about his days as an assistant district attorney at the
time of the Watts riots twenty years earlier. "When will we learn?" he
asks. "I'm beginning to believe there's too much law and not enough
justice." Noble intentions notwithstanding, too much of this episode
seemed self-congratulatory. But to its credit, the series followed
through on some of these story lines in future episodes, especially
when Rollins's political campaign turned dirty and ugly. The social atmosphere—and slipping ratings—made the creators realize their dera-

cializing edict had to be reversed. The race theme also made *L.A. Law* an even better show; like *Hill Street Blues*, one of the best series of the decade.

The supposedly color-blind casting of African American actors some-times gave a series some intriguing subtexts. Certainly, few characters could have been harder to figure out than Anthony Bouvier on the sit-com *Designing Women*. Centering on four women at the decorating firm Sugarbakers (set in a comfortable suburban Atlanta town house), *Designing Women* featured Anthony (first as a recurring character, then as a regular) as an ex-con working as a handyman for the women. Originally, Anthony was not written as a Black character. But actor Me-shach Taylor's audition was so strong that he was hired. Sitcom creator (and co-executive producer) Linda Bloodworth-Thomason could pride herself on hiring the right actor for the role, regardless of race. But race popped up inadvertently, especially with the recurring joke on the series about Anthony's "unfortunate incarceration." African American viewers questioned why Anthony was an ex-con. Once again, a Black male was associated with crime; once again, drawn as a possible social misfit. Anthony's past could easily have been changed without altering the character. (Anthony hardly seemed like a man with such a past any-way.) Some civil rights groups also protested about this former jailbird now working contentedly for four Southern white women. It simply pointed up the fact that, as in the past, race does play a part in shaping audience perception.

Viewers also had questions about Anthony's sexuality. On a very popular episode, Anthony found himself snowbound in a motel room with the voluptuous, sexy Suzanne Sugarbaker (Delta Burke). The two spend their time talking, learning more about one another. Anthony never expressed the least romantic interest in Suzanne—or any of the other women. Nor did they express any such interest in him. All of this, coupled with Anthony's interest in fashion, led some viewers to assume that Anthony was gay and that the show's creators didn't have the guts to just come out and say it.

Eventually, as if to alleviate viewer concerns (or fears), the writers developed another life for Anthony. Anthony returned to college, grad-uated, and then became a partner in the design firm. During the

1989–90 season, Olivia Brown played his girlfriend. Later Jackee Harry briefly appeared as Anthony's fiancée. When that relationship didn't work out, the writers resorted to another plot device for Anthony. While on a trip to Las Vegas with his designing women friends, he awakens in his hotel room—to learn that he's married a leggy showgirl named Etienne (Sheryl Lee Ralph)! He's not sure what happened! Anthony's marriage might have worked better had the writers taken a different route.

Previously, Meshach Taylor appeared on such television shows as *Barney Miller, M*A*S*H, Lou Grant,* and in a regular role on the short-lived sitcom *Buffalo Bill.* Once he began work on *Designing Women* (at age forty-one), Taylor, aware of viewer perceptions, understood how he would have to navigate his way around the scripts. With his double takes and his common sense amid some of the storms at the design firm, Taylor presented an Anthony who saw through the conflicts and rivalries, the pretensions and vulnerabilities of these successful white women. His lack of interest in the women seemed due to his preoccupation with getting his work done and going about his life (even though we didn't know that life at first). If anything, he led us to believe he felt a tad sorry for these weary white broads.

TV Movies

The era's television movies continued to examine the nation's racial dilemmas. Some like *White Mama* (starring Bette Davis as an impoverished widow who bonds with a Black teenager played by Ernest Harin) and *Jimmy B. and Andre* (the tale of an older white widower who bonds with a Black ten-year-old) were rather innocuous melodramas, stressing again the idea of brotherhood.

Issue-oriented dramas, based on real events, started appearing early in the decade. The 1980 *Attica,* directed by Marvin J. Chomsky, was a rather fevered dramatization of the 1971 uprisings at the New York state penitentiary. Its cast included Morgan Freeman, Roger E. Mosley, and Glynn Turman. *The Atlanta Child Murders* sprang from the headlines about the mysterious killings of young African American children in Atlanta. The story of the historic 1957 school desegregation in Little Rock was told in *Crisis at Central High.* The drama spent most of its time following the *valiant* efforts of the *valiant* white teacher Elizabeth

Huckaby (Joanne Woodward) to reassure the Black students—and to keep a lid on the violent emotions of whites in the community.

Something similar—a typical, jaundiced TV perspective—was at the heart of *Grambling's White Tiger*, which most African American viewers tuned in to hoping to learn more about the remarkable football team of the Black college, Grambling State in Louisiana. A legendary hero for many Black Americans, Grambling's coach, Eddie Robinson, had led the school's football team to an astounding number of victories, and at a time when many African American athletes still were not welcomed at the big white universities, Robinson had trained a number of athletic stars who later were recruited by the NFL. Under the direction of Georg Stanford Brown, Harry Belafonte made a rare television appearance playing Robinson. But what did the drama do? Rather than turning all its attention to Robinson and the school, as if their struggles weren't dramatic enough, it focused on Bruce Jenner as the only white on Grambling's team. For many, it seemed just another white boy movie.

The Jesse Owens Story, which starred Dorian Harewood in the title role, proved more effective in telling its story of the American star of the 1936 Berlin Olympics, tracing his life from his college days to his later years when he was almost shockingly exploited.

Other dramas based on true stories followed. *Johnnie Mae Gibson: FBI*—with Howard Rollins, Lynn Whitfield, and Richard Lawson under Bill Duke's direction—dramatized the experiences of the first Black female FBI agent. The drama *Guyana Tragedy: The Story of Jim Jones*, directed by William A. Graham and written by Ernest Tidyman, was based on the true story of cult leader Jim Jones (played by Powers Boothe), who led more than 900 of his followers, many of whom were African American, to mass suicide in 1979. Fortunately, the story was developed strongly enough so that viewers had a sense of the mania that drove the followers to such a desperate final act. Both Rosalind Cash and Madge Sinclair were to capture both the intensity and the dreamy self-destructive romanticism of their characters.

In the 1980s, the networks also aired a familiar genre, the Old South Plantation drama. No matter how hard they tried, these presentations never escaped the old stereotypes. A well-publicized drama like *Beulah Land* proved hopelessly dated and embarrassing. Even before *Beulah Land* was completed, groups protested against it.

But David Wolper's star-studded, elaborate twelve-hour miniseries adaptation of John Jakes's popular pre-Civil War novel *North and South* drew high ratings. Though it attempted to update the genre by uncovering the sadism and corruption of the Old South, the miniseries was tied to past images without much of anything original to say—and without many African American actors in the cast. British actress Lesley-Anne Down was cast as a lovely Southern belle, Madeline Fabray LaMotte, who unknowingly carries a dark secret. Her loyal servant, a mammy if ever there was one, played by a lively Olivia Cole, was aware of the secret and determined that it never be revealed, especially to Madeline's burly brute of a husband, Justin LaMotte (David Carradine). Poor Olivia even goes to her death—she's pushed down a stairway—while trying to protect Madeline. The secret? In a very clever performance, Elizabeth Taylor, as a glamorous New Orleans madam, inadvertently reveals that the pretty but mysterious Madeline had a *negra* mother. (Ironically, the bearer of the secret, the dark-haired Elizabeth Taylor, looked as if she might have a touch of the Creole herself.) Afterward Madeline endures a multitude of indignities. That *negra blood* can do all sorts of devilish things to a person's mind. *Newsweek* compared *North and South* with the execrable *Beulah Land*, which also "reduced the antebellum slave experience to an Aunt Jemima/Uncle Remus cliché," adding that the drama's "Scarlett clone comes with a black mammy who, sounding more like Hattie McDaniel than the original, is given to such chidings as 'You better dresses, chile, or we be late fo' de barbecue.' "

Also in the cast was Georg Stanford Brown as a very dignified slave, who marries an abolitionist named Virgilia (Kirstie Alley)! But, of course, they must suffer dire consequences. Poor Brown is quickly killed off. Afterward Alley's Virgilia, who always seemed a tad neurotic, goes completely bonkers. As it refuses to depict her as a sane, well-balanced white woman, the drama's subliminal suggestion is that she'd have to be cuckoo to marry a Negro. Virgilia is last seen in the 1986 twelve-hour sequel, *North and South, Book II*, which covered the years of the Civil War. Here she was taken before a firing squad and executed. The fates of Alley and Brown, however, are far worse than the suffering Madeline's. Since she's played by a real white actress, she can finally be reunited with her true love, the sensitive and kindly Confederate officer Patrick Swayze. Aware of Madeline's mixed racial heritage, Swayze nonetheless seems totally ignorant of the fact that they are now an interracial couple. Though corny and melodramatic, the first *North and South* was also sometimes more fun than it had a right to be. Interestingly, perhaps to avoid controversy, the sequel, *North and South, Book II*—which was patently routine—had no major African American characters, other than Madeline. But, of course, she doesn't count!

Two of the era's most interesting and offbeat dramas were *Sophisticated Gents* and *Sister, Sister*, each of which sat on NBC's shelves long after their completion. Both had been produced under the aegis of Fred Silverman, who, after the extraordinary success of *Roots*, believed, when he took over the programming schedule at NBC, there was still a huge audience for African American material. But once the TV films were completed, the network reportedly thought both were duds. Neither was aired until Silverman left NBC and his successor Grant Tinker arrived and decided to unload his predecessor's leftover baggage. In the end, though, *Sophisticated Gents* and *Sister, Sister* proved fascinating to African American viewers.

Based on the novel *The Junior Bachelor Society* by African American writer John A. Williams and directed by Harry Falk with a script by that movie rebel Melvin Van Peebles, *Sophisticated Gents* focused on the lives of a group of African American men. Having all participated as boys on an athletic team, the men meet again for a reunion honoring their coach on his seventieth birthday. He was the man who first made them believe in themselves and who helped guide them on their road to manhood. Now middle-aged, they are a diverse crew, representing a wide range of African American male attitudes, aspirations, and frustrations. One is a college professor (Ron O'Neal); another, a playwright (Dick Anthony Williams); another, a gay concert performer (Raymond St. Jacques), married to a white woman; another, a postal worker (Thalmus Rasulala), also married to a white woman; still another, the editor of a Black magazine (Robert Hooks). Paul Winfield played the president of the group. Bernie Casey and Roosevelt Grier portrayed other members. Van Peebles himself played the character Moon, another former member who is now a pimp wanted for murder. Throughout, the men examine the drift of their lives, their relationships with one another and with the women in their lives. Each also has to deal with his place in American society.

Uneven, unwieldy, and something of a maverick adolescent fantasy,

Van Peebles's script never conforms to the standard kind of formulaic TV drama. The character that the drama seems to identify with most, as its heroic individualist who understands most clearly the African American male's struggle in a culture that attempts to emasculate him, is Moon. You almost have to laugh at Van Peebles's stubborn attraction to this type of character. There are echoes of his movie hero Sweetback here. Yet *Sophisticated Gents* never fails to engage. Its actors seem to take pleasure in just about every line of dialogue and each scene in which they can express their frustrations and anger. Often there appears to be a movie within the movie: the actors themselves seem energized at having the chance perhaps to comment—in a sense—on their own dilemmas in an entertainment industry that has never fully understood or valued their talents.

Though *Sophisticated Gents* is told very much from a male point of view, it also was enlivened by the performances of its actresses: Denise Nicholas, Janet MacLachlan, Bibi Besch, and that underrated goddess of high-tuned attitudinizing, the rapturous Rosalind Cash. Like Warhol stars, all the performers sometimes appear more caught up in their individual moments than in the drama itself.

Directed by John Berry from a script by Maya Angelou, *Sister, Sister* also focused on a reunion—that of three sisters in their North Carolina home following the death of their father. They too examine the drift of their lives. Hovering over them are thoughts of their deceased parents: the difficult father and the passive mother who died mysteriously in a church fire. In one scene after another, the women confront each other, uncovering one another's secrets, lies, yearnings, and vulnerabilities. As the oldest sister—a frustrated, prim spinster who had remained home to care for the father she did not particularly like—Diahann Carroll was perhaps the perfect representation of old-style, rigid Black middle-class life. The youngest sister, caught in the throes of first love, was played by Irene Cara.

After having lived a life of abandon in Chicago, Rosalind Cash, the middle sister, returns home with her young son and seems hell-bent on shattering everyone else's illusions. This proved to be one of Cash's most exciting performances. Born in Atlantic City in 1938 and having acted successfully on the New York stage, Cash had a career of highs and lows. Her work with the Negro Ensemble Company had garnered her great attention. Tall and angular with dark dramatic eyes and a lush sensual mouth, she wore her hair for years in a large Afro (later, before it was fashionable, in dreadlocks) and was considered a beauty in theater circles—as well as an emblem of the new gritty Black theater of the late 1960s and early 1970s. In the 1970s, she went to Hollywood, where she starred opposite Charlton Heston in *The Omega Man* and also gave a very intense, moody performance in the Black melodrama *Melinda* as well as in *The New Centurions* with George C. Scott. By all rights, she should have become a real movie star. In temperament and attitude, she resembled Susan Hayward. Both seemed to be restless, knowing women, easily wounded, and ever ready to express their emotional distress and pain. Cash was best at revealing explosive pent-up emotions. Like Hayward again, Cash rarely had the roles her talents were worthy

Rosalind Cash

of. Ultimately, her movie career petered out, and she worked more on television, in everything from appearances on *The Mary Tyler Moore Show*, *Starsky and Hutch*, and *Police Story* to *thirtysomething*, *China Beach*, *Hill Street Blues*, and *A Different World*.

Cash was keenly aware that challenging roles rarely came down the pike; when she found a decent part as in *Sister, Sister*, one senses her al-most clutching it, not willing to let go until she's given it everything she's got. Though *Sister, Sister* had far too many climaxes, revelations, and confrontations, Cash brings her distinct energy and insights to every sequence; often appearing to revel in her character's sluttiness; a sign of sheer rebellion for Cash.

The high point comes when she has her final confrontation with her older sister Carroll. Here were two actresses with entirely different styles: Carroll, a goddess of glitz and glamour and tight reserve, seem-ingly fearful of losing control and her own sense of identity; Cash, ea-gerly rushing into chaos and anarchy, believing that only an odyssey of darkness can deliver one to the light. Cash has such a volcanic force as she lashes out at Carroll that one might feel she's attacking not only the character but the other actress's acting style and point of view. One might quickly declare Cash the winner. But Diahann Carroll reaches deep inside herself to pull up a long-festering anger and discontent, and ultimately she rises to Cash's acting challenge. Big emotions like these were rarely seen on television. Also in this all-star cast were Dick Anthony Williams, Robert Hooks, Paul Winfield, Christoff St. John (as Cash's young son), and Alvin Childress.

Following *Sister, Sister*, Rosalind Cash worked on television in such productions as *Go Tell It on the Mountain* and *A Dangerous Affair*. Then in 1995 while appearing as Mary Mae Ward in the daytime soap *General Hospital*, Cash died at age fifty-six.

PBS afforded some African American directors, many of whom had made feature films, the opportunity to work on more challenging projects, often with casts of talented actors. Bill Duke's *The Killing Floor*, set in the stockyards of Chicago, focused on interracial union organizing during World War I. Duke also directed a rather heavy-handed 1989 version of *A Raisin in the Sun* with Danny Glover and Esther Rolle. Far more interesting was his expanded adaptation of Jeff Stetson's 1987 one-act play *The Meeting*, which dramatized an imagi-nary 1965 meeting between Martin Luther King Jr. and Malcolm X.

Best known for directing such films of the 1970s as *Which Way Is Up?, Greased Lightning*, and *Car Wash*, Michael Schultz directed *For Us the Living*, a 1983 dramatization of the life of slain civil rights leader

Medgar Evers, based on a book by his widow, Myrlie Evers. The cast included Howard Rollins Jr. (as Evers), a miscast Irene Cara (as Myrlie), Janet MacLachlan, Roscoe Lee Browne, Margaret Avery, Paul Winfield, and a young Laurence Fishburne (then billed as Larry Fishburne).

Gordon Parks directed Avery Brooks, Rhetta Greene, John Saxon, Janet League, and Joe Seneca in *Solomon Northrup's Odyssey*. Set in the 1840s, it was the story of a Northern-born Black man (Brooks) who was kidnapped and put into slavery. Writer Samm-Art Williams also scripted *Charlotte Forten's Mission: Experiment in Freedom*, which featured Melba Moore as the real-life educated young Black woman who journeyed to the South—an island off Georgia—to teach freed slaves during the Civil War.

But perhaps most impressive was Stan Lathan's 1984 adaptation of James Baldwin's autobiographical *Go Tell It on the Mountain* for *American Playhouse*. James Bond III portrayed the troubled young boy trying to come to terms with his harsh, disciplinarian stepfather, played with great power by Paul Winfield. Also in the cast were Rosalind Cash, Ruby Dee, Alfre Woodard, Olivia Cole, and Linda Hopkins.

Other TV movies were vehicles for television's Black stars. Louis Gossett Jr. became a fairly hot television property in the 1980s, starring not only in his series *Gideon Oliver* but also in a lineup of important TV features, including: *The Father Clements Story*, based on the fight of a Chicago priest to adopt a teenager, played by Malcolm-Jamal Warner; *Sadat*, which starred Gossett as the Egyptian leader; *The Fourth of July*; the HBO movie *The Guardian; Don't Look Back: The Story of Leroy "Satchel" Paige*, in which Gossett played the Negro baseball league star Paige; and the offbeat *Sam Found Out: A Triple Play*, written by Terence McNally and Wendy Wasserstein. In *Sam Found Out*, Gossett, cast opposite Liza Minnelli, played a klutzy student in a New York dance class. His instructor, Minnelli, is a starry-eyed romantic enraptured by old Hollywood musicals. As it turns out, Gossett is actually a wealthy African prince who, smitten with Minnelli, pleads with her to come away with him to his kingdom. Though it was a tribute to Gossett's talent that Minnelli decided to cast an African American actor as her romantic ideal, Black viewers no doubt would have preferred to see him falling for some ravishing African American beauty.

A promising—but ultimately disappointing project—was *Roots:*

The Gift in 1988. Gossett re-created his role as Fiddler, with LeVar Burton reprising his role as the young Kunta Kinte. With hopes that ratings lightning would strike again, ABC heavily promoted this drama based on a story by Alex Haley but written by D. M. Eyre Jr. and directed by Kevin Hooks. Unlike the earlier *Roots*, which might best be described as fictionalized history, *Roots: The Gift* was pure fiction. Set in 1775, it recounted a journey taken by Kunta Kinte and Fiddler with their white master to a neighboring plantation for a Christmas celebration. There, they become involved with the efforts of the plantation owner's young Harvard-educated son to lead slaves to freedom through the Underground Railroad. (It did not seem to matter to scriptwriter Eyre that the Underground Railroad didn't exist at this point in history.)

With few surprises and few emotional jolts, *Roots: The Gift* was serviceable TV. Everything seemed sanitized, polite, genteel, and at times implausible. But that shrewd old master Gossett was able to come up with some wonderful line readings. When Kunta tries to help a Black man disentangle himself from a bounty hunter's net, the angered bounty hunter asks Fiddler, "You in charge of this boy?" Aware of the consequences Kunta could face, Gossett's Fiddler quickly answered, "Yes, ma'am. It's so cold that his poor brains is froze. I'm gonna take the boy home." As in the original, Gossett cues us in to the quick way Fiddler's mind works, to his ability to play the accepted social role of deferential servant while covertly asserting himself and here saving Kunta from disaster. Of course, the real problem with *Roots: The Gift* was that we were left to think that Kunta might escape someday. But we know, from having seen the original, that he never will.

Gossett's best TV film of the era—and one of the decade's better Black-oriented TV movies—was the 1987 *A Gathering of Old Men*. Based on the novel by Ernest Gaines, adapted for television by Charles Fuller (the Pulitzer Prize-winning playwright of *A Soldier's Play*), and directed by Volker Schlondorff, *A Gathering of Old Men*, set in rural Louisiana, told the story of a group of older African American males who, having lived quiet submissive lives, courageously assert themselves after a white racist has been murdered. An elderly Black man, Mathu (Gossett), says he has committed the crime. But a young white woman (Holly Hunter), who was raised by Mathu following the death of her parents, rouses the other men, all of whom assume responsibility for the killing. Throughout, *A Gathering of Old Men* keeps its earnest white heroine front and center. At times slow and meandering, the drama nonetheless worked up some heat, and its cast included some very fine performers: Julius Harris, Joe Seneca, Woody Strode, Richard Widmark, and Papa John Creach.

Unfortunately, the pedestrian quality of many of Gossett's other TV movies took its toll on his career. He always remained likable as a tough but fair, gutsy guy; a man whose fundamental decency and honesty were the hallmarks of his identity. But in time, just as his feature films became weaker and he in turn became a weaker box-office name (to the point where most of his work was on television), Gossett, by the late 1980s and 1990s, was no longer a surefire TV viewer winner.

The same was true of Billy Dee Williams. Perhaps always too glamorous and too much of a larger-than-life sex symbol for television and the movies, Williams played a character with some bite in *Chiefs*. But mostly he was stuck with lackluster roles in such productions as *Oceans of Fire* and *The Return of the Desperate*. For African American viewers, he could still set pulses pounding when he played himself in guest appearances on such Black sitcoms as *The Jeffersons, 227*, and *Martin*. In the 1990s, he appeared in the syndicated program *Lonesome Dove: The Series*.

Faring better on television, at least in terms of finding continual employment, was Paul Winfield. More a character actor than a lead, he now usually played supporting roles in such TV films as *Breathing Lessons, White Dwarf*, and *The Assassination File*. When he appeared in a series, it often was unsettling to watch this highly skilled technician in shlock material. In 1987, he was cast as the Mirror in the modern fairy tale series *The Charmings*, later appeared in *227*, and then made periodic appearances in the celestial ranks of *Touched by an Angel*. A role with substance like that of Isaac Twine in episodes of the series *Wiseguy* was rare. When one watched a dramatic series like *Under One Roof*, you wondered why, instead of casting a fake old windbag like James Earl Jones as the paterfamilias, the producers hadn't had the sense to have hired Winfield.

Television regulars like Ruby Dee and Ossie Davis worked throughout the decade. By now, the couple, still better known within the African American community than in the mainstream one, were considered by Black viewers to be something of acting elder statespeople. They had survived many lean years yet managed to keep their integrity intact. Still, the pair was aware of their position within the entertainment industry.

"Do you know that I feel like I should be where Anne Bancroft or Jane Fonda is now?" Ruby Dee said in 1980. "Ossie and I make 90 percent of our money every year doing poetry readings at colleges. We aren't allowed to practice our craft. Sometimes the parts we are offered are so ridiculous that we wouldn't play them. Young people think of us as successful, but as the older generation used to say, 'We're only doing all right for colored.' "

In the 1980s, the two appeared together in the drama *All God's Children* as well as their talk show *Ossie and Ruby* and later the TV dramas *Lincoln*, *The Ernest Green Story*, and *The Stand*. Dee played supporting roles in a number of TV dramas, including *The Atlanta Child Murders*, and the starring role as Zora Neale Hurston in *Zora Is My Name*. In 1991 she would win an Emmy as Outstanding Supporting Actress in a Miniseries or Special for her performance in *Decoration Day*.

Davis also played a supporting role as the friendly Oz Jackson in the Burt Reynolds series *B. L. Stryker*. He represented the familiar kindhearted, wise, older Black man whom the younger white hero can trust. From 1990 to 1994, Davis also worked with Reynolds again in the series *Evening Shade* and later had a recurring role as a judge on the series *John Grisham's The Client*. Watching Davis in these later years could be a gratifying experience, to see the way he had grown as an actor, so assured in what he was doing that he could create a character with a minimum of strokes, paring away the dialogue to speak eloquently through a glance or a nod. Of course, when he did speak, there was that deep, theatrical voice that now also had been scaled down perfectly to answer the intimate demands of the tiny tube.

The Cosby Show's Keshia Knight Pulliam was the only Black child star of the late 1980s who appeared in movies clearly developed around her. Based on the Hans Christian Andersen fairy tale but now set in New England in the 1920s, *The Little Match Girl* cast Pulliam as an orphan of the streets, who is rescued and brought into a wealthy white family's home. Naturally, the dear little thing brings joy and sunshine into everybody's life. Yet no one seems to question what this little Black child is doing in this place that seems so lily-white. Sentimental, hokey, and devoid of any reality, *The Little Match Girl* nonetheless aired just before Christmas 1987 and did well in the ratings.

Fortunately, Pulliam's other big TV movie of the period, *Polly* in 1989, directed by Debbie Allen, sought to contextualize her in an African American setting. This musical *Polly* cast Pulliam as little Pollyanna, who comes to live in an Alabama town in the 1950s. Pulliam's co-stars included Phylicia Rashad, Dorian Harewood, Celeste Holm (the only major white performer in the production), Brock Peters, Larry Riley, and Butterfly McQueen. Lots of handclapping and some energetic choreography (by Allen) gave the drama some spice. And Pulliam was convincing and charming. A sequel, *Polly—Comin' Home!*, appeared a year later.

Whoopi Goldberg turned her sights to television, portraying a working single parent in *Kiss Shot* opposite Dorian Harewood and Dennis Franz. Goldberg also appeared as a bartender in some episodes of the syndicated series *Star Trek: The Next Generation*, which didn't seem the best of career moves. Critic Roger Ebert once pointed out that Goldberg was sometimes treated by film directors as if she were a creature from Planet X. Her movies had frequently desexed her, depicting her as an oddball loner, out of sync and style with the rest of society. By choosing to work in a series about intergalactic, otherwordly figures, Goldberg seemed to feed into the stereotype the entertainment industry had found for her. Her decision to play a rather oddball but ordinary mother in *Kiss Shot*, no matter how disappointing that TV movie turned out, was an interesting choice. It was also good to see her with a leading man. Goldberg appeared infatuated with television, turning up in several other productions, including HBO's *In the Gloaming* and a revamped version of the game show *Hollywood Squares*.

TV viewers also became familiar with Robin Givens. When she appeared as one of Faye Dunaway's high-priced call girls in the TV movie *Beverly Hills Madam*, Givens presented an image of a narcissistic, calculating, and manipulative young woman. While Black women had often been depicted as sexual predators, Givens created a predatory female but one with a tough intelligence; you felt she'd never be trampled on by a man. Givens, however, was better known for her role in the series *Head of the Class*, the story of honor students at a special high school.

But her television image as a smart yet wholesome girl was soon at odds with her media persona: first as the girlfriend and then the wife of boxing champion Mike Tyson. Their initial pledges of undying love as well as their public spats and eventual separation and divorce made them tasty fodder for the tabloids—as well as the evening news broadcasts. No doubt the high point of their turbulent public soap opera came with their widely seen appearance on ABC's *20/20*. Interviewed by Barbara Walters, Givens spoke of physical abuse from Tyson while he silently sat by, almost dumbly. Afterward Givens emerged as a woman that the nation loved to hate; she was perceived as little more than a conniving, moneygrubbing witch. She would have been perfect as one of those bitchy villainesses on the nighttime soaps.

Givens was the first of a new kind of Black media figure: the woman who becomes known to the public because of scandal rather than any role or her talent. Past divas like Billie Holiday, Josephine Baker, and Dorothy Dandridge all had turbulent lives that fascinated the public. But the public was intrigued by the turmoil only because it had first been struck by the women's talents. Even the scandal that exploded over the nude pictures of Vanessa Williams in *Penthouse* magazine interested the public because it knew her as the first Black Miss America. But no one really knew anything of Robin Givens before the Givens/Tyson headlines. She had become the first Black woman on television whose off-screen image alone had given her the kind of notoriety that some network executives felt might lure viewers to their TV sets.

The 1989 TV film *Penthouse* was an attempt to cash in on that viewer interest in Givens. Cast appropriately as the pampered daughter of a wealthy executive (Robert Guillaume), Givens's character finds herself held captive and terrorized in her father's swanky apartment by a psychotic young white man. Though well promoted, *Penthouse* proved disappointing, partly again because the material obviously hadn't been written with African American characters in mind. Givens's role could have been easily played by any of Hollywood's blond beauties, a Linda Evans or a Donna Mills. Unfortunately, the film didn't draw out the right kind of bitchy drive that viewers expected of Givens, who was the victim for too long. And no one in his right mind would ever want to see Robin Givens as a victim.

Other Black stars turned up in TV movies. Carl Weathers starred with Robert Urich in a tepid remake of the 1958 Sidney Poitier/Tony Curtis film *The Defiant Ones*. Danny Glover appeared in the Old West miniseries *Lonesome Dove*, which was produced by Suzanne de Passe and pulled in huge ratings. He also co-starred with Alfre Woodard in the HBO drama *Mandela*. Eddie Murphy produced the TV comedy *What's Alan Watching?* and also did a satiric cameo in it as an imprisoned James Brown.

CAN WE TALK?: OPRAH AND THE RISE
OF THE NEW BLACK INTERVIEWERS

Of the era's Black TV movies and African American stars, none was more successful than Oprah Winfrey in *The Women of Brewster Place*. By the time it appeared, Winfrey had already emerged as a cultural phenomenon.

Winfrey was one of a new group of African American TV interviewers/hosts to reach a huge television audience. Among that group were Bryant Gumbel, Ed Bradley, and Arsenio Hall, all of whom ushered in new images of African Americans on the tube. On *The Today Show*, Bryant Gumbel had helped America wake up every morning with his cool, fiercely articulate style. He clearly enjoyed his position as the man in charge, who called the shots and never took any guff from anybody. When Gumbel had to conduct fluff interviews with some film or pop star, he could be patently phony. He would sometimes make some *seemingly* important or insightful statement about something the star had done, then he'd follow up with a fake boyish "Why?"

But when it came to social or political issues, Gumbel could be a supremely tough and intelligent interviewer, quick on the draw with the follow-up questions and, rare for morning personalities at the time, often not backing down from getting the facts. He was the best of the morning talk hosts of his era. Yet though viewers respected him, many considered him arrogant, and try as he might with his bright morning smiles, he never seemed warm. And in some circles, he was not considered "Black enough." Rapper Ice T criticized Gumbel for not being a hero for young African American kids because he came across "like a square white wannabe." "If you take a Black child and put him in a Simi Valley home and keep him there—don't let him associate with kids in the 'hood—he will grow up to to be like Bryant Gumbel," he said. "To me, Gumbel is the epitome of a black-skinned white person—his speech, his talk and how he carries himself." He added that on television Gumbel "portrays a dude who gave up all his black culture to get a job." Though one might understand the point Ice T was trying to make, the criticism, no matter how one felt about Gumbel, was unfair and overlooked Gumbel's accomplishments and importance. Gumbel had introduced a new kind of polish and assertiveness. He really helped propel African American male images—as informed authority figures—forward.

60 Minutes' Ed Bradley, however, introduced a different type of polish and assertiveness *without* alienating any segment of the African American community. Perhaps Bradley, with his beard and the public's awareness of his experiences as a correspondent in Vietnam (and his *past look*—the scraggly Afro), was perceived as being more genuine, more of a manly man, more of a brother who'd made it to the top without losing a degree of his ethnicity. Yet Bradley also had a worldly sophistication that made his interviews all the more thorough and penetrating. Never did he come across as the kind of man who could be hoodwinked.

Without being especially funny or truly cool, Arsenio Hall reached a large, hip audience in the late 1980s, and in the process became the first African American star of a hit late-night talk show. Though its reign at the top was comparatively short, *The Arsenio Hall Show* drew a high-voltage live audience with an unparalleled energy level. It also introduced viewers to unusual guests (from the rappers to an actress/writer like Anna Deavere Smith) who were really altering the nation's popular culture. Sometimes Hall seemed corny when interviewing his guests. Other times—with a star like Eddie Murphy—he came across as mock macho and surprisingly homophobic. Still other times, he appeared like a giddy star gazer, and overly impressed not only with the star but with his own emerging celebrity. But young audiences liked the show and, for a time, identified with him. Once it left the airways, however, Hall found it hard to duplicate its appeal. After the failure of his 1997 sitcom *Arsenio* with Vivica A. Fox, he began to look like a pop anachronism. Yet he held on to his career and later he appeared in the action series *Martial Laws.*

But the greatest television surprise in the late 1980s was the unprecedented success of Oprah Winfrey. Having begun her career in 1973 (at age nineteen) as a reporter/anchor for Nashville's CBS affiliate, Winfrey rose up the broadcast ranks when she landed a co-anchor news position on Baltimore's ABC affiliate and also hosted the local talk show *People Are Talking*, from 1977 to 1983. In 1984, she moved to Chicago as the star of *A.M. Chicago*. It was there that composer Quincy Jones saw Winfrey's show and decided she was perfect for the role of Sofia in the forthcoming film *The Color Purple*, which he was co-producing. Winfrey's performance in the film won her an Oscar nomination as Best Supporting Actress of 1985.

The Winfrey story might have ended there. But rather than sitting it out in Hollywood, waiting for roles (the best of which might have been as some jolly helpmate on a sitcom), she shrewdly made the most of the Oscar publicity and maneuvered to have her local Chicago show syndicated. In time, she also redid her look: her Afro gave way to a full head of splashy hair, her makeup looked meticulously applied, and her clothes were chosen with an eye on swanky—yet nonthreatening—glamour. Once the syndicated show debuted, Oprah Winfrey was on her way to becoming a household name. In the beginning, many tuned in just to see what she was all about. Those viewers ended up staying with the show—in droves. She landed in ratings heaven and reached (in daytime TV) a greater audience than many primetime stars could hope for. She also emerged as a potent force in television, a media superstar, her face glowing from the covers of such publications as *Ms., Essence, People, Us*, and even *The National Enquirer. Forbes* would include her in its yearly lists of America's highest-paid celebrities.

Just what was it about Winfrey that proved so attractive to viewers? What enabled her to succeed where other women like Barbara McNair, Pearl Bailey, and Della Reese (all of whom had briefly hosted daytime talk shows) had failed to click? Some felt that her self-deprecating humor was the basis of her appeal. She never hesitated to let her public know of her romantic hassles or weight problems. For her fans, such talk made Oprah seem like a woman enlivened by candor and down-home earthiness. Viewers could easily identify with her vulnerabilities. For her critics, though, she sometimes seemed a replay of the large, cheery, nurturing Black woman—something of an updated mammy figure—who understood and patiently comforted her troubled or anxious white guests—and who was not any type of sexual threat. In a cover story for *The New York Times Magazine*, writer Barbara Grizzuti Harrison perhaps cruelly and perhaps unfairly attributed part of Oprah's success with white viewers to her nurturing disposition and the fact that the oppressor wants to believe he's loved by the oppressed. "In a racist society, the majority needs, and seeks, from time to time," wrote Harrison, "proof that they are loved by the minority whom they have so long been accustomed to oppress, to fear exaggeratedly, or to treat with real or assumed disdain. They need that love, and they need to love in return in order to believe that they are good. Oprah Winfrey—a one-person demilitarized zone—has served that purpose."

As was the case with most African American stars, Black and white audiences responded to Winfrey in different manners. Contrary to Harrison's comments, many Black women admired Winfrey's spunk and drive; her uncanny ability to reinvent herself. Winfrey also had to be credited with displaying fundamental common sense and intelligence, with being able to put her guests and her in-studio audience at ease, and with adroitly and smoothly moving her show along at a fast clip. Forming her own production house, Harpo Productions, she also created a power base for herself, from which she controlled her image and used her clout to bring her own projects to fruition.

Her first primetime production (she served as its executive producer and star) was the four-hour, two-part television miniseries *The Women of Brewster Place.* Based on the novel by African American writer Gloria Naylor and featuring an all-star cast that included Cicely Tyson, Lonette McKee, Paula Kelly, Jackée, Olivia Cole, Lynn Whitfield, Robin Givens, Paul Winfield, and Moses Gunn, *The Women of Brewster Place* marked television's first attempt in several years to dramatize the experiences and conflicts of African American women, joining a short lineup of such rare productions as *The Autobiography of Miss Jane Pittman, Backstairs at the White House, The Hollow Image,* and *Sister, Sister.*

The Women of Brewster Place followed the lives of a disparate group of women living in tenements—on a dead-end street—in an unnamed city. At the center was the long-suffering Mattie Michael (Winfrey), who has had a steady string of disappointments and abuses: she is seduced, impregnated, and deserted by a handsome young man; she is violently beaten by her unforgiving father (Paul Winfield) when she refuses to name the father of the child she is carrying; years later, she loses her home after being deserted by her son; finally, she ends up an asexual communal matriarch on Brewster Place.

There Mattie interacted with other women, also battered by life, most of them misled or mistreated by men: Etta Mae (Jackée), an aging good-time gal, who foolishly embarked on a hopeless relationship with a shifty minister (Douglas Turner Ward); Ceil (Lynn Whitfield), a delicate young woman who lost her little daughter and was abandoned by her insensitive husband (William Allen Young); Cora Lee (Phyllis Yvonne Stickney), a contented welfare mother who could not stop having children; Lorraine (Lonette McKee) and Theresa (Paula Kelly), two lesbian lovers, in search of the freedom to live their lives without public censure; and Kiswana (Robin Givens), a hip young middle-class woman who tries to organize the tenants of Brewster Place into fighting for their rights. All the women had compelling stories. Yet the director (Donna Deitch) and writer (Karen Hall) seemed unable to pause for any moments of reflection within a narrative that leapt from one high-voltage sequence to the next.

Oprah arrives: Talk show hostess turned TV
dramatic actress and power broker with
The Women of Brewster Place

Generally, the critics deplored the melodrama. *Daily Variety* wrote that "the stories are overly familiar, and the overall concept achingly routine." The severest criticism of *The Women of Brewster Place* was for its depiction of the Black male characters, who, wrote John J. O'Connor, "almost without exception, are dismissed as irresponsible, even vicious louts. . . . Viewers may find themselves wondering how black society has ever managed to produce any men deserving respect."

Though the men of Naylor's novel were often ruthless, coldhearted, and reckless, usually (though not always) the tone of Naylor's prose enabled readers to be shocked by the males' behavior without viewing them simply as brutal caricatures. One of the few admirable men of the TV production was Kiswana's young boyfriend. Moses Gunn as an old janitor, drunk and defeated by life, also created a likable and moving character. But mostly the camera rushed in, reveling in the vulgarity and cruelty of the men, so much so that viewers sometimes lost sight of the inner torment of the women. Possibly the ugliest male was the young delinquent C.C. (Glenn Plummer), who savagely attacked the lesbian Lorraine. Curiously, after the attack, he vanished, never pursued or caught, leaving in his wake a rather frightening subtext: there is a violent young African American man somewhere out there, roaming your city streets.

What kept viewers tuned in was the outline of Naylor's story (as well as the need by many to see some comment on the tensions and conflicts of African American women) *and* the performances, some of which—such as Olivia Cole's destructive busybody Miss Sophie—were overblown and verbose but always interesting. Though Jackée's character was not greatly different from her Sandra on *227*, she was lively and fit in with the melodramatic conception. In a telling scene between Robin Givens and a supremely confident Cicely Tyson (who played Givens's mother), you immediately saw the difference between a young aspiring star and an authentic, mature actress who knows how to work her way around a dim line of dialogue. Yet appropriately wired up, Givens understood intuitively that she didn't have to act; it was more important to give a junior league star performance, which she did convincingly. Perhaps most striking was Lonette McKee, long-limbed, fiery, and sexy. Her work recalled her kinetic performance in the film *Sparkle* but with a deepened vulnerability and emotional pain. For her performance as Theresa, Paula Kelly walked off with an Emmy nomination as Outstanding Supporting Actress in a Miniseries or Special.

The critics praised the performers. In *New York* magazine, John Leonard wrote that "the magic of the acting almost covers over the holes in the mini-series." Though he found the drama predictable, he believed it sang "some ancient truths about the seasons of grief and the cycles of renewal. . . . And there hasn't been so glorious an assemblage of black acting talent all in one place at the same time on television since CBS canceled *Frank's Place.*" *The Women of Brewster Place* won an Emmy nomination as Outstanding Miniseries. Later Winfrey created a short-lived half-hour dramatic series based on the Naylor book called *Brewster Place.*

Winfrey's unique and historic position in American television history was solidified with this miniseries. In the past, an actress like Cicely Tyson had been the impetus behind such TV movies as *A Woman Called Moses* and *The Marva Collins Story.* But Winfrey went further.

In retrospect, the 1980s proved to be more of a breakthrough era for television than most might have expected. Shows like *Hill Street Blues, St. Elsewhere,* and *L.A. Law* revealed that workplace series were more realistic and perceptive when African American characters were included in the cast and that race—whether as text or subtext—remained a potent subject, even if a series chose to ignore it. Performers like Philip Michael Thomas and Diahann Carroll (in *Dynasty*) brought Black style and glamour—as well as Black sexuality—into American living rooms. *The Cosby Show* and *Frank's Place*—each in its own way—indicated the way innovative Black programs could invigorate the primetime schedule, while shows like *Amen* and *227* revealed that African American viewers still responded to lively old-style sitcoms where tempers could flare and bold personalities could flourish. The TV movie—whether it be *Sister, Sister, Sophisticated Gents,* or *The Women of Brewster Place*—still offered Black actors and actresses their best opportunities for unusual and striking dramatic roles. Finally, most important for television history, in the 1980s both Winfrey and Cosby became true power brokers, able to exert a creative control previously denied to most African Americans in Hollywood and attaining an immense popularity with audiences, white and Black. Later, Cosby even set out to purchase NBC. In some respects, they set the tone, pace, and perspective for the next decade, when even more African American directors, writers, and producers would work within the industry. The success of Cosby and Winfrey also indicated—for years to come, for better or worse—that the real foundation for a Black power broker still too often was built on his or her superstardom as a performer.

5. THE 1990s: FREE-FOR-ALLS

The restless, politically contentious 1990s closed a century *and* a millennium. The decade was a heady mix of pessimistic low expectations and surprisingly, by decade's end, high hopes for the future. In the early years, as the Bush era came to a close, Americans were faced with a war in the Persian Gulf, unprecedented unemployment statistics, and vast company layoffs as corporations talked of downsizing. The national mood changed, however, once William Jefferson Clinton assumed the presidency with ambitious plans to boost the economy and reform health care. As Clinton appointed more African Americans and women to his cabinet than any American President before him, he looked as if he really might be able to overhaul history and lead (as he would say in his reelection campaign) to a bridge to the next century. The good news was that the economy soared, unemployment was at record lows, and Wall Street profits were at record highs. But along with the boom years came a series of White House scandals that ultimately led to the historic impeachment hearings of William Jefferson Clinton, the President of the United States. Though Clinton remained in office, and high in the opinion polls, the pundits cried that permanent damage had been done to the presidency—and the country.

In the early 1990s, the nation seemed to have mixed feelings about race, racial problems, and racial/cultural identities. Some preferred to believe, as they had in the 1980s, that America had outgrown its racial divisions and conflicts. Affirmative action and quotas, they contended, were unfair and unnecessary. But an entirely different mood arose at colleges and universities, where a traditional Eurocentric view of history and culture was challenged. The rise of multicultural studies marked the new view of the American experience as a mosaic of cultural contributions and insights, its very fabric woven together by the input of Native Americans, Africans, Asians, and Europeans. A new generation of African Americans was more conscious of its cultural roots in this Afrocentric era. Young rap/hip-hop artists celebrated Black life and culture and also examined—with hard-hitting lyrics— long-held American social/political injustices and inequities.

Throughout the era, the nation was stunned by a series of events— many televised—in which race reared its ugly head. Television viewers could daily turn on the tube and witness the Clarence Thomas/Anita Hill hearings, in which Thomas referred to the Senate investigation of him on charges of sexual harassment as a "high-tech lynching," while Hill emerged as a solitary figure being judged not by her peers but by a panel of senators that was all male and all white. In March 1991, the nightly news shows broadcast a videotape of four white Los Angeles police officers brutally beating African American motorist Rodney King. Little more than a year later, in April 1992, after those same police officers were acquitted in a state trial on charges of having used excessive force on King, civil disorders erupted in Los Angeles's African American community. Fifty-three Americans ended up dead while property damaged totaled some $1 billion. Riots also broke out in other parts of the country. At the end of the 1990s, the nation would learn of a shockingly vicious hate crime in Texas. A Black man was chained to a pickup truck by three white men who then dragged him to his death. Mainstream America was forced to acknowledge that the nation's racial attitudes had not changed as much as many might have hoped.

In one way or another, all these events would affect television's primetime African American images.

But in this new decade, television programming was also affected by further changes in the medium itself as the networks continued to see an erosion of their viewership. By 1990, the number of households wired for cable rose from 20 percent to 37. In turn, the networks'

67 percent share of American homes slipped to 57 percent. Viewers in more than half of those cable-wired households could choose from some fifty channels. The once seemingly undifferentiated TV audience that the three networks had always catered to could now tune in to cable's Black Entertainment Television or the Food Channel or the Sci-Fi Channel or the History Channel, all of which successfully tapped the tastes of specific viewers. Many established cable networks like Lifetime also offered original productions. In the summer of 1998, cable would triumph when it "captured more TV households than ABC, NBC, CBS and Fox combined *for the entire month of August.*" By the end of the decade, the future for the networks looked even bleaker. Of the nation's 100 million households with television, some 70 million would have cable.

With all the changes in viewer tastes and habits as the twentieth century drew to a close, network television often appeared frantic in both its search for and its avoidance of shows centered on African Americans. TV power brokers like Cosby and Oprah still found the networks receptive to just about anything they wanted to do. A newcomer like Will Smith looked as if he were his network's darling. For a brief spell, the network Black-cast series was also fashionable. But as the decade progressed, the three major networks, unable to come up with hit Black shows, reverted to form and played it safe, airing fewer and fewer Black-cast series. In their place the new "alternative" networks like Fox and later UPN and WB became known for taking a chance on weekly Black material. These networks solidified their power bases by courting the African American audience, but often with controversial images that might have made Kingfish and Sapphire blush.

New stars of the era would not be only the African American actors featured in dramatic network programs like *I'll Fly Away* or *ER*. Several new TV stars—Martin Lawrence, Queen Latifah, and Brandy—would come from such alternative network sitcoms as *Martin, Living Single,* and *Moesha.* Along with new stars, the era also saw the rise of even more African American producers and directors. Thomas Carter, Keenen Ivory Wayans, Damon Wayans, Eddie Murphy, Quincy Jones, Eriq La Salle, Martin Lawrence, Malcolm-Jamal Warner, and Eddie Griffith all had producing or directing credits. (With the notable exception of Oprah Winfrey, women, for the most part, were missing from the list.) Sometimes the new producers or directors came up with imaginative work. Other times they offered stale replays of the old formulas. Still, the era opened with a trio of diverse series—*Brewster Place, Equal Justice*, and *In Living Color.*

NEW SERIES, NEW CONTROL

Following her miniseries *The Women of Brewster Place*, Oprah Winfrey returned to the characters of Gloria Naylor's novel with a weekly half-hour drama called *Brewster Place.* Winfrey repeated her role as the dowdy and stoic Mattie Michael, a long-suffering Black heroine if ever there was one. Also included in this series were Mattie's friend the lively, sexy Etta Mae (now played by Brenda Pressley); the busybody Miss Sophie (again played by Olivia Cole); the young, socially conscious Kiswana Browne (Rachael Crawford), and her militant boyfriend Abshu Kamau (Kelly Neal).

Brewster Place opened in an undesignated inner city in 1967, a time (as we hear on the radio) when a young boxer named Cassius Clay has lost his title because of his refusal to fight in Vietnam and when politician Adam Clayton Powell is embroiled in a scandal. In this world, Mattie Michael, forlorn and at loose ends after having lost her job in a beauty parlor, is urged by her friend Etta Mae to take over an Italian restaurant that is about to close. Afraid of risks and commitments, Mattie has never really recovered from the heartache caused when her son vanished with her life's savings. But Etta Mae, blessed with some TV-land homespun wisdom, tells Mattie, "A broken heart doesn't have to be a cold one." Together, so Etta Mae reasons, she and Mattie can run a successful soul food eatery. Of course, once Mattie opened the restaurant, viewers saw her dealing weekly with the lives and conflicts of the customers who wandered into her place, most just plain-folk inhabitants of Mattie's Brewster community.

Brewster Place had noble intentions: it sought to give television viewers a dramatic Black series with *positive* images and some sense, no matter how simplified, of African American history. Gone were some of the controversial aspects of the original miniseries (such as the lesbian characters and the brutal bucklike males). Added here was the sympathetic character Ralph Thomas (John Cothran Jr.), a widower cousin of Mattie's who arrives from the South with three children to care for. But in the long run, *Brewster Place* seemed devoid of personality. Its characters, setting, and conflicts lacked any distinctive resonance or urgency. It had none of the ugly emotional loose ends that can draw viewers into a story.

"Instead of a cold, hard look at life in the ghetto, 'Brewster Place' now has a warm and soft one—like a black inner city version of 'The Waltons,' " wrote David Bianculli in the *New York Post*. "Winfrey has made it a small, typical-TV shadow of Naylor's original vision." In *New York*, John Leonard complained that as an actress Winfrey was unable "to modulate herself anywhere between extremes of hallelujahs and despair. She suffers, or she affirms, like a seesaw. I'm not asking for a machine-gun spray of sitcom laughs, just imagination and intelligence. Maybe her fans will watch her in anything but compared with *Brewster Place*, Oprah's talk show is depth psychology."

A fundamental mistake with *Brewster Place* may also have been its half-hour length. Traditionally, more serious television fare (like such dramatic shows of the 1990s as *ER* or *The Practice*) flourished best in the hour format. Generally, the half-hour format worked well for sitcoms, few of which could sustain their humor and high jinks longer. After less than three months, *Brewster Place* was off the air.

Despite this failure, Oprah Winfrey remained as much a cultural phenomenon as she had been in the 1980s. In the early years of the decade, her talk show continued to be a big hit. In 1993, she conducted a ninety-minute primetime interview with Michael Jackson that drew in a huge audience. In the midst of the interview, when actress Elizabeth Taylor suddenly appeared, viewers saw three of the great pop icons of the twentieth century. Surprisingly, there were no ego clashes, each personality aware and respectful of the other's star power. Viewers may have found it bizarre that the three-way conversation seemed so normal, almost mundane. Any really serious questions anyone might have had—about Jackson's life and the pressures of his extraodinary fame— could be easily brushed aside as stars made a Personal Appearance for millions in their homes. Curiously enough, though Taylor and Jackson seemed to have scaled down their personas for the tube, you could never doubt their hot explosive magnitude. These were not the kind of stars who would be welcomed weekly in American homes. Oprah, however, remained a *cool* personality who was true to the demands of television and indeed would be welcomed back to households (the very next day in fact). She asked the kind of questions that any average viewer might have. The ratings soared—rivaling those of the Super Bowl—with the show reaching 36.5 million households.

Oprah, superstar, icon, and an unprecedented cultural phenomenon

Oprah's fans had no problem watching her shift gears. Much like Cicely Tyson in the late 1970s/early 1980s, Winfrey can be credited with popularizing the Black Woman's film on television. Usually, Winfrey's films stressed the traditional theme of (motherly) self-sacrifice. Her dramatic role in the 1993 TV movie *There Are No Children Here*, directed by African American Anita Addison, pulled in huge ratings. Here she played an inner-city mother struggling to shield her sons from the grim and violent realities of contemporary urban life. Maya Angelou appeared as Winfrey's grandmother. Another dramatic role followed in the 1997 television film *Oprah Winfrey Presents: Before Women Had Wings*, produced by Winfrey's production company. Winfrey appeared as Miss Zara, a kindly woman who, having been abandoned by her daughter, befriends a troubled young white girl suffering emotional abuse from her mother. Eventually, that dear Miss Zara intervenes to help the girl's mother as well. This, of course, was the typical Winfrey role: the warmhearted, nurturing soul who seems to have a life only when she's helping someone else. Viewers ate it up. This was the Oprah they wanted to see, a character that was in many ways an extension of Oprah's daytime persona. Later in the decade, her production company also produced *Oprah Winfrey Presents: The Wedding.* Though Winfrey did not appear in this two-part drama, her very association with it—the Oprah Seal of Approval—guaranteed its success. The same was true of *Oprah Winfrey Presents: Tuesdays with Morrie* in 1999.

Throughout the decade, Winfrey's face continued to grace the covers of innumerable magazines: *People, Ebony, In Style, Ladies' Home Journal,* and *McCall's.* A very glamorous Winfrey also appeared on the cover of *Vogue.* The tabloids continued to report on everything about her, from her struggles with her weight to her ongoing romance with Stedman Graham.

Was Oprah also America's most influential woman? Some thought so, especially in 1996 when Winfrey launched her own monthly television book club with stunning success. The sales of such selections as Jacquelyn Mitchard's *The Deep End of the Ocean* and Toni Morrison's *Song of Solomon* soared. It looked as if television's most famous diva could even get Americans to do the unthinkable: to briefly turn off the tube and read again. With her appearance on the series *Ellen,* she also seemed to help Americans deal better with the controversial issue of a sitcom character's lesbianism. When Ellen DeGeneres's character Ellen finds herself attracted to another young woman, whom does she rush off to talk to? Why, it's Oprah, who plays her therapist.

Winfrey's power was never more apparent than with the broadcast of her program on mad cow disease in April 1996. Terrified of the symptoms of the disease, Winfrey told viewers, "It just stopped me cold from eating another hamburger! I'm stopped!" Afterward sales of beef plummeted. An enraged group of Texas cattlemen sued her for $12 million, claiming her comments had cost them at least that much. Flying to Amarillo, Texas, Winfrey testified at the trial. She also brought her television staff to tape *The Oprah Winfrey Show* in Texas for the duration of the case.

Fans swamped her with requests for tickets to the show. Daily, they stood outside the courthouse to catch a glimpse of her. The evening news shows (as well as newspapers around the country) reported on the trial and all the attendant excitement. The president of the local chamber of commerce informed chamber employees that they were *not* to attend tapings of her program. Amarillo stood by its beef producers, he explained, adding that "we are not going to have any red-carpet roll-outs, key to the city, flowers" for Ms. Winfrey. But *The New York Times* reported that "he quickly rescinded his order, especially after the president of the local chapter of the National Association for the Advancement of Colored People said he was 'dismayed, shocked and mystified' by it." In the end, Winfrey was cleared of any liability for lower beef sales as a result of her remarks.

On her talk show, Winfrey's image remained that of a warm, insightful Black woman blessed with a traditional American aggressiveness and a common sense that made her seem wise—as she discussed problems that affected all Americans, from abusive relationships and tensions among siblings to low self-esteem. Yet rarely was there anything profound about what Oprah said. Nor did she send out complicated messages. Too great an intelligence might have made her a threat. Winfrey posed no sexual threat either. As Winfrey's weight fluctuated, some women no doubt saw in her what they believed was the vulnerable yet better part of themselves. Her fans also loved her success: the stories of her homes, her clothes, her shopping sprees.

She also handled the issue of race in the shrewdest manner. Never was she an overethnicized diva. Never did anyone think of her as a homegrown homegirl. Nor did she comes across as some backwoods country girl. To her credit, Oprah never denied the issue of race in America. One of her most widely seen programs recorded her 1987 trip to Forsyth County, Georgia, where white racists were marching. She could also be very funny when she dropped her stentorian tones and spoke Black vernacular. For her viewers, it was a sign of Oprah being *real*, shooting through the bull in a way a white talk show host could not. Oprah seemed to enjoy letting her viewers know where she came from and what she had overcome. It was such an *American* story; one that in her hands extolled the same concerns and values that *all* Americans had. At the same time, her story never had a residue of resentment or anger; Oprah had *overcome* all that.

During the decade, chinks in the Winfrey armor sometimes showed. Her 1998 television presentation *Oprah Winfrey Presents: David and Lisa*, a remake of the 1963 film, was a ratings disappointment. Most disheartening for her had to be the commercial failure of her 1998 film version of Toni Morrison's novel *Beloved*, in which she starred. She had optioned the novel in 1987, but it took years for the film to reach movie screens. Though heavily publicized by both Oprah and the Disney studio, the drama met with mixed reviews while movie audiences seemed to avoid it at all cost. By the end of the decade, her talk show would also slip in the ratings, affected by competition from raunchier talkfests like *The Ricki Lake Show* and especially *The Jerry Springer Show*. Still, at the start of the twenty-first century, Winfrey became a partner in Oxygen Media, a new cable network geared to female viewers. She also launched a hugely successful magazine for women called *O*.

Ultimately, Oprah would always be Oprah. She had too many triumphs, had been too much a part of the national collective consciousness, for her light ever to be dimmed. Even should she have one failure after another, that too now would be a part of the Oprah story.

Like *Brewster Place*, the dramatic legal series *Equal Justice* had a short run. Its protagonists, a group of young lawyers in a district attorney's office in Pittsburgh, were a mixed bag: a bright, dedicated Black attorney (Joe Morton); a decent, seasoned pro (Cotter Smith), aware of the legal system's flaws; a recent law school grad, nervous and insecure on her first important job (Sarah Jessica Parker); a pipe-smoking, pompous chauvinist (Barry Miller); a handsome young ladies' man (James Wilder); and a serious young woman (Jane Kaczmarek) who specializes in sex crimes.

Much like *Hill Street Blues*, *Equal Justice* often explored social/political issues affecting large urban areas: police brutality, drugs, rape, racial tensions. Its premiere episode dramatized the trial of four white policemen accused of murdering a Black teenager. Among those characters following the case was an opportunistic, media fiend of a Black minister, no doubt inspired by perceptions of the Reverend Al Sharpton of New York City.

Darker and grungier than the slick and glitzy *L.A. Law*, *Equal Justice* had as its executive producer thirty-six-year-old Thomas Carter. Having begun his career as an actor on *The White Shadow*, Carter had already distinguished himself as an Emmy-nominated television director. Like such African American directors as Ivan Dixon, Georg Stanford Brown, and Stan Lathan, Carter could direct any type of television program; he had helmed some ten episodes of *Hill Street Blues* and also the pilots for such nonblack series as *Miami Vice, St. Elsewhere, Midnight Caller, A Day in the Life,* and *Glory Days.* But by becoming the executive producer of *Equal Justice*—the most powerful creative position on episodic television (more so than that of the director)—Thomas Carter emerged as one of the most important African Americans working in primetime television. Directing some episodes of *Equal Justice* himself, Carter also gave assignments to such Black directors as Kevin Hooks and Eric Laneuville.

Thomas Carter's Equal Justice *with Cotter Smith, George DiCenzo, Joe Morton, James Wilder, and Barry Miller*

For the African American audience, *Equal Justice*'s most interesting character may well have been the Black attorney, Mike. Originally, the character was conceived as an Italian named Michael Corelli, a Vietnam vet who was an opera buff and a gourmet cook. When African American actor Joe Morton auditioned for a guest spot on the first episode, he expressed his interest in playing the prosecutor. "They made it clear there wasn't much chance of me getting the character because the network wouldn't want a Black actor in the role," Morton said. But Carter decided to go with Morton. "Joe, I think," said Carter, "would not have been cast had I not been there."

Director/Producer Thomas Carter

It was a shrewd move. Afterward the character's name was changed to Michael James. But little else was done to alter him. His musical tastes were not changed to rhythm and blues to make the character seem more "Black." This could have easily backfired. Michael James might have come across as another of television's colorless Black men without racial/cultural anchors. But Morton himself was able to convey, through his style, speech, and mannerisms, a man rooted in an African American cultural experience. At times the opera and food bit seemed fake but not because they were the interests of an African American character. Rather they appeared to be the now rather dopey standard television flourishes to make a character seem "unusual."

When African American actress Vanessa Bell Calloway was cast as Delia, Morton's love interest, Black viewers became all the more interested in *Equal Justice* because, so Carter believed, even at this late date it was still unusual to see Black characters in love on a primetime drama. Consequently, when Delia was killed off, there was "an enormous response from the people who were really, really upset with us that the character had died." People of color, even in 1990, still found "a great paucity of real-life characters that reflect their lives," said Carter.

Equal Justice lasted a little over a year. But it was another attempt to bring a serious, adult African American male character to the weekly primetime schedule—and to often place him front and center even within this ensemble cast.

The comedy series *In Living Color*, which aired on Fox, was a great hit that helped boost the ratings of this then aspiring fourth network. Its creator was thirty-one-year-old African American writer/director Keenen Ivory Wayans. He came to this series with an impressive list of credentials on projects that appealed to young, rather hip African American audiences. He was the director of the Blaxploitation parody *I'm Gonna Git You Sucka*, the co-writer of Robert Townsend's movie-colony satire *Hollywood Shuffle*, and the co-producer and co-writer of *Eddie Murphy Raw*. He also worked with Robert Townsend on the HBO special *Robert Townsend and His Partners in Crime*.

A comedy show no doubt inspired by the irreverent madness of *Saturday Night Live*, *In Living Color* took irreverence to new heights with skits that were sometimes outrageous, sometimes fresh, and often inventive, fast-moving, and clever. Enlivened by a Black sensibility with a talented group of newcomers that included Damon Wayans, Kim Coles, and Jim Carrey, *In Living Color* also sometimes played with or parodied stereotypes and racial misconceptions. A skit called "Riding Miss Daisy" was a wicked send-up of that favorite film of the conservative Bush era, *Driving Miss Daisy*. Here the servile, seemingly sexless and self-sacrificing chauffeur, Hoke, informs his passenger, Miss Daisy, that he knows exactly what she needs. Thereafter he jumps into the back with his prim employer—and begins pumping away on her. Characters such as Homey the Clown immediately won audience favor.

In Living Color also audaciously poked fun at some major (and previously untouchable) African American icons. A *Love Connection* par-

Helping to put Fox TV on the map: In Living Color *with (clockwise) David Alan Grier, Kelly Coffield, Damon Wayans, Keenen Ivory Wayans, Tommy Davidson, Jim Carrey, Kim Wayans, and T'Keyah "Crystal" Keymah*

ody on the first episode lampooned boxer Mike Tyson and his wife, Robin Givens. Oprah Winfrey was also mercilessly satirized. Don King was parodied in a skit called "Don King: The Early Years." Also examined under this comic microscope were Arsenio Hall interviewing D.C. mayor Marion Barry, and in a now classic *Star Trek* parody called "The Wrath of Farrakhan," Black Muslim minister Louis Farrakhan no doubt saw himself caricatured for the first time on television. Here *In Living Color* was at its best with a really brittle, iconoclastic edge and beat.

The critics were enthusiastic. "Who says the variety show is dead?" *Variety* asked in its review. "As Keenen Ivory Wayans demonstrates, all a variety show needs to succeed is to be funny, contemporary, and hot. And *In Living Color* is all three." In *The New York Times*, critic John J.

O'Connor called *In Living Color* "one of the freshest new shows of the year" with a "first-rate repertory company."

Critics' praise aside, the quality of *In Living Color* varied. Some skits, such as one dealing with a colorized version of *Casablanca*, fell flat. Other skits and characters proved disturbing and unsettling, notably Anton, a homeless character who smells and revels in vulgarities. For some viewers, the Anton skits came across as a cruel, insensitive comment on a very real and serious social problem in America. The same was true of the show's disabled character Handi-Man (he's an action hero who suffers from cerebral palsy) and the loony burn victim Fire Marshal Bill. Maybe some things *aren't* funny. Yet this humor prefigured that of a late 1990s hit gross-out movie like *There's Something About Mary*.

Other skits were built around a character named Wanda Wayne, which featured actor Jamie Foxx in drag as a bucktoothed, bug-eyed, misshapen woman looking for love, naturally in all the wrong places. Repeatedly, the Wanda skits made fun of physical unattractiveness. The routines were almost sadistic in the way that Wanda was set up for a fall or defeat. Had this material not been so popular, one might have simply dismissed the routines as hopelessly dated. They sent out the same dumb, hack message time and again that, even in a postfeminist age, women were judged on their appearance, on their ability to please a man.

Then, too, there was criticism of two of the series's most popular characters: the gay critics Blaine Edwards (Damon Wayans) and Antoine Merriweather (David Alan Grier) in the "Men on Film" sketches. Their mannerisms and gestures seemed straight out of "swishville" while their movie reviews were spiked with sometimes hilarious sexual innuendos. If a movie was considered any good, then it had to turn them on. Gay groups complained. So did some critics, who found Blaine Edwards and Antoine Merriweather to be "mincing stereotypes who seem wholly unaware of the age of AIDS. Their potential to give offense is certainly enormous." *Variety* commented that the show's "black humor wouldn't be all that funny coming from nonblack artists, and likewise its gay humor is of questionable taste coming from artists who are not avowedly gay." Damon Wayans was also "singled out as a prime candidate for some consciousness raising, especially when it comes to women and gay men."

African American critics also often felt uneasy with *In Living Color.* On the television program *20/20,* Black psychiatrist Alvin Poussaint of the Harvard Medical School blasted the show for playing on old stereotypes about Black incompetence. One series of skits revolved around a prisoner who can't master the basics of the English language, butchering it as much as the poor characters on *Amos 'n' Andy.* But, surely, that criticism about Black incompetence could not have applied to any characters more than it did to the two panhandlers in the Homeboy Shopping Network skits. Peddling an array of "hot" stolen items from the back of a truck, the two men urge their viewers to phone in orders for merchandise from a nearby pay phone. "We take an exaggerated stereotype and really have fun with it," said Keenen Wayans, in defense of his series and such characters. "If I take something and ridicule it to such a degree that people could never look at it as anything real, then it really helps to destroy a preconceived notion." If only that were the case. Unfortunately, the Homeboy Shopping Network skits didn't appear to satirize a single misconception that much of white America may have had about African American males being petty thieves and crooks. Instead the routines affirmed the old stereotypes without offering any insight or a new perspective. Interestingly enough, the Homeboy Shopping Network routines were indeed *inside* humor, the kind of comments and jokes some African Americans might have made among themselves. Like *Amos 'n' Andy* in 1950s television land, the material would be read differently by white viewers and a segment of the African American community. But even as late as the 1990s, some African American viewers felt uncomfortable at seeing such skits in a medium that remained fundamentally white.

Who exactly created the images on *In Living Color*? That was the question many asked. Though Keenen Ivory Wayans was the executive producer, writer, and star, *New York* magazine reported that at one time "the thirteen-person writing staff includes three blacks, in addition to Wayans and his brother Damon. (Still, three of the writers—all white—are from Harvard.)" Keenen Wayans admitted at one point that he was searching for more African American writers, although he commented that "there aren't many black writers in Hollywood. You have to search other places." That led some to wonder precisely what type of insights some members of the writing staff brought to the street characters that populated so much of this series. In this light, some of *In Living Color*'s skits and perspective were all the more questionable.

Nonetheless, *In Living Color* sometimes shot into the top fifteen of the Nielsen ratings, won an Emmy in 1990 as Outstanding Variety, Music or Comedy Series, and ran for four seasons. Its extraordinary success with a younger audience helped put Fox on the map. The series also launched the careers of the Wayans siblings—Keenen, Damon, Shawn, and the underrated Kim—as well as Tommy Davidson, David Alan Grier, Kim Coles, Jim Carrey, and T'Keyah "Crystal" Keymah, all of whom continued working in television. Davidson appeared in such films as *Strictly Business* and *Booty Call* as well as the series *Between Brothers*. At one point, he was also an Ed McMahon-like sidekick on *The Magic Show*. Grier—a graduate of the Yale drama school and the son of a prominent African American psychiatrist—starred in the disappointing series *The Preston Episodes* and *Damon*. Coles and Keymah fared better with their roles on the respective sitcoms *Living Single* and *Cosby*. Keenen Ivory Wayans appeared in the films *A Low Down Dirty Shame* and *Glimmer Man*, then starred in his own talk program, *The Keenen Ivory Wayans Show*, which failed to win big numbers. But by the summer of 2000, he had directed the hit feature film *Scary Movie*, intended more for a general audience than for an exclusively African American one.

Most predicted a major career for Damon Wayans, possibly the most talented of the Wayans family. After appearing in such films as *Blankman* and *Major Payne*, Wayans starred in the sitcom *Damon*. But it barely lasted a season. He also was the executive producer of the short-lived dramatic series *413 Hope Street*. Afterward he announced, "I'll never be on television again." He added that network executives "say they want to push the envelope and they want to do something new, but the truth is, they just want the same old thing." Shawn Wayans had better luck. He teamed up with younger brother Marlon for the dopey sitcom *The Wayans Bros*. Ironically, the biggest star to come out of *In Living Color* was white performer Jim Carrey.

Also appearing in the early 1990s was the dramatic series *Gabriel's Fire*, the story of a Black ex-con (yet another one!), played by James Earl Jones. Of course, there was an expected TV-style twist. Originally,

Gabriel Bird had been a dedicated cop. But during a botched raid, he saw his white partner about to ruthlessly kill an innocent mother and child. To save them, Gabriel shot and killed the officer. But when he was put on trial, the jury didn't see his act as heroic. Consequently, he served twenty years—as a model prisoner—until a savvy young white attorney named Victoria (Laila Robbins) reviewed his case and won him a release. Though Gabriel had mixed feelings about his return to society, the attorney persuaded him to become a private investigator for her. Together they often worked on cases to help women and minorities.

Though *Gabriel's Fire* toyed with the interracial bonding theme, mainstream viewers need have no fears of anything more intimate. There was no hint whatsoever of any romantic interest in the Bird/Victoria relationship. But, wisely, the creators developed another relationship for Gabriel. Frequently, he spent time at a café run by the "Empress" Josephine Austin, played in high, haughty diva style by the incomparable Madge Sinclair. In the hands of a less talented and interesting actress, Josephine might have been simply a cardboard love interest. But Sinclair, now having been in Hollywood for over fifteen years, aware that she had to make the best out of whatever came her way, turned Josephine into one of television's most enjoyable female characters.

Not taking any guff from anybody, Sinclair gave a performance that young Black actresses should have studied closely. Never did she let attitude become overdone: no excessive hands on the hips, no mean scowls when a man doesn't please her. Instead she turned a Hollywood fantasy into a flesh-and-blood woman. In her scenes with Jones, Sinclair was so natural that Jones seemed forced to bring himself down a few pegs from his usual bombast. Surprisingly, he was rather likable.

Gabriel's Fire didn't have the contemporary beat and style of the post-*Hill Street Blues* dramas like *Equal Justice*. Though not as enjoyably old-fashioned and quaint as *Matlock*, it still looked at times as if it should have been produced a decade or two earlier. No doubt it appealed more to viewers a tad older (which, in television terms, means their early thirties), especially African American ones.

In its second season, the show was retitled *Pros and Cons*. Actress Laila Robbins was dropped from the cast, replaced by Richard Crenna as an aging private eye named Mitch O'Hannon. Now living in Los Angeles, Gabriel Bird teams with O'Hannon to form their own agency, called O'Hannon and Bird, and *Pros and Cons* reverted to the standard Black male/white male formula. Jones's Bird now smiled a lot, too much really. Fortunately, Sinclair's Empress Josephine remained in the cast. She and Bird married that second season. But the revamped version, dry and tired without any sparks, lasted but one season.

Most series were business as usual. Redd Foxx starred in the sitcom *The Royal Family*, which co-starred Della Reese and was executive-produced by Eddie Murphy. Foxx and Reese argued, fumed, and fumbled a lot. Nothing new here. But because the performers were energetic and appealing, *The Royal Family* might have lasted longer had Foxx not died during production. For a brief spell, the series continued with Reese as the star.

Other sitcoms appeared and then quickly disappeared. The series *Sugar and Spice* asked the question what happens when a high-spirited aspiring singer and a strict divorcée become surrogate parents to a niece who has just lost her mother? Well, not much happens that's of interest, at least not as it was handled on this wacked-out series, which starred Loretta Devine (as the singer) and Vickilyn Reynolds (as the divorcée). It had about a two-month run.

Then there was the summer replacement *Singer & Sons*. About all that was noteworthy here was that it marked the return of Esther Rolle to series television. But after seeing Rolle in dramas like *I Know Why the Caged Bird Sings* and her Emmy-winning performance in *The Summer of My German Soldier*, viewers must have found it sad to watch her playing yet another comic housekeeper. Here she works for the owner (Harold Gould) of a Jewish deli who laments that he has no sons to pass his family business on to. Rolle's character Sarah suggests he hire her sons, played by Bobby Hosea and Tommy Ford. Of course, this was to be a culture-clash comedy, kosher versus soul food. What could be funnier than two Black dudes in a Jewish deli? Actually, viewers knew there was much that was funnier. On other channels. *Singer & Sons* expired after three weeks.

Another sitcom, *True Colors*—from the Fox Television Network—was centered on an interracial marriage. The topic was still relatively taboo for television, although it had been touched on in such series as *The Jeffersons* and *The Days and Nights of Molly Dodd*. In the latter series, its free-spirited heroine Molly (a precursor to Ally McBeal in the late 1990s) had a relationship with—and a child by—a young Black detective (Richard Lawson). For the time, *Molly Dodd* handled the subject sensitively. But before the two could marry, the Black character died—rather conveniently. Later *Ally McBeal* would also feature its heroine Ally (Calista Flockhart) in the arms of a handsome Black doctor (Jesse Martin). But *Ally McBeal* would depict the relationship as problematic, not because of the racial issue, but because of Ally's eccentricities.

True Color's marriage was between a widowed Black dentist, Ron Freeman (Frankie Faison, later replaced by Cleavon Little), and a divorced white kindergarten teacher, Ellen Davis Freeman (Stephanie Faracy). Each has children by their previous marriages; the wife, a daughter; the husband, two sons. Always nosing around and disapproving of the match was the wife's opinionated mother.

Usually, whenever the series attempted a trenchant social comment, it undercut itself. That was evident on an episode that finds Freeman's younger son, Lester (Adam Jeffries), feeling dejected. He sits at home reading *The Autobiography of Malcolm X*. (Interestingly, at this point in television history, the name of Malcolm X was now acceptable—and even *respectable*—for primetime. In fact, his name was tossed into the dialogue of one show or another whenever the writers wanted viewers to appreciate such a program for its "honesty" and "courage." One only wonders what Malcolm X himself would have thought of some of these programs.) No doubt politically awakened by Malcolm, Lester soon was criticizing interracial marriages—and the rest of the family. He called his brother a clown in blackface; his sister, a bleeding liberal. But how was this political dissent resolved? In the most annoyingly simple-headed and illogical way. Lester comes to his senses after he has missed his own birthday party. "Cake and ice cream, evidently, beat Malcolm X any day—on a television sitcom," wrote John J. O'Connor.

TAKING HIP-HOP MAINSTREAM: *THE FRESH PRINCE OF BEL-AIR*

But in the early 1990s, nothing drew more attention than the sitcom *The Fresh Prince of Bel-Air*. Its story was the traditional fish-out-of-water concept but with an ersatz rap sensibility. Its hero was teenage Will, played by rapper Will Smith, who, after a minor brush with trouble in his West Philadelphia 'hood, is sent by his mother to live with well-to-do relatives, the Banks family, in Bel Air. The head of the Banks household is Uncle Philip (James Avery), a successful attorney, who is as pompous as he is affluent. His wife is the more down-to-earth Aunt Viv (Janet Hubert, later Janet Hubert-Whitten). The children are a motley lot: Carlton (Alfonso Ribeiro), a preppy teenager consumed with grades and career goals; Hilary (Karyn Parsons), a snotty Valley Girl type concerned mostly with shopping and her social status; and the youngest, Ashley (Tatyana M. Ali), sweet and unaffected and the one family member Will immediately connects to. There is also the hoity-toity butler Geoffrey (Joseph Marcell). As Will contends with a new way of life and a new set of attitudes and values, *The Fresh Prince of Bel-Air* became a comedy of culture clashes, a comic test of wills for Will and the other family members.

Culture clash: Hip-Hop vs. the Black Bourgeoisie in
The Fresh Prince of Bel-Air *with Karyn Parsons,*
Tatyana M. Ali, Will Smith, and Alfonso Ribeiro

The Fresh Prince of Bel-Air sprang from the real-life experiences of then thirty-two-year-old African American music executive Benny Medina, whose bio read like something out of a Hollywood movie. Following the death of his mother, a very young Medina was raised in various juvenile detention centers in California until he met Jack Elliot, a white composer who lived with his family in Beverly Hills. Medina persuaded Elliot to let him move in with the family. Exposed to a whole new world, Medina attended Beverly Hills High School. He never forgot the effect of his early years, the change in lifestyles, in cultural attitudes and traditions. After he began a career in the entertainment industry, Medina decided his life was perfect material for a television series.

Medina submitted the concept to Quincy Jones, whose production company was looking for television projects. Jones liked Medina's idea but shrewdly decided on an important change that would give the concept a contemporary kick. The family that the kid would go to live with would not be white but Black. Lynn Hirschberg reported that Jones then took Medina with him for an appointment at the office of NBC's programming wizard Brandon Tartikoff. There Medina had to pitch the idea to Tartikoff and other NBC executives. "You've got eight minutes," Tartikoff told him at the start of the meeting. Medina then launched into a discussion of the projected series.

"My eyes glazed over while he was talking," Tartikoff recalled. "My eyes were still semi-glazed when I said, 'Who would play you?' "

Aware of the ever-changing youth culture—and the effect that hiphop had on it *and* television—NBC had already been interested in finding a show with the new hip-hop sensibility. By now, rap music had moved into the cultural mainstream. Along with the music came a style of dress, a spirit, an attitude. "There was a drumbeat out there," said NBC's Warren Littlefield. "And we wanted to find a way to get that on the schedule." NBC had seen the numbers for MTV's *Yo! MTV Raps*, which was one of that cable channel's highest-rated shows. (It was, of course, ironic that MTV had scored so high with a show featuring African American music stars. Initially, MTV hadn't wanted to play videos by Black performers, assuming that their viewers had no interest in Black stars or Black music. Only after Michael Jackson's record company had threatened to pull its videos by white stars if MTV didn't air Jackson's videos did MTV change its tune. When Jackson's music proved extraordinarily popular, the cable station reevaluated its position on Black stars.)

Medina decided upon the young rapper Will Smith as the star of the show. Once Smith auditioned for a group of NBC executives at the Bel Air home of Quincy Jones, NBC became excited about the series *and* Smith. At twenty-one, Smith already had a very successful career. He had grown up in Philadelphia, where he had been nicknamed Prince—for Prince Charming—while in grade school. Like most kids of his generation, he liked rap, and by age fourteen, Smith teamed with his friend Jeff Townes in a rap act known as DJ Jazzy Jeff and the Fresh Prince. Their first single was released in 1987. The next year their songs "Parents Just Don't Understand" and "A Nightmare on My Street" became hits. In 1989, DJ Jazzy Jeff and the Fresh Prince became the first rappers to win a Grammy.

Though most music insiders conceded that the two had taken rap mainstream, others felt they had merely popularized rap (and diluted its gut power and political subversiveness) for a fundamentally middle-class (and often white) audience. "They're a Cosby-family kind of rap group," said rapper Fab 5 Freddy. "They don't really reflect the majority of black people in an urban situation." Kid of the group Kid 'n Play commented, "[DJ and Fresh Prince] are good friends of mine, but they can't get arrested in a black town right now." None of this criticism had any effect whatsoever on NBC executives.

To get the program ready for the fall, NBC had to move quickly. Andy and Susan Borowitz, both Harvard-educated and upper-middle-class, were signed to develop the series. Previously, Andy Borowitz had co-produced and written the NBC series *Day by Day*. Susan Borowitz had been a writer-producer for *Family Ties*. They first heard of the proposed show at NBC Productions' weekly breakfast. Brandon Tartikoff walked up to them and said, "Did you hear the news? You've inherited a rap group." They immediately went to work on the pilot.

Afterward, when the nation's television journalists converged at Los Angeles's Century Plaza Hotel for NBC's press tour to announce the new fall lineup, many bluntly asked the Borowitzes what qualified them to depict the African American experience. When asked to define hip-hop, Andy Borowitz responded, "It's a subculture of rap. It shows racial pride. There's a manner of dress. In Philadelphia, they wear monochromatic sweat clothes—"

Will Smith, also present, then interrupted. "Mon-o-Crao-mat-IC!" he said. "What is mon-o-Crao-ma-tic?" The journalists laughed as Smith successfully deflected attention away from the obvious.

But the questions remained about the series's creators. "I was very reluctant about them," Benny Medina said. "I thought, I better make sure I'm really connected with the show. I mean, this is a lot different than *The Jeffersons*. This is deep, and you better be sensitive to it, because you're only a step away from offending somebody all the time. I just didn't understand how the Borowitzes could have the right sensibilities." Eventually, Medina felt comfortable with the Borowitzes. The couple strove to prove other Doubting Thomases wrong and also to counter attitudes of some NBC executives. Andy Borowitz recalled, "Somebody at the network said, 'The whole issue of black identity seems very controversial to me.'"

Susan Borowitz explained, "The question we were trying to address is: Does every one of the have-nots want to be where the Cosbys are? No. They have a very strong code. So then the question becomes: How do you succeed in a white man's world and stay Black?"

Good questions. But despite the Borowitzes' intentions, the initial episodes of *The Fresh Prince of Bel-Air* were full of missteps and misconceptions about middle-class African American life, some of which would plague the series throughout its run; others would be realigned and reconfigured in order not to offend the African American audience.

On the first episode, Will, arriving at the Banks home, was presented as a jivey, pushy, clowny know-it-all, who struts about in blue shorts, a striped green shirt, green socks, athletic shoes, and a baseball cap. Rather than being funny, he seemed merely silly. Frequently, the dialogue was embarrassing as it strained to make Will hip-hop hip, familiar with the vernacular of the 'hood. "Will will be going to Bel Air Academy," Uncle Philip tells his white lawyer. "Good for you, Will," says the lawyer. "I used to fence at Bel Air." Will responds, "Really? How much you think we could get for that stereo?" A totally witless line of dialogue.

For those who saw Benny Medina promote the series in an interview on *The Today Show*, the Will persona seemed all the more misconceived. Medina came across as intelligent, articulate, and shrewd without any signs of a clichéd rap attitude and without any of the mannerisms of Hollywood's fixed image of a homeboy. The real Medina was a distinct *person*. His TV counterpart was a type, closer to J.J. on *Good Times* than to Theo on *The Cosby Show*.

In the early episodes, Will struck some viewers as being far too disrespectful of the Banks family. He came across as rude, immature, and not at all the kind of Black kid whose mother, in sending him to relatives, would have insisted that he mind his manners. One only has to compare Will's early encounters and exchanges in the Banks household with those of Pam with the Huxtables. Sweetly deferential, Pam revealed her feelings and attitudes only *after* the Huxtables were out of the house. Will had been an arrogant cuss from the git-go.

At the same time, the series's creators didn't understand what the Black Bourgeoisie was all about. Though some might believe the Black middle class simply imitated the values and attitudes of whites (partly true), the Black Bourgeoisie also had its own set of standards and values, its own set of references and priorities, which were distinct unto itself. In the early 1990s, these were people who indeed may have wanted their children to attend top private schools; who themselves may have lobbied for an entrée to the "best" social clubs, neighborhoods, and restaurants. Yet they did not necessarily want to be white. Nor did they—in their pursuit of the almighty American Dream—want to completely abandon African American culture and an African American middle-class lifestyle.

Traditionally, these were people who had their own social clubs, their own set of equally successful African American friends, their own rituals, their own hierarchy. All sorts of status symbols came into play, everything from hair texture to skin tone to the use of language. For decades, the Black Bourgeoisie also had its own top schools, not Harvard or Yale, but historically Black colleges like Morehouse, Howard, Lincoln, and Fisk. The Black middle class also prided itself on knowledge of *its* literature, be it the work of Paul Laurence Dunbar, Langston Hughes, or Countee Cullen. Or *its* artists like Horace Pippin and Augusta Savage. Or its great concert hall performers like Marian Anderson, Roland Hayes, and Paul Robeson. And the Black Bourgeoisie had a distinct social philosophy regarding the importance of all African Americans doing something to further the race, not hinder it. Acutely aware of racism, the Black Bourgeoisie adhered to W. E. B. Du Bois's Talented Tenth theory, seeing themselves as leaders who had to set or preserve standards for the *rest* of the race.

It was true that in the late 1960s and 1970s, the old-guard Black Bourgeoisie had changed in some ways, indeed was more integrated into the system. Its children had also rebelled against its pretensions. But the Black Bourgeoisie's traditional values died hard. *The Fresh Prince of Bel-Air* seemed to have no awareness of those values and traditions, which series like *The Cosby Show* and *A Different World* had so effortlessly articulated.

Without those traditional anchors, too often the scripts (*not* the actors) made the Banks family look like a white family with some color smeared onto them. Hilary's Valley Girl accent, interests, and obsessions were funny but never seemed quite right. The butler, Geoffrey, came across as some stock fixture out of a Depression-era film about a proper British servant working for the scatterbrained idle rich. (Florence of *The Jeffersons* was closer to the mark in expressing the attitudes of a Black domestic working for a Black family.) Only Tatyana Ali as Ashley struck one as possibly an authentic representation of a middle-class Black teenager, although the scripts tended to depict her as a family anomaly because she was so down-to-earth.

Some steps were taken to give the character Uncle Philip some semblance of a cultural identity. "I remind you of where you came from and what you used to be," the brash Will tells Philip on the first episode. "Somewhere between Princeton and the office, you got soft. You forgot who you are and where you came from." Fortunately, the writers let Philip respond. "You think you're so wise," he says. "Let me tell you something, son. I grew up on the streets, just like you. I encountered bigotry you couldn't imagine. Now you have a nice poster of Malcolm X on your wall. I heard the brother speak. I read every word he wrote. Believe me, I know where I came from." He adds, "So before you criticize somebody you find out what he's all about." Playing the scene with a degree of commitment, James Avery looked like an actor almost overjoyed to have dialogue he could work with. But one had to ask: If the character was so committed, why hadn't he been able to pass on even a glimmer of Black history, let alone his own personal one, to his children? Activists from the 1960s were notorious for letting their kids know of their radical glory days. Even if the children rebelled against the radicalism of their parents (or countered it with a political conservatism of their own, like Alex Keaton on *Family Ties*), at least they knew why they wanted to divorce themselves from their parents' pasts. But in those early episodes, the dim Banks kids didn't seem to have been told anything.

Worse was the depiction of Carlton for too much of the series. Here was an intelligent, articulate, goal-oriented, ambitious young African American male. Yet young Black viewers were never given the chance to identify with him. Instead he was written as the jerk, the nerd, the pampered, self-delusionary sellout. Will was set up as the ideal normal teen, uninhibited and high-spirited. *The Fresh Prince of Bel-Air* made a mistake similar to that of *Good Times:* its primary young Black male was a clown.

People, which called the show a "black version of *The Beverly Hillbillies*," commented, "The comic tension grows out of seeing this jive jester in an antiques-filled drawing room." Of course, the magazine had its point. But the writers of *The Fresh Prince of Bel-Air* also used the character Will to make fun of the Banks elders, which apparently alienated "a good many viewers" who, as John J. O'Connor observed, "may not necessarily like the idea of solid upper-middle-class citizens being turned into buffoons to be sneered at by a smart aleck."

The producers realized early that the series needed some work. Samm-Art Williams signed on as a producer and also wrote for the show. Jeff Melman was brought on to direct episodes.

The fundamental problems didn't go away. On another episode, a friend from Philip and Viv's radical days showed up at the house, on the run from the law. When she and Will talked, the subject of 1960s-style political engagement emerged as she spoke of Angela Davis. But the writers still couldn't get it right. After coming up with this cultural reference, about all the writers could do was have Will comically comment on her huge Afro. Was this the best that could be said of Angela Davis? Here was only one of many times when pertinent African American cultural references were introduced, then trivialized for a quick, cheap joke that in the long run wasn't funny at all.

Another episode ended beautifully with the family gathered around Aunt Viv as she read a poem by Amiri Baraka. It was an unusual moment for a sitcom (reminiscent of the reading of Langston Hughes's poem "The Negro Speaks of Rivers" on *A Man Called Hawk*). But this quiet, reflective pause was undercut when the director immediately cut to Will, who looked into the camera and said, "If you'd like to learn more about poetry, you can reach us at . . ." Then he laughs, "Psych!" He grins and says, "We just kidding. Good night, you all." Then he waves to the audience.

On another episode, Will and Carlton are stopped by white cops, who assume the two are in a stolen car. Victims of racial profiling, they end up in jail. Much like the pseudo-serious episodes of *Good Times*, the episode was never wholly convincing. Yet it marked an attempt by the writers to extend the formula, to comment on current events in American life. But too often in the beginning the series was guilty of the same mistaken judgment as the white cops: it too fell back on the familiar image of inner-city kids who were, in some way or another, dim-witted jokesters or people associated with crime. When Will's friend Ice Tray (played by Don Cheadle) visits from Philadelphia, he comments on his (lack of) education. Questioned about school, Ice Tray says proudly, "I don't bother it. And it don't bother me. I've been held back in the tenth grade three times in a row. My motto is when I find a grade I like, I stick with it." On one episode, another of Will's inner-city pals, Jazz, played by Smith's music partner Jeff Townes, suggests they play basketball in his neighborhood. "Of course, we can only play half court," he says. "They use the other half to sell stolen appliances."

During the 1990–94 seasons, Townes appeared in a number of episodes. Clearly, the writers saw him as a raunchier counterpoint to Will. Through the camaraderie of Smith and Townes, the writers hoped to capture a rap sensibility—that sense of rebellion and a questioning of the system. But *The Fresh Prince of Bel-Air* failed as true hip-hop comedy. "What the creators of this new sitcom have done," wrote critic David Bianculli, "is to take a popular performer of rap music and build a totally nonthreatening comedy about him."

Benny Medina seemed to agree. "Will is not threatening," he said. "As the show develops, we will start to deal with some of the same things as N.W.A., Public Enemy, Ice Cube and artists with a much more radical way of communicating their life style." That never happened.

Will Smith's inexperience as an actor also showed. *TV Guide* commented, "For all his success, it is clear that the kid who steps in front of the cameras on a Hollywood sound stage is a novice at acting. The voice doesn't carry far enough: floor marks are missed." The periodical remarked that the director "needs to prod and cajole a more animated performance out of him." "We are seeing an improvement every day," executive producer Andy Borowitz said at the time. "He has a natural ability [but] it's not like we pulled some schmo off the street." Though the Will character was toned down, he never evolved into another be-ing, a really adult figure.

With its exaggerations and absurdities, *The Fresh Prince of Bel-Air* seemed to descend into farce. No doubt it was precisely this comic-book style that made younger viewers tune in. *Variety* reported that in its first season the series was "a solid performance. . . . It won its time slot five of eight weeks this season and has drawn strong shares among teens and young adults, its target audience." It did better than such other series as *Ferris Bueller, Parker Lewis Can't Lose*, and *Hull High.*

Will Smith himself was aware of the problems. "Early on I began to see that sitcoms are part of a system of built-in mediocrity," he said. "But for the first seasons, I stayed cool and didn't say much. I studied the genre, the structure of the scripts. When I did comment, I wanted to come from a place of knowledge and understanding, rather than in-stinct, even though my original instincts were right on. Because of that, I now have the freedom to act on those instincts. I've been given input. I've placed myself in a position where I can make demands. As a result, the scripts have improved. I'm happier with the show, and so is every-one else. The stories are more natural, more human. I want my charac-ter to be warm and living, to display integrity and, of course, to be funny. But funny doesn't come first. Integrity does." As time moved on, the series improved and had a run of six seasons.

Though Hilary and Geoffrey were never explained, the characters were accepted without being questioned. Both actress Karyn Parsons and actor Alfonso Ribeiro (who had formerly appeared on the sitcom *Silver Spoons*) were skilled young showbiz performers who could play off one another splendidly; never stepping on one another's lines; never missing a beat of the rhythm they established. Janet Hubert-Whitten brought a straightforward, brisk intelligence to her character, Vivian. A former member of the Alvin Ailey dance company, she once said she liked the role because "I play an upscale mom and I'm dark-skinned. So many Black people come up to me after the taping and say, 'It's so nice to see us portrayed on TV in all our different colors and types.'" *Essence* reported that initially the casting agents had wanted a "green-eyed, long-haired Black woman" for the part. Hubert-Whitten recalled, "Right before I got this part, I had just lost out on a soap because I was too dark. I came home and just cried. It hurts to the bone. . . . You can take the chains off arms but not off minds." During the fourth season,

Hubert-Whitten was replaced in the role of Vivian Banks by Daphne Maxwell Reid.

In time, Will and Carlton became friends. They graduated from prep school and enrolled at the University of Los Angeles. Will also eventually married his girlfriend Lisa (Nia Long). Throughout, the series never lived up to its real promise as a sharp, incisive, satirical study in culture clashes; at its best, as *Cable Guide* commented, *The Fresh Prince of Bel-Air* introduced "sassy street styles to white America in a safe party context." Yet Will Smith connected exceedingly well with young viewers, Black and white.

Once *The Fresh Prince of Bel-Air* left the air, one wondered if Will Smith would suffer the fate of other series' stars. Would he be unable to break free of his television persona? A few years later, Smith emerged as a box office movie star in such films as *Independence Day*, *Men in Black*, and *Enemy of the State*. *The Fresh Prince of Bel-Air* had clearly set the stage for his stardom.

In the season following the premiere of *The Fresh Prince of Bel-Air*, the race theme became fairly fashionable on episodes of some television series, especially after the news broadcasts of the videotape of white police officers assaulting Black motorist Rodney King. But too often on sitcoms, the topic of race or racism appeared to be used simply as a convenient prop for the basic television-style jokes and gags. That was clear on the short-lived series *Teech*. In the opening scene of the premiere episode, Teech, its central character, a Black music teacher who is hired at a preppy all-white boys' school, arrives for his first day of work. The headmaster's secretary, however, assumes he's a workman and promptly informs him that he must go "around to the back, use the service entrance, don't walk on the grass, pick up the fruit, talk to the students or eat lunch in plain view of anyone." In turn, he asks her, "Can I plant watermelon seeds on the back forty?" Not a very funny line. The problem with a show like *Teech* was that the race theme—even now, years after the groundbreaking *All in the Family*—didn't carry much weight in the sitcom format that had a manic need for quick laughs.

In the early 1990s, the theme was handled better in special episodes of dramatic series like *The Trials of Rosie O'Neill* and *Quantum Leap*.

This was also the period when *L.A. Law* also showed some muscle in commenting on race. Ironically, during the 1990–91 season, seven of its twenty-two episodes explored problems of race in one form or another. Quite a reversal for a series that had initially sought to deracialize its one important Black character, Jonathan Rollins.

The next season, following the 1992 disorders in Los Angeles, television was even quicker to reflect the unrest. Quick to exploit it too. On the two-part episode of *A Different World* titled *Honeymoon in Los Angeles: The Simi Side of Life*, newlyweds Whitley and Dwayne, back on Hillman's campus, recalled their honeymoon in Los Angeles when they witnessed firsthand the explosive disorders. On *The Fresh Prince of Bel-Air*, the Banks family returned to its old neighborhood in South Central to help clean up. But they also had to examine their own attitudes about their roots. The hero of *Doogie Howser, M.D.* also examined his feelings on race (his basic social unawareness) when he saw victims of the disorders in the emergency room of the hospital where he worked. Even *Knots Landing* had a special episode built around the devastation in Los Angeles. Despite the earnestness, the episodes seemed mighty tame.

LOOKING TO THE PAST:
HOMEFRONT AND *I'LL FLY AWAY*

But during the early years of the new decade, the race issue appeared as a recurring theme on two new dramatic series, *Homefront* and *I'll Fly Away*. Coming from the producers of *Knots Landing*, *Homefront* was a post-World War II drama set in 1945 in a small industrial town, River Run, Ohio. Focusing on the problems of Americans at a time when the nation was experiencing great social change, *Homefront* concentrated on three families: the affluent white Sloans, who own the town's big factory; the blue-color Metcalfs, also white, who work in the factory; and the Black Davises, who work for the Sloans. Abe Davis (Dick Anthony Williams) is their chauffeur and handyman; his wife, Gloria (Hattie Winston), is their housekeeper.

Homefront proved both interesting and frustrating in the way it explored race relations and attitudes. Returning to River Run was the Davises' war hero son Robert (Sterling Macer Jr.). Ambitious and ready

Looking back at racism and the American family: I'll Fly Away,
*with (front row) Ashlee Levitch, Sam Waterston, John Aaron
Bennett, (back row) Jeremy London, and Regina Taylor
as the domestic Lilly Harper*

for a new day in the land of the free and the home of the brave, he
applies for a position at his hometown's factory. But he's not even considered qualified for the assembly line. Instead he's offered a job as a
janitor. Later, his father, who fails to persuade his boss Sloan to do better by his son, takes another route. He establishes communication with
a "system within the system," composed of former Black service workers who have contacts with influential whites; through their help, a call
is made to Sloan from the office of none other than Eleanor Roosevelt.
Robert gets his production-line job. But he is hounded and harassed by
the white workers. Though the racial tensions might strike us as realistic, the earlier solution—the call from the office of Mrs. Roosevelt, who
indeed in real life had spoken out about opportunities for African
American veterans—strikes us as pure Hollywood-style hokum.

But Robert faced other problems. When Gina, the pregnant young widow of the Sloans' son, is kicked out of their home, the kindly Davis family takes her in. Robert and Gina have a platonic friendship that some whites misinterpret. When Robert is brutally beaten by some white police officers, Gina decides to live elsewhere.

Television viewers may have been heartened by the fact that *Homefront* was not depicting its Black residents as simply passive happy folks without social/racial problems. But the series seemed smug and far too self-congratulatory about its social conscience when, in fact, its brand of social comment had appeared in movies years earlier, during the actual postwar era. Occasionally, *Homefront did* slip into a view of fundamentally passive Black characters. When the factory boss—a blatant bigot and a union basher—takes his Black chauffeur aside so they can discuss the best way to handle their wives, you know it's trying to show that "human" or gender "commonalities" transcend racial differences, and you don't believe a minute of it. It's not hard to understand why some critics complained that *Homefront*'s race relations "seem to unfold in a never-never land."

Homefront looked as if it would pick up steam early in its second season when war hero Robert brought his war bride—a young French woman—Perrette (Perrey Reeves) to River Run. This might have emerged as series television's most provocative exploration of society's attitudes (Black and white) on interracial marriages. The couple is repeatedly subjected to racist taunts. At a baseball game, they are hassled. At home, they receive hate calls and hate mail. Yet the writers of *Homefront* seemed to have forgotten what Robert had already experienced when Gina lived at his family's home. Why would he even bother to bring his young bride to this hotbed of small-town racism? "He seems unaware of the problems this may cause," commented writer Mimi White, "despite the beating he received the previous season. Instead, memory is superseded by a repetition compulsion focused on the dramatic and eroticized charge to be gained by interracial coupling."

Nonetheless, *Homefront* quickly disposed of this plot line. Robert and wife were written out of the series. "It came as a surprise to me," actor Sterling Macer said. "I realize they had to do some cutting due to the budget, but I have a tough time knowing that one of the characters they found most expendable was the only strong, young African-

American on the show, the only one who challenges racial barriers and has a vision of equality for the future." The racial focus was back on the Davis parents. *Homefront* folded after its second season.

The hour-long dramatic series *I'll Fly Away* proved more successful in examining America's tangled race relations—and also in presenting a moving image of an African American woman. Like *Homefront*, it was set safely in the past; in the small Georgia town of Bryland in the late 1950s/early 1960s during the rise of the civil rights era. Exploring the attitudes of Black and white as the nation underwent social and political changes, much of *I'll Fly Away* focused on the family life of a prosecuting attorney, Forrest Bedford (Sam Waterston). When his emotionally fragile wife suffers a breakdown and becomes a patient in a sanitarium, Bedford hires a Black maid, Lilly Harper (Regina Taylor), to manage his home and care for his three children.

Sensitive, poetic, proud, and uncompromising, Lilly was not the typical self-sacrificing, love-thy-massa movie/TV African American domestic. From the start, she was drawn as a character who refused to be taken for granted. Or to let herself be the invisible woman. On the day that Bedford interviews and then hires her for the job in his home, she is acutely aware that this white man, who prides himself on being fair and a liberal, has never once said her name. Finally, she looks directly at him and says, "I'm Lilly." After he has explained his wife's condition, Lilly also tells Bedford that "everybody has their difficulties, don't they, sir?" Later, when the oldest Bedford child, Nathan (Jeremy London), a teenager going through the pangs and pains of adolescence, makes it clear that he regards Lilly as little more than a piece of furniture in the home, she calmly tells him, "You don't know I'm here. But I'm here." Fortunately, the director knew when to focus the camera on Lilly. The close-ups of Taylor's Lilly became quietly powerful moments that said far more than the dialogue.

In time, Lilly grows fond of the youngest Bedford child, six-year-old John Morgan (John Aaron Bennett), who, confused by his mother's absence, is in need of an understanding ear. At first, you fear that Lilly will become doggedly devoted to the child, and find yourself holding back emotionally, not wanting to give in to a familiar sentimental relationship. But the scenes between the two were sensitively done and marked by Lilly's awareness of the delicate line she must walk in balancing her work and her personal life.

Lilly always understood her place in Southern culture. Here *I'll Fly Away* dramatized a fact that most African Americans were aware of but had rarely seen articulated on the primetime series in such thoughtful terms: that while Lilly becomes well aware of the Bedfords' conflicts and contradictions, their dilemmas and yearnings, they know very little about her, the Black woman in their midst. Lilly also sees the contrast between the Bedfords' comfortable middle-class way of life and her own. *I'll Fly Away* never let the viewer forget that once Lilly left the Bedford household, she returned to her modest home in the colored part of town. Lilly was given a love life for a time with a musician named Clarence, played by Dorian Harewood. But mostly and most memorably, Lilly was shown with her six-year-old daughter, Aldaine (originally played by Zelda Harris; later Rae'ven Kelly), and her father (Bill Cobbs), with whom she lives.

For Lilly, there are often intense, emotionally conflicted moments when she has to "explain" the world to her daughter. On one episode, Aldaine mistakenly thinks a cowboy hat is for her. Lilly must tell her that, actually, it belongs to the privileged Bedford child John Morgan. When Lilly has taken Aldaine to work with her, she knows her daughter doesn't understand why they must leave by the back door at the end of the day. Filming the sequence had been painful for actress Regina Taylor. "It shook me," said Taylor. "How do you explain that to a child? The daily indignities—how do you survive them?" Such telling, subtly effective moments were at the heart of the series.

Throughout, Lilly observes the world around her, always questioning and reflecting on the people she meets, the community where she lives, and, ultimately, the meaning of her life. Through Lilly, *I'll Fly Away* repeatedly reminded its viewers of the racism that infected the land and culture.

The premiere episode dealt with the trial of a white bus driver accused of negligence in the death of several Black passengers on his vehicle. Prosecuting the case is Forrest Bedford, who knows he can never get a guilty verdict from the all-white jury. The bus company finally offers a settlement. But the African American minister, who has led a protest about the incident in the colored community, refuses it. Later there is a mass candlelight gathering. No one speaks. No one moves.

On another episode, a Black military man was viciously shot and killed in his car by a group of white men, out for sport.

I'll Fly Away also explored the clear racial divisions in Lilly's daily life. On an episode in which Bedford's wife, after having been released from the sanitarium, is killed in a car accident, Lilly and another Black domestic discuss the matter in the kitchen of the Bedford home. As they prepare food to be served to the white mourners gathered there, the two women also discuss the murder of the Black military man. We see that one death means so much to the white community; another, so little. Perhaps most perceptive was an episode that dramatized a white child's curiosity about blackness.

Created by John Falsey and Joshua Brand (both of whom also created the series *St. Elsewhere, Northern Exposure,* and *A Year in the Life*), *I'll Fly Away* was originally conceived as a family drama set in South Africa. But Brand knew the networks would never accept such a concept. "They're going to go, 'What, are you *crazy?*' so we don't say *that* to them but in effect it's a similar situation," Brand said. "American society [had been] essentially an apartheid society, and, as in South Africa, there are changes that people are trying to make that should be made."

When the NBC affiliates were informed that the network considered replacing the series *Matlock* with *I'll Fly Away,* Brand recalled that "the affiliates got upset and they said, '*Race,* what are you going to do?'; 'We're going to get hit over the head' and 'I don't want to turn on my television and hear that stuff again.' And then [NBC] showed [the pilot] to them, and people loved it."

Yet admirable as *I'll Fly Away* was, it was, in many respects, like *Homefront,* a safe, even self-congratulatory show with its racial tensions neatly tucked in the past, enabling audiences to pride themselves on the way that America had overcome its Jim Crow laws, its racially stratified South, and its view of African American women. Its hero, Forrest, seemed to spring from the hip of *To Kill a Mockingbird*'s Atticus Finch: the noble white male, who represents the best of white America; an idealized liberal character. He may be conflicted or confused by racial issues, such as during the time he opposed Lilly's attempts to distribute voter-rights information to other Black domestics. But ultimately Forrest will always do the right thing and, in essence, be something of a savior for the Black community. Its solemn pace and rhythm made *I'll Fly Away* all the more dreamlike, as one could hypnotically lose himself/herself in a fundamentally soothing show. The perpetrators of really vicious acts seem to be aberrations rather than "normal" folks who might be racist to the core.

But ultimately what saved *I'll Fly Away* and made it really effective and often moving, far more so than most primetime fare, was the creators' commitment to their material, and the fine performances. One couldn't help but agree with *Newsday* critic Marvin Kitman when he wrote, "Watching [Sam] Waterston is like watching water drip." Yet despite Waterston's meticulously slow buildup of character and situation, he created a credible and at times, regardless of the idealization, a complicated man.

No one found fault with Regina Taylor, though. "I haven't seen a more powerful performance," wrote Kitman. "As Lilly, Ms. Taylor is superb, conveying a mixture of strong intelligence and simmering anger with a complete absence of extraneous fuss," wrote John J. O'Connor.

By the time she appeared in *I'll Fly Away*, Taylor was thirty years old. Having grown up mostly in Dallas, she originally planned to become a journalist. But after only one acting class at Southern Methodist University, she chose a different path. To earn a living while pursuing an acting career in New York, she worked many jobs, including one as a maid. Later she became a member of New York's Shakespeare Festival Company, played Juliet on Broadway, and wrote a play, *Watermelon Rinds*. She found work in the film *Lean on Me*, and the TV movies *The Howard Beach Story* and *Concealed Enemies*.

I'll Fly Away marked Taylor's first important television role. But she had doubts about playing a maid. She was well aware that most dramas frequently denied such women intelligence and independence and a point of view. (Hattie Winston had the same reservations about her maid character on *Homefront*.) But once Taylor read the script and talked to the producers, she accepted the part. "My motto is 'Off with the head rag,' " she said. "It's important to me that Lilly not get stuck in some Mammy myth. . . . There's a richness in her culture that she's at the center of. She knows that certain things are wrong. How do you dare express that out loud?"

Taylor began by digging into her family history: stories she knew about her grandmother, who helped raise her; about her aunt, who was a maid; and about her mother, Nell Taylor, a retired government worker and poet. "They did a lot of footwork to get me where I am. My grandmother was fiercely independent and headstrong. She had her own mind, and a wonderful heart. My mother went to college. But she would apply for certain jobs, and they would tell her she could work in the kitchen," said Taylor. "In a way, by playing Lilly, I've put on [their] shoes."

Despite her strengths, Lilly was frequently presented as the passive observer, similar to the young Jane Pittman. Yet Taylor always suggested a woman who understood that the key to her survival at times lay in her reserve *and* her caution. Taylor's Lilly knows she can never reveal much about herself to the whites for whom she works as well as to members of her own community. With her own father, Lilly can be guarded. Taylor was at her best in a sequence when two FBI agents visit Lilly's home to question her about Forrest Bedford, who is being considered for an appointment as a United States attorney. Asked if Bedford is a member of the Communist Party, she answers no. Asked then if she knows what the Communist Party is, she responds, "I know."

Then one agent says, "Mr. Bedford's considered a hero in your community, isn't he?"

"My feeling about Mr. Bedford is that folks, the white people in town, think we think that. But we don't."

When an agent presses her, "Is he still a champion of the rights of the colored?" she tells him, "No. I think I ought to know when my rights are being championed and when they aren't."

Once the FBI agents have left, Lilly's father expresses surprise at some of her answers, saying she may have cost Bedford the new job. Lilly, however, lets him know she felt she was being set up. "They wanted me to say Mr. Bedford is the kind of man who would enforce the law even if it meant being on the side of the colored. 'Cause I think maybe they're not."

It was a good strong moment that revealed Lilly's shrewd insights and her ability to quickly assess a situation. But one wonders why the script did not develop the scene in such a way that her father, rather than coming across as being naive about the agents and Lilly's strategy, instead might have understood every word Lilly had uttered; that the two of them could have been joint conspirators in resistance to two corrupt, racist white FBI agents.

Taylor created a woman who seemed scared by life, aware she can take only so many chances. On one episode, actress Mary Alice made a guest appearance as a friend who stops by Lilly's home to sell her cosmetics. At the time, Lilly is getting over her romance with the musician Clarence. When Mary Alice's character comments on Lilly's personal life, saying that she's heard Lilly and Clarence have parted company, Lilly's mood changes. We feel her stiffening. This woman has stepped over a line into Lilly's private, guarded territory. With the subtlest change in her tone, Taylor's Lilly says firmly that she doesn't want to buy any cosmetics.

At the episode's conclusion, Lilly, having reflected on the joys and sorrows of life following a visit to the sanitarium where Mrs. Bedford is institutionalized, stops by Mary Alice's home. She is formal as she says, "I know it's late but I was wondering if we might have a visit." She then says she wants to purchase some cosmetics. When Mary Alice asks what she has in mind, Lilly again says formally, "I was hoping you could tell me, being specifically trained." As Mary Alice applies makeup to Lilly's face, the two talk casually. Then Lilly opens up, as much as she can. "It's a fact," she says, "since Clarence left, I've hardly slept. I've let myself go. It's hard to think your heart can do that."

She also comments on the Bedfords. "What a mess of loneliness and desolation," she says. "A bunch of white folks without their minds." Then she softly adds, "It makes you think, you know. At least, I know what love is. I got people I care about and memories that make me warm when I do recall them. It just makes you think that."

"I know," says Mary Alice.

Lilly then breaks down and cries. "Clarence, you know, he opened me up. I've been shut down too long." It was a quietly significant sequence; a poignant portrait of two African American women sharing the most intimate of moments. The episode was written by African American Kevin Arkadie.

For Lilly, though, her real intimate is the journal she keeps. Only there—in Lilly's voice-overs that closed each episode—is she free to sort out her feelings, to really let her guard down. At the close of the episode in which she mourns the end of her romance with Clarence, Lilly says plaintively, "The old people say you can visit the corpse of one you knew in life and who was pleasantly disposed toward you. When nobody's looking, you ask that they take your sickness along with them. Even as a child, that seemed to me wrong. I believe our dead should and do go up to the stars. Clean and clear and light and finally free of foolish sorrow."

Throughout, Taylor was an actress of great interior powers, similar to Gloria Foster and especially Cicely Tyson. One questioned, though, if Taylor had the range of a Cicely Tyson. *I'll Fly Away* never afforded her the opportunities to open up in other ways, especially to fully express her sexuality. Or to unleash her anger. Not until later with a performance in a film like *Clockers* did audiences see the other moods—and the other type of power—that Regina Taylor could convey.

The critics' reactions to *I'll Fly Away* were mixed. "Here's the only show of the new season taking the high road. Unfortunately, a serious tone and important themes don't make this drama, from the creators of *Northern Exposure*, compelling," wrote a critic for *People*.

Newsweek, however, praised it as the "season's only class act." John J. O'Connor called it "a fine and in many unexpected ways a powerful new series." But O'Connor questioned if viewers would accept it. "Can a thoughtful, leisurely paced drama about racial and social issues in the late 1950s compete with the plethora of current network shows marketing little more than zippy, mindless one-liners?" he wrote. "Anyone concerned about the future of television will certainly hope so, despite dismaying odds."

I'll Fly Away won the Peabody Award, three Humanitas Awards, and twenty-three Emmy nominations. But the series never pulled in large ratings. General viewers may have found the pace too slow and the drama itself too much of a period piece (which seldom fares well in a series). Some African American viewers may have taken one look and decided they weren't interested in a maid drama. Even those Black viewers who watched the show regularly—primarily because it was just about the only series with a Black woman at its center—no doubt would have preferred that Lilly have another occupation. Then, too, in later episodes, viewers saw less of Lilly. *I'll Fly Away* chose to focus on Nathan and his friend Paul Slocum. After two seasons, NBC dropped the series. Later PBS reran *I'll Fly Away* in its entirety and also aired an original two-hour episode titled *Then and Now* that concluded the story.

The concluding episode—a story told in flashbacks—opened with an older Lilly, now a published writer, who discusses events of the past with her grandson Lewis. The writers opened the character up, letting her become a more fully developed participant as she recalls an inci-dent—in 1962—when her father, Lewis, celebrated his seventy-second birthday. The elder Lewis has witnessed two white men abducting an African American youth, who is visiting from Detroit. The young man has made "unacceptable" comments to a white Southern woman. Sur-prisingly, *Then and Now* stressed the nobility of its white character Bedford, who encourages Lilly's father to testify against two white men who are on trial accused of having lynched the young Black. (The episode is loosely drawn from the lynching case of Emmett Till.) In past episodes, her father had never been the activist that Lilly was in her earlier efforts at voter registration. Nor had Bedford been encouraging of her activism. As one critic commented: "All of this is displaced or rewritten in the final movie, which shifts the burden of activism from Lilly and other African American women in the community to the pa-triarchal figures of Forrest and Lilly's father. The final episode 'forgets' its own fictional past by situating patriarchy, especially Southern white patriarchy, squarely at the center of the narrative of civil rights progress." Still, Regina Taylor's Lilly remained one of the era's most compelling characters—and one of the few important dramatic Black female characters in primetime series during the 1990s.

There was also—briefly—the indomitable Cicely Tyson on *Sweet Jus-tice,* her first series role since her days on *East Side, West Side.* Like *In the Heat of the Night, Sweet Justice* was set in the New South. It's a place where the old guard (some of the diehard white leftovers from the era of *I'll Fly Away*) are still uneasy about the shift in racial dynamics. Here a disillusioned onetime Wall Street lawyer, Kate Delacroy (Melissa Gilbert), returns, hoping that now back in her hometown she'll find herself. Her father (Ronny Cox), a powerful conservative lawyer, pres-sures her to come into his firm. Instead Kate joins the law offices of Black attorney Carrie Grace Battle (Tyson), much to the bewilderment of her father. Years earlier, at the height of the civil rights movement in the South, Kate's mother had marched with Carrie, whose own hus-band was slain during the era. Kate's father has never forgotten nor ap-parently forgiven Carrie for her fiery protest days. She "dragged us kicking and screaming into the new South," he says. "Some of us didn't think there was anything wrong with the old."

That description alone was enough to make viewers sit up and take notice. Just one glimpse of Tyson—who looked magnificent, a mature beauty with a streak of gray strategically placed right above the middle of her forehead, the eyes as luminous and penetrating as ever—was enough to draw one in. Dressed in sleek, sophisticated suits, she looked like a fashion plate. And her supposedly "modest" home, out of which she worked with her dedicated staff, was an elegant, well-appointed setting. This may well have been Tyson's most glamorous television role. In some episodes, Michael Warren appeared as an African American community leader and love interest for Carrie. Tyson herself—energetic and bristling with that no-nonsense, exacting intelligence of hers—seemed primed for action: charming and gracious in social situations but also shrewd and calculating in her courtroom sequences. She clearly relished playing a woman so much in charge of any given situation.

But *Sweet Justice* never gave Tyson enough to do. On one episode, she defended a homeless man who liked to order fine meals at fancy restaurants. When the check arrived, he could not pay the bill. Not a particularly compelling case. Other courtroom sequences had more bite, the episode that focused on Carrie's successful reopening of the thirty-year-old killing of a civil rights leader by a local, now elderly, bigot. Another two-part episode that introduced Carrie's daughter (Charlayne Woodard) and grandchild (Rae'ven Allen) looked promising. But Carrie's attempt to work out her strained relationship with her daughter was a subplot. Mainly the great Tyson served as a wise counselor for Kate Delacroy; she was there primarily to help bring the emotionally restless Delacroy to maturity. Viewers were back with another Black/white bonding tale with most of the emphasis on the white heroine. Interestingly enough, Cree Summer, formerly Freddie on *A Different World*, played a young single mother who works on Carrie's staff. The drama might have had a whole other tone had the scripts further developed Carrie's friendship with this young Black woman. Had Tyson and Summer been cast in mother surrogate/daughter roles (or Tyson and Woodard as mother and daughter), *Sweet Justice* might have become the kind of successful "woman's series" that *Judging Amy* emerged as in early 2000. Or it might have been the kind of tense, engrossing, primarily Black-cast drama that later *City of Angels* strove to be. *Sweet Justice* ran for one season. For Tyson, as in past decades, her best work would come in television movies of the era.

NETWORK MISCALCULATIONS: FINDING SITCOMS FOR CHANGING TIMES, CHANGING AUDIENCES

During the early to mid-1990s, the networks became conscious of a significant Black audience. A 1990 Nielsen study had revealed some startling information on viewing habits in African American homes. Though the overall audience for the networks continued to decline, African Americans, it was discovered, were watching television in record numbers. Non-Black households averaged 47 hours a week of television. But in African American households, viewers averaged nearly 70 hours of television viewing a week. Other numbers also proved surprising: Blacks between the ages of two and seventeen viewed 68 percent more television than other viewers in that age range. At the same time, while general audiences tuned in to cable in significant numbers, Black viewers stuck with the networks. In the end, though Black Americans represented 12 percent of the nation's population, they comprised more than 20 percent of a network's primetime audience. In Black households, the most popular programs were *The Cosby Show*, *A Different World*, and *The Fresh Prince of Bel-Air*, all of which aired on NBC.

Network programmers searched for shows that appealed specifically to Black viewers. "They don't constitute *enough* percentage of the audience so that mass media can be successful by targeting them exclusively," said David Poltrack, CBS senior vice president for planning and research, "but, as has been seen with the large number of successful Black-cast shows, the strong support of the Black population plus the ability of those shows to cross over and attract a significant white audience has brought them to the forefront."

Once again, the Black show was fashionable on the networks, albeit briefly.

Such new series as *Here and Now*, *Out All Night*, *Hangin' with Mr. Cooper*, *Rhythm & Blues*, and *Thea* were feverish attempts by the networks to reach African American households—mainly through programming aimed at the young. Executive-produced by Bill Cosby and airing on NBC, *Here and Now* starred former *Cosby Show* kid Malcolm-Jamal Warner as a psychology graduate student named A.J. who works with troubled kids at a youth center in Manhattan. He lives with a family friend, his "Uncle" Sydney (Charles Brown), whose daughter he has a crush on. Mainly, though, A.J. tries to reach inner-city kids. *Here and Now* often looked like a project designed to put Warner's former character Theo in a new context: to deidealize the world a Theo-style character lives in, to be more realistic about the problems he must face.

One noticed the supposedly hip, "youth appeal" language Warner's character A.J. now used as he greeted people with a "Yo, how you living!" or a "Hey, man!" But A.J. (as well as the series) also understood the way language could be sexist and demeaning. In one episode, A.J. reprimanded one of the kids for referring to a girl's "booty." The boy had to leave the center. Afterward, his brother, a drug dealer, confronted A.J., who did not back down from his position. Young African American women have to be respected. For a later generation, this sequence might look sweetly naive, especially when a well-publicized Black-cast film like *Booty Call* was later released without any protest. Still, one could appreciate the sentiments, the earnest Cosby-like attempt to maintain certain standards amid a rapidly changing youth culture.

But *Here and Now* also relied on old images. No doubt again to appeal to hip-hop audiences, the series introduced the character "T" as a sidekick for A.J. A former delinquent who sometimes sported a floppy pimp-style hat and often clowned around, "T," upon seeing A.J. confront the drug dealer, was scared out of his wits and hid behind a counter. To succeed, *Here and Now* needed stronger scripts and perhaps even a different premise. Within a few months, it was off the air.

Out All Night didn't fare much better. It just proved to be more offensive. The series starred pop diva Patti LaBelle as a former singing star who opens a club in L.A. After a young college grad named Jeff (Morris Chestnut) persuades her to let him manage the place, she takes him and his buddy Vidal (Duane Martin) under her wing. She even sets them up in an apartment building she owns. Weekly, LaBelle nurtured the guys like mad, to the point where she began to look a little mad herself. Doesn't this woman have anything better to do? Weekly, too, Vidal let everyone know how horny he was, especially as he eyed LaBelle's fashion stylist daughter (Vivica A. Fox).

Out All Night's executive producers, Andy and Susan Borowitz, who had also been the creators of *The Fresh Prince of Bel-Air*, hadn't a clue about the series's characters or their situation. One critic credited them with "inventing much of the language that passes for black English on

TV today, which is Esperanto to some viewers." In its attempts to be young, hip, and sexy, some of Vidal's dialogue was painful. All it did was to create one more Black male character living in a state of perpetual adolescence, unable to look at a woman without thinking about a way to maneuver her into the sack; even at that, he didn't have enough sense to know how to court a woman in a way that might make her willing to be his bedmate. "Right now I'm delivering pizza [for a living]," Vidal tells a pretty female. "And in my personal life as well as in my work, I deliver hot and on top." Another time, Vidal, while wearing a sweatshirt that reads "Just Do Me," announces, "This girl walked by in a dress so tight—POW—I could see her heart beat."

About the best things the series offered were guest appearances by African American music stars: Luther Vandross; the trio TLC; Dionne Warwick; and Gladys Knight. But even they couldn't save the show. *The Hollywood Reporter* commented on the series's "insistence on clanging, buffoonish characterizations." *Out All Night* died after its first season.

Rhythm & Blues was another music-oriented sitcom with yet another set of dimly conceived characters. Having inherited a radio station from her late husband and desperate to reverse sagging ratings, Veronica Washington (Anna Maria Horsford) hires a deejay after hearing an audition tape in which he does a wicked parody of Michael Jackson. Though she's never seen the deejay, she grooves to his name— Bobby Soul—and knows this has to be one baad brother. When he arrives at the station, she's shocked to see that soul brother Bobby (Roger Kabler) is not exactly what she thought. He's white! Thereafter she tries to fire him, but Bobby, who does impressions of everybody from Redd Foxx to Harry Belafonte, wins the support of the radio staff and listeners. He's one funky white boy that all the colored folks dig. The staff's approval, unfortunately, makes them appear simpleminded: they don't seem aware of how condescending he is.

Thereafter *Rhythm & Blues* recounted Bobby Soul's adventures at the station with the usual television wanna-be eccentrics: the Love Man (Troy Curvey Jr.), a heavyset deejay, who's often surrounded by various ladies; the sales manager Don (poor talented Ron Glass); the sincere program director Colette (Vanessa Bell Calloway); and Ziggy (Christopher Babers), Mrs. Washington's son, who, thinking of himself as Jamaican, repeatedly uses a West Indian accent. Every one of them seems to be suffering from some kind of dementia.

Sandwiched between the NBC hits *A Different World* and *Cheers,* *Rhythm & Blues* was in the right place. But viewers and critics alike were turned off by it. *Variety* wrote that the show had "all the emotional complexity of a jingle." The paper also pointed out what should have been obvious to the people who created it; namely, that there was "something disconcerting about [Bobby Soul's] role: The idea of a conquering Caucasian hero amidst a black staff dilutes the strength of a show that teasingly suggests it will turn racial clichés on their head." Critic David Bianculli expressed similar sentiments. "You want condescension? Step right up," he wrote. "You want a show where African Americans are cast in subservient roles to a white star? Be my guest. You want the most insulting sitcom premise of the season? This is it." After less than two months, *Rhythm & Blues* died.

Finally, during the 1992–93 season, ABC aired *Hangin' with Mr. Cooper,* a sitcom that in some respects looked like a replay of *Three's Company.* A former NBA player, Mark Cooper (stand-up comic Mark Curry), moves in with an old friend (Dawnn Lewis) and a curvaceous stockbroker (Holly Robinson). Though the supposedly adult characters are concerned about their careers, the writers seemed more interested in having them talk about sex in dialogue that was dim-witted and flat. Says Robinson of Cooper's physique: "He's got a butt that makes me wish I was his wallet." Throughout, the camera ogled Robinson as much as Cooper did. But then as one critic commented: "It's hard not to get attention, though, when you wear dresses small and tight enough to double as headbands." When he's not ogling Robinson, Curry's Cooper teaches high school students. But his behavior isn't much different from theirs. When he can't get a student to behave, Cooper glues the kid to his chair! He's yet another primetime African American male adolescent.

Even before *Hangin' with Mr. Cooper* aired, the network saw problems. A high-level studio executive informed *Variety* that the series was "the essence of what bad, Black racist comedy done by a purely white producer looks like. It's about a Black guy with an overactive libido living with two women with big tits. Oh, and there's a palliative: He teaches school, so people don't feel so bad watching him trying to fornicate." Executive producer and creator Jeff Franklin left the series. Afterward there was a scramble to make changes.

During the second season, new characters, played by Raven-Symone (formerly of *The Cosby Show*) and Nell Carter (playing the principal at Cooper's school), were introduced. Emerging as more of a family show but aimed primarily at kids, *Hangin' with Mr. Cooper*, unlike the other new Black-cast series, endured for several seasons.

The next season, ABC aired *Thea*, the tale of yet another hefty mother. She's a widow with four kids to raise and keep out of trouble. Like the title character on *Roseanne*, the heroine struggles to make ends meet. Not only does she work as a cashier at a supermarket; she also takes management courses at night and works part-time as a hairdresser. But unlike *Roseanne*, *Thea* was one joke after another. Thea herself (Thea Vidale) was little more than another nurturing mammy figure, full of basic love and joy. Playing Thea's daughter was a very young Brandy Norwood, who later in the decade would become a pop diva and also the star of the series *Moesha*. That was about the only noteworthy aspect of the series. Within six months, *Thea* expired.

Having decided to program shows for the African American audience, the networks, however, failed to come up with innovative concepts; programs that also might cross racial/cultural lines and appeal to broad audiences, young and old, Black and white. It seemed to have slipped the minds of network programmers that the most successful of all African American series, *The Cosby Show*, had scored so high precisely because it was not created to appeal simply to the young. Worse, the new series reverted to pre-Cosby-era images. "Nearly two decades ago, in a TV era replete with ethnic stereotypes," wrote a critic for *Newsweek*, "a teenager named J.J. strutted through the ABC series *Good Times* flashing a flubber-lipped grin and punctuating the air with his catch phrase, 'Dy-no-MITE!' But if anyone thought such caricatures of African American life had gone the way of Fred Sanford's junkyard truck, they haven't taken a look at prime time this year."

Bill Cosby also lashed out at the new series at a dinner marking his induction into the Television Hall of Fame. Calling them "drive-by images," he said that the new shows presented Blacks who "think funny about theft." "They think funny about gross movements towards the female. How many times has the punch line been, 'We're going to kick butt'? How many times has the punch line been about genitalia or big breasts?" Later Cosby said, "The racial stupidity is even worse than the racial grossness. And this isn't Stepin Fetchit, man, this is network television. . . . They see the pimp, the deal, the strutting street kid. What they never see, because they never look for it, is the hard-working mother and father upstairs who are trying to move up and out."

The age-old question arose as to why there were no African American dramatic series. "We are relegated to comedy," said Susan Fales, the executive producer of *A Different World*. "We are not regarded as interesting enough for drama." Many African American writers and producers also questioned why Black shows were seldom seen on primetime after 9 p.m. The 8–9 p.m. time slot often was reserved, as *Variety* noted, for "broad and slapstick sitcoms."

FLEDGLING FOX: BUILDING A BLACK VIEWER BASE

While the shows on the major networks proved short-lived, the still new network Fox had better luck with a run of new Black-cast series. As it struggled to be a contender in the network arena, Fox realized it needed a solid viewer *block* that would ensure strong ratings. After its success with a youth-oriented show like *21 Jump Street* (which also pulled in young Black viewers) and *In Living Color*, Fox again tapped into that potential African American viewer block with its first successful Black sitcom, *Roc*, in 1991.

Charles Dutton as Roc

Roc told the story of a Baltimore garbage collector, Roc Emerson (Charles Dutton), who lives with his extended family: his wife, Eleanor (Ella Joyce), a nurse; his retired father, Andrew (Carl Gordon); and his brother Joey (Rocky Carroll), an unemployed trumpet player. Weekly, Roc navigated his way through social and economic problems. He and other family members were vocal about the fact that the Bush administration had forgotten them (and much of Black America). Throughout, he tries counseling his wayward brother Joey. Roc and the rest of the Emersons must also adjust to a changing society. On one episode, the entire family was overjoyed at hearing the news that Dad's younger brother was finally getting married. But when the brother (Richard Roundtree) showed up, the family learned that his betrothed was not only white but also another man. As the series moved on, an assertive Roc—troubled by drugs and crime in his neighborhood—took more control over his life and community. He ran for the city council on a strong anticrime campaign. A series with a social conscience, Roc was a tribute to the common working-class man doing the best he could and pushing himself to do more; puzzled and frustrated by life, but never defeated. "I ain't got that worked out yet," was his catchphrase.

Roc also treated its characters thoughtfully, refusing to trivialize their lives. The only problem was that on occasion the series was not especially funny. It was really an issue-oriented program. But it couldn't smoothly blend its mix of comedy and drama as Frank's Place had often done. Frequently, the writing was didactic "with one manufactured problem a week neatly resolved before the final credits." Sometimes, too, the performances didn't seem scaled for the medium. The actors (many of whom had appeared on Broadway in August Wilson's drama The Piano Lesson) often overpunched and overdramatized their lines, projecting way out there when they should have pulled in and minimized. Still, Roc seemed an authentic comment on the lives of the type of people television usually ignored. Though never a major hit, Roc ran for three seasons. When Fox announced the series's cancellation, twenty-nine African American members of Congress—the Black Caucus—asked Fox to keep Roc on the air, calling it a "disturbing prospect to lose a series respected by the Black community."

Ultimately, a great deal of Roc's appeal could be attributed to its star, Charles Dutton. His career already had been one of the more fascinating in television. Born in Baltimore in 1951 and nicknamed Roc, the twelve-year-old Dutton, in and out of trouble, had been sent to reform school. Five years later, during a fight with another young Black man, Dutton had stabbed the man in self-defense. He was sentenced to five years in prison (with two years suspended) for manslaughter. After eighteen months, he was released. But later he was arrested and rein-carcerated for possession of a deadly weapon. While in solitary confine-ment, he read his first play, *Day of Absence* by African American playwright Douglas Turner Ward. Later he staged it with other inmates. His prison group also performed Shakespeare.

Upon his release, Dutton studied drama at Towson State University in Maryland. "For the first time I felt free," said Dutton. "But when I graduated in '78, my whole world stopped. Where do I go from here? By then I knew I was born to be an actor, but no one else knew that. I was terrified I'd end up back on the streets." For two years, he was adrift. Then a Towson professor suggested Dutton apply to the Yale drama school. To his surprise, Dutton was admitted to Yale in the fall of 1980. "One of my friends thought I said I was going to *jail* in Connecti-cut," said Dutton. " '*Yale*, stupid,' I told him. 'Sure, Roc, you're going to Yale.' " Three years later he graduated. Afterward he plowed ahead in search of work in the theater. The break came with a leading role in the Broadway production of August Wilson's *Ma Rainey's Black Bottom*. The critics hailed Dutton's electrifying performance.

Roc marked a new career direction for Dutton. Though his televi-sion performances were often stagy, he improved with time. Able to adroitly move from broad comedy to serious social comment, he cre-ated a man who seemed all heart, all fundamental decency; a character with everyday dreams and longings that many middle-class families could identify with.

Afterward Dutton continued to work in films (*Mississippi Masala, Cookie's Fortune, Nick of Time*) and such television programs as *Jack Reed: A Search for Justice, Zooman, True Women,* and *The Sixties.* He also directed *The Corner* for HBO in 2000.

Fox Television, however, out to land a ratings jackpot, veered away from socially committed Black humor as it aired a series of comedies aimed primarily at the young: *Martin, Townsend Television, Living Sin-gle, The Sinbad Show,* and *South Central.* Looking like a watered-down and sanitized version of *In Living Color, Townsend Television* was the brainchild of Robert Townsend, who previously had directed the film *Hollywood Shuffle*, a send-up of Black movie stereotypes. The series lasted only a few months.

South Central didn't do much better. Initially, creators Michael Weithorn and Ralph Farquhar developed the show for CBS. It was the story of a single African American woman struggling to raise her three children. The network wanted more comedy, less drama. "Make it a Black *Roseanne*," one CBS executive said. The network, said Weithorn, could not comprehend "the idea of poverty." On the pilot episode, the daughter Tasha pled for a special Cross Colours jacket, which her unemployed mother could not afford. Weithorn recalled, "We got notes asking, 'Why doesn't the mother put it on her credit card?' " Finally, CBS dropped plans to air the show. Fox picked it up. But the series never jelled. Jokes about gunfire in the 'hood fell flat. *South Central* would have worked better as a weekly drama.

Fox's dramatic sci-fi series *M.A.N.T.I.S.*, which starred Carl Lumbly as a brilliant scientist, also quickly expired.

MARTIN MANIA: THE RISE OF MARTIN LAWRENCE

But Fox hit pay dirt—and heated controversy—with the sitcom *Martin*. The series chronicled the adventures of Insane Martin Payne (Martin Lawrence), the host of a talk show at the Detroit radio station WZUP. Away from work, Martin pursues, beds, and eventually weds the girl of his dreams, Gina (Tisha Campbell), a marketing executive. Also around are Martin's friends Tommy (Thomas Mikal Ford) and Cole (Carl Anthony Payne Jr.) as well as Gina's secretary and close friend, Pam (Tichina Arnold). There were also such characters as Sheneneh Jenkins, Jerome, security guard Otis, and Martin's mother, Mrs. Payne, all of whom were played by Martin Lawrence.

Martin Lawrence was already known for his stand-up comedy. Lawrence had been born Martin Fitzgerald Lawrence (named, so he said, after Martin Luther King Jr. and John Fitzgerald Kennedy) in 1965 in Frankfurt, Germany, where his father, John, was stationed in the air force. By the time Martin was seven, his parents divorced. While his mother, Chlora, took her other children to live in Landover, Maryland, a suburb of Washington, D.C., Martin was left with his father but joined his siblings when he was in the third grade. To keep the family afloat, Chlora Lawrence worked various jobs as a cashier and in department stores.

TV's bad boy, Martin Lawrence

As a heavy, hyperactive kid nicknamed Chubby, Martin was so disruptive at school that his teachers sometimes permitted him to tell the class jokes if he promised to be quiet afterward. At home, Lawrence watched Jimmie Walker on *Good Times* (maybe that was his biggest mistake), Redd Foxx, and Richard Pryor, all of whom, along with Eddie Murphy, would be influences. "Richard taught me that honest emotions about sex could be really funny on stage," said Lawrence. Slimming down to some ninety pounds at age fifteen, he became a Golden Gloves boxer. Upon graduation from high school in 1984, he performed at local clubs while working as a janitor at a five-and-dime.

The big break came with a 1987 appearance on television's *Star Search*. Not long afterward, he won a supporting role in the syndicated series *What's Happening Now!!* Spike Lee cast him in *Do the Right Thing*. Then came roles in the movies *House Party* and *Boomerang*.

Lawrence continued performing stand-up comedy routines in which he created energetic minidramas, often centered on relationships. He acted all the parts. Discussing a variety of subjects from racism to the use of condoms, he could be both macho and sensitive. When addressing the subject of male sexual boasts, he seemed surprisingly candid. "Brothers, quit braggin' [about your equipment]," he once said. Then he confessed to being minimally endowed. "But I *work* with what I've got," he said. Audiences loved the honesty. "He is *so* large. He's like the first in a new wave of comics behind Robin Harris," said producer Russell Simmons. "He's part of a whole new generation that is a little freer. The energy is different. It's not shock humor. The language is so natural." Still, Lawrence was criticized for his "woman-hating" material. Often Lawrence could revel in graphic discussions about feminine hygiene, odors, and yeast infections.

His stand-up performances reached a wider audience when he became the host of HBO's sexually explicit *Def Comedy Jam*. In many respects, that series served as a launching pad for *Martin*. *Def Comedy Jam*'s executive producer, Stan Lathan, called him "a mirror of the current hip-hop generation. The kids are all trying to maintain this macho exterior even though they have a lot of inner sensitivity and insecurities."

Much as Lawrence had done in concerts, his sitcom *Martin* was intended as a new take on contemporary relationships and friendships, done with a hip-hop beat and rhythm. It also set out to comically dramatize the rather traditional sexual/gender attitudes of a young African American male. On its premiere episode, radio host Martin, who specializes in talk about romance and relationships, discussed male sensitivity on the air. When a male listener admits to crying, Martin gets his dander up. What is the world coming to? "You shave your face or your bikini line?" he asks. "Stand up, pull your pants down, man, and look at the front of your drawers. You're missing a flap, girlfriend." Throughout the series, the openly sexist Martin battled his girlfriend Gina for the upper hand. Though she fought him, and though Martin was sometimes made to look foolish, the series glorified rather than challenged his attitudes, not only with Gina but with the world at large.

From the start, the reviewers—to put it mildly—*hated* the series.

"Clearly, 'Martin' intends to mine the same misogynistic mucho-macho vein that is a hallmark of 'Def Comedy,' " wrote the *New York Post*'s Michele Greppi. "It deserves a deaf ear."

In the *Los Angeles Times*, television critic Howard Rosenberg wrote of the racism of a "world-class crude" episode in which an oversexed Martin struggles to forgo having sex—for two weeks—with his girl-friend, Gina. "Bumping, grinding and pawing, he was all over her in public—his body pumping like a piston, his tongue thrusting lewdly—acting generally like an animal. 'I'm telling you, baby, I gots to have it!' " At one point, as a desperate Martin tries to calm himself down, Gina discovers he is wearing an ice pack on his penis. "That the half hour was endorsed by Fox's standards and practices department for airing at all was bad enough," wrote Rosenberg. "That it was on at 8 p.m.—and thus potentially available to young kids galore—made it an even greater abomination." He added that perhaps "the bottom line here *is* the bottom line, that anything goes on Fox when it comes to making a buck."

Everything about the show seemed caricatured. In the first year, the primary set—Martin's living room—with its bold colors (purples, yel-lows, greens) looked like something out of a cartoon. The acting too was fast-paced and frenetic, with most cast members playing to the manic rhythm established by Lawrence. There never seemed to be a quiet moment when a character could relax and—heaven forbid—re-flect about what he/she was saying. Worse, the scripts presented the characters with too broad a stroke. Martin's friend Cole, with his over-sized clothes and his large hats, seemed so dim-witted that one won-dered how he survived in the world. Certainly, he didn't look as if he could function in any workplace; one more sign that Black males had nothing to contribute to establishment culture. (Watching actor Payne, viewers must have asked how an actor who was so appealing and re-freshing on *The Cosby Show* could have sunk so low. His saving grace was his vulnerability: he almost looked helpless. Somehow he never lost his fundamental charm.) On the other hand, Tommy appeared as if he *might* be on the ball; certainly he wasn't childlike like Cole and cer-tainly he had more common sense than Martin. But no one was sure where Tommy worked. Or if he worked at all. It was as bad as the situ-ation with Kingfish.

Then there was Gina's friend Pam, decked out in her tighter than skintight dresses while the camera gave viewers a lingering, leering look at her. She became the butt of Martin's repeated jokes. The two regularly traded insults. Of course, bickering Black couples were a staple of Black sitcoms: Kingfish and Sapphire; Fred Sanford and Aunt Esther; George Jefferson and Florence. But Sapphire was usually on Kingfish's back because of something stupid he had done. George Jefferson's criticism of Florence—for not being able to cook, for being lazy, or for being late—grew out of his belief that she failed to meet her responsibilities as an employee in his home. In turn, she criticized him for being cheap and pretentious.

But Martin's criticisms of Pam were usually tied to her looks. Or her attributes (or lack of) as a woman. He talked about her bad breath, her nappy hair, her figure—and compared her to a horse and a camel. "Why can't I find at least a half decent man?" Pam once asked Gina. "Don't you have any mirrors at home?" said Martin. Pam could match him in the insult department. She made fun of his size and other male inadequacies. For Martin, Gina was always the ideal woman; Pam, the unpleasant leftover, a disgrace to the other sex. Because of the casting, the subtext of the Martin/Pam spats seemed to comment on color. Once again, a lighter African American woman, Gina, played by the lighter actress Tisha Campbell, was the dreamgirl; Pam, played by the browner Tichina Arnold, became a Black woman who cannot meet certain physical standards. As much as Martin yelled and screamed at Pam, he could never directly refer to her color as a sign of her lack of beauty. Never could he call her a *dark* heifer or a *Black* witch. That would have alienated the African American viewer. But for many, color preference was tied in to those battles. In this respect, *Martin* could be pernicious and poisonous.

The characters played by Lawrence himself were the most blatant caricatures. The jivey Jerome, who looked like a reject from *Superfly*, was as sexist as Martin. One afternoon when he eyed Gina walking off with Pam, he felt compelled to *compliment* her by saying, "Girl, you sure is *swollen*." Unlike Richard Pryor, who could uncover the pathos or pain inside his winos and junkies, Lawrence could never invest a character like Jerome with any insights. At the same time, as his character Mother Emma Payne badgered and blasted Gina (whom she felt was totally inappropriate for her baby Martin), she was one more old-style mammy, a direct descendant of Sapphire's Mama.

Much the same might be said of Sheneneh, one of Lawrence's best-known creations. Living across the hall from Martin, Sheneneh sashayed about wearing opulent extensions in her hair, tight short skirts to emphasize her bulging hips and bodacious backside, tight blouses to showcase her ample breasts. Like Martin's mother, she despised Gina.

Part of the cruel fun was watching Sheneneh dump on Gina and other women. On one episode, the conniving Sheneneh took advantage of Gina and forced her to work in Sheneneh's Sho' Nuf Hair Salon. All sorts of comic horrors transpire here. First Gina was told she must have a professional look. The next thing we know, we see Gina *coiffed* in out-sized curly braids. A customer, Mira, said she needed a pedicure because her corns were fixing to pop. "Why don't you take your shoes off, so we can get started," she was told. "They are off," the woman answered. Sheneneh then used an electric power tool to work on the woman's feet.

Shortly afterward, Mira told Gina, "Look, I got to get my perm. I can't sit here all day. I got *mens* waiting to see me." Gina gave her a perm but without a neutralizer. Mira ended up practically bald, except for patches of hair above her ears and long hair in the back. Sheneneh, however, persuaded Mira that she looked stylish. But Sheneneh let Gina know that Mira "was tore up from the floor up. I damn near threw up."

Throughout, *Martin*'s misogyny was apparent (and, sadly, part of the appeal for some misguided males). The series delighted in turning Sheneneh and other women (with the notable exception of Gina and perhaps Pam) into grotesque figures; objects of tawdry jokes and scorn. With her extensions, her eye pops, her competitive attitude toward Gina and other women, Sheneneh was a ribald parody of a pushy, know-it-all, forever attitudinizing, desperately trying-to-be-hip, always-in-your-face young urban Black woman.

Yet *Martin* quickly emerged as a very popular hit. Perhaps young viewers were drawn in by the simple fact that *Martin* was far franker about sex (and the fact that the hero had to have it) than previous Black sitcoms. At times, Martin, like other Black male characters on sitcoms, seemed a tad obsessed with sex. But for viewers, what distinguished Martin was indeed the relationship with Gina. The story line of three of the most popular earlier episodes centered on Martin and Gina as they fought, broke up, and then got back together. Before the final episode, viewers were invited to vote, via a 900 number, on which of the two should apologize. The verdict: Martin should get on his knees. Viewers were always willing to forgive him his trespasses. Hip, loose, free, and very up-front about his desires, he may have struck the young as being an assault (much like Kingfish) on traditional, polite bourgeois society.

Another aspect of his appeal—though his critics would be loath to admit it—was that Martin had a joie de vivre that was infectious; he was something of the indomitable optimist (the opposite of the beleaguered, sometimes cornered Kingfish) with catchphrases that encapsulated his energy and perspective on life. "You go, girl!" "You so crazy!" "Wass Up!" and "Don't go there" caught on and entered the popular lexicon of people who didn't even know of the series.

Martin Lawrence's looks no doubt led viewers not only to feel sorry for him but also to patronize him. Thin and short with large eyes and protruding ears, he was never anyone's idea of a hunk (which, of course, made his slams against Pam seem all the more absurd). All mouth, he was a fiercely unthreatening hero. In this respect, he was obviously similar to Sherman Hemsley's George Jefferson but without the charm or wily intelligence and without the wicked way of turning a line inside out. Martin Lawrence usually bopped and hopped his way through a performance, using his energy rather than any acting talent to create his character. Nonetheless, had the character Martin been tall, muscular, deep-voiced, less hyper, he might have been scary and totally unacceptable. No one would sit by and listen to a buck figure express some of the sexist sentiments of a Martin.

For the same reason, Lawrence no doubt succeeded with his characters Sheneneh, Jerome, and Mama Payne. Despite the fact that they're cruel parodies, they're such outlandish clowns that it's hard not to laugh at them, even though you do so at your own peril. In the minds of viewers, these characters were all the same person: It's Martin—the perpetual runty adolescent—dressed up in the clothes and makeup of Mommy and her friends. You almost feel sorry for this overcaffeinated adolescent's desperate need to get attention—by any means necessary. Yet viewers were always drawn to him. Later in movies like *Life*, Lawrence also extended his talents as an actor.

The demographics indicated that *Martin* was popular with those

18- to 49-year-old viewers that pleased advertisers. To appeal to them even more, the series featured such guest stars as rappers Snoop Doggy Dogg and Biggie Smalls as well as football star Randall Cunningham. But the series also found favor with even younger viewers. *Martin* ranked in the top five among viewers age 12 to 17 and in the top ten with ages 2 to 11. "I'm huge with the under-5 crowd," said star Martin Lawrence. One only wonders about the ideas those poor kids came away with.

As *Martin* continued its run, it was toned down. Later episodes were better, yet more traditional television fare, at times as much influenced by *I Love Lucy* as episodes of *227* and *Amen*. A memorable episode featured Marla Gibbs as an exacting drill sergeant of a housekeeper determined to make Martin and Gina stick to a schedule. The episode played on our knowledge of Gibbs's TV career from the days of *The Jeffersons* to *227*. In some episodes, Judyann Elder and J. A. Preston had funny bits as the parents of Gina. Here the series touched on class friction within the African American community. Some characters on *Martin* almost started to look like actual human beings.

In time, viewers became as familiar with the off-screen Martin Lawrence as with the character he played. The success of the series and the new fame that grew out of it appeared to take a toll on him. He became a favorite of the gossips and the tabloids. In 1993, the press reported that he dumped his manager and co-creator of *Martin*, Topper Carew. The next year, a story broke that Lawrence had failed to perform concert dates in Cleveland, Atlanta, and Buffalo. Lawrence, along with his agent and tour promoter, was sued for fraud and breach of contract for the cancellation of the concerts. Later came news that Lawrence had been arrested after he stood at a busy Los Angeles intersection, screaming and ranting incoherently at passersby. Police discovered that he was carrying a concealed weapon. Another arrest came in August 1996 at California's Burbank airport. There he was charged with carrying a loaded handgun in his luggage. Most damaging to his professional image was a sexual harassment suit filed by his TV co-star Tisha Campbell. Campbell left the show but later returned just before its last episodes were filmed.

By the fifth season, the overall ratings for *Martin* plunged. It ranked number 106 out of approximately 130 shows. Yet Lawrence's Black constituency stuck with the program. It was the third most watched show by African Americans. Still, that couldn't save it. Fox dropped the sit-com in August 1997. Afterward its reruns scored well in syndication.

SISTA FRIENDLY: QUEEN LATIFAH AND *LIVING SINGLE*

Fox's other hit sitcom was *Living Single,* which focused on a group of young professional African American women. At the center was Khadi-jah James (Queen Latifah), the editor of her own magazine *Flavor* (or *Flava*). Living with her were her secretary and cousin Synclaire (Kim Coles) and their friend Regine (Kim Fields), who worked at a woman's boutique. Often hanging out in the apartment was another friend, a lawyer named Maxine (Erika Alexander). Upstairs were the roommates Kyle (T. C. Carson), an egotistical financial planner, and Overton (John Henton), a handyman. Initially influenced by *Designing Women, Living Single* also anticipated the super-hit *Friends.* Here too was a comic commentary on the relationships of a group of young friends, who spent a great deal of time together, sharing their passions and enthusi-asms, their doubts and goals.

Queen Latifah, a high priestess of hip-hop who
unexpectedly became a television star

The critics were not kind to the show. "Though all the roommates have college degrees and upscale jobs," wrote Harry Waters in *Newsweek*, "they behave like man-crazy Fly Girls." Bill Cosby also was critical. "Suppose I did a sitcom about four African-American women like Fox's *Living Single*?" he said. "In my show, two of them might be sitting around discussing men all the time. But the other two women are going someplace: something else is happening in their lives. Is that too much to ask?"

No, it wasn't. There was much to complain about. Not only did *Living Single* seem taken up with too much talk about romance and sex, but some of the characters were also blatant gender stereotypes. Like her predecessor Sandra on *227*, Kim Fields's Regine was forever on the prowl for a man with money. Those who had enjoyed Fields as Tootie on *Facts of Life* asked wistfully where that sweet teenager had gone.

Even ditzier was Synclaire, who harked back (as did Regine) to movie and TV fixtures of the 1950s: Synclaire was part Marilyn Monroe, part Jayne Mansfield, and part Marie Wilson on TV's *My Friend Irma*. Part of her was also *Three's Company*'s Suzanne Somers. Not much about the character seemed original. You had to ask why a Black woman on television should be stuck with a white woman's formulaic leftovers. At the same time, Overton was a warm-hearted dunce.

Often Erika Alexander's Maxine seemed to break past molds. A divorce attorney, she was smart, shrewd, articulate. The series also tried to say something more serious about Max when she developed a drinking problem and lost her job. Yet Max's strength was often undercut by the antics the scripts put her through. Namely, she was a foodaholic, gobbling up just about anything in sight. Each time you saw her stuff something into her mouth, you winced, for the actress as much as for the character. It was one more feeble attempt at presenting a character with "lovable" idiosyncrasies.

Yet formulaic television that it was, *Living Single* could grow on you. Once Synclaire and Overton saw stars in one another's eyes, they became a very amusing, nutty pair, splendidly attuned to one another's rhythm and perspective. They gave love a good name. And when Max and Kyle (who later became lovers) verbally sparred with one another, it was a pop/hip-hop version of Beatrice and Benedict.

But *Living Single*'s most interesting character was Queen Latifah's Khadijah, who injected a new sensibility into the old formula. By the time she hit the airwaves, Queen Latifah already was a heroine for record buyers. Born Dana Owens, the daughter of a police officer father and a high school art teacher mother, she grew up in East Orange, New Jersey. Something of a tomboy accustomed to doing things girls were not supposed to do, she was a power forward on her high school basketball team. As a teenager, Dana took the Arabic name Latifah, which means "delicate and sensitive," because she felt it defined the real person inside her that few saw. Later she audaciously added the Queen. With two friends, she formed a rhyming group called Ladies Fresh.

Upon graduating from high school in 1987, she worked as a cashier at Burger King and The Wiz. She also briefly attended Manhattan Community College, wrote songs, and performed rap with local groups. Through a friend, one of her demo tapes fell into the hands of MTV host Fab 5 Freddy. Not long afterward she won a record contract. In 1989 her album *All Hail the Queen* was released. It was a smash. Later she had another hit with *Black Reign*.

Some in the rap world griped that she wasn't edgy or daring. "Latifah's not a revolutionary. She's a pop artist," said James Bernard, the executive editor of the rap magazine *Source*. "Which isn't bad, but it's not [as if she were] Ice Cube." Still, in the male-dominated world of rap, here came the conquering Queen, a young woman almost six feet tall (and proud of it) who wore African-style power turbans. On stage, she was all confidence and self-assertion, a bodacious sista sending out the word that the brothers better take stock. She was a hip-hop feminist of sorts, and her songs "Ladies First," "Fly Girl," and "The Evil That Men Do" clicked with female listeners. Later she had a hit titled "U.N.I.T.Y. (Who You Calling a Bitch?)." Latifah also pursued an acting career and won roles in the movies *Jungle Fever* and *House Party 2*.

When she came to television in *Living Single*, Queen Latifah carried her rap image with her. She automatically represented a hip, postfeminist young African American woman, who was upwardly mobile and economically secure. Yet the scripts sometimes drew Khadijah as a traditional nurturer as she counseled the other women on their problems. For a time, it also didn't look as if she'd have a love life. Once she finally had a successful relationship, it was with a man in the music promotion business who was often away. Sometimes, too, the writers made unexpected mistakes, undervaluing the independence of the character and the actress. On one episode, Khadijah depends on Kyle to help her maintain a budget. Why would a woman who runs her own magazine need a man to tell her how to manage her money? Still, her character was the most mature of the lot, and the anchor in the series.

Created and executive-produced by Yvette Lee Bowser (formerly a writer for *A Different World*), *Living Single* steadily improved, becoming for a time the number one show with Black viewers. Sometimes it focused on more serious social issues, as in the episode on which Khadijah was accused of sexual harassment by a male employee whom she had fired.

A mix of TV-style generations at the wedding of the characters
Overton and Synclaire on Living Single: *(back row)*
Queen Latifah, T. C. Carson, Erika Alexander, Kim Fields, and
(front row) Antonio Fargas (Huggy Bear of Starsky *and* Hutch*),*
Gladys Knight, John Henton, Kim Coles, Denise Nicholas,
and Ron O'Neal (of Superfly*)*

The look of the women proved important to Black viewers. Latifah and Kim Coles, both of whom might be described as full-figured women, seemed comfortable with their bodies—their hips, their breasts. Also comfortable with those bodies was the camera, which never turned the women into physically grotesque heroines as had been the case with heavier women on other series. Nor did *Living Single* fall into a color trap; it never adhered to the light-bright beauty standards of a *Martin.*

Martin and *Living Single* ran into the late years of the decade. They were joined by a lineup of other Black-oriented sitcoms: *The Gregory Hines Show, Arsenio Hall* (starring Hall with Vivica A. Fox), *Getting Personal* (with Vivica A. Fox and Duane Martin), *Skip Chaser,* and *The Hughleys.* All except *The Hughleys* expired quickly. Throughout the decade, other series featured offbeat Black supporting characters. On the Linda Bloodworth-Thomason series *Hearts Afire,* the liberal white character Georgie travels and lives with the Black woman who raised her, Miss Lula (Beah Richards). Another character refers to her as Georgie's mammy. On another Bloodworth-Thomason series, *Evening Shade,* which was set in the South and starred Burt Reynolds, Ossie Davis was cast as the philosophical Ponder Blue (the proprietor of the Ponder Blue Barbecue Villa, where the locals hang out), who narrated the series. On both Bloodworth-Thomason series, the African American characters seemed to have been created mainly to certify the liberalism of key white characters. (That also might be said of the character Anthony on *Designing Women.*) But as James Wolcott pointed out, the bizarre Miss Lula doesn't even seem to do that; instead, in the first episode, "she's an exhibit from the Colored Museum, stored upstairs for safekeeping." Robert Guillaume played a testy executive producer of a nightly cable sports news show on *Sports News.* On the Michael J. Fox political sitcom *Spin City,* actor Michael Boatman played a gay assistant in the office of the city's mayor. At a time when there was such a hullabaloo about the lesbian character Ellen on the sitcom *Ellen,* the Boatman character functioned weekly with nary a word said.

TOUCHED BY AN ANGEL: A HEAVENLY NURTURER TAKES FLIGHT

But none of these characters had the impact of Della Reese on *Touched by an Angel.* By this time in her career, sixty-one-year-old Della Reese, though not yet a full-fledged TV star, was known to viewers. She had been a performer for almost fifty years. Born Deloreese Patricia Early, she had grown up in Detroit, the daughter of steel mill workers. As a child, she began to sing. But her great joy was going to the movies with her mother, whom she adored. Later she was surprised to learn that the woman she thought was her mother was actually her grandmother. At age thirteen, the precocious Deloreese toured with gospel star Mahalia Jackson's singing group. When she later performed on her own, she used the professional name Della Reese. For years, she did not seem to be getting anywhere with her career. That changed when her pop single "Don't You Know" became a hit. But the real break came when Ed Sullivan took a professional interest in her career. He featured Reese frequently on his variety show, introducing her to the television audience.

Della Reese as star of Touched by an Angel *with Roma Downey, and earlier in her career with Mike Douglas on* The Mike Douglas Show

Reese also played Vegas, where she faced the same discrimination as other African American stars of the era. "In those days, Black entertainers could work on the Strip but we couldn't go in the casino, nor could we eat or sleep in those hotels," she recalled. "The only place to stay was all the way across town at a hotel aptly named the Dust Bowl." Once while appearing at a Vegas club with an Ed Sullivan revue, she ordered a slice of cheesecake for her dressing room. But the establishment refused to place her order. Sullivan himself intervened. Reese recalled that every night thereafter, Sullivan and his wife took her for a late meal to an all-white restaurant, where the other diners always stared.

Reese had her share of personal problems. After an abusive first marriage, she suffered a near-fatal accident. After her recovery, she suffered a massive aneurysm. Again her physicians were not sure she would live, and if so, if she would regain her memory or be able to speak. Yet miraculously she pulled through. Reese also faced financial difficulties—and mounting problems with the IRS.

Her career underwent its greatest change when nightclubs went out of vogue and musical tastes changed. She then searched for acting roles. "I had good training for it. I was always a stylist, a lyricist. I became acquainted with the words in order to convince you I must believe in what I'm singing," she said. "That's what acting is: believing. It was just like one thing flowing into another. It was finding another rhythm so you could take the music out." But her acting career went nowhere until African American casting director Reuben Cannon secured her a role on an episode of *The Mod Squad*. In 1969, she also became the first African American woman to host her own syndicated talk show, *Della*. Later she was the first woman to host *The Tonight Show*. "I worked my way up, step by step, bit by bit," said Reese. Gradually, she won regular roles in the series *Chico and the Man*, *It Takes Two* (on which she played a judge), *Charlie & Co.* (as the feisty Aunt Rachel), and *The Royal Family*. She made guest appearances on *Designing Women*, *L.A. Law*, and *Night Court*. By the 1990s, television viewers knew Reese, not as the svelte, glamorous torch singer of the Sullivan years, but as an older, larger, sometimes boisterous and sharp-tongued, sometimes lusty middle-aged woman. That proved perfect for *Touched by an Angel*.

Touched by an Angel seemed part soap saga, part inspirational uplift tale. Weekly, a trio of angels (originally, it was just two) went undercover, posing as nurses or teachers or whatever, as they entered the lives of troubled, often desperate people. Two parents, unable to accept the death of their son, chewed away at one another until the angels showed them the light. A terminally ill man found relief for his passage into the next world only after the angels appeared. Actress Roma Downey played the younger angel, Monica, who always looked as if she was new on the job and had to learn the ropes. Reese played the older Tess, a heavenly supervisor of sorts who *don't take no nonsense, honey, from nobody.* A third angel, played by John Dye, balanced the two, although he was also mindful of his manners when around Tess.

When *Touched by an Angel* first aired on Wednesdays opposite *Roseanne*, it was clobbered in the ratings. The critics dismissed it too. "It's so goody-goody and lovey-dovey," said Tom Shales of *The Washington Post*, "[and] such a throwback to something Michael Landon did much better [in the 1980s series *Highway to Heaven*]." But somehow *Touched by an Angel* survived, was rescheduled for Saturday evenings to come after *Dr. Quinn, Medicine Woman*, and won a following. When CBS made the bold move of scheduling it at eight o'clock on Sunday evenings, following *60 Minutes*, *Touched by an Angel* soared in the ratings, hitting the number two spot and thereafter usually landing in the top ten.

Seeing Reese as Tess, some may have felt that Beulah had simply gone on to heaven. During the credits, Tess wrapped her arms lovingly around young Monica. Reese's voice was heard on the soundtrack singing "Walk by Me." *Touched by an Angel* succeeded for an age apparently in need of some pop enlightenment and that stressed the idea of spiritual regeneration. Much of its appeal could also be attributed to Reese. Viewers may not have known the particulars of Della Reese's story (as they had decades before with Ethel Waters). But Reese projected the headstrong strength of someone who, having suffered, will no longer suppress her feelings or ideals—and who also will brook no bull from anyone. Yet she also seemed fair, decent, and, as was true of the archetype that Tess embodied, comforting.

Later generations may find the series sentimental and hokey to the core. But viewers of the 1990s still responded to the *people* on-screen (the messages or personal histories emanating from them) as much as to their characters. Even at the end of the century, viewers still seemed to want their all-knowing, all-seeing, all-hearing, all-understanding Black earth mother figures. *Touched by an Angel* revitalized Reese's career, leading to roles in such TV movies as *Big Brother Jake*, *A Match Made in Heaven*, and *Mama Flora's Family*.

THOSE UPSTARTS: UPN AND WB

By the later years of the 1990s, the three major networks lost interest in Black series—and generally in the African American audience as well.

But eyeing Fox's success with *Martin* and *Living Single*, two upstart networks, WB and UPN, each founded in 1995, built their power bases on Black or "ethnic" programming, or, as some industry insiders called it, "narrow-casting." Programmers at these two new networks were aware that shows designed for African American audiences appealed not only to Black and urban viewers (the group that watched the most television) but often enough to a young white audience too. "Younger viewers—kids and teens—see a lot of trends starting with Blacks in music and other forms of entertainment," said Steven Sternberg, a senior partner with BJK7E Media, a buying service for advertisers. Hopeful of being in on the new trends, the kids watched the Black shows.

Thus, while the major networks assumed that Black programming was the kiss of death, the upstarts capitalized on it. UPN aired such series as *Moesha, Malcolm & Eddie, Sparks, Goode Behavior, Homeboys in Outer Space, Good News*, and *Between Brothers*. When NBC dropped the sitcom *In the House*, UPN picked it up. WB's series included *The Wayans Bros., The Jamie Foxx Show, The Steve Harvey Show, Smart Guy*, and *The Parent 'Hood*. When ABC dumped *Sister, Sister* and when NBC dropped *For Your Love*, WB aired the shows. It was a striking cultural phenomenon. But critics cried that Black programs were being ghettoized on these networks and that the African American audience was being exploited with an array of old-style stereotypes.

The quality of the shows varied. Most had dim-witted stories and characters. A series like *Goode Behavior* starred Sherman Hemsley as a jailbird con man who was released on parole. Where does he have to live? In the house of his son, a college professor (Dorien Wilson). Not an especially funny situation. And did viewers need to see yet another Black con? *Sparks* starred James Avery as an attorney who heads a "walk-in law firm" with his two dense sons (Miguel A. Nunez and Terrence Howard), who spend most of their time panting for a sexy lawyer played by Robin Givens. ("Sexist Malarkey," said *Entertainment Weekly*.) *Good News* centered on a young minister (David Ramsey) who takes over an exuberant congregation eager to perform gospel songs in praise of the Lord. Lead actor Ramsey proved appealing. The music was fine. But the whole affair would have been better had it simply been a Sunday morning gospel hour.

Other series were no better. *The Jamie Foxx Show* cast its star Foxx as a young man who, while trying to break into show business, works at the hotel owned by his aunt (Ellia English) and testy uncle (Garrett Morris). While no one could ever accuse Foxx of lacking energy and drive, he often looked desperate as he tried injecting life into humorless dialogue. On one episode, when he had to explain how he got a ride from a train station, he was saddled with some unspeakable lines. "I caught this ride, you know, with two brothers . . . ," he said, "they was in a white Ford Bronco, had a police escort . . . everybody was waving, you know. It was like they knew me. They had signs talking 'bout 'Go O. Jamie.' " Could it get any worse? Unfortunately, yes.

There was also *The Wayans Bros.* Dumb and Dumber was one thing. Dumber and Dumbest was another. Focusing on the misadventures of two nitwit brothers, the series revolved around gags and jokes about women and bathrooms. Playing the father of the two was John Witherspoon. Everything about him was crude, lewd, vulgar. Here was another talented comic trapped in unimaginative material.

Like *Martin*, most of these shows centered on young urban males. Most were horny. Most were sexist. Most were almost neurotically energetic. The women were comic foils. While the older ones were often the heavy, nurturing mamas, the younger ones were usually required to do little more than strut about in the requisite short, tight dresses. Sometimes they had attitude as they peddled the independent woman line. But after one look at the young women, you knew what they were there for. When viewers saw an actress like the stunner Garcelle Beauvais on a program like *The Jamie Foxx Show*, they could only shake their heads and ask, "Is this what becomes of a sophisticated, sexy African American woman?"

On many of these shows, African American cultural references and vernacular flew all over the place. Even a comment about Puffy (Sean Puffy Combs) or Left Eye (of the singing group TLC) on an episode of *The Steve Harvey Show* was no doubt a reference that the major networks might have found (at the time) too obscure for mainstream viewers. In time, many of the cultural references were to earlier Black television programs (rather than African American social or political figures). Still, young African American audiences understood such references. Like African American viewers of the past when watching Eddie "Rochester" Anderson on *The Jack Benny Show* or Amanda Randolph on *The Danny Thomas Show*, they responded to the rhythm and attitude of the performers; the way they used language, gestures, mannerisms—a whole assortment of cultural signs—to communicate. These were great points of identification for African American viewers. But unlike some earlier Black television performers, the new ones too often pushed language and mannerisms to an extreme, dangerously close to caricature. Here *less* definitely would have been more. The new shows also often failed to establish a real context for any of this seemingly unleashable energy.

There were some exceptions. *Sister, Sister,* which starred real-life twins Tia and Tamera Mowry, was a fairly earnest show about Black teenage girls coming of age. Playing their parents were those TV veterans of an earlier age (the 1980s!) Jackee Harry and Tim Reid. What a pleasure it must have been for Jackee to finally shed some of her man-crazy, money-hungry antics. She even directed episodes of the show. *Smart Guy* also had its appeal. The brother of the Mowry twins, Tahj Mowry, starred as a child prodigy who ends up in high school with his older siblings. *The Parent 'Hood,* starring Robert Townsend, was another Black family comedy.

One of the better new shows was *Moesha.* Created by Ralph Farquhar (who had developed *South Central*), Sara V. Finney, and Vida Spears, the series told the story of a teenager with the expected teen problems of boys, dating, parents, school, sex. Starring teenage singing star Brandy in the title role, *Moesha* dramatized its events from the point of view of its heroine rather than from that of the parents (as was the case with *The Cosby Show*).

On one episode, Moesha decides to lose her virginity. But she knows not to do so without taking precautions. Discussing the matter with her girlfriends, she's surprised to learn that one has already done the dirty deed. Later Moesha consults a physician for advice and contraceptives. Upon learning that the teenager is on birth-control pills, Moesha's stepmother is shocked and hurt that the girl did not discuss anything with her. She also doesn't want Moesha to become sexually active at this point in her life. Always, *Moesha* stressed that its heroine could talk to her parents (Sheryl Lee Ralph and William Allen Young), even though she might not realize it at first. Though her boyfriend is already sexually experienced, ultimately the episode kept its heroine chaste. Moesha decides she wants to wait. Here *Moesha* clearly maintained that old double standard. But, frankly, its audience preferred it that way.

Later in its run, *Moesha* attempted to deal more seriously with its characters when the father's nephew Dorien (Ray J) comes to live with the family. But Dorien, Moesha, and the rest of the family are stunned to learn that Dorien is actually the illegitimate son of Moesha's father. The episodes dramatizing the revelation skillfully walked that delicate tightrope, focusing on a serious subject without trivializing it. The series was one of the few programs that sensitively dramatized the experiences of an African American teenage girl. For a spell, *Moesha* became one of UPN's most popular series. It led to a spin-off, the ribald sitcom *The Parkers*, starring Countess Vaughn and that skilled comedienne Mo'Nique.

Regardless of the quality of the programs, they reached their intended audience. While NBC had 14 percent more white households tuning in than Black ones, UPN drew 52 percent more African American households than white ones. Fox had 105 percent more Black homes. The WB network had an astounding 586 percent higher Black viewership. Ultimately, the new networks also revealed a clear split in viewing habits of the nation, Black and white. While such shows as *Seinfeld, Friends,* and *Frasier* were among the top ten for white viewers, they scored at the bottom of the list in Black homes.

At one point, *The Steve Harvey Show* (another of the better shows) was the number one program for Black viewers. Comedian Steve Harvey played Steve Hightower, a former lead singer in a soul group, who becomes a high school music teacher in Chicago. There, he matches wits with the school's principal, Regina (Wendy Raquel Robinson), and a lineup of other characters: Cedric (played by Cedric "The Entertainer"), the overweight sports coach; Lovita (Terri J. Vaughn), the principal's simp secretary, who becomes involved with Cedric (and later marries him); and the student Romeo (Merlin Santana), a not very bright ladies' man. The two important white characters—the students Bullethead and Lydia—were often the silliest in the cast but very appealing nonetheless. In some respects, Harvey's Hightower was the most mature male character on these new sitcoms. Yet at times his adult image was undercut by his language and attitudes. On an episode when he's concerned about his young niece, he discusses the matter with the principal, Regina, saying, "She just ain't like a regular teenager. She don't talk back. She don't roll her eyes." Though generally his rhythmic use of Black vernacular is appealing and a

The Steve Harvey Show, *scoring number one with African American viewers but almost unknown by the general television audience*

clear cultural sign, one is still grateful that he doesn't teach English. Often, too, as was true of past Black-cast sitcoms, the female lead character, Regina, is more sensible and mature than Hightower. Yet the writers frequently depicted Regina as being rather uptight. Hightower's sexism often went unchallenged. Still, for most episodes, African American director Stan Lathan kept the show moving at a brisk pace, and the actors held on to their dignity. And on some episodes, an African American female writer like Josslyn Luckett created more engaging dialogue and perspectives for the female characters on the show.

Yet, successful as *The Steve Harvey Show* was with Black audiences, most white viewers didn't even know of its existence. The same was true of many other Black-cast series, such as UPN's *Between Brothers*, which at one point also scored number one in Black households. All these programs on the alternative networks were still pitched at young viewers. WB admitted that the demographic it sought was the 18- to 34-year-old viewers.

For older African American viewers (those in their thirties and above) and more educated ones in search of more adult fare, the Black-cast shows presented a too narrow, too reductive definition of Black life—as little more than an urban, jivey, jokester experience. But mainly, simply by the fact that they were sitcoms, the new shows still promoted the idea, as had the shows of earlier decades, that for Black Americans life was a laughfest.

WORKPLACE DRAMAS, ENSEMBLE CASTS, 1990s STYLE

More serious African American characters and situations—which indeed appealed to older, more educated African American viewers—turned up on the hour-long dramatic series of the 1990s: such programs as *N.Y.P.D. Blue*, *Law & Order*, *Homicide: Life on the Streets*, *ER*, *New York Undercover*, *Chicago Hope*, *Brooklyn South*, *Third Watch*, and *The Practice*. (Or HBO's *Oz*.) For the most part, these were well-written, well-directed, and tensely acted programs in which issues of race were sometimes examined. Yet good as the programs were, Black viewers often yearned to know more about the Black characters. In a series like David Kelley's *The Practice*, the Black lawyers Eugene and Rebecca often appeared deracialized; the series rarely commented on race as a factor in their lives. In fact, it dramatized little about their personal lives. Viewers knew that Eugene had a son. But episodes were not developed around Eugene's personal situation until well into the run of the series. At that time, his teenage son Kendall was arrested on a drug charge. Afterward Eugene's ex-wife took him to court, seeking full custody of the boy. The actors on Kelley's series—Steve Harris, Lisa Gay Hamilton, as well as Lisa Nicole Carson and Jesse Martin on *Ally McBeal*—were strong enough to create credible characters. But where these characters came from culturally was anybody's guess.

On such series as *Law & Order* and *N.Y.P.D. Blue*, the African American characters were too often confined to the sidelines. The long-running *Law & Order* included Black actor Richard Brooks as assistant district attorney Paul Robinette in its original cast. But only after Brooks, having left the series, returned for a guest appearance did viewers get to see Robinette actually try a case. Apparently in an attempt to appeal more to female viewers, the Robinette character was replaced by a female assistant district attorney in the series's fourth season. Also brought in to play police lieutenant Anita Van Buren was S. Epatha Merkerson, a stage-trained African American actress who had appeared on Broadway in *The Piano Lesson* and in Spike Lee's film *She's Gotta Have It*. Brisk, intelligent, and sensitive, she quickly emerged as one of the more intriguing Black female characters on episodic television.

The early days of N.Y.P.D. Blue *with David Caruso as Detective John Kelly and the underused James McDaniel as Lieutenant Arthur Fancy*

Many viewers probably waited for "special" episodes that would focus on her. On the episode *Black Tie*, Van Buren had to deal with Detective Mike Logan's discomfort at having a woman in charge. On another, *Competence*, Van Buren briefly moved center stage. While at an ATM machine, she was held up by two teens. Pulling out her revolver, she ended up killing another teen, a mentally handicapped boy. As the case was investigated, her professionalism was questioned within the department. She also had to face the dead boy's mother: one African American woman trying to explain her tragic mistake to another. Merkerson and Black actress Lisa Louise Langfold played the scene beautifully, subtly shading it without overdrawn histrionics. But usually Merkerson seemed underused.

"Why am I in a position of authority yet you rarely see me on-screen?" actress Merkerson once complained. "You can write stories for me without them necessarily being about a Black issue, but it never happens that way." Aware that her Van Buren could always be counted on for counseling and common sense, Merkerson was also conscious of the character's earth mother qualities. "I think that's why Van Buren has been made Black and female," she said, adding that the earth mother was "another role we tend to find ourselves in: 'Come and tell me the problems and I'll help you out.' You know, 'Come sit on Mammy's knee.'"

With its minimalist scripts (sticking mainly to the story at hand with few diversions) and with its use of handheld cameras (early episodes were shot by cinematographer Ernest Dickerson), *Law & Order* had a documentary feel that lifted it above the ranks of general episodic television. To its credit, *Law & Order* was willing to focus on complex racial issues. One episode that examined a case of sexual harassment seemed drawn from the Anita Hill/Clarence Thomas headlines. Yet it was dramatized in an unexpected way. Regina Taylor guest-starred as a woman who accused her former boss, now a prominent liberal white city councilman, of having demanded sex in return for a partnership at his law firm. In her courtroom testimony, Taylor's character spoke chillingly of her humiliation. But then the script shrewdly moved from a comment on gender issues in the workplace to racial ones. Still another episode drew on the riots in Brooklyn's Crown Heights. A Black adolescent was killed in a hit-and-run accident. But the Jewish driver of the car was not indicted. Afterward a Black minister (no doubt inspired by New York's Reverend Al Sharpton) led a protest. A riot ensued in which an Italian man, mistaken for the Jewish driver, was killed by a young Black man. The African American lawyer Shambala Green (a recurring character played by Lorraine Toussaint) defended the youth. Ultimately, the episode commented on the once bonded, now strained, relations between the African American and Jewish communities. Another episode, which focused on the assassination of an African American leader, possibly by an organization fighting for the rights of African Americans, called to mind the assassination of Malcolm X—and the past rumors of the Nation of Islam's involvement. Later in its run, *Law & Order* added African American actor Jesse L. Martin to its cast.

Among the characters on Steven Bochco's *N.Y.P.D. Blue* was the African American police lieutenant Arthur Fancy (James McDaniel). Though the series explored the troubled private lives of its cop heroes, usually little of Fancy's life was dramatized. Generally, Fancy was depicted as a taciturn, exacting, strictly-by-the-book officer who once fired a detective who had an affair with an informant. Co-creator David Milch felt that Fancy was a character "who, by his own account, says he has trained himself not to want things he can't have, which in a way is one of the strategies of Blacks in America." But Milch was also aware of the limitations of the role. "We knew it would be a feat of acting to sustain such a character over the first episodes, [but] Jimmy is like a Zen actor," said Milch. "He accomplishes an enormous amount with a minimal amount of effort." "[Fancy] has a certain type of sanity the others don't," said actor McDaniel. "I can provide exposition the others can't. To a certain extent it's boring stuff, but it's challenging for me as an actor."

But on some sequences, he was featured more prominently as the series sought to examine the feelings of a Black man in a profession considered hostile and unjust to African American men. At one point, a Black character berated Fancy, saying, "You ain't nothing but an Uncle Tom." Fancy himself questioned his role as a Black cop in the police department, especially when he was faced with Officer Andy Sipowicz's racism.

N.Y.P.D. Blue was rather bold in depicting Sipowicz—one of its central characters—as a man who struggled not only with his alcoholism but with his racial attitudes as well. This was best dramatized in an episode when Sipowicz has a heated confrontation with another Black character. The angry Black man yells at Sipowicz, "I don't have to go anywhere with you. You're dealing with that one nigger in a thousand who knows what you can and cannot do." Sipowicz responds, without thinking, we assume: "I'm dealing with the nigger whose big mouth is responsible for this mess." The scene was written in such a way that many viewers may have felt Sipowicz was provoked into using the word.

Nonetheless, the episode reveals—in a rather self-congratulatory way—the more acceptable responses of other characters. Sipowicz's partner, Bobby Simone (Jimmy Smits), tells him, "I was not comfortable with those words. I am not comfortable with the thoughts behind it. I just want you to understand that." At home, Sipowicz discusses the racial incident that *provoked* him into using the N-word. He asks his wife if she's ever heard him say it. She answers that she hasn't. But she has seen him use certain gestures when talking about African Americans. "It's code," he tells her. "So you don't have to say it." "Don't ever show it to our child," she then says. "Don't teach him to think in that way." Viewers may have felt that Sipowicz was too likable and vulnerable to be a Mark Fuhrman. But upon closer examination, Sipowicz may have more of an affinity to Fuhrman than we'd like to admit.

But for African American viewers, it was more intriguing to watch Fancy's response to Sipowicz. Often without uttering a word of dialogue, McDaniel looked as if he were wearied by the daily accretion of racism he must deal with—or ignore—to get his job done. When he gets into an argument with Sipowicz, he lets it be known that should Sipowicz be removed from the precinct, "They'll send me another like you. Only worse." Then he says, "Maybe you can't handle a Black man being your boss."

On another episode, Sipowicz arrests an innocent African American man in a murder case. Though the man eventually gets off, Sipowicz is blind to his own bigotry. The episode ended with Fancy taking him to a restaurant in Harlem where Sipowicz is the only white man. When the two talk, Sipowicz says "it doesn't matter" whether or not he is a racist as long as he is fair when he does his job. Fancy says to him, "You're uncomfortable in this restaurant, but imagine how you'd feel if these waiters had badges and guns." Not only does Fancy refute Sipowicz's point of view but he makes him consider how his life would be if he were African American and on the other side of the law. Still, effective as this scene was, it said more about Sipowicz than about Fancy. Though *N.Y.P.D. Blue* frequently featured Black guest stars, it didn't add another Black character—Baldwin Jones, played by Henry Simmons—until its seventh season.

Among *N.Y.P.D. Blue's* strongest assets was African American director Paris Barclay, who won Emmys two years in a row for his work on the series. So, too, was African American writer Kevin Arkadie.

Based on the book *Homicide: A Year on the Killing Streets* by Baltimore *Sun* crime reporter David Simon and executive-produced by

Barry Levinson and Tom Fontana, the gritty police show *Homicide* was set in Baltimore. Known for its quirky look and sound—the handheld camera shots, the jump cuts, and the blues or rock music pulsating on the soundtrack—it was a drama less interested in highly developed story lines than in its idiosyncratic characters. The detectives did not so much solve cases as close them. Sometimes a case went from one week to the next. Often justice was ambiguous. On some occasions, the cast of *Law & Order* was brought on as the characters of the two series joined forces to resolve a case. Always the detectives had short fuses, ready to explode not only with the criminals that they sometimes could not bring to justice but with one another as well.

Homicide could boast of three important African American characters, played by actors Yaphet Kotto, Clark Johnson, and Andre Braugher. Later Giancarlo Esposito and Michael Michele joined the cast. Such African American actors as Erik Todd Dellums, Clayton LeBoeuf, and Al Freeman Jr. also appeared on some episodes in supporting roles. Like *The Defenders* and *N.Y.P.D. Blue*, *Homicide* also featured a number of African Americans in guest roles: James Earl Jones, Lynn Thigpen, Alfre Woodard, Chris Rock, Gloria Reuben, and Melvin Van Peebles. So many African American faces appeared that some critics mistakenly considered *Homicide* a Black show. Never was it situated enough in an African American cultural context to be *that*. But its Black protagonists as well as some of its story lines were startlingly new for television.

Most of the attention was focused on Andre Braugher—"one of television's most thoughtful, deeply realized characters," wrote Caryn James—as the lapsed Catholic detective Frank Pembleton. Critic John Leonard called Braugher "the best actor on series television." Other critics agreed. Earlier in his career, Braugher had played a cop on *Kojak* during the 1989–90 season. But he had hated the producers' conception of his character as a bed-hopping womanizer. On *Homicide*, Pembleton is a family man who struggles with himself to remain that. Hot-tempered and moody yet philosophical, he's keenly aware of the toll his job has taken on his home life. He's a man who's wound up so tight that we can feel the knot in his stomach. Yet as gifted an actor as Braugher was, he could also overplay his hand. His use of language and his delivery, his movements and his moods themselves, sometimes became almost archly stylized. Even when he uttered intentionally mundane dialogue, Braugher aimed for bravura effects. In turn, he occasionally became a lot of hot brilliant flash; an actor who seemed to enjoy hearing the sound of his own voice; savoring his own dulcet tones. Yet all of those effects, ironically, made him compellingly watchable. Later, Braugher starred in the series *Gideon's Crossing*.

Often overlooked was the sturdy presence of Yaphet Kotto as Lieutenant Al "Gee" Giardello, the half African American, half Italian lieutenant who gave the men their orders and who also understood their weaknesses and their frustrations. Having worked in theater, movies, and television for years, Kotto brought an assured maturity to the part and the series itself; his was the perceptive intelligence in the squad room that held everything together. Kotto also wrote for the series. Clark Johnson as the streetwise Meldrick Lewis contrasted effectively with both Kotto and Braugher.

Homicide's real surprise came in its sixth season with the arrival of actress Michael Michele. Almost everyone wondered how this stunner would make it in the gritty testosterone world of *Homicide*. Previously, Michele had played a pampered rich girl in the glossy nighttime series *Central Park West*. As she gossiped or partied or commiserated with her white friends on that earlier show, as she became involved with the wealthy father of a friend, her character was one of television's most culturally unanchored heroines. Nothing explained how this young Black woman became so entangled in this world of wealth and privilege. (The character didn't even have the basic cultural demarcations of *Dynasty*'s Dominique.) Michele seemed as if she had never experienced any crisis more serious than not being able to find the right lip gloss. She also appeared for a season on *New York Undercover*.

When she showed up in *Homicide*, she was still a stunner: tall, angular, and haughty, although not as glamorous. Wisely, the series didn't try to camouflage her looks. It was explained that she was a former beauty queen who has to prove herself to the guys in the homicide unit. Somehow Michele pared herself down to essentials, emerging as a tough, resilient heroine.

Despite its innovations and unusual characters, *Homicide* never had high ratings. It was always more of a critic's favorite than an audience's.

Of these dramatic shows, *New York Undercover* and *ER* had a greater impact with African American viewers. A cop show with a healthy dose of weekly action, *New York Undercover*—created by Dick Wolf and

Kevin Arkadie—was one of the rare dramatic series that Fox pitched at African American viewers. Within its traditional formula, its younger hip cop detective heroes, the African American J.C. (Malik Yoba) and the Latino Eddie (Michael DeLorenzo), appealed to a young audience. So too did its use of music (jazz, rap, rhythm and blues), its sexy, fast-paced New York setting, and its cinema verité style. Later joining the cast were Lauren Velez and Tommy Ford (showing off his acting skills in a way that *Martin* didn't permit).

ER'S BENTON AND BOULET:
MAKING THE MOST OUT OF MARGINALIZED LIVES

Created by best-selling author Michael Crichton, *ER* was an innovative doctors' series that shot to the top of the ratings, emerging at the end of its first season as the highest-rated new drama in television history. Set in the emergency unit of Chicago's County General Hospital, the series dramatized the experiences of a group of (relatively) young doctors who struggle not only to save lives but to work out their own personal dilemmas. Among the group was the African American surgeon Peter Benton (Eriq La Salle). For Black viewers, Benton quickly became both an exciting and frustrating hero. On the one hand, you had to respect the skills of this hardworking professional, demanding the best of himself and those around him. Seeing Benton (like seeing his predecessor played by Denzel Washington on *St. Elsewhere*), you realized that television images of African American men indeed had inched forward. Yet in an unexpected way, Peter Benton sometimes appeared to embody a familiar 1960s-style media type: the angry young Black man. Benton was a man with a scowl; a surly sourpuss if ever there was one.

For too long, the series did not explain Benton's tensions and anger; or put them into a context that gave them meaning. As was true of most of these nighttime dramas, *ER* was eager to comment on the lives of the major white characters: the heartthrob Dr. Ross (George Clooney), the sensitive Dr. Greene (Anthony Edwards), the emotionally fragile nurse Hathaway (Julianna Margulies), the young, eager-to-please resident John Carter (Noah Wyle), the earnest physician Dr. Lewis (Sherry Stringfield). Viewers learned about Dr. Ross's relation-

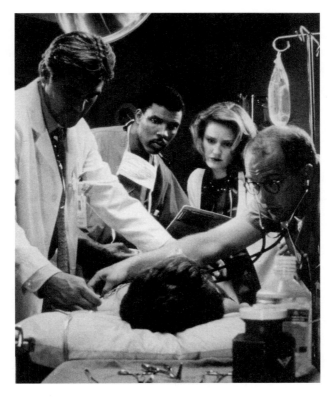

"Why is Dr. Peter Benton angry?": ER's Eriq La Salle (second from left) with George Clooney, Sherry Stringfield, and Anthony Edwards

ships with various women, Greene's problems with his lawyer wife, and Hathaway's shaky romance with a physician as well as her once devastating relationship with Dr. Ross. Those characters also frequently befriended each other. Yet except for his relationship with the resident under his supervision, Carter, who idolized him and was almost desperate to please him, Benton was left isolated. With Benton and Carter, *ER* wisely refused to go the bonding route. It was altogether realistic that the Black Benton might not care to develop a personal relationship with a white colleague. But there was no one at the hospital that he seemed close to. When African American actresses like C.C.H. Pounder and the striking Tyra Ferrell made guest appearances as physicians, you hoped Benton might express his feelings about being the only African American doctor on the ER team; perhaps then we'd understand the source of his anger or alienation. But no such thing happened. He remained as removed from them as from everyone else. Where did this man go after he left the hospital?

A semblance of a home life was created for Benton when that great marvel of an actress Beah Richards appeared in various episodes as his elderly mother. As the warm and even-tempered mother, who was revealed to be suffering from Alzheimer's disease, Richards created a stunning portrait of a woman fearful of losing control over not only her life but her very sense of identity. Together, Benton and his sister (Khandi Alexander) were faced with the painful decision to put their mother into a nursing home. At the end of that episode, Benton was seen massaging his mother's feet while looking over a family photo album. "Your talent is God's gift to you," Richards tells him. "What you do with it is your gift back to God." It was a beautiful moment. But the scene said more about the mother than the son. Ving Rhames also appeared as Benton's brother-in-law Walter. Yet even with his family Benton was still a cipher.

Eventually, *ER* gave Benton a love life. He first became involved with his mother's caretaker, a married woman, Jeanie Boulet (Gloria Reuben). In his intimate scenes with Boulet, La Salle's Benton remained remote, frustrating viewers all the more. Whereas the sadness and disillusionment in actor George Clooney's eyes had lifted his Dr. Ross womanizer character out of a one-dimensional cad category (the writers seemed to write with Clooney, the man, in mind to create a fully dimensional, engaging hero), La Salle appeared unable to infuse a flat character with some personal warmth or idiosyncrasies. "Benton is probably the most misunderstood [character]," wrote *Jet*, "as he rarely allows his wall of defense to come down."

Later the writers created two other romances for Benton: first with Carla (Lisa Nicole Carson), with whom he has a son, Reese, but to whom he cannot commit; then an interracial affair with a British doctor, Elizabeth Corday (Alex Kingston). Significantly, Corday pursues him, trying her best to get him to let his guard down. But he's still a stiff. His most spontaneous moment came on a Halloween episode. During the closing segment, viewers saw Benton dressed as movie hero Shaft (with Isaac Hayes's music in the background). It provided the Benton character with a great cultural reference (which otherwise was usually missing).

In the third season, an episode of *ER* finally commented on the subject that many African American viewers were most curious about: Benton's feelings about race. A young African American intern at the hospital, Dennis Gant (Omar Epps), wants very much to connect to Benton. But Benton is always tough on him (as much so as he was with Carter). Finally, in a telling sequence, when the two are alone, Gant confronts Benton. Benton asks if Gant checked "Black" on his medical school application. When Gant replies yes, Benton informs him that everyone will assume Gant is there because of a quota system, not because of merit. Therefore Gant must work harder and be better to prove them wrong. It was one of the rare times when viewers felt they had been given some concrete comment on Benton's feelings of (racial) isolation as the only African American doctor on the ER staff. In time, Benton's one-note remoteness became, to put it politely, uninteresting.

Later the writers tried softening the Benton character as he struggled to accept his young son's deafness. But it wasn't a particularly engrossing plot development. In the fifth season, an entire episode of *ER* was devoted to Benton. When asked during an appearance on *The Today Show* why it had taken so long for a special episode on Benton, actor La Salle answered, "I don't know. You'd have to ask the producers. They've done it with every original member of the cast. They've actually done it multiple times. For five years, I said, 'Okay, guys, I'm on the show as well.' " La Salle admitted he had to put his foot down. "I think it was a bit unfortunate that it gets to that level. But I think it's really about that this is an ensemble show. And the word 'ensemble' implies fair treatment and equality. I think we're here. And it's a great challenge. I'm definitely glad and pleased with the show. But it was a struggle."

To his credit, La Salle also voiced his other concerns about *ER*. "As an African American man, it becomes a bit offensive if the negative things are all you're showing," he said. "Because in real life we romance and get on each other's nerves and laugh and do all the things that any other race of people do." He urged the writers to drop the romantic story line between Benton and the white Corday. "So if the only time you show a balanced relationship is in an interracial relationship whether it's conscious or subconscious, it sends a message I'm not comfortable with. [The writers] were sending a message that I didn't want to be a part of, which was the only time that this man becomes human and tender and vulnerable and open is when he falls in love with a white woman." He added that his relationships with African American women on the series had been dysfunctional. "One was an adulterous relationship with Jeanie Boulet and then the next relationship I got into was with Carla. And unfortunately the writing there was, every time you see them they're either fighting or [having sex]." The writers dropped the Benton/Corday story line. Later a romance was developed for Benton and a new character, Dr. Cleo Finch, played by African American actress Michael Michele.

Like *Hill Street Blues*, *ER* sometimes fell back on familiar, even stock characterizations of urban African Americans. On one episode, two young Black men were brought into the emergency room, each with gunshot wounds. Two young Black women—who visit the men—argue and get into a shoving match. They are asked to leave the room. But in the hospital corridor they begin to fight and are told to get out of the hospital or the police and security will be called. Later one of the women is brought back to the hospital with stab wounds, apparently having been attacked by the other woman. On another episode, Carter ends up in the inner city, where he stumbles across two Black children sitting on a doorstep outside a doorway. He walks inside the house to find their tubercular mother breathing heavily. As he attempts to help, a Black man suddenly appears, demanding to know what Carter is doing in his home. Though Carter says he only wants to help the woman get medical treatment, the man—irrationally—insists that he leave.

During the fifth season, new cast members Djimon Hounsou and Akosua Busia played a married West African couple who are political refugees from Nigeria, where Hounsou was tortured. He's a janitor at the hospital; she works in the cafeteria's food service. One day she confides in the nurse Hathaway that she was raped while in Nigeria but thus far she has been unable to tell her husband. She fears his reaction. Later she ends up with a knife wound to the chest and wheeled into the emergency room on a gurney. We learn that her husband "freaked out" and we assume he attacked her. Though this story line later had a surprising twist, you wonder why all these episodes relied on a continuing depiction of a world of crime or violence for these Black characters.

Still, despite its shortcomings, *ER* reached a segment of the African American community. Part of the appeal was that *ER* also developed a fine lineup of Black supporting players: Yvette Freeman as nurse Haleh Adams; Deezer D. as nurse Malik McGrath; Conni Marie Brazelton as nurse Conni Oligario; guest star C. C. H. Pounder as Dr. Angela Hicks. Freeman with her short Afro, Brazelton with her dreads, Pounder with her traditional coif all provided the workplace with an interesting visual comment on the various styles and looks of African American women.

Certainly, the most moving story line for an African American woman centered on Jeanie Boulet. Married to a man who has cheated on her, she ends up briefly in the arms of Benton. Later working as a physician's assistant, Jeanie solemnly walks through the corridors, hallways, and elevators of the hospital, always ready to help others. Jeanie's story attained a distinct emotional power when she learned that she was HIV-positive. Fearful of losing her job, she keeps her condition a secret. There was some grumbling that *ER*'s depiction of an HIV-positive Black character was a negative comment on the African American community, especially since she contracted the disease from her husband, a promiscuous Black man. But the Black characters on *ER*, like the white ones, had to have problems, great and small. AIDS was a real problem within the African American and Latino communities, and *ER* neither sensationalized nor exploited the subject. Yet television's one primetime weekly African American heroine—who was mature, sophisticated, *and* sexual—looked as if she might disappear.

Though Gloria Reuben was not an especially expressive actress (with her flat voice, she spoke almost in a monotone), her passivity and melancholic air worked beautifully for the character. Some of the most affecting moments of the television season were those when the camera came in close to record Reuben/Jeanie's despair. You felt you were losing something special, right before your eyes. You dreaded seeing her die. Then the writers did an unexpected thing. They let the character live with her disease. Eventually, little was said about her condition. Then, without much fanfare, the character married and was written out of the series. But no viewer ever forgot Boulet.

Despite the limitations of the hour-long dramatic ensemble series, these remained the only weekly programs that African Americans could turn to for serious, mature Black characters. Such dramatic Black

*Gloria Reuben as the HIV-positive Jeanie Boulet
on* ER, *one of the era's most moving characters*

series as *Under One Roof,* Thomas Carter's multigenerational family story, and *413 Hope Street,* executive-produced by Damon Wayans, disappeared quickly from the primetime schedule. Set in a crisis center with a mixed but predominantly Black cast, *413 Hope Street* had promise. It scored well with Black viewers, becoming their third most watched show. But when *413 Hope Street* failed to bring in the big ratings, Fox, rather than giving the series time to find a broader audience, dropped it. Black dramatic series still could not survive on the primetime schedule.

COSBY RETURNS

Toward the end of the decade, Bill Cosby, that thirty-year veteran of television, also appeared in a new sitcom, *Cosby.* It followed a string of disappointments. After *The Cosby Show,* he had appeared in *The Cosby Mysteries.* Playing a criminologist and forensic expert in New York's police department, Cosby as Guy Hanks weekly solved crimes in a fashion similar to Jessica Fletcher on *Murder, She Wrote* and Quincy on *Quincy, M.E.* His supporting cast included: James Naughton as his colleague; Rita Moreno as his housekeeper; Dante Beze as a street kid who helped him solve cases; and later Lynn Whitfield as his friend and the widow of his partner. Clearly not a Black-cast show, *The Cosby Mysteries* had some good moments and might have developed into a slick whodunit that appealed to older viewers, in the vein of programs like *Matlock* and *Murder, She Wrote*. But *The Cosby Mysteries* lasted only one season. Cosby also starred in syndicated versions of the old Groucho Marx show *You Bet Your Life* and Art Linkletter's *Kids Say the Darndest Things*. These were not hits either.

His new series *Cosby* revolved around the life of Hilton Lucas, a sixty-year-old airline employee who, after thirty years, was fired when the company decided to downsize. Now his days were spent at his home in Queens with his wife, Ruthie (Phylicia Rashad), who has to listen to the steady gripes of a man with too much time on his hands. Also in and out of the Lucas household were Ruthie's deadpan friend Pauline (Madeline Kahn); the Lucases' grown law school graduate daughter, Erica (T'Keyah "Crystal" Keymah); and neighbor Griffin (Doug E. Doug), who has a crush on Erica.

The British sitcom *One Foot in the Grave*, on which *Cosby* was based, had been a dark comedy about a man who finds himself a displaced and disgruntled failure in a culture that does not seem to have a place for him. Apparently, the first script for *Cosby* by writer/executive producer Richard Day had the same tone as the original sitcom. Cosby, however, could not see himself playing such a character. Day explained that "when pressed I think he lost his nerve because he's had a lot of success with a very lovable persona. He threw the script out and said everyone would reject him if he played that character. He outlined a new tone for the show which was essentially *The Cosby Show* where he was a lovable, retired guy full of wisdom. So I wrote another script. . . . I'm not going to say it was bad, but I wouldn't watch it—there just wasn't any conflict." Day was fired. New writer Dennis Klein was brought in. The Lucas character was softened. The tone of the show was brighter.

Cosby met with some harsh reviews. Some critics felt it was still too dark a show for America's favorite father figure. Others believed it had no bite. "Cosby has lost his bearings," wrote Ken Tucker in *Entertainment Weekly*. "Where's the beguilingly goofy guy from *The Cosby Show*, the smiling father figure from all those Jell-O commercials, the dignified cool cat from *I Spy*? Gone, gone. Instead we get a poker-faced grump." In *The New Yorker*, James Wolcott, who had a different view, wrote that *Cosby* "seems to take place in a Sesame Street neighborhood of quaint flopsy-mopsy characters." He added that the program was "oddly unsettled—patchy, yet pushy. It stresses its harmlessness to a nervous degree. It's nice to the point of intimidation. . . . Perhaps Cosby is so beholden to the idea of success that he can't express the frustration born of a sense of failure (anyone who has been fired knows that you feel like a failure, even if it wasn't your fault), or perhaps he can't play against the grain because he's been such a dapper pro for so long that he's worn the grain smooth."

Viewers tuned in the first week, pushing *Cosby* to the eighth most watched show of the week. But afterward the numbers fell significantly. Even softened, Hilton was too much a curmudgeon for many viewers. In time, the series changed. Hilton remained an intensely likable character without those dark edges. Some episodes required him to perform slapstick, which seemed to be the kind of humor the young Cosby had avoided at all costs. Occasionally, there were some very sweet, warm moments between Hilton and his daughter. But the relationship between Hilton and Griffin became a focal point as this odd couple bonded. (Cosby seemed to take an interest in the career of this young comedian, who had previously appeared on the sitcom *Where I Live*, much as Cosby had with Sinbad in the 1980s.) Later more children appeared on the show, which made *Cosby* look more like a traditional sitcom. But most important, *Cosby*, though not a ratings winner like *The Cosby Show*, survived for four seasons.

Like other great stars with careers spanning decades, Cosby—now as much an American institution as Lucille Ball and Jackie Gleason—understood why viewers liked him and he went with his instincts. For older viewers, *Cosby* was likable television that summoned up a series of associations from the past. Indeed, Scotty had grown up, had played the field and learned more about family and community ties under the guise of being Chet Kincaid, and had then assumed his acceptable roles of father and husband as Cliff Huxtable. Now that same recurring character—that enduring persona that had been in American homes since 1965—had become on *Cosby* a grandfatherly figure, free of some past restraints and responsibilities and now able, with Griffin by his side, to live out a second childhood of sorts. Though his critics might have their points about his being too wholesome and without the kind of anger that the real Cosby could exhibit in real life on matters racial and otherwise, Cosby had refused to violate the very characteristics that viewers, Black and white, valued in him. Even at the tail end of the twentieth century, he remained one of the few African American television stars with the clout to determine his own destiny on television and off.

During the closing years of the decade, two new Black-oriented sitcoms drew protests from the African American community. The story of Desmond Pfeiffer (Chi McBride), a proper, aristocratic British butler and aide to Abraham Lincoln during the Civil War, *The Secret Diary of Desmond Pfeiffer* was criticized because of its jokes about slavery. In a scene in which butler Pfeiffer relaxes, Lincoln's chef tells him abruptly, "The slaves haven't been emancipated yet, Pfeiffer. Get your feet off that table." Though the series was deadly *unfunny*, the Beverly Hills/Hollywood chapter of the NAACP wanted it taken off the air. It ended up dying because of audience apathy.

Also drawing criticism was the foamation (stop-motion animation done with foam/latex puppets) sitcom *The PJs*, a domestic tale about Thurgood Stubbs, the superintendent of a housing project. Eddie Murphy supplied the voice for Stubbs and was also one of the creators and executive producers of the series. When Thurgood goes out for a neighborhood stroll, he mutters, "The gunfire is coming from the west tonight." At one point, he finds himself near the intersection of Al Sharpton Boulevard and Alvin Ailey Alley. His running comment is "Bless my Soul Train." Throughout, there were jokes about the multiple strokes of an elderly woman and the habits of a junkie as well as welfare benefits. "I kind of scratch my head why Eddie Murphy's doing this," said Spike Lee, "because it shows no love at all for Black people. I'm not saying we're above being made fun of, but it's really hateful toward Black people." Oddly enough, though, *The PJs* had moments of a distinct ethnic cultural awareness. Loretta Devine, who supplied the voice of Thurgood's patient wife, also had some surprisingly touching sequences. The problem was that Murphy saw something inherently undignified about his Black characters and settings. The only real affection he had for his characters grew out of their coarseness or ignorance. Otherwise Murphy failed to come up with any insights or significant observations. The show did well in the ratings among viewers in the 18- to 49-year-old category.

Even more typed than shows like *The Secret Diary of Desmond Pfeiffer* and *The PJs* was Phil Morris's role as the lawyer Jackie Chiles on *Seinfeld* and later in Honda Odyssey minivan commercials. Though supposedly satirizing attorney Johnnie Cochran, Chiles's thick dialect and broad, stagy double takes harked back to Kingfish on *Amos 'n' Andy*. One would like to think it was an homage to poor Kingfish. Actually, it *was* Kingfish, 1990s style. Seeing these antics, many viewers might have felt television images had not progressed at all.

By the last season of the decade, the networks drew criticism from the NAACP, as well as from groups representing Latinos and Asian Americans, for the lack of minority representation in the new prime-time series. No new African American series appeared on any of the three major networks' 1999–2000 season debuts. The situation was reminiscent of those protests over *Amos 'n' Andy* in the 1950s. Stung by the criticism, the networks quickly rewrote scripts to include African American or other minority characters in such new shows as *The West Wing, Judging Amy,* and *Family Law* as well as in a returning series like *Suddenly Susan*. In early 2000, Steven Bochco and Paris Barclay developed the medical drama *City of Angels*, which featured a mostly African American cast. Early episodes, however, were misshapen and uneven. The writers weren't able to establish a consistent tone. Sometimes *City of Angels* was straightforward (but predictable) hospital fare. An older patient (Fran Bennett) worries about her grandchildren—and their drug-addicted mother. Other times, the series turned mindlessly quirky. The hospital's chairman—who has a foot fetish—requests that a female administrator give him one of her shoes. A patient has had a Golden Globe Award shoved into his rectum. The lead characters were depicted as do-gooders with far too noble profiles.

TV Movies

Away from the primetime series, Black performers and some African American directors found varied work on the networks' movies. Still favored were dramatizations of true stories about African Americans. Among the more prominent were *Murder in Mississippi* (the story of the young civil rights activists James Chaney, Mickey Schwerner, and Andrew Goodman, who were murdered near Philadelphia, Mississippi, in 1964) and Mike Newell's two-part *Common Ground* (which focused on three families living in Boston during the city's troubled period of school desegregation in the 1960s). *The Howard Beach Story: Making the Case for Murder* was another drama centered on a real-life racial incident.

Other real-life dramatizations focused on celebrities. Fox aired a quickly made *O. J. Simpson Story,* which capitalized on the media frenzy surrounding the trial of former football player Simpson for the murder his former wife, Nicole Brown Simpson. *The O. J. Simpson Story* couldn't even muster up enough energy to successfully exploit its subject. Also routine was another celebrity tale, *Bad As I Wanna Be: The Dennis Rodman Story*, starring newcomer Dwayne Adway. For better or worse, these celebrity sagas—as well as others that followed *Little Richard* in the next century—indicated that indeed African Americans had attained the kind of fame or notoriety that had previously been reserved for white stars.

Two miniseries that scored high in the ratings, surprising the networks, were *The Jacksons: An American Family* and *The Temptations*. Old-fashioned melodramas that were executive-produced by Suzanne de Passe, both owed much to their Motown soundtracks and to their viewers' memories of the singing styles and personal tribulations of these two very famous singing groups. *The Jacksons* told the then well-known story of Joe and Katherine Jackson and their talented children. Most of the focus was rightly placed on Michael, the gifted and gloved weird one. Jason Weaver turned in a highly kinetic and convincing performance as Michael. Portraying Katherine Jackson was Angela Bassett just before her days of movie stardom. (Bassett had also appeared in such TV movies as *Heroes of Desert Storm* as well as in episodes of *Tour of Duty, The Cosby Show, Spenser: For Hire, thirtysomething*, and *Alien Nation*.) The real surprise was Lawrence-Hilton Jacobs as the foul-tempered Joe Jackson, who pushes his kids to stardom, unconcerned about the price they have to pay. Many viewers remembered Jacobs from his days as Freddie "Boom-Boom" Washington on *Welcome Back, Kotter.* Probably most were unaware of his role on the series *Alien Nation.* Here was an excellent example of TV as a great mass communal event where viewers opened their arms to a member of the "family"— Jacobs—who had been away too long.

Viewers, white and Black, tuned in to *The Temptations*—the story of the five original members of the singing group: their problems with their families, women, Motown, and one another. Yet despite its popularity, *The Temptations* never rose above a standard rags-to-riches-to-heartache movie musical. Paul Williams, who committed suicide by putting a gun to his head, might have been a harrowing figure. Viewers might have experienced the terror of an imprisoning fame, and the tragic desperation of a man who can't cope with life off-stage; who perhaps needs an entertainment-induced world of illusions to feel real. Some might say that's asking too much of television. But the Motown heroes and heroines—from Marvin Gaye to Mary Wells to Tammi Terrell—became legendary pop gods and goddesses not only because of their music but also because of their battles with Motown and the terrifying turns that their lives took. Yet the Temptations' music remained so melodic and energetic—and the re-creations of the choreography for the group were so smooth and slick—that much as viewers might reject the hack story line, they couldn't move away from the set. And actor Leon Robinson—billed simply as Leon—succeeded in expressing some of the maddening drive and self-destructive vitality of that other tragic Temptation hero, David Ruffin.

Just as old-time Motown found favor with television viewers, so did old-time Alex Haley. Dramatizations of two of his books—*Queen* and *Mama Flora's Family*—turned up on the primetime network schedule. The story of Haley's mother's family, the miniseries *Queen* traced the life of a slave girl (Halle Berry), who is the daughter of a slave mother and the son of the plantation owner. With its all-star cast that included Ossie Davis, Paul Winfield, Jasmine Guy, Lonette McKee, Ann-Margret, Danny Glover, Tim Daly, and Dennis Haysbert, *Queen* probably should have been made at least a decade earlier, shortly after *Roots*, when this type of material was still new to television. By 1993, you felt you had already seen the story. For the most part, *Queen*, directed by John Erman, failed to be compelling television. "The real problem with *Queen* is Queen," wrote John Leonard. "Growing up, going mad, Berry is affecting. In between, she is inchoate." The only fireworks came from Lonette McKee in a brief but memorable star turn as a high-yeller woman who is passing for white. When she learns that Berry has foolishly revealed her racial identity, McKee lashes into the girl. Watching McKee, one was reminded of Rosalind Cash's *lash* scenes with Diahann Carroll in *Sister, Sister:* it's a demonstration of a volcanic actress challenging a rather placid one to match her intensity and power.

The 1998 *Mama Flora's Family* also often covered familiar terrain. Featuring an all-star cast that included Cicely Tyson, Mario Van Peebles, Blair Underwood, and Della Reese, the drama traced the life of another Haley ancestor, Flora, from the late nineteenth century into the early twentieth. When the young impoverished Flora (Erika Alexander) is sent to work for a wealthy Black family, she succumbs to the wily advances of the family's handsome young son (Shemar Moore). Deflowered and then rejected by him, a pregnant Flora returns home. But once she gives birth to a son, her former lover arrives and quickly takes the child. Here *Mama Flora's Family* offered an unusual view of social/racial history. In old films and television shows, the villain would have been the handsome son of the plantation owner. But for the pop audience, Haley's unflattering portrait of the old-guard Black bourgeoisie was used to dramatize issues of color and class within the African American community.

In the mid-1990s, a major television event was the broadcast of the eight-hour miniseries *Scarlett*, the sequel to *Gone With the Wind*. For African American viewers, the question was not so much what has happened to Scarlett, Rhett, and Ashley but rather what filmmakers in the late twentieth century were going to do with the stereotypical Black characters Mammy, Prissy, and Pork. *Scarlett* worked its way around the problematic Yankees-is-coming Prissy by simply eliminating the character. Gone too was Pork. But, surprisingly, Big Sam, a minor character best remembered for having rescued Scarlett from a nasty encounter near shantytown, survived, thanks to a miraculous transformation: from the part Tom, part noble buck of actor Everett Brown to the smooth sophistication of Paul Winfield. Now Big Sam is an astute lumber entrepreneur!

Scarlett also kept Mammy around but quickly put her to death.

Playing the powerhouse Hattie McDaniel role was the tube's Esther Rolle, who had a deathbed scene in which she asks to see the face of that old devil himself—who but?—Mister Rhett. Once Rhett shows up, Mammy dear lets him know she'd like to be buried in that red silk petticoat he once gave her. Not a word about Mammy's own family, even after all these years. Nor was this a performance with any shadings or subliminal suggestions of hostility and anger. Now that she was about to go on to her heavenly reward, it might have been terrific fun to hear Mammy tell both Scarlett and Rhett exactly where they could go.

During the 1990s, PBS offered viewers a few sturdy dramas but was hardly as vital as in the past. Among the dramas were *Zora Is My Name* and *Simple Justice*. Directed by Neema Barnette, *Zora Is My Name* explored the life of Harlem Renaissance writer Zora Neale Hurston. Ruby Dee and Beah Richards were among the cast. Based on the book by Theodore Rosengarten, *All God's Dangers* starred Cleavon Little as the former slave/sharecropper recalling the stormy events of his life.

CABLE MOVIES

Many of the more talked-about television movies appeared on cable. TNT aired *The Court-Martial of Jackie Robinson*, which recounted Robinson's experiences as a young soldier faced with bigotry while stationed at Fort Riley, Kansas, in the 1940s. Andre Braugher starred as Robinson. TNT also aired *Heat Wave*. Directed by Kevin Hooks with an all-star cast that included Cicely Tyson, Blair Underwood, James Earl Jones, and Margaret Avery, it dramatized the experiences of journalist Robert Richardson during the Watts uprisings in 1965. *Assault at West Point: The Court-Martial of Johnson Whittaker* featured Samuel L. Jackson, Al Freeman Jr., Sam Waterston, Seth Gilliam, and Eddie Bracken in a drama centered on the experiences of the first Black cadet at West Point. *The Buffalo Soldiers*, starring Danny Glover, also aired on TNT. Showtime broadcast *Mr. and Mrs. Loving*, a tale about an interracial marriage, starring Lela Rochon, Timothy Hutton, Isaiah Washington, and Ruby Dee.

Leading the pack of cable stations that aired Black TV movies was

HBO taps the African American audience: Lynn Whitfield in The Josephine Baker Story

HBO. Aware of its large African American viewership, which turned shows like *Def Comedy Jams* and later *The Chris Rock Show* into bona fide hits, HBO had great success with *The Josephine Baker Story*. Not only did the film turn actress Lynn Whitfield into a TV star; it also walked away with Emmys: Best Director for Brian Gibson; Outstanding Actress for Whitfield. The enthusiastic viewer response indicated that there was an eager African American audience in search of alternative films that the networks would never touch. Other HBO Black dramas, some based on true stories, followed: *The Tuskegee Airmen*, starring Laurence Fishburne, Andre Braugher, Allen Payne, and Malcolm-Jamal Warner as the World War II unit of African American pilots; *Don King: Only in America*, an uneven but engrossing, quasi-Brechtian study of the controversial boxing promoter starring Ving Rhames; *Against the Wall*, a prison drama featuring Samuel L. Jackson; *Miss Evers' Boys*, starring Laurence Fishburne and Alfre Woodard in a drama about young African American men whose syphilis deliberately went untreated during an experiment in the South in the Depression era; *Criminal Justice* with Forest Whitaker and Rosie Perez; and *A Lesson Before Dying*, based on a novel by Ernest Gaines and starring Don Cheadle, Cicely Tyson, Irma P. Hall, and Mekhi Phifer. *Introducing Dorothy Dandridge* turned Halle Berry into a full-fledged television star; she won an Emmy for her performance as the tragic pioneering African American film actress.

HBO highly promoted this latter film, shrewdly using all the publicity surrounding the eagerness of some of Hollywood's top African American actresses to play the role of Dandridge: from Whitney Houston to Jasmine Guy, Vanessa Williams, and that sweet-tempered pop goddess Janet Jackson. The end results were mixed. Though Berry gave a heartfelt performance and was also the executive producer, the script turned the complex Dandridge's tumultuous larger-than-life experiences into a conventional saga. "Its portrait of Dandridge is simplified," wrote Caryn James. The drama earnestly attempted to reveal the racism Dandridge endured as a nightclub star, but it proved timid in attacking the racist attitudes of the movie industry, which had clearly led to the actress's decline. Still, the ratings were high, indicating that the fundamental story of Dandridge was of great importance and interest to the African American audience. Ironically, *Introducing Dorothy Dandridge* was a drama the major networks had shown no interest in.

African American directors also found work on HBO and other cable outlets. *One False Move* filmmaker Carl Franklin directed the well-received *Laurel Avenue*, a Black family drama that was better than anything the networks offered during the era. Actors Eriq La Salle and Charles Dutton directed the respective HBO features *Rebound: The Legend of Earl (the Goat) Manigault* and *First Time Felon*. Dutton later directed the cable series *The Corner*, an examination of life in the ghetto in Baltimore—in which he drew disturbing and moving performances from T. K. Carter and Khandi Alexander. His work also won him a Best Director Emmy. Actor Andre Braugher directed *Love Songs* for Showtime. Before he directed the feature film *How Stella Got Her Groove Back*, Kevin Sullivan directed *Soul of the Game*, a drama about the Negro baseball leagues starring Delroy Lindo, Blair Underwood, and Mykelti Williamson. Best known for her film *I Like It Like That*, Darnell Martin proved, with her pilot (and other episodes) of the prison series *Oz*, that, contrary to popular notions, a woman could direct a strong, *manly* dramatic series. Eric Laneuville directed Mary Tyler Moore in Lifetime's *Stolen Babies*, which starred Mary Tyler Moore in a tale about an illegal adoption ring in the 1940s. Mario and Melvin Van Peebles co-directed Showtime's *Gang in Blue*.

Some directors like Darnell Martin also worked well on network shows. Martin directed episodes of *ER*. Michael Schultz tried resurrecting some of the gritty fervor of Blaxploitation cinema with *Hammer, Slammer & Slade*—with 1970s action star Jim Brown—which was produced by Keenen Ivory Wayans's Ivory Way Productions. Schultz also directed episodes of *Touched by an Angel*. With a script by Richard Wesley, Kevin Hooks directed *Murder Without Motive: The Edmund Perry Story*, which examined the life of teenager Edmund Perry, who during a break from his studies at Phillips Academy was shot in a botched robbery. Filmmaker Charles Burnett directed the highly praised *Nightjohn* for the Disney Channel as well as the uneven *Oprah Winfrey Presents: The Wedding* for ABC. Debbie Allen brought her direct but energetic style not only to episodes of *A Different World*, *The Fresh Prince of Bel-Air*, and *In the House* but also to the TV movies *Polly—Comin' Home!* and *Stompin' at the Savoy*. Neema Barnette also directed *Run for the Dream: The Gail Devers Story*, *Sin & Redemption*, and *Scattered Dreams* as well as episodes of *A Different World*, *Diagnosis Murder*, *Deadly Games*, and *The Cosby Mysteries*.

Director Kevin Hooks

Television provided a lifeline to some of these filmmakers when the big movie projects proved slow in coming.

Stars also found better opportunities to showcase their talents in television movies. Having rarely appeared on the tube during the years of his heady movie stardom, Sidney Poitier found some solid roles in television during his later years. In 1991, he starred as Thurgood Marshall in the two-part network drama *Separate But Equal.* Later he played Nelson Mandela, in the Showtime production *Mandela and De Klerk* in 1997. He repeated his role as the teacher Mark Thackeray in the TV sequel *To Sir with Love II.* He also appeared in the Western *Children of the Dust*, as the psychiatrist in *Oprah Winfrey Presents: David and Lisa*, and with his daughter Sydney Poitier in the Showtime production of *Free of Eden.* In CBS's *The Simple Life of Noah Dearborn*, Poitier gave one of his most affecting television performances. Directed by Gregg Champion, this old-fashioned melodrama cast Poitier as a stubborn loner, a magical carpenter who can work wonders with wood, hammer, nail, and lathe. Noah was like an older, weathered version of the almost saintly characters Sidney Poitier had played in the 1950s/1960s. But Poitier the actor understood the beauty of silences and soaks up every minute of screen time.

That giddy cross-dresser RuPaul also found television surprisingly receptive to his talents. Standing well over six feet tall (with his high heels about seven feet tall), with full breasts and near-platinum blond hair, RuPaul liked to boast of being the world's most famous drag queen. After his celebrated disco recordings, RuPaul, still in full drag regalia, came to the tube. He made guest appearances on the sitcom *Sister, Sister* and the daytime soap *All My Children*. Then he temporarily dropped his queen persona to appear in a serious role as a man opposite Linda Hamilton in the USA Channel's *A Mother's Prayer*. Then came *The RuPaul Show* for VH1. If anything, his success marked some type of shift in national attitudes, at least among a segment of younger viewers. RuPaul became a real-life advertisement for that pop belief of the 1990s that indeed you could be whatever/whomever you wanted to be.

Television movies also injected some new energy into the careers of a number of African American actresses. It even looked as if television might see a resurgence of the Black Woman's Film (like those that Cicely Tyson had done so effectively in the 1970s and early 1980s). One of the big stars to appear in women's pictures was Diana Ross. Ever since her highfalutin Motown years with the Supremes, Ross had been a television fixture. The Supremes had turned up on such variety programs as *The Ed Sullivan Show* as well as in an episode of the series *Tarzan* in which they played nuns. Later, as a solo performer, Ross starred in her own specials on the networks and cable. In the 1970s, she even had the ultimate television celebrity interview with Barbara Walters. After her dramatic performances in such features as *Lady Sings the Blues, Mahogany*, and the musical *The Wiz*, Diana Ross, who for years dreamed of playing Josephine Baker, seemed forgotten by the film industry. Ross shrewdly turned to the tiny screen for the dramatic roles that otherwise eluded her. First came the starring role as a paranoid schizophrenic in *Out of Darkness* in 1994. Five years later, she appeared with Brandy as estranged mother and daughter pop stars in *Double Platinum*.

Lynn Whitfield was another actress who scurried about the film colony for years in search of a role that would bring her attention. She had first become interested in acting as a little girl in Baton Rouge, Louisiana. When director Otto Preminger came to town to shoot scenes of his film *Hurry Sundown,* Whitfield's dentist father moonlighted as a talent scout, finding local Blacks to work as extras in the movie, which starred Jane Fonda, Michael Caine, Faye Dunaway, and African American performers Robert Hooks and Diahann Carroll. Whitfield's father also asked her if she'd like to work in the movie. "When he told me I'd be sitting in a courtroom with no lines, or singing with a lot of other children, I just shook my head," she recalled. "Even at that age, I had such a developed sense about what I was going to be: a movie star, not an extra in Diahann's movie."

But as an adult her roles in such films as *Silverado* and *Doctor Detroit* had taken her nowhere. The same was true of a string of roles in such television productions as *For Colored Girls Who Have Considered Suicide When the Rainbow Is Enuf* and *The George McKenna Story.* Even her surprise leading role in *Johnnie Mae Gibson: FBI* didn't give her career any kind of push. Finally, *The Josephine Baker Story* turned her career around. When word first leaked out that she would star in the TV film, many wondered why the role of the fiercely energetic, hotly sexual, and charismatic *La Bakair* was going to the rather laid-back, passive Whitfield. Whitfield, however, had the last laugh. The drama itself was rather standard television docudrama, but Whitfield's Emmy win gave her career a boost.

Afterward she emerged as a star *of sorts.* More people knew who she was. But the plum roles still didn't come her way. With the exception of *Eve's Bayou,* she was left dangling in mundane or misconceived films like *Gone Fishin',* *A Thin Line Between Love and Hate,* and *Stepmom.* She had the good sense to keep working in television even when she had to take a backseat to a star like Vanessa Williams in a TV movie like *Stompin' at the Savoy.* She also appeared on *The Cosby Mysteries.* What saved Whitfield's career was cable. Viewers saw her away from the networks in a series of melodramas, some of which were old-style women's pictures: Showtime's *Taking the Heat* and *Love Songs,* HBO's *State of Emergency,* Lifetime's *Sophie and the Moonhanger* and its *Dangerous Evidence: The Lori Jackson Story* (in which she played a civil rights activist fighting to overturn the rape conviction of a Black marine, played by Richard Yearwood).

By the end of the decade, she appeared in the successful TV films *Oprah Winfrey Presents: The Wedding* and *Deep in My Heart*, the latter the story of a biracial child born to a young Irish Catholic woman who is raped by an unknown Black man. (Though based on a true story, it presented viewers with yet another image of a Black rapist.) When the girl's mother puts her up for adoption, Whitfield appears as a foster mother who takes the child into her home—and later tries to adopt her. But she's disillusioned and angered when a social worker sends the girl to a white family instead. Years later Whitfield sees her again (the role now played by Gloria Reuben). *Deep in My Heart* touched on the issues of class, identity, and culture facing biracial children in America. But it succeeded primarily as a mother/daughter melodrama with a standout performance by Anne Bancroft (as the birth mother of the girl in later years) and a rather felt one by Whitfield.

In the 1990s, an actress like Vanessa Williams might have become a one-of-a-kind sexy, sophisticated television star had she not appeared to be far more interested in a music as well as a movie career (in films like *Hoodlum, Erasure,* and *Dancin'*). Still, she appeared in such TV movies as *Perry Mason: The Case of the Silenced Singer* and *Sidney Sheldon's Nothing Lasts Forever* as well as a guest shot on the series *L.A. Doctors*. Her performance in TV's *Stompin' at the Savoy* had drive and heat, and never did she exude a lusher sensuality and old-time movie glamour than as Calypso in *The Odyssey*.

Late in the decade, Ruby Dee, Diahann Carroll, and newcomer Audra McDonald scored high ratings in the CBS movie *Having Our Say: The Delany Sisters' First 100 Years*. The drama was produced by Camille Cosby.

But the biggest pop star to work on the tube in the 1990s was Whitney Houston, who appeared in the Rodgers and Hammerstein musical *Cinderella* on The Wonderful World of Disney, which she also co-executive-produced with Debra Martin Chase. The musical *Cinderella* had first appeared on television starring Julie Andrews in 1957. Another version starring Lesley Ann Warren had aired in 1965. Both productions were helped immensely by their leading ladies. The score itself was not top-drawer Rodgers and Hammerstein. This new, highly unusual, rather daring multicultural production caught most viewers and critics off guard. Before its airing, the new *Cinderella* struck some as a disaster in the making, primarily because of its unusual casting. Brandy was to be Cinderella. Cast as her Wicked Stepmother was white actress Bernadette Peters. One of the evil Stepsisters was to be white; the other, Black. How would viewers respond to the white Peters berating poor little Black Brandy? But perhaps because *Cinderella* was indeed a fairy tale set in a never-never land, viewers accepted the production's cast without any troubling second thoughts. Playing the Prince was newcomer Paolo Montalban. Playing his mother was a very funny Whoopi Goldberg. Appearing as the Fairy Godmother was a resplendent Houston. Songs such as "The Sweetest Songs" were added to this new version.

It was a significant cultural sign that an African American actress was now playing the classic fairy-tale princess. Critic Caryn James commented that the "new version has a social conscience," "a feminist twist." She added: "The matter-of-fact racial casting works so smoothly that it becomes one of the show's happiest effects. There is no cause to wonder why one stepsister is black and one white. The entire kingdom is blissfully multiethnic." Viewers both Black and white seemed entranced. ABC estimated that about 60 million viewers saw at least some of the program, which attracted 70 percent of girls under the age of eighteen.

Finally, for a star like Cicely Tyson, the decade had its ups and downs. Fortunately, Tyson, though never inundated with challenging scripts, worked consistently (at a time in her life when some of her contemporaries looked ready to give up on their careers) in such TV films as *Heat Wave, When No One Would Listen, Widow, Lily in Winter*, and *The Price of Heaven*. Frequently, her followers must have questioned why she appeared in a TV film like *Always Outnumbered*, in which she had so little to do. Or why she signed on for a routine TV film like Showtime's *Riot*. But Tyson understood that an actress, to remain a viable presence in Hollywood, has to keep working, has to be seen, has to remind the industry that she's still around. Yet she also held on to her career by selectively choosing projects which she felt had some meaning and by often accepting supporting roles.

Sometimes she came up with winners. Her performance in *The Oldest Living Confederate Widow Tells All* won her an Emmy. Her film *Mrs. Scrooge* had two notable surprises. First, this version of Charles

A multicultural version of Cinderella *with Whitney Houston and Brandy: seen by nearly 60 million viewers and attracting 70 percent of girls in the nation under the age of eighteen*

Dickens's *Christmas Carol*, updated with Tyson cast as the coldhearted Mrs. Scrooge, was directed by John Korty, who had previously directed *The Autobiography of Miss Jane Pittman*. Some may have wondered how Korty became involved in this seemingly slight production. But the second surprise was that *Mrs. Scrooge* was actually an entertaining, lively film, graced by Tyson's utterly charming and well-thought-out performance. In key scenes, she still had that "tight reserve" that Pauline Kael had written about years earlier. Seeing her drop that reserve—when an enlightened Mrs. Scrooge awakens on Christmas morning—was part of the great pleasure. Korty understood the fact that the grande dame of high drama could also be deliriously funny (without being campy) and could transform serviceable dialogue into meaningful moments. After all these years, Tyson could still surprise us. Throughout, Tyson, as in earlier eras, remained a commanding presence and still an unlikely icon. A newer generation may not have been as familiar with her. But as soon as anyone saw Cicely Tyson, you understood here was an actress bigger and better than any role she might be playing.

By the end of the 1990s, television had undergone yet more significant transitions. Too often in the past, primetime had been locked in a time warp, only commenting on social issues belatedly, too long after the initial impact of significant social/political change in America. But with some of the dramas of the 1990s like *Law & Order, N.Y.P.D. Blue,* and *Homicide: Life on the Street* (as occasionally with past shows like *The Defenders* and *East Side, West Side* as well as *Hill Street Blues*), the networks seemed to be slowly coming of age; to be catching up, even if only in pop terms, with the various social shifts of American life. The new networks and cable had given viewers programming choices previously unthought of. Cable movies had explored more serious and unusual subject matter than general network fare—whether it be a conventional narrative like *The Josephine Baker Story* or a more experimental one like *Don King: Only in America.* At the same time, would anyone have imagined that, on certain nights, you could turn on a station like WB or UPN and view Black programs running back to back? With some of the new Black-cast series like *Moesha* and *The Steve Harvey Show*, which might not have existed without *The Cosby Show*, television also depicted amusing aspects of African American life without completely caricaturing characters or situations.

Yet though television of the 1990s offered more choices for viewers, those choices still had not been varied enough. For the most part, primetime television—even on the cable stations and the new networks—still failed to answer the needs of African American viewers for more realistic or satisfying shows about African Americans.

Surprisingly, by the tail end of the decade, researchers saw a new trend in viewing habits. The number one show for African Americans was *The Parkers*, which aired on UPN, as did such other programs on the Black top ten lists as *Moesha* and *Grown Ups*. But after the dramatic split between the tastes of Black and white audiences through the mid into the late 1990s, research by the Manhattan-based media group TN Media revealed that the network most watched by African Americans in the fall of 1999 was CBS. On the top ten list for African Americans were the CBS programs *60 Minutes* (seventh place), *Touched by an Angel* (ninth place), and *Walker, Texas Ranger* (tenth place). Among the top twenty were such other CBS programs as *Cosby, Kids Say the Darndest Things*, and the *CBS Sunday Movie*—as well as NBC's *ER* and ABC's *The Practice*. Part of the great racial divide on television had narrowed. Black viewers were willing to watch non-Black programs (it helped if the cast included an African American). Yet white viewers still avoided such Black programs as *The Parkers* and *The Steve Harvey Show*, although both included white supporting performers in their casts. If anything, television remained in transition at the close of the 1990s. Though the big three networks were no longer as powerful as in the past, they still influenced mass viewer tastes and attitudes.

And so as the twenty-first century began, primetime television viewing had been—for many African Americans—a frustrating and exasperating experience; a mixed bag of sorts with its failures and odd accomplishments. Much of primetime television history had been a series of hack concepts and stereotyped images. Throughout various decades, television programming, with its steady lineup of Black sitcoms and its lack of serious weekly African American dramas, had reflected the evasions and fantasies of a nation trying, more often than not, to ignore or suppress its feelings and fears about race; to duck the important social/political questions. Television still had a long way to go in honestly and sensitively recording African American life; to do so it would still need an influx of African Americans behind the camera; far more writers, directors, and producers. Artists like Thomas Carter or Paris Barclay or Stan Lathan or the power brokers like Cosby and Winfrey. More programmers and casting directors too. More executives at the networks.

Still, as the twenty-first century began, there had already been promising signs for primetime television's future. Some unexpected achievements still resonate. Performers like Ethel Waters or Cicely Tyson or Bill Cosby or a lesser-known actress like Madge Sinclair or Rosalind Cash, had often moved and entertained viewers, transforming the medium with their highly personal or idiosyncratic visions and styles. They had also proved, from mid-century on, that the people we saw still could mean more than the stories they were saddled with— that those people could enliven the tube with their unexpected personal power.

Sometimes it was simply the power to make us *like* them the way Eddie Anderson did as Rochester on *The Jack Benny Show* or as Amanda Randolph did as Louise on *The Danny Thomas Show*. Sometimes it was the power, no matter what the role, or in spite of it, to stun us with their rapid delivery of dialogue, their perfect timing, their masterly double takes, whether it was Marla Gibbs and Sherman Hemsley on *The Jeffersons* or Redd Foxx on *Sanford and Son* or Jackée on *227*.

Other times, it was the power to *intrigue* us, making us curious and wanting to know more, as Juano Hernandez had done in *Escape Route* or as the young Bill Cosby did in *I Spy*. Other times—as Howard Rollins did on *In the Heat of the Night*—it was the power to make us feel intuitively that behind the story on the tube there was another far more affecting narrative. Then sometimes—like Ethel Waters or like Cicely Tyson as Miss Jane walking to the fountain or like John Amos and that multitalented cast in *Roots* or like Regina Taylor as the poetic Lilly in *I'll Fly Away*—it was the power to *move* us in the most personal way.

It's undeniable now that—from television's early history up to the start of the new century—key African American performers have used their fierce talents to tell us a story of their own. In that way, they were able to transcend television's own distortions and dishonesties, its myths and misconceptions about African Americans. That in itself had made television, on occasion, a surprising emotionally rousing experience that caused millions of us to sit up and take notice in our living rooms. That in itself was another bridge to the new century, and the new millennium.

NOTES

Some sources are of special note. Tim Brooks and Earle Marsh's *Complete Directory to Prime Time Network TV Shows* and Alex McNeil's *Total Television* were excellent references for checking dates, schedules, and casts of network programs. J. Fred MacDonald's *Blacks and White TV* provided a fine general overview of the African American presence in television. Todd Gitlin's comments on *Hill Street Blues* were extremely helpful in my discussion of the series. Lynn Hirschberg also provided a fine chronology on the genesis of *The Fresh Prince of Bel-Air*. Some of the comments on *A Different World*, *Frank's Place*, *The Women of Brewster Place*, *Equal Justice*, and *In Living Color* appeared in a different form in my television essays in *The Black Arts Annuals: 1987–1988*, *1988–1989*, and *1989–1990*.

1. The 1950s: Scraps

9 Results offered sharp contrasts: "Television Reviews: Ethel Waters," *Variety*, June 28, 1939.

16 Hazel Scott has a: "Television Reviews: Hazel Scott," *Variety*, April 19, 1950.

18 have never entertained: "Hazel Scott Makes Denials at Inquiry," *The New York Times*, September 23, 1950.

18 Redlist Costs Hazel Scott: Hugh Deane, "Redlist Costs Hazel Scott Job," *The Compass*, September 17, 1950.

23 Except for a few: Bert., "Television Reviews: Beulah," *Variety*, October 11, 1950.

23 With Miss Waters playing: "Ethel Waters as Beulah," *The New York Times*, October 4, 1950.

24 There is still no: Ethel Waters and Charles Samuels, *His Eye Is on the Sparrow* (New York: Doubleday, 1951).

25 white folks kitchen comedy: "Louise Beavers Takes Over 'Beulah' TV Role," *Jet*, March 27, 1952.

27 There are three things: " 'Amos 'n' Andy' on Television," *Ebony*, May 1951.

32 the perpetuation of stereotyped: Rose., "Television Reviews: Amos 'n' Andy Show," *Variety*, July 4, 1951.

32 The fact remains that: Ibid.

33 Why the *Amos 'n' Andy*: *Amos 'n' Andy* Clippings File at the Schomburg Center for Research in Black Culture.

35 a cute and amusing: Billy Rowe, "Billy Rowe's Notebook," *The Pittsburgh Courier*, July 7, 1951.

37 truly wonderful, deeply moving: Hift, "Television Reviews: Amos 'n' Andy," *Variety*, December 31, 1952.

38 is such a mixture: Margo Jefferson, "Seducified by a Minstrel Show," *The New York Times*, May 22, 1994.

50 Whenever Danny or any: Sheldon Leonard, *And the Show Goes On: Broadway and Hollywood Adventures* (New York: Limelight Editions, 1995).

50 Miss Randolph, at 70: "People Are Talking About," *Jet*, July 28, 1966.

57 all the black actors: Etta James and David Ritz, *Rage to Survive* (New York: Villard Books, 1995).

57 wall of frustration: Hy Gardner, "The Editor's Corner," *New York Herald Tribune*, September 18–24, 1955.

60 I was totally bowled: Diahann Carroll with Ross Firestone, *Diahann!* (Boston: Little, Brown and Company, 1986).

61 half crazy with frustration: Ibid.

61 there was really no: Ibid.

61 A good try, and: Chan., "Tele Follow-up Comment," *Variety*, March 9, 1955.

62 As nearly as can: Tau., "Tele Follow-up Comment," *Variety*, October 12, 1955.

66 programs such as this: "TV's New Policy for Negroes," *Jet*, November 24, 1955.

66 Philco was threatened with: Sidney Poitier, *This Life* (New York: Alfred A. Knopf, 1980).

67 For me . . . it was: Ibid.

67 TV's New Policy for: "TV's New Policy for Negroes," *Jet*, November 24, 1955.

69 a very headstrong lady: Guy Flatley, "At the Movies: 'Julia' Stirs Images of Other Films for Fred Zinnemann," *The New York Times*, September 30, 1977.

69 Ethel Waters regrettably had: Jack Gould, "TV: Faulkner's 'Sound and Fury,' " *The New York Times*, December 7, 1955.

69 Courage should be made: "Tele Follow-up Comment: Playwrights '56," *Variety*, December 14, 1955.

73 I am unemployed . . . No: " 'Stormy Weather' Has Waters singing 'Blues,' " New York *Journal-American*, January 3, 1957.

73 The woman who, during: "Ethel Waters a Winner," *The New York Times*, January 9, 1957.

75 He was completely at: Gros., "Television Reviews: Nat King Cole," *Variety*, November 7, 1956.

76 I like Nat Cole: "Did Bias Banish Nat's TV Show?" *Jet*, March 4, 1965.

76 I think Nat could: Ibid.

77 If I could have: Nat King Cole (As Told to Lerone Bennett), "Why I Quit My TV Show," *Ebony*, February 1958.

77 Madison Avenue, the center: Ibid.

78 unquestionably one of the: Jack Gould, "The Green Pastures," *The New York Times*, October 27, 1957.

78 The initial performance of: Jack Gould, "TV: Treasure of Medium," *The New York Times*, March 24, 1959.

82 The great Juano Hernandez: Pauline Kael, *I Lost It at the Movies* (Boston: Little, Brown and Company, in association with the Atlantic Monthly Press, 1965).

85 on becoming the first: "Can Sammy Davis Jr. Crash Network TV?" *Ebony*, October 1954.

88 Naughty little television comes: Tube., "Tele Follow-up Comment: Dick Powell's Zane Grey Theater," *Variety*, November 18, 1959.

88 Davis, who probably hasn't: Ibid.

2. The 1960s: Social Symbols

92 There is no case: Lerone Bennett, *Before the Mayflower: A History of Black America* (Chicago: Johnson Publishing Co., Inc., 1987).

103 persuasive and mature in: Rose., "Tele Follow-up Comment: The Nurses," *Variety*, May 5, 1963.

108 A sensational phoney: "TV Reviews: East Side, West Side," *New York Herald Tribune*, September 24, 1963.

109 came right out of: Barbara Delatiner, "On Television: CBS Show Circles Race Issue with Clichés," New York *Newsday*, November 5, 1963.

109 Drama of protest, a: Jack Gould, "TV: A Drama of Protest," *The New York Times*, November 5, 1963.

110 For the first time: Horo., "Tele Follow-up Comment: East Side, West Side," *Variety*, November 6, 1963.

110 as forceful a piece: "TV: All Around Town," *The Village Voice*, January 9, 1964.

110 We feel this city: Richard Doan, "A CBS Show Stars 2 Negroes: Atlanta Blacks It Out," *New York Herald Tribune*, November 5, 1963.

111 a good actress: "TV: All Around Town," *The Village Voice*, January 9, 1964.

111 her tight reserve slightly: Pauline Kael, "Cicely Tyson Goes to the Fountain," *The New Yorker*, January 28, 1974.

111 I really didn't do: Cicely Tyson comment to Donald Bogle.

112 A Negro actress was: Alan Patureau, "Dixie Boycott Killed TV Series: Susskind," New York *Newsday*, February 4, 1964.

112 Negro characters. We've had: Edith Efron, "Who Killed Neil Brock?" *TV Guide*, March 28, 1964.

112 Two years ago, if: Barry Farrell, "Life TV Review: TV Drama Cops Out on the Racial Problem," *Life*, May 1, 1964.

113 Ivan felt very unused: Brenda Scott Royce, *Hogan's Heroes: Behind the Scenes at Stalag 13!* (Los Angeles: Renaissance Books, 1998).

113 When I started: Charles Hobson, "The Success of Ivan Dixon," *Black Stars*, October 1976.

114 Ivan was a truly: Sidney Poitier, *This Life* (New York: Alfred A. Knopf, 1980).

114 the triumphant arrival of: Ibid.

117 If I would do: Mel Watkins, *On the Real Side: Laughing, Lying, and Signifying—the Underground Tradition of African-American Humor That Transformed American Culture, from Slavery to Richard Pryor* (New York: Simon & Schuster, 1994).

117 He was doing a: Sheldon Leonard, *And the Show Goes On: Broadway and Hollywood Adventures* (New York: Limelight Editions, 1995).

118 We're afraid of that: Ibid.

119 I had a computer: Ibid.

119 loved it with one: Ibid.

120 Ivan Dixon, in a: "I Spy," *New York Herald Tribune*, September 16, 1965.

120 Cicely Tyson was cool: Bill. "Television Reviews: I Spy," *Variety*, September 9, 1965.

120 Whatever the cause of: J.M.C., "I Spy," *Christian Science Monitor*, September 17, 1965.

121 a show in search: "I Spy," *The New York Times*, September 16, 1965.

121 The network and producer: Bill., "Television Reviews: I Spy," *Variety*, September 22, 1965.

121 Everybody told us we: "I Spy: Comedian Bill Cosby Is First Negro Co-star in TV Network Series," *Ebony*, September 1965.

122 Negroes like Martin Luther King: Ibid.

124 toe-to-toe slugfest: "Bill Cosby Finally Makes Love on I Spy," *Jet*, June 30, 1968.

125 Because I was first: Alan Ebert, "Bill Cosby: A Piece of the Action," *Essence*, December 1977.

125 But if I dressed: Ibid.

127 I got on the: Dick Hobson, "On Maneuvers with Hari Rhodes," *TV Guide*, April 20, 1968.

128 If Greg Morris turned: Patrick J. White, *The Complete Mission: Impossible Dossier* (New York: Avon Books, 1991).

128 Some people wrote resenting: Ibid.

129 demolition, construction, counterfeiting, metallurgy: Ibid.

129 in tunnels, elevator shafts: Ibid.

129 shot (three times), beaten: Ibid.

132 Gene and I agreed: Nichelle Nichols, *Beyond Uhura: Star Trek and Other Memories* (New York: G. P. Putnam's Sons, 1994).

132 The network men had: Ibid.

133 Given the fact that: Ibid.

133 The network suits, who: Ibid.

134 *Plato's Stepchildren* first aired: Ibid.

134 I'm a white Southern: Ibid.

135 You cannot, and you: Ibid.

135 A New Star in: *Ebony*, January 1967.

136 He's great but he's: Arnold Perl, "TV Mailbag: 'A Lovely Man,' " *The New York Times*, July 5, 1970.

137 a new criteria concerning: "Frank Silvera, Actor-Director, Electrocuted in Coast Mishap," *The New York Times*, June 12, 1970.

141 We're going to show: Robert Lewis Shayon, "TV-Radio: 'Julia' Symposium: An Opportunity Lost," *The Saturday Review*, May 25, 1968.

142 is a far, far: Robert Lewis Shayon, "TV-Radio: 'Julia': Breakthrough or Letdown?" *The Saturday Review*, April 20, 1968.

142 I would think that: Robert Lewis Shayon, "TV-Radio: 'Julia': A Political Revenge," *The Saturday Review*, July 20, 1968.

142 *Julia* is politically oriented: Ibid.

142 launched a full-scale assault: Diahann Carroll, with Ross Firestone, *Diahann!* (Boston: Little, Brown and Company, 1986).

144 The star, Diahann Carroll: Joan Walker, *Cue*, October 5, 1968.

144 Watts it ain't: Bill., "Television Reviews: Julia," *Variety*, September 25, 1968.

144 For years we've been: "Heavily Burdened," New York *Daily News*, September 25, 1968.

145 Meant to be both: " 'Julia': Television Network Introduces First Black Family Series," *Ebony*, November 1968.

145 Well, I suppose this: Carroll and Firestone, *Diahann!*

145 By now there was: Ibid.

145 There was no question: Ibid.

146 for blatant examples of: Ibid.

146 sometimes we ran into: Ibid.

146 I'm John Wayne and: Ibid.

150 would not recognize a: Scott Haller, "Diahann Carroll Dresses Up 'Dynasty,' " *People*, May 14, 1984.

151 What captured my attention: Carroll and Firestone, *Diahann!*

151 had also worn me: Ibid.

152 I was always torn: Edith Efron, "Success Is Not Her Problem," *TV Guide*, May 27, 1967.

153 How could I portray: Edmund Newton, "Diahann!" *Essence*, October 1984.

153 I ask what she: Carolyn See, "I'm a Black Woman with a White Image," *TV Guide*, March 14, 1970.

154 Of course! *Of course*: Ibid.

154 Times have been trying: Robert A. DeLeon, "Diahann Carroll: I've Been Black All the Time," *Jet*, April 3, 1975.

154 Her critics argue that: Ibid.

154 I am not about: Ibid.

157 We were stuck with: Dick Hobson, "The Show with a Split Personality," *TV Guide*, July 3, 1971.

157 Here was the TV: Robert Lewis Shayon, "TV-Radio: Mod vs. The Squad," *The Saturday Review*, November 23, 1968.

158 *The Mod Squad* was: Tim Brooks and Earle Marsh, *The Complete Directory to Prime Time Network and Cable TV Shows, 1946–Present* (New York: Ballantine Books, 1999).

158 aid and comfort to: "Why Mod Squad Turns on Young TV Viewers," *Jet*, October 29, 1970.

159 I try to keep: Judy Stone, "Television: Young Cops with a Soul," *The New York Times*, September 22, 1968.

160 because for the first: Dick Hobson, "The Odyssey of a Black Man in 'White Man's Television,' " *TV Guide*, March 1, 1969.

160 I, Otis Young, black: Ibid.

160 Bill did not play: Ibid.

161 We didn't want the: Ibid.

163 a nice, liberal-oriented: John Oliver Killens, "Our Struggle Is Not to Be White Men in Black Skin," *TV Guide*, July 25, 1970.

164 an extraordinarily attractive young: Joan Walker, "TV Notes," *Cue*, November 1, 1969.

168 opportunity to give: Tom Mackin, "Bill Cosby Speaks Out," *Newark Evening News*, July 7, 1969.

3. The 1970s: Jokesters

174 too risqué: Judy Stone, " 'Barefoot' Stubs a Toe," *TV Guide*, October 10, 1970.

174 honest and true to: Ibid.

174 I want to tell: Ibid.

175 the Uncle Tom bit: Ibid.

176 so poor even the: "When You're Hot, You're Hot," *Time*, January 31, 1972.

177 Generally, it only takes: Ibid.

177 what my thing was: Ibid.

178 The head-to-toe: Ibid.

180 Television's First Black Superstar: Ibid.

180 It should be noted: Bill., "Television Reviews: The Flip Wilson Show," *Variety*, September 24, 1969.

181 There is a certain: Lerone Bennett, "The Emancipation Orgasm: Sweetback in Wonderland," *Ebony*, September 1971.

181 I have feelings about: "When You're Hot, You're Hot."

185 a junkie shoot up: Donna McCroban, *Prime Time Our Time: America's Life and Times Through the Prism of Television* (Rocklin, CA.: Prima Publishing & Communications, 1990).

185 the Romans let human: Ibid.

186 He's a wholly ignorant: Charles L. Sanders, "Is Archie Bunker the Real White America?" *Ebony*, June 1972.

186 call a spade a: Laura Hobson, "As I Listened to Archie Say 'Hebe,' " *The New York Times*, September 12, 1971.

186 What shall we do: Sally Bedell Smith, *In All His Glory: The Life of William S. Paley, the Legendary Tycoon and His Brilliant Circle* (New York: Simon and Schuster, 1990).

189 one of the brightest: Louie Robinson, "Sanford and Son: Redd Foxx and Demond Wilson Wake Up TV's Jaded Audience," *Ebony*, July 1972.

189 I called it a: Kay Gardella, "Meet NBC's Sanford and Son," New York *Sunday News*, February 6, 1972.

189 white to the core: Eugenia Collier, " 'Sanford and Son' Is White to the Core," *The New York Times*, June 17, 1973.

194 the funniest dishwasher on: Malcolm X, with the assistance of Alex Haley, *The Autobiography of Malcolm X* (New York: Grove Press, 1965).

195 Redd was the comedic: Bill Davidson, "The World's Funniest Dishwasher Is Still Cleaning Up," *TV Guide*, March 17, 1973.

195 He was the first: Ibid.

195 Do your *real* act: Ibid.

195 I was scared: Ibid.

196 made it in twelve: "All in the Black Family," *Time*, April 17, 1972.

196 I've been cheated more: Nick Ravo, "Redd Foxx, Cantankerous Master of Bawdy Humor, Is Dead at 68," *The New York Times*, October 13, 1991.

198 I kept telling them: Judy Stone, "Florida Finds Good Times in Chicago," *The New York Times*, May 5, 1974.

200 On the one side: John J. O'Connor, "Good Times for the Black Image," *The New York Times*, February 2, 1975.

200 the tube's best effort: Louie Robinson, "Bad Times on the 'Good Times' Set," *Ebony*, September 1975.

203 He's 18 and he: Ibid.

204 it might mean: Mel Tapley, "Is 'Good Times' a Fatherless Family?" New York *Amsterdam News*, May 22, 1976.

206 but there's got: Robinson, "Bad Times on the 'Good Times' Set."

212 this show is not: Cleveland Amory, "Review: The Jeffersons," *TV Guide*, February 22, 1975.

212 those who may still: Louie Robinson, "The Jeffersons: A Look at Life on Black America's New Striver's Row," *Ebony*, January 1976.

213 There were no pallid: Bonnie Allen, "Movin' On Up: The Jeffersons," *Essence*, October 1981.

213 but nobody laughs at: Ibid.

219 displays the slyest wit: Peter Andrews, "Television: The Bad and the Beautiful," *The Saturday Review*, April 12, 1980.

220 The fans of: Dick Adler, "You Can't Put *That* John Shaft on TV," *TV Guide*, April 20, 1974.

221 Whether at home or: John J. O'Connor, "TV: Tenafly, Black Detective, Arrives," *The New York Times*, February 14, 1973.

226 What about the kid?: Sally Bedell, *Up the Tube: Prime-Time TV in the Silverman Years* (New York: The Viking Press, 1981).

233 strutted through this role: Tim Brooks and Earle Marsh, *The Complete Directory to Prime Time Network and Cable TV Shows, 1946–Present* (New York: Ballantine Books, 1999).

237 quite possibly the finest: Pauline Kael, "Cicely Tyson Goes to the Fountain," *The New Yorker*, January 28, 1974.

237 Cicely Tyson transforms the: John J. O'Connor, "TV: Splendid 'Jane Pittman' Relates Black History," January 31, 1974.

237 I'm sure God didn't: Kay Gardella, "Cicely Tyson: Actress by Accident, Star by Design," New York *Daily News*, January 6, 1974.

242 violated two long-standing: Bedell, *Up the Tube*.

242 dramatic portrayals of nonwhites: Ibid.

242 because his lips were: Ibid.

243 made a difference: David Wolper, with Quincy Troupe, *The Inside Story of TV's "Roots"* (New York: Warner Books, 1978).

243 Our concern: Bedell, *Up the Tube*.

243 I think we fooled: Ibid.

243 To spread it out: Ibid.

243 they would only lose: Ibid.

243 I did not have: Ibid.

4. The 1980s: Superstars

255 a performance of wide: Bok., "Television Reviews: Palmerstown, U.S.A.," *Variety*, March 26, 1980.

257 Instead of writing letters: Bever-Leigh Banfield, "Feeling Fit and Fabulous," *Essence*, January 1984.

258 So blacks don't want: Suzanne Adelson, "Feasting on TV Stardom and a New Marriage, Nell Carter Celebrates Life in, Well, Fat City," *People*, June 21, 1981.

258 I did coke all: "Oh, the Troubles She's Seen," *People*, February 28, 1994.

261 When people see me: Kenneth Turan, "He's the Tallest 40 Inches in Hollywood," *TV Guide*, January 14, 1984.

261 Everyone thinks it's this: Ibid.

262 the first one we: Andy Meisler, "The Rise and Fall—and Rise Again—of Diahann Carroll," *TV Guide*, March 23, 1985.

262 A lot of people: Lee Margulies, "Black Dynasty," *Us*, October 22, 1984.

262 where a Black could: "Diahann Carroll Dresses Up 'Dynasty,' " *People*, May 14, 1984.

263 a blow against one: Ibid.

263 the show's ratings zoomed: Charles Sanders, "Newest Sassy, Sexy Couple on 'Dynasty,' " *Ebony*, October 1984.

263 first Black bitch: Edmund Newton, "Diahann!" *Essence*, October 1984.

264 between 8 p.m. and: Thomas Morgan, "The Black Viewers' New Allure for the Networks," *The New York Times*, December 1, 1986.

264 They can make the: Ibid.

268 not for her magnetic: Ellen Torgerson Shaw, "Fine Actress, Great Cheekbones, Sexpot with a Sense of Humor . . . ," *TV Guide*, April 17, 1982.

268 Black American accent: Patricia Jones, "Madge Sinclair: A Working Woman On-screen and Off," *Essence*, March 1982.

268 Why isn't she famous?: Ellen Torgerson Shaw, "Fine Actress, Great Cheekbones . . ."

269 If I were a: Ibid.

274 We were not trying: Todd Gitlin, *Inside Prime Time* (New York: Pantheon Books, 1983).

274 Our quarrel with them: Ibid.

274 a mixture of various: Ibid.

274 problems that we might: Ibid.

274 wholly unrecognizable: Ibid.

274 unfashionably liberal: Ibid.

274 In the end, loyalty: Ibid.

276 There's no way you're: Ibid.

280 the culmination in popular: Stephen Holden, "A Hit Show Spawns a Hit Album," *The New York Times*, December 22, 1985.

281 What I wanted to: Richard Corliss, "Cool Cops, Hot Show," *Time*, September 16, 1985.

283 I'm American gumbo: Corliss, "Cool Cops, Hot Show."

284 The relationship of Crockett: Roger Simon, "What's Black and Blue and Hurtin' All Over? *Miami Vice*, Pal!" *TV Guide*, March 21, 1987.

285 The Tubbs character is: Jeff Silverman, "Virtue and 'Vice,' " *Us*, February 9, 1987.

285 What had been an: Gary Deeb, "Ad-'Vice' to 'Miami': Put Themes Out Front," *New York Post*, August 26, 1986.

285 Philip Michael Thomas: Is There: *TV Guide*, October 21, 1989.

285 I realize how important: "Don't Be So Modest, Phil!" *TV Guide*, August 17, 1985.

285 I have a game: Nancy Collins, "The Rolling Stone Interview: Don Johnson," *Rolling Stone*, November 7, 1985.

285 put a lot of: Ibid.

288 "reghettoizing" commercials: "Charge Black 'Ghetto' for TV Com'l Voices," *Variety*, July 21, 1970.

288 blurbs aimed specifically at: Ibid.

288 to affect Negro accents: Ibid.

289 by turns combative, defensive: Harry F. Waters, "Bill Cosby Comes Home," *Newsweek*, November 5, 1984.

289 "Egomania" and "arrogance" are: Harry F. Waters, "Cosby's Fast Track," *Newsweek*, September 2, 1985.

289 too many of these: Ibid.

289 I hate it when: Ibid.

290 Anyone hearing that the: Ibid.

293 a source of unconcealed: Waters, "Bill Cosby Comes Home."

293 My one rule is: Waters, "Cosby's Fast Track."

293 irresistibly charming, flawlessly executed: Waters, "Bill Cosby Comes Home."

293 a supersitcom, funny, fast-paced: Jeff Jarvis, "Tube: The Cosby Show," *People*, September 24, 1984.

293 *The Cosby Show* is: John J. O'Connor, "Bill Cosby's Triumph," *The New York Times*, May 9, 1985.

294 If black people fail: Jeff Donn, " 'Cosby' Study Sparks Race Debate," *New York Post*, April 28, 1992.

294 *Leave It to Beaver*: Waters, "Cosby's Fast Track."

294 subscribes too readily to: Tom Carson, "Cosby Knows Best," *The Village Voice*, October 1984.

297 appear to endorse controversial: Waters, "Cosby's Fast Track."

299 Some people have said: Sally Bedell Smith, "Cosby Puts His Stamp on a TV Hit," *The New York Times*, November 18, 1984.

302 Usually, the fathers in: Peter J. Boyer, "TV Turns to the Hard-Boiled Male," *The New York Times*, February 16, 1986.

302 running out of steam?: John J. O'Connor, "An Update on 'The Cosby Show,' " *The New York Times*, January 21, 1988.

303 Before the demographically divvied: Kate Meyers, "Cosby's Last 'Show,' " *Entertainment Weekly*, May 3, 1996.

306 just a bit touchy: Lorene Cary, "I Am No Tonto," *TV Guide*, December 6, 1986.

306 tried (unsuccessfully) to mimic: Ibid.

306 I *still* can't tell: Ibid.

306 My Hawk is easier: Ibid.

306 In large measure, Avery: Ibid.

306 Hey! I am not: Ibid.

306 blues hero . . . You see: Ibid.

306 One of the neater: John J. O'Connor, "TV Weekend: 'Spenser: For Hire,' in Series Debut on ABC," *The New York Times*, September 20, 1985.

307 Played to a spiffily: John J. O'Connor, "TV Reviews: Private-Eye Drama, ABC's 'Spenser: For Hire,' " *The New York Times*, July 1, 1986.

309 On *The Jeffersons* supporting: Jeff Jarvis, "Tube: 227," *People*, September 16, 1985.

311 temptress Sandra has shades: Michael McWilliams, "Television: Second to None," *Rolling Stone*, April 23, 1987.

314 I was holding down: Pam Johnson, "Grapevine: Showstopper Anna Maria Horsford," *Essence*, July 1987.

315 As Thelma . . . Horsford plays: McWilliams, "Television: Second to None."

317 a vulnerable "Cosby" spinoff: Kay Gardella, "Thursday Night Combat: 'Tour of Duty' Goes to War with 'Cos' & Daughter," New York *Daily News*, September 24, 1987.

317 I have a confession: Marvin Kitman, "A 'Different' Sort of Spin-Off from Cosby," New York *Newsday*, undated, *A Different World* clippings file at the Library of Performing Arts at Lincoln Center.

326 strongly to Blacks of: David Bianculli, "TV: CBS Programmers Map Fall Campaign," *New York Post*, August 7, 1987.

328 So far as entertainment: Merrill Panitt, "In the Heat of the Night," *TV Guide*, December 3, 1988.

331 a cross between Pee-wee: Joy Horowitz, "Snookums! Steve Urkel Is a Hit," *The New York Times*, April 17, 1991.

332 the diversity within the: Ibid.

332 He's not up on: Ibid.

332 broadly caricatured antics: John J. O'Connor, "Blacks on TV: Scrambled Signals," *The New York Times*, October 29, 1991.

336 We didn't originally put: Harry F. Waters, with Janet Huck, "Lust for Law: Prime Time's Hottest Series Has Sex, Style and Plenty of Smarts," *Newsweek*, November 16, 1987.

346 reduced the antebellum slave: Harry F. Waters, "A Terrible Unswift Sword," *Newsweek*, November 4, 1985.

354 Do you know that: Robert Ward, "We've Won Some of the Battles," *TV Guide*, March 22, 1980.

357 like a square white: Ice T and Heidi Siegmund, *The Ice Opinion* (New York: St. Martin's Press, 1994).

360 In a racist society: Barbara Grizzuti Harrison, "The Importance of Being Oprah," *The New York Times Magazine*, June 11, 1989.

362 the stories are overly: Tone. "Telefilm Reviews: An ABC Novel for Television— The Women of Brewster Place," *Daily Variety*, March 17, 1989.

362 almost without exception, are: John J. O'Connor, "TV Views: In 'Brewster Place,' Women Lead the Way," *The New York Times*, March 19, 1989.

363 the magic of the: John Leonard, "Television's Character Building," *New York*, March 20, 1989.

5. The 1990s: Free-for-alls

367 captured more TV households: Johnnie L. Roberts, "Fraying Nets," *Newsweek*, December 28, 1998–January 4, 1999.

369 Instead of a cold: David Bianculli, "Inner City Oprah," *New York Post*, May 1, 1990.

369 to modulate herself anywhere: John Leonard, "Television's Soap Oprah," *New York*, May 7, 1990.

372 we are not going: Sam Howe Verhovek, "Talk of the Town: Burgers v. Oprah," *The New York Times*, January 21, 1998.

372 he quickly rescinded his: Ibid.

375 They made it clear: Mike Duffy, "TV/Cable: Always on the Case: Joe Morton as a Top Attorney in *Equal Justice*," New York *Daily News*, April 29, 1990.

375 Joe, I think . . . would: Marc Gunther, "Black Producers Add a Fresh Nuance," *The New York Times*, August 26, 1990.

376 an enormous response from: Ibid.

376 a great paucity of: Ibid.

377 Who says the variety: Bier, "Television Reviews: In Living Color," *Variety*, April 25, 1990.

378 one of the freshest: John J. O'Connor, "Bringing a Black Sensibility to Comedy in a Series," *The New York Times*, May 29, 1990.

378 mincing stereotypes who seem: Ibid.

378 black humor wouldn't be: Bier, "Television Reviews: In Living Color," *Variety*, April 25, 1990.

378 singled out as a: O'Connor, "Bringing a Black Sensibility to Comedy in a Series."

379 We take an exaggerated: Gunther, "Black Producers Add a Fresh Nuance."

379 the thirteen-person writing staff: Dinitia Smith, "Color Them Funny: Keenen Ivory Wayans and TV's New Black Comedy Hit," *New York*, October 8, 1990.

379 there aren't many black: Ibid.

380 I'll never be on: Lisa Ferguson, "Fed-up Damon Wayans Kisses TV 'Goodbye,' " *New York Post*, September 4, 1998.

383 Cake and ice cream: John J. O'Connor, "Blacks on TV: Scrambled Signals," *The New York Times*, October 27, 1991.

385 You've got eight minutes: Lynn Hirschberg, "Yo, NBC!" *Vanity Fair*, October 1990.

385 My eyes glazed over: Ibid.

385 There was a drumbeat: Ibid.

386 They're a Cosby-family kind: Ibid.

386 [DJ and Fresh Prince]: Ibid.

386 Did you hear the: Ibid.

386 It's a subculture of: Ibid.

386 Mon-o-Crao-mat-IC: Ibid.

387 I was very reluctant: Ibid.

387 Somebody at the network: Ibid.

387 The question we were: Ibid.

390 a black version of: "Fresh Prince of Bel-Air," *People*, September 9, 1990.

390 a good many viewers: John J. O'Connor, "Review/Television: Black Sitcoms Steeped in Concept," *The New York Times*, October 4, 1990.

391 What the creators of: David Bianculli, "TV: Yo! Check This Show," *New York Post*, September 10, 1990.

391 Will is not threatening: Larry Rother, " 'Fresh Prince of Bel-Air' Puts Rap in Mainstream," *The New York Times*, September 17, 1990.

391 For all his success: Joanna Elm, "Dweeb or Dude?" *TV Guide*, October 13, 1990.

392 a solid performance. . . . It's: "NBC Invites 'Carol,' 'Fresh Prince' Back," *Variety*, November 26, 1990.

392 Early on I began: David Ritz, "Will Power," *Essence*, February 1993.

392 I play an upscale: Benilde Little, "Profile: Janet Hubert," *Essence*, December 1990.

392 green-eyed, long-haired: Ibid.

392 Right before I got: Ibid.

393 sassy street styles: "Broadcast News," *Cable Guide*, September 1990.

396 seem to unfold in: O'Connor, "Blacks on TV: Scrambled Signals."

396 He seems unaware of: Mimi White, "Reliving the Past Over and Over Again," in Sasha Torres, ed., *Living Color: Race and Television in the United States* (Durham: Duke University Press, 1998).

396 It came as a: "Grapevine: Taking Affront with *Homefront*," *TV Guide*, October 3, 1992.

398 It shook me: Sara Rimer, "Star of New TV Series Taps Harsh Memories of School Integration," *The New York Times*, October 22, 1991.

399 They're going to go: Judith Michaelson, "TV Adjusts Its Mirror," *Los Angeles Times*, September 22, 1991.

399 the affiliates got upset: Ibid.

400 Watching [Sam] Waterston is: Marvin Kitman, "The Marvin Kitman Show: 'Fly Away' Soars as Drama," New York *Newsday*, October 7, 1991.

400 I haven't seen a: Ibid.

400 As Lilly, Ms. Taylor: John J. O'Connor, "Review/Television: Racial Issues of the 1950's, as People Lived Them," *The New York Times*, October 7, 1991.

400 My motto is "Off: Rimer, "Star of New TV Series Taps Harsh Memories of School Integration."

401 They did a lot: Ibid.

403 Here's the only show: "Picks and Pans: I'll Fly Away," *People*, October 28, 1991.

403 season's only class act: Harry F. Waters, "That Old Familiar Feeling," *Newsweek*, September 9, 1991.

403 a fine and in: O'Connor, "Racial Issues of the 1950's, as People Lived Them."

404 All of this is: White, "Reliving the Past Over and Over Again."

406 They don't constitute *enough*: Michaelson, "TV Adjusts Its Mirror."

407 inventing much of the: Marvin Kitman, "The Marvin Kitman Show: New Comedies on the Block," New York *Newsday*, August 27, 1992.

408 insistence on clanging, buffoonish: Miles Beller, "TV Review: Out All Night," *The Hollywood Reporter*, September 18, 1992.

409 all the emotional complexity: Roberta Bernstein, "Television Review: Rhythm & Blues," *Variety*, September 2, 1992.

409 You want condescension? Step: David Bianculli, "TV & Radio: Rhythm and Boos," *New York Post*, September 24, 1992.

409 It's hard not to: David Bianculli, "TV & Radio: 'Cooper Stupor,' " *New York Post*, September 24, 1992.

409 the essence of what: John Broadie, "Blacks to Tube: Get Real," *Variety*, September 7, 1992.

410 Nearly two decades ago: Joshua Hammer, "Must Blacks Be Buffoons?" *Newsweek*, October 26, 1992.

410 drive-by images: Ibid.

410 The racial stupidity is: "Bill Cosby Sees Red over TV Stereotypes," *New York Post*, November 29, 1993.

411 We are relegated to: Broadie, "Blacks to Tube: Get Real."

412 with one manufactured problem: O'Connor, "Blacks on TV: Scrambled Signals."

412 disturbing prospect to lose: Lynn Elber, "Beware of Falling 'Roc,'" *New York Post*, May 21, 1994.

413 For the first time: Ross Wetzsteon, "Up from Solitary: Charles Dutton's Rocky Road from Prison to Broadway," *New York*, May 7, 1990.

413 One of my friends: Ibid.

414 Make it a Black: Harry F. Waters, "Black Is Bountiful," *Newsweek*, December 6, 1993.

415 Richard taught me that: Mark Stuart Gill, "He's Half Macho Man, Half Teddy Bear," *The New York Times*, August 1, 1993.

416 He is *so* large: Esther Everem, "The Brother from the Corner: Martin Lawrence Succeeds by Just Being Himself," New York *Newsday*, April 29, 1993.

416 a mirror of the: Gill, "He's Half Macho Man, Half Teddy Bear."

417 Clearly, "Martin" intends to: Michele Greppi, "TV & Radio: 'Martin' Should Be Soon Partin'," *New York Post*, August 27, 1992.

417 world-class crude: Howard Rosenberg, "A New Low on the Taste Meter," *Los Angeles Times*, December 15, 1993.

421 I'm huge with the: Gill, "He's Half Macho Man, Half Teddy Bear."

423 Though all the roommates: Waters, "Black Is Bountiful."

423 Suppose I did a: Ibid.

424 Latifah's not a revolutionary: Andy Meisler, "The Ever-Expanding Realm of Queen Latifah," *The New York Times*, January 9, 1994.

426 she's an exhibit from the: James Wolcott, "On Television: Designing Couple," *The New Yorker*, October 12, 1992.

427 In those days, Black: Bob Thomas, "'Angel' Della's Bumpy Road to TV Heaven," *New York Post*, October 24, 1997.

428 I had good training: Ibid.

428 I worked my way: Ibid.

429 It's so goody-goody: Michael A. Lipton, "Heaven Help Us," *People*, February 22, 1999.

430 Younger viewers—kids and: Bill Carter, "Two Upstart Networks Courting Black Viewers," *The New York Times*, October 7, 1996.

430 Sexist Malarkey: "Beyond the Big 4," *Entertainment Weekly*, September 13, 1996.

437 Why am I in: Kevin Courrier and Susan Green, *Law & Order: The Unofficial Companion* (Los Angeles: Renaissance Books, 1998).

438 who, by his own: Verne Gay, "A Patient 'Blues' Man," New York *Newsday*, April 5, 1994.

438 [Fancy] has a certain: Ibid.

440 one of television's most: Caryn James, "Critic's Choice/Television: Officer's Last Harangue," *The New York Times*, May 8, 1998.

440 the best actor on: John Leonard, "Television: Swept Away," *New York*, June 10, 1996.

444 Benton is probably the: "Eriq La Salle and Gloria Reuben Help Make 'ER' a Top-Rated TV Series," *Jet*, February 17, 1997.

445 As an African American: Michael Starr, "Why the Romance Went Out of 'ER,' " *New York Post*, April 14, 1999.

449 when pressed I think: Michael Starr, "Cosby Removes Producer over 'Grave' Disagreement," *New York Post*, April 9, 1996.

450 Cosby has lost his: Ken Tucker, "Cos and Defects," *Entertainment Weekly*, September 27, 1996.

450 seems to take place: James Wolcott, "The Dad Trap: Is Cosby's America's Most Repressed Father?" *The New Yorker*, October 14, 1996.

451 I kind of scratch: Lawrie Mifflin, "TV Notes: Of Race and Roles," *The New York Times*, January 20, 1999.

455 The real problem: John Leonard, "Television: Week of the Woman," *New York*, February 15, 1993.

458 Its portrait of Dandridge: Caryn James, "TV Weekend: After Climb to Stardom, A Tumble, Then Death," *The New York Times*, August 20, 1999.

462 When he told me: "A Diva with a Difference," *New York Post*, November 5, 1997.

464 new version has a: Caryn James, "TV Weekend: The Glass Slipper Fits with a 90's Conscience," *The New York Times*, October 31, 1997.

BIBLIOGRAPHY

See the Notes for articles and other sources.

Agee, James. *On Film.* Boston: Beacon Press, 1968.

Altschuler, Glenn C., and David I. Grossvogel. *Changing Channels: America in TV Guide.* Urbana: University of Illinois Press, 1992.

Andrews, Bart, and Ahrgus Juilliard. *Holy Mackerel!: The Amos 'n' Story.* New York: E. P. Dutton, 1986.

Andrews, William L., and Frances Smith Foster and Trudier Harris. *The Oxford Companion to African American Literature.* New York: Oxford University Press, 1997.

Arlen, Michael J. *Living-Room War.* Syracuse, N.Y.: Syracuse University Press, 1997.

Barnouw, Erik. *Tube of Plenty: The Evolution of American Television.* 2nd rev. ed.; New York: Oxford University Press, 1990.

Bedell, Sally. *Up the Tube: Prime-Time TV in the Silverman Years.* New York: Viking Press, 1981.

Bennett, Jr., Lerone. *Before the Mayflower: A History of Black America.* Chicago: Johnson Publishing Co., Inc., 1987.

Bogle, Donald. *Blacks in American Films and Television: An Illustrated Encyclopedia.* New York: Fireside Books, 1990.

———. *Dorothy Dandridge: A Biography.* New York: Amistad Press, 1997.

———. *Toms, Coons, Mulattoes, Mammies, & Bucks: An Interpretive History of Blacks in American Films.* New York: Continuum Publishing, 1994.

Carroll, Diahann, and Ross Firestone. *Diahann!* Boston: Little, Brown and Company, 1986.

Cooper, Ralph, with Steve Dougherty. *Amateur Night at the Apollo: Ralph Cooper Pre-*

sents Five Decades of Great Entertainment. New York: HarperCollins Publishers, 1990.

Courrier, Kevin, and Susan Green. *Law & Order: The Unofficial Companion.* Los Angeles: Renaissance Books, 1998.

Dates, Jannette L., and William Barlow, eds. *Split Image: African Americans in the Mass Media.* Washington, DC: Howard University Press, 1990.

Foxx, Redd, and Norma Miller. *The Redd Foxx Encyclopedia of Black Humor.* Pasadena, Calif.: Ward Ritchie Press, 1977.

Gitlin, Todd. *Inside Prime Time.* New York: Pantheon Books, 1983.

Greenfield, Jeff. *Television: The First Fifty Years.* New York: Crescent Books, 1981.

Gross, Edward, and Mark A. Altman. *Captains' Logs: The Unauthorized Complete Trek Voyages.* Boston: Little, Brown and Company, 1995.

Ice T and Heidi Siegmund. *The Ice Opinion.* New York: St. Martin's Press, 1994.

James, Etta, and David Ritz. *Rage to Survive.* New York: Villard Books, 1995.

Jones, Gerard. *Honey, I'm Home!* New York: St. Martin's Press, 1993.

Jones, LeRoi. *Blues People: Negro Music in White America.* New York: William Morrow & Co., 1963.

Kael, Pauline. *Kiss Kiss Bang Bang.* Boston: Little, Brown and Company in association with the Atlantic Monthly Press, 1968.

Kalat, David P. *Homicide: Life on the Street: The Unofficial Companion.* Los Angeles: Renaissance Books, 1998.

Katz, William Loren. *The Black West: A Documentary Pictorial History.* Garden City, New York: Doubleday & Company, Inc., 1971.

MacDonald, J. Fred. *Blacks and White TV: African Americans in Television Since 1948.* 2nd ed.; Chicago: Nelson-Hall Publishers, 1992.

McNeil, Alex. *Total Television.* 4th ed.; New York: Penguin Books, 1996.

Mr. T. *The Man with the Gold: An Autobiography.* New York: St. Martin's Press, 1984.

Nichols, Nichelle. *Beyond Uhura: Star Trek and Other Memories.* New York: G. P. Putnam's Sons, 1994.

Price, Joe X. *Redd Foxx, B.S. (Before Sanford).* Chicago: Contemporary Books, 1979.

Reese, Della, with Franklin Lett and Mim Eichler. *Angels Along the Way: My Life with Help from Above.* New York: G. P. Putnam's Sons, 1997.

Riggs, Marlon. *Color Adjustment* (Video). San Francisco: California Newsreel, 1991.

Robertson, Ed. *The Fugitive Recaptured: The 30th Anniversary Companion to a Television Classic.* Los Angeles: Pomegranate Press, 1993.

Royce, Brenda Scott. *Hogan's Heroes: Behind the Scenes at Stalag 13!* Los Angeles: Renaissance Books, 1998.

Smith, Sally Bedell. *In All His Glory: The Life of William S. Paley, the Legendary Tycoon and His Brilliant Circle.* New York: Simon and Schuster, 1990.

Spelling, Aaron, with Jefferson Graham. *Aaron Spelling: A Prime-Time Life.* New York: St. Martin's Press, 1996.

Spignesi, Stephen. *The ER Companion: An Unauthorized Guide.* New York: A Citadel Press Book Published by the Carol Publishing Group, 1996.

Stempel, Tom. *Storytellers to the Nation: A History of American Television Writing.* New York: Continuum Publishing, 1992.

Tartikoff, Brandon, and Charles Leerhsen. *The Last Great Ride.* New York: Turtle Bay Books, 1992.

Thompson, Robert J. *Television's Second Golden Age: From Hill Street Blues to ER.* Syracuse, N.Y.: Syracuse University Press, 1996.

Torres, Sasha, ed. *Living Color: Race and Television in the United States.* Durham, N.C.: Duke University Press, 1998.

Wertheim, Arthur Frank. *Radio Comedy.* New York: Oxford University Press, 1979.

White, Patrick J. *The Complete Mission: Impossible Dossier.* New York: Avon Books, 1991.

Wolper, David, with Quincy Troupe. *The Inside Story of TV's "Roots."* New York: Warner Books, 1978.

Zicree, Marc Scott. *The Twilight Zone Companion.* Los Angeles: Silman-James Press, 1992.

Zook, Kristal Brent. *Color by Fox: The Fox Network and the Revolution in Black Television.* New York: Oxford University Press, 1999.

ACKNOWLEDGMENTS

There are many people to thank for their assistance and generosity during the period that I researched and wrote *Primetime Blues*.

Foremost, I want to thank my researcher Phil Bertelsen, who did an excellent job of finding key information on various programs and personalities. He also read an early draft of the manuscript and made perceptive comments. I was just sorry he was unable to continue working on the project. But when your researcher goes off to direct a movie, you can't argue with that.

I am also indebted to Ned Comstock at the University of Southern California's Cinema/TV Library, who, as always, was especially helpful. Zoe Burman at the UCLA Film/Television Archives also was helpful, setting up screenings for me of past television shows. I'd like to extend my gratitude to the staffs at the Museum of Television and Radio, especially Michelle Glanville; at the Schomburg Center for Research in Black Culture; at the Billy Rose Theatre Collection at the Library of Performing Arts at Lincoln Center; and at the Margaret Herrick Library of the Academy of Motion Pictures Arts and Sciences in Los Angeles. Howard Mandelbaum of Photofest was of great assistance in tracking down rare television stills.

In Los Angeles, my friend Jerald Silverhardt of MB Artists Management proved more useful than he may have realized. He kept me informed of the activities of various production companies, directors, writers, producers, and performers. Because he knows the industry inside out, it was always good to discuss new programs with him and to hear the industry buzz on various projects. The same was true of my conversations with Janet Alhanti, who is one of the country's finest acting teachers and coaches. It was extremely useful to discuss the work of various actors and actresses. Janet knows exactly what can go right—or disastrously wrong—in a performance. I value all of her insights.

It was also helpful to discuss various ideas with my good friend Debra Martin Chase of BrownHouse Productions. She has a clear understanding and appreciation for old Hollywood and the problems so many earlier African American actors and actresses had to endure. I also frequently discussed in detail various sitcom episodes with Leah Hunter of BrownHouse, who has an almost encyclopedic knowledge of programs, past and present.

My friend Cheryll Greene proved helpful in sharing her impressions of recent television programs. She also read an early draft of the manuscript and offered very intelligent and insightful comments. My good friend Bruce Goldstein at New York's Film Forum remains a fountain of knowledge, not only on American movie history but also on the early years of television.

I'd like to express my gratitude to Ayana Charleston and Hassan Charleston for their assistance with the research—and for their enthusiasm throughout the writing of this book. Another researcher, Knox Robinson, also proved very skillful at digging up all the TV reviews, interviews, and articles I requested. Even I was surprised at what he was able to find. I'd also like to thank several former students for the research they compiled: Charles Adams, Cheryl Williams, Awura-Adzua Backman, Michael Gerber, Erica Freeman, Vincent Roth, and Hayley Thomas. Former student Asia Slowe did an especially fine job of tracking down articles in *TV Guide*.

No book is ever completed without the help of friends and associates. I feel fortunate in having friends and associates who have been able to deal with and also respect my idiosyncrasies. So I have to express my gratitude to the following: my great friend Sarah Orrick Thompson; Ronald Mason, who helped me surf the Internet in search of information on African American performers and directors; Harry Ford III; Joerg Klebe; Jeanne Moutoussamy Ashe; Barbara Reynolds;

Herma Ross Shorty; Alan Sukoenig and Hiroko Hatanaka; Robert Katz and Jay Peterson of VHI; Pele Charleston of E! Entertainment; Evander Lomke; Carol Scott Leonard; Gwen Leonard; Sally Placksin; Harold and Fayard Nicholas; Rigmor Newman Nicholas; Emery Wimbish; H. Alfred Farrell; Anna Deavere Smith; Martin Radburd; Bettina Batchleor; Jacqueline Mosley; Roslynne Bogle; Jeanne Charleston; Janet Schenck; Susan Peterson; Ann Marie Cunningham; Harold Jovien; Daniel Beer; Peg Henehan; Bob Silverstein; Clisson Woods; David Aglow; the director William Greaves and his wife, Louise; Ivan Dixon; Neema Barnette; Linda Tarrant-Reid (who helped me find a new researcher); Dorothy McConnell; Gerald and Irene Mayer; Kathe Sandler; television veteran and good friend Marian Etoile Watson; and that marvel of intelligence and insight, the great Geri Branton. And, of course, Charlotte and the very elusive Peggy.

I'd also like to thank my colleagues at New York University's Tisch School of the Arts: Dean Mary Schmidt Campbell, who is always encouraging; my friend and the former chair of the Dramatic Writing Department, Janet Neipris; the current chair of the Dramatic Writing Department, Mark Dickerman; David Ranghelli; Susan Dwyer; my former teaching assistants Josslyn Luckett (now a writer for *The Steve Harvey Show*), Myla Churchill, and Anne Washburn; and my former students Jennifer Chen and Kyona Levine. I also want to extend my gratitude to Audrey Smith Bey and Gale Elleson in the Afro-American Studies Program at the University of Pennsylvania.

As always, my agent, Marie Dutton Brown of Marie Brown Literary Associates, proved encouraging and helpful. She has always been the perfect person to discuss any professional problem or hassle with. Her insights and fundamental optimism always make any difficult situation seem less so. I'd also like to thank her staff—past and present—for their assistance: Lesley Ann Brown, Lisa Davis, David Jackson, and Joana Blankman.

The staff of Farrar, Straus & Giroux has been of great assistance, especially Robyn Creswell, Peter Miller, copy editor Jack Lynch, and Rahel Lerner.

Finally, I must thank my editor, Elisabeth Kallick Dyssegaard, who, throughout the long period that it took me to complete this book, has always been encouraging and thoughtful. I've appreciated and valued her comments and suggestions, all of which have been intelligent and perceptive. I also have to thank her for her great patience. Somehow she coped with various delays. A writer feels mighty fortunate if he has a sensitive and informed editor. Elisabeth has been that—and so much more. I cannot thank her enough.

INDEX

DATE DUE
